CHILDREN (SCOTLA

Revised Edition

Kenneth McK. Norrie, LL.B., Ph.D.

Professor of Law at the University of Strathclyde

W. GREEN/Sweet & Maxwell
EDINBURGH
1998

First published 1995
Reprinted 1996, 1997
Revised Edition 1998
Reprinted 2000
Reprinted 2001
Reprinted 2002

Published in 1998 by W. Green & Sons Ltd
21 Alva Street
Edinburgh EH2 4PS

Typeset by
Medip Communications Ltd, Frome, Somerset

Printed in England by
Athenæum Press Ltd, Gateshead, Tyne & Wear

No natural forests were destroyed to make this product.
Only farmed timber was used and replanted.

A catalogue record for this book is available from the British Library

ISBN 0414 012 80 1

CHILDREN (SCOTLAND) ACT 1995*

(1995, c. 36)

ARRANGEMENT OF SECTIONS

PART I

PARENTS, CHILDREN AND GUARDIANS

Parental responsibilities and parental rights

PART II

PROMOTION OF CHILDREN'S WELFARE BY LOCAL AUTHORITIES AND BY CHILDREN'S HEARINGS ETC.

CHAPTER 1

SUPPORT FOR CHILDREN AND THEIR FAMILIES

Introductory

1

CHAPTER 2

CHILDREN'S HEARINGS

Constitution of children's hearings

Qualifications, employment and duties of reporters

Safeguards for children

Conduct of proceedings at and in connection with children's hearing

102. Removal of duty to report on operation of Children Act 1975.
103. Interpretation, rules, regulations and Parliamentary control.
104. Financial provision.
105. Extent, short title, minor and consequential amendments, repeals and commencement.

SCHEDULES:
   Schedule 1—Children's Panels.
   Schedule 2—Amendments of the Adoption (Scotland) Act 1978.
   Schedule 3—Transitional Provisions and Savings.
   Schedule 4—Minor and Consequential Amendments.
   Schedule 5—Repeals.

An Act to reform the law of Scotland relating to children, to the adoption of children and to young persons who as children have been looked after by a local authority; to make new provision as respects the relationship between parent and child and guardian and child in the law of Scotland; to make provision as respects residential establishments for children and certain other residential establishments; and for connected purposes.

[July 19, 1995]

PARLIAMENTARY DEBATES
   Hansard, H.C. Vol. 252, col. 555, Vol. 259, cols 25–146, Vol. 263, col. 1739. H.L. Vol. 564, cols 13–23, 37–58; Vol. 565, cols 1109–1153, 1200–1236, 1792.
   The Committee Stage in the House of Commons took place in Special Standing Committee on January 25, February 6, 13, 21, 23 and 28 and March 2, 7, 9 and 14, 1995. The Committee Stage in the House of Lords took place in a Committee of the Whole House off the Floor of the House on June 6, 7 and 13, 1995.

INTRODUCTION AND GENERAL NOTE
   Before the passing of the present Act, Scottish child law had been in a state of flux for some time past. Society had changed—and continues to change—dramatically since the basic precepts of family law were laid down, and the position and status and role of children in our society is very different today from what they were earlier in the 20th century. Even as recently as 1986, when the Law Reform (Parent and Child) (Scotland) Act 1986 was passed, it was considered appropriate to talk exclusively in terms of the rights that parents had in and over their children. Now, society more and more sees children as individual persons in their own right and perceives the nature of the parent-child relationship as in essence one of responsibility rather than one of right. There has been a clear shift from parental rights to children's rights, a shift heralded in domestic law by the House of Lords' decision in the case of *Gillick v. West Norfolk & Wisbeck Area Health Authority* [1985] 3 W.L.R. 830, [1986] A.C. 112, and in international law by the United Nations *Convention on the Rights of the Child* (see para. D.146). This Convention evidenced a growing awareness in the international community of the fact that children have rights as children and not only the basic human rights they have as members of the human race. The Convention's implementation by the British Government (on December 16, 1991, a few months after the coming into force of the English Children Act 1989) had the effect of rendering a number of provisions in the existing Scots domestic law incompatible with the U.K.'s international obligations. Scots child law therefore required amendment not only to take account of the change in the social perception of the status of children in Scotland but also to allow Scots law to consist with the terms of the UN Convention. In 1992 the Scottish Law Commission produced their *Report on Family Law* (Scot. Law Com. No. 135, May 1992), in which many suggestions for major change were made, and upon which Part I of the present Act is based.
   In the field of child protection Scots law had a difficult few years in the early 1990s. The children's hearing system, established by the Social Work (Scotland) Act 1968 and in operation since 1971, was much admired and free of significant criticism in its first 20 years. However, in the early 1990s a number of high profile cases highlighted some serious problems that did exist in the system. Various inquiries were established to scrutinise different aspects of the system and to suggest possible improvements, and extremely useful reports followed. These included the Clyde Report (*Report of the Inquiry into the Removal of Children From Orkney in February 1991* (1992–1993 H.C. 195)), the Kearney Report (*Report of the Inquiry into Child Care Policies in Fife* (1992–1993 H.C. 191)), and the Finlayson Report (*Reporters to Children's Panels: Their*

Children (Scotland) Act 1995

Role, Function and Accountability, Scottish Office, 1992). The Government reacted to these reports by producing the White Paper, *Scotland's Children: Proposals for Child Care Policy and Law*, 1993, Cm. 2286. The bulk of Part II gives effect to the proposals contained therein. In addition, new rules were created in order to deal with the problems that led to the highly contentious litigation in the cases of *Sloan v. B*, 1991 S.L.T. 530 (the Orkney case), *L., Petrs*, 1993 S.L.T. 1310 and 1342 (the Ayrshire case) and *D. v. Grampian Regional Council*, 1995 S.L.T. 519.

Scots child law is unlikely to be the subject of as substantial a piece of legislation as the present Act for a very long time. Yet the law itself is unlikely to remain static. The coming into force of the Act means that its provisions will be the subject of developing judicial scrutiny, which, in time, will clarify some of the more significant drafting ambiguities. Further legislation is required to remove one hideous flaw. The shift from parental rights to parental responsibilities cannot be taken seriously as long as a third of all fathers (the unmarried ones) are expressly and deliberately absolved of their responsibilities. This matter is considered in greater depth in the notes to section 3. The impact of the European Convention on Human Rights on Scottish child law is unlikely to be any less significant than in other areas of private law. The potential for conflict between the rights-based perspective of the Convention and the welfare-based perspective of much of our domestic law is obvious. The implementation of the Convention might well create the environment which necessitates a more radical reappraisal of the basic principles of child law than even the present Act constitutes.

ARRANGEMENT OF THE ACT

Part I—Parents, Children and Guardians
Part I of the Act, dealing with private law matters, contains in many respects the most fundamental alterations to the law as it previously stood, with the replacement of custody and access with "residence" and "contact" and the setting out of a much more clearly defined list of orders available to a court in dealing with private law matters. Replacing the appropriate provisions of the Law Reform (Parent and Child) (Scotland) Act 1986 and, it would seem, what remained of the common law, this Part sets out the parental responsibilities and parental rights that mothers and good fathers will have in relation to their children, who is to have these responsibilities and rights, and how they can be acquired, lost and regulated. The important s.11 specifies the types of order that a court can make in relation to parental responsibilities and parental rights, who can apply for them and on what terms such orders can be made. It is provided in that section that three "overarching principles" must inform the court's decision-making: that is to say (i) the welfare of the child is to be the court's paramount consideration, (ii) the court may make an order only when persuaded that to do so is better than making no order at all, and (iii) the child is to be given an opportunity to express views on the decisions the court has to make and the court must take appropriate account of these views.

In addition, the law of guardianship in Scotland, which had sat uneasily with the indigenous offices of tutory and curatory and which had been left anchorless on the abolition of these offices in 1991, is at last clarified. It is made plain that a guardian is (in the absence of statutory provision or court order defining it otherwise) a parent-substitute, with all the responsibilities and rights of a mother or good father. Provisions in this Part set out the effect of guardianship and detail the rules for the appointment and termination of appointment of guardians. Again, the common law is superseded by the comprehensive statutory provisions. There is also a much needed modernisation of the rules on administration of children's property.

Part II—Promotion of Children's Welfare by Local Authorities and by Children's Hearings etc.
This is by far the largest Part of the Act, though the changes it introduces are, perhaps, less fundamental than those in Pt I. Much of this Part is a re-enactment, and tidying, of the Social Work (Scotland) Act 1968 (c. 49), though a number of important amendments to the rules contained therein have been made. The duties that local authorities have towards children in their areas are specified and clarified; and in a significant change in terminology, designed to update the law and make it more accessible, the statute moves away from the notion of children "in care" to a notion of children being "looked after" or "accommodated" by local authorities. The aim here is to remove the stigma felt by many to attach to the previous status of children "in care".

The children's hearing system survives much as it was before, though the legal provisions applicable to that system are significantly tidied and updated. A number of new powers are granted to children's hearings such as to call for an early review, to appoint a safeguarder on a broader basis, and to give advice on various matters, though the philosophy behind the system traced to the Kilbrandon Report of 1964, remains intact. The most important changes in this

Part are in the creation of a number of new orders that the sheriff can make in relation to children who are in need of some form of emergency, short-term, protection. In particular the sheriff is given power to make child assessment orders to assess the physical or emotional wellbeing of a child, child protection orders (which replace the old place of safety orders), and exclusion orders (excluding a named person from a child's home). Also, the sheriff can make a parental responsibilities order, which replaces local authorities' power to assume to themselves parental rights and powers.

As under Pt I, there are three similar "overarching principles" which courts and children's hearings must apply whenever they are called upon under this Part to make decisions relating to children: (i) that the welfare of the child is the court's or children's hearing's paramount consideration, (ii) that the child is to be given an opportunity to express views on the decision the sheriff or children's hearing have to make and appropriate account will be taken of these views, and (iii) that the sheriff or children's hearing will not make an order unless persuaded that to do so is better for the child than making no order at all. The underlying philosophy throughout the Act—and not only this Part—is that children are best looked after by their parents, that the state should interfere in the upbringing of children only when this is necessary for the protection of children's welfare, and that when such interference is necessary it should be to the minimum extent required to achieve its purpose.

Part III—Adoption

Part III of the Act and Sched. 2 amend the law of adoption as it is contained in the Adoption (Scotland) Act 1978 (c. 28) in a number of important respects. The most significant of these changes is the provision allowing a step-parent to adopt a child alone, without having to bring in her or his spouse (the natural parent) as a co-applicant. In addition, in order to bring Scots law into line with the UN Convention on the Rights of the Child, the child's welfare is made the paramount consideration in the whole adoption process. The right of the child to express views is strengthened and regard must be had to the child's religious persuasion, racial origin and cultural and linguistic background. These matters are all fully explored in Plumtree's annotations to the Adoption (Scotland) Act 1978 to be found at paras A.444–A.530. The full treatment of adoption there means that it is no longer necessary to give the matter detailed treatment within the present annotations.

Part IV—General and Supplemental

The normal general provisions are contained in this Part, though in addition there is an amendment to the Registration of Births, Deaths and Marriages (Scotland) Act 1965 (c. 49) to take account of the fact that some parents who will be obliged to register births are themselves children (*i.e.* persons under the age of 16 years). This fact is reflected in other provisions in the present Act, as will be made clear at the appropriate points in the following annotations.

Developments Since 1995

Part I of the Children (Scotland) Act came into effect on November 1, 1996, and the bulk of the remainder came into effect on April 1, 1997. Since these dates there has been little judicial discussion of the Act, though some provisions have already been amended by statute. Most notably the Criminal Procedure (Scotland) Act 1995 repealed s.49 of the present Act and replaced the rules therein relating to remits and referrals for advice from the sheriff court with new rules now contained in s.49 of the Criminal Procedure (Scotland) Act 1995. In addition, the various rules and regulations made necessary by the Act have also now been brought into force.

ABBREVIATIONS

The 1968 Act	: Social Work (Scotland) Act 1968.
The 1986 Act	: Law Reform (Parent and Child) (Scotland) (Scotland) Act 1986.
O.C.R. 1993	: Act of Sederunt (Sheriff Court Ordinary Cause Rules) 1993 (S.I. 1993 No. 1956).
R.C. 1994	: Rules of the Court of Session 1994 (S.I. 1994 No. 1443).
The 1996 Rules	: Children's Hearings (Scotland) Rules 1996 (S.I. 1996 No. 3261 (s.251)).
A.S. 1997	: Act of Sederunt (Child Care and Maintenance Rules) 1997 (S.I. 1997 No. 291 (s.191)).
The UN Convention	: The United Nations *Convention on the Rights of the Child* (28 International Legal Materials 1448).
Scot. Law Com. No. 135	: Scottish Law Commission *Report on Family Law* (May 1992).

PART I

PARENTS, CHILDREN AND GUARDIANS

Parental responsibilities and parental rights

Parental responsibilities

1.—(1) Subject to section 3(1)(b) and (3) of this Act, a parent has in relation to his child the responsibility—

(a) to safeguard and promote the child's health, development and welfare;

(b) to provide, in a manner appropriate to the stage of development of the child—
    (i) direction;
    (ii) guidance,
    to the child;

(c) if the child is not living with the parent, to maintain personal relations and direct contact with the child on a regular basis; and

(d) to act as the child's legal representative,

but only in so far as compliance with this section is practicable and in the interests of the child.

(2) "Child" means for the purposes of—

(a) paragraphs (a), (b)(i), (c) and (d) of subsection (1) above, a person under the age of sixteen years;

(b) paragraph (b)(ii) of that subsection, a person under the age of eighteen years.

(3) The responsibilities mentioned in paragraphs (a) to (d) of subsection (1) above are in this Act referred to as "parental responsibilities"; and the child, or any person acting on his behalf, shall have title to sue, or to defend, in any proceedings as respects those responsibilities.

(4) The parental responsibilities supersede any analogous duties imposed on a parent at common law; but this section is without prejudice to any other duty so imposed on him or to any duty imposed on him by, under or by virtue of any other provision of this Act or of any other enactment.

DEFINITIONS
    "child": ss.1(2), 15(1).
    "parent": s.15(1).
    "parental responsibilities": s.1(3).

GENERAL NOTE
    See Scot. Law Com. No. 135, paras 2.1–2.13.
    Though statute law before the passing of this Act was worded in terms of parental rights, it has long been understood that "parental rights exist for the benefit of the child and they are justified only in so far as they enable the parent to perform his duties towards the child" (*per* Lord Fraser of Tullybelton in *Gillick v. West Norfolk & Wisbech Area Health Authority* [1985] 3 W.L.R. 830 at 841; see also Stair I, v, 1 and Erskine I, vi, 53). The aim of the current provision is to emphasise that a parent's primary relationship to her child is one of responsibility, and that this responsibility flows from being a parent. There are still parental rights recognised by the law and dealt with in s.2 below, but the change in terminology from rights alone to both responsibilities and rights is designed to remove the common misunderstanding, given credence by the terms of the 1986 Act, that parents have rights in, rather than duties and powers towards, their children.

Subs. (1)
    This subsection tells us what mothers and good fathers are expected to do and how they are expected to act in relation to their children. Much of the language used in this subsection can be traced to the UN Convention on the Rights of the Child. That Convention is worded in terms of the child's rights while the present provision is worded in terms of the parents' responsibilities; the statute should, however, be interpreted in the light of the Convention since Parliament has clearly designed this Act to give effect to it.

There are four parental responsibilities which can shortly be referred to as the responsibilities: (1) to safeguard and promote the child's health, development and welfare, (2) to provide the child with direction and guidance, (3) to maintain personal relations and direct contact with the child, and (4) to act as the child's legal representative. It is provided that the parent must fulfil these responsibilities in so far as it is practicable for her to do so and in so far as it is in the interests of the child for her to do so. A parent need not act as the child's legal representative if it is not in the child's interests, say, to raise an action which has little chance of success. Nor need the parent do any more than is practicable in all the circumstances. So the responsibility, for example, to maintain direct contact with the child will be affected by where the child lives, how old she or he is, and whether the child her or himself wants to maintain contact. There will be no breach of this responsibility if the child lives in Australia and the parent living in Scotland can afford few long distance telephone calls.

Subject to s.3(1)(b). Section 3(1)(b) provides that a father who is not married to the child's mother will not have parental responsibilities or parental rights in relation to the child unless he obtains an order from the court granting them under s.11 below, or he enters into an agreement with the mother under s.4 below. If these requirements are not satisfied the father is absolved of his parental responsibilities. This position breaches the U.K.'s international obligations under the UN Convention, for reasons which are explored more fully in the General Note to s.3 below.

Direction and guidance. Art. 5 of the UN Convention requires that the parent or guardian of a child has a duty to provide appropriate direction and guidance to the child. Direction differs from guidance in that the former implies instruction while the latter implies advice. They are treated differently in the present statute with subs. (2) below providing that the parent is obliged to direct the child until the age of 16 and is obliged to guide the child until the age of 18.

Maintain personal relations and direct contact. This parental responsibility reflects the child's right, protected by Art. 9(3) of the UN Convention, to personal relations and direct contact with both parents on a regular basis. The exclusion of the unmarried father from this responsibility breaches the child's right under the Convention.

Legal representation. The responsibility of legal representation is the duty to act on behalf of the child in transactions having legal effect, such as entering into contracts, raising and defending actions, granting discharges etc.

Subs. (2)

Instead of specifying at what age the various parental responsibilities come to an end, the Act follows the rather clumsy approach previously adopted by the 1986 Act of defining a child differently depending upon which parental responsibility is at issue. All bar one of the parental responsibilities end when the child attains the age of 16 years. The exception is the responsibility to give guidance (i.e. advice), which lasts until the child is 18 years old. It is, however, difficult to see what content this responsibility has since the parental right to give guidance ends on the child's 16th birthday (see s.2(7) below).

Under the age of. A person attains a particular age at the beginning of the relevant anniversary of the date of her or his birth: Age of Legal Capacity (Scotland) Act 1991 (c. 50), s.6(1).

Subs. (3)

This subsection gives the child title to sue or defend in any proceeding relating to parental responsibilities. A child is given title to seek an order under s.11 below by subss (3) and (5) of that section. This provision gives the child title to defend such an action, and title to sue or defend in any proceedings other than s.11 actions which will affect the exercise of parental responsibilities or which arise from such exercise, such as applications for parental responsibilities orders and child protection orders. It might also include actions by the child for breach of a parental responsibility. A breach of parental responsibilities has not yet been held to give rise to delictual liability in Scots law, though there is no reason in principle why it should not do so. There is nothing to stop a child suing a parent for damages in reparation, and if the child suffers a legally recognised loss through a failure by the parent in her duty to promote the child's welfare then liability might well be recognised. It would, however, be surprising if the Act intended to create a new form of liability but did so only here in relation to title to sue. The liability must be regarded as based on common law, and the effect of this provision is to put the child's title to sue in her or his own name beyond doubt.

Any person acting on his behalf. The child is not given any legal capacity by this Act that she or he does not otherwise have, and it follows that someone else will often have to act on behalf of the child in enforcing a parental responsibility. The legal representative of the child has title to sue under this provision but cannot be the only person included: if the action concerned liability arising out of legal representation, then that representative is hardly the appropriate person to join issue on behalf of the child. It is submitted that title to take a matter to court inheres in any person claiming to act on behalf of the child, even when they are not exercising any parental responsibility or parental right. The court will appoint a curator *ad litem* in such cases.

Subs. (4)

The common law is superseded by this Act in relation to parental responsibilities, and the duties that parents have towards their children are now to be found exclusively in this Act, or in other statutory provisions (such as the obligation of child support in the Child Support Act 1991 (c. 48), or the obligation to educate a child of school age in the Education (Scotland) Act 1980 (c. 44), s.30).

Parental rights

2.—(1) Subject to section 3(1)(b) and (3) of this Act, a parent, in order to enable him to fulfil his parental responsibilities in relation to his child, has the right—

   (a) to have the child living with him or otherwise to regulate the child's residence;
   (b) to control, direct or guide, in a manner appropriate to the stage of development of the child, the child's upbringing;
   (c) if the child is not living with him, to maintain personal relations and direct contact with the child on a regular basis; and
   (d) to act as the child's legal representative.

   (2) Subject to subsection (3) below, where two or more persons have a parental right as respects a child, each of them may exercise that right without the consent of the other or, as the case may be, of any of the others, unless any decree or deed conferring the right, or regulating its exercise, otherwise provides.

   (3) Without prejudice to any court order, no person shall be entitled to remove a child habitually resident in Scotland from, or to retain any such child outwith, the United Kingdom without the consent of a person described in subsection (6) below.

   (4) The rights mentioned in paragraphs (a) to (d) of subsection (1) above are in this Act referred to as "parental rights"; and a parent, or any person acting on his behalf, shall have title to sue, or to defend, in any proceedings as respects those rights.

   (5) The parental rights supersede any analogous rights enjoyed by a parent at common law; but this section is without prejudice to any other right so enjoyed by him or to any right enjoyed by him by, under or by virtue of any other provision of this Act or of any other enactment.

   (6) The description of a person referred to in subsection (3) above is a person (whether or not a parent of the child) who for the time being has and is exercising in relation to him a right mentioned in paragraph (a) or (c) of subsection (1) above; except that, where both the child's parents are persons so described, the consent required for his removal or retention shall be that of them both.

   (7) In this section, "child" means a person under the age of sixteen years.

DEFINITIONS
   "child": ss.2(7), 15(1).
   "parent": s.15(1).
   "parental responsibilities": s.1(3).
   "parental rights": s.2(4).

GENERAL NOTE
   See Scot. Law Com. No. 135, paras 2.14–2.35.
   Under the 1986 Act the parental rights were "guardianship, custody or access", together with "any right or authority relating to the welfare or upbringing of a child conferred on a parent by any rule of law" (s.8). The aim of the present provision is to put all parental rights onto a statutory basis, to declare that they exist only for the purpose of enabling the parent to fulfil her parental responsibilities, and to set out as clearly as possible the content of each of these rights.

Subs. (1)

The four parental rights are listed here, and there are no others: they may shortly be referred to as the rights (1) to regulate the child's residence, (2) to direct or guide her or his development and upbringing, (3) to maintain personal relations and direct contact with the child, and (4) to act as the child's legal representative. It will be noticed that all four reflect the parental responsibilities listed in s.1 above. So the right to have the child living with the parent exists in order that the parent has the practical power to safeguard and promote the child's health, development and welfare; the right to control the child's upbringing is granted in order to allow the parent to fulfil the obligation to provide direction and guidance; the right to maintain personal relations is granted to allow the parent to fulfil her obligation of maintaining personal relations; and the right to act as legal representative is granted to allow the fulfilling of the obligation to act as legal representative.

In order to enable him to fulfil his parental responsibilities. The exercise of any particular parental right is valid only in so far as it is directed towards the fulfilling of one or more of the parental responsibilities.

Has the right. As under the 1986 Act, the use of the word "right" in this context is inept since the interest recognised by this section is not a "right" in any normal sense of the word. An action to enforce the "right" will not be determined according to the strength of its validity but according to the welfare of the child; breach of the "right" will not give rise to an action for damages (*McKeen v. Chief Constable of Lothian and Borders Police*, 1994 S.L.T. 93). Rather, the so-called parental rights are really more in the nature of powers or capabilities, that is to say the ability to act in ways that the law will recognise and give effect to. "Parental power" would have been a more apt phrase to use.

Legal representative. A parent has the right to act as the child's legal representative, *i.e.* to enter into transactions having legal effect on behalf of the child. It sometimes happens, however, that the parent is herself a child (*i.e.* a person under the age of 16) and may well lack legal capacity to undertake legal transactions, whether on behalf of herself or of her child. (A father under the age of 16 would not have parental rights since he would not be married and the court is highly unlikely to grant such a father parental rights.) Either this provision is inept in relation to the under-16-year-old mother, or it confers full legal capacity on such a person to act on behalf of her child. Neither of these interpretations is satisfactory. If the provision is inept, this runs the risk of a child of a mother under 16 having no legal representative until the court appoints one. And if a mother under the age of 16 has full capacity to enter into contracts on behalf of her child it would be a strange law which prohibited her from entering into contracts on her own behalf. The solution, though it is slightly clumsy, must be as follows. The process of acting as a legal representative is itself a transaction having legal effect; if a mother under 16 has no capacity to undertake a particular transaction it has to be undertaken by her own legal representative (*i.e.*, normally, her own parent, or the baby's grandparent). The responsibility and the right to act as a child's legal representative passes through the young parent to the young parent's legal representatives, who therefore have the responsibility and the right to act on behalf not only of their own child but also of their filial grandchild. A mother under 16 can act on behalf of her child on terms which are not unreasonable and in circumstances in which it is common for persons of her age and circumstances to transact (Age of Legal Capacity (Scotland) Act 1991 (c. 50), s.2(1)).

Subs. (2)

This replaces s.2(4) of the 1986 Act, and has the same effect. A person exercising one of the powers recognised by this section can do so on their own without consulting any other person with the same powers, and it follows that in cases of disagreement the advantage is given to the person who takes the initiative. If, for example, married parents disagree as to the school the child is to attend, either can, against the wishes of the other, enrol the child into the school of their choice. However, s.6(1) below imposes an obligation on any person exercising a parental responsibility or parental right to have regard to the views of any other person with parental responsibilities and parental rights: see the General Note to that section. An alteration to the old s.2(4) is that this provision is made subject to the immediately following subsection.

Any decree or deed. The decree would be granted in terms of s.11; the deed would be one governed by the rules in s.7.

Subss. (3) and (6)

One of the most contentious areas of law in recent years has concerned international child abduction, and the problems of one parent removing the child from the jurisdiction before the court has resolved the issue of the child's residence. Removal of a child from the jurisdiction in defiance of a court order, or without the appropriate consent when there is a court order, is an offence (Child Abduction Act 1984 (c. 37), s.6). In addition, a "wrongful removal or retention", within the terms of the Hague Convention on International Child Abduction (brought into our law by the Child Abduction and Custody Act 1985 (c. 60)) requires the authorities of the jurisdiction to which the child has been taken to order the immediate return of the child. The provisions in subss (3) and (6) make clear that removal by one parent with parental responsibilities and parental rights without the consent of the other parent with parental responsibilities and parental rights amounts to a "wrongful removal" for the purposes of the Hague Convention even although the removing parent is exercising her or his right to determine the child's residence. In other words, one parent has a veto on the removal of the child from the jurisdiction by the other parent. And that veto is given to parents with *either* the right to determine the child's residence *or* the right to maintain personal relations and direct contact with the child. For further exploration of this issue, see Norrie, "The Hague Convention, Rights of Contact, and s.2(3) and (6) of the Children (Scotland) Act 1995", 1997 S.L.T. (News) 173.

No person. This includes, but is not limited to, the person who has parental rights under this section.

Remove a child. In its terms this provision is wide enough to cover both a removal with an intention of permanency, and removal for a foreseeably short term, such as a holiday.

Habitually resident. See the General Note to s.14(1) below.

Retain any such child. The notion of retention has been dealt with in a number of cases raised under the Hague Convention on International Child Abduction and the present provision is likely to be interpreted consistently with that Convention, as enacted in the Child Abduction and Custody Act 1985 (c. 60). See for example *H. (Minors) (Abduction: Custody Rights), Re* [1991] 2 A.C. 476, *Findlay v. Findlay*, 1994 S.L.T. 709.

Consent. It is not laid down how consent to the removal of the child is to be evidenced, and it can be assumed, therefore, that it is open to proof *prout de jure*. A number of cases have arisen under the Hague Convention, in which it is a defence to an application for the return of the child that the parent from whom she or he was removed consented to the removal. See for example *Zenel v. Haddow*, 1993 S.L.T. 975. Acquiescence may infer consent; see *Robertson v. Robertson*, 1998 S.L.T. 468; see also the House of Lord's decision in *Re H and Others (Minors) (Abduction: Acquiescence)* [1997] 2 All E.R. 225.

Subs. (4)

Title to sue, or to defend, in any proceedings. Section 11(3) gives the parent title to seek an order under s.11, and this section gives the parent title to defend such an action, and title to sue or defend any other action which will affect the exercise of parental responsibilities or which arises from such exercise, such as, for example, a parental responsibilities order or a child protection order.

Parent. Though defined in s.15 as "genetic parent", it is clear that the context here requires the word to be limited to parent with parental responsibilities and parental rights (*i.e.* it initially excludes the father who is not married to the mother at the appropriate time).

Subs. (5)

Like s.1(4) in relation to parental responsibilities, s.2(5) ensures that parental rights come solely from the present Act or any other Act of Parliament and not from the common law, which is entirely superseded in so far as it existed before the coming into force of the present Act (thereby tidying up the confused position under s.8 of the 1986 Act). Sheriff Kelbie, in a commentary on *D.G. v. Templeton*, 1998 S.C.L.R. 180, suggests that the common law right of a parent physically to chastise a child has been superseded by this provision and that such chastisement is now lawful only insofar as it is an exercise of one or more of the rights listed in subs. (1) above, which exercise is lawful only in order to fulfil one or more of the responsibilities listed in s.1(1) above. This must be so and, as Sheriff Kelbie suggests, sheriffs who hold the exercise of a parental right to be lawful ought to make findings of fact as to which parental responsibility or parental right the activity found lawful relates to.

Subs. (7)

All parental rights cease on the child's 16th birthday (including the right to give guidance, notwithstanding that the responsibility to give guidance lasts until the child's 18th birthday: see note to s.1(2) above).

Provisions relating both to parental responsibilities and to parental rights

3.—(1) Notwithstanding section 1(1) of the Law Reform (Parent and Child) (Scotland) Act 1986 (provision for disregarding whether a person's parents are not, or have not been, married to one another in establishing the legal relationship between him and any other person)—

(a) a child's mother has parental responsibilities and parental rights in relation to him whether or not she is or has been married to his father; and

(b) without prejudice to any arrangements which may be made under subsection (5) below and subject to any agreement which may be made under section 4 of this Act, his father has such responsibilities and rights in relation to him only if married to the mother at the time of the child's conception or subsequently.

(2) For the purposes of subsection (1)(b) above, the father shall be regarded as having been married to the mother at any time when he was a party to a purported marriage with her which was—

(a) voidable; or

(b) void but believed by them (whether by error of fact or of law) in good faith at that time to be valid.

(3) Subsection (1) above is without prejudice to any order made under section 11 of this Act or section 3(1) of the said Act of 1986 (provision analogous to the said section 11 but repealed by this Act) or to any other order, disposal or resolution affecting parental responsibilities or parental rights; and nothing in subsection (1) above or in this Part of this Act shall affect any other—

(a) enactment (including any other provision of this Act or of that Act); or

(b) rule of law,

by, under or by virtue of which a person may have imposed on him (or be relieved of) parental responsibilities or may be granted (or be deprived of) parental rights.

(4) The fact that a person has parental responsibilities or parental rights in relation to a child shall not entitle that person to act in any way which would be incompatible with any court order relating to the child or the child's property, or with any supervision requirement made under section 70 of this Act.

(5) Without prejudice to section 4(1) of this Act, a person who has parental responsibilities or parental rights in relation to a child shall not abdicate those responsibilities or rights to anyone else but may arrange for some or all of them to be fulfilled or exercised on his behalf; and without prejudice to that generality any such arrangement may be made with a person who already has parental responsibilities or parental rights in relation to the child concerned.

(6) The making of an arrangement under subsection (5) above shall not affect any liability arising from a failure to fulfil parental responsibilities; and where any arrangements so made are such that the child is a foster child for the purposes of the Foster Children (Scotland) Act 1984, those arrangements are subject to the provisions of that Act.

DEFINITIONS
"parent": s.15(1).
"parental responsibilities": s.1(3).
"parental rights": s.2(4).
"person": s.15(4).

GENERAL NOTE

In *Marckx v. Belgium* [1980] 2 E.H.R.R. 330 the European Court of Human Rights held that Belgian legislation which drew a distinction between the "legitimate" and the "illegitimate" family constituted discrimination in violation of Art. 14 of the European Convention on Human Rights (ECHR), by virtue of the lack of any objective and reasonable justification for the difference in treatment accorded by Belgian law. In relation to Scots law the 1986 Act attempted to remove all the civil disabilities attaching to the children of unmarried parents, and while it achieved that limited aim it did not, as is sometimes claimed, abolish the status of "illegitimacy". Apart from the various rules in relation to domicile and succession (see Wilkinson and Norrie, *Parent and Child* (1993, W. Green) at pp. 5–10), the terminology is still used in, for example, the Adoption (Scotland) Act 1978 (c. 28) and can still be found in recent judicial dicta (see for example Lord Jauncey in *D v. Grampian Regional Council*, 1995 S.L.T. 519 at p. 520). In addition and most importantly, under the 1986 Act the unmarried father was denied parental rights in relation to his child. The Scottish Law Commission (Scot. Law Com. No. 135 at paras 2.50 and 17.10) had recommended that the status of illegitimacy be abolished and with it the discrimination against unmarried fathers. The Government rejected that recommendation and the present provision re-enacts the 1986 Act, with minimal improvements (and indeed an added disadvantage) in the position of the unmarried father. In doing so, the UK remains in clear breach of its international obligations.

In *McMichael v. U.K.*, (1995) 20 E.H.R.R. 205 the applicant had argued that his exclusion from a children's hearing considering the case of his child, on the basis that he was not married to the mother, was discriminatory and therefore in violation of Art. 14 ECHR, but the Court unanimously held that the 1986 provisions were not discriminatory. The aim of the legislation was to identify meritorious fathers and the Court held that the conditions they had to satisfy before obtaining parental rights were proportionate to that legitimate aim. This decision may well be inconsistent with the Court's slightly earlier ruling in *Schmidt v. Germany* (1994) 18 E.H.R.R. 513 in which it was held that very weighty reasons would have to be established before the Court could accept that a difference of treatment based exclusively on the ground of sex was compatible with the European Convention on Human Rights. The *McMichael* case was not argued on that basis but on the basis of discrimination between unmarried and married men. The decision might well have been different had the questions asked in the case been these: why should men have to prove their parenting merit when women do not? And why is marriage in itself a determinant of paternal merit?

Even if it is conceded that married parents should be treated differently from unmarried parents, there is no justification in treating the children of unmarried parents differently from the children of married parents. Article 18 of the UN Convention on the Rights of the Child provides for the recognition of the principle that both parents have common responsibilities for the upbringing and development of the child. This is based on the proposition that all children have the right to look to at least two adults for protection and guidance (a proposition, incidentally, given explicit statutory recognition in the U.K. by s.13(5) of the Human Fertilisation and Embryology Act 1990 (c. 37)). The child of the unmarried father can look only to her or his mother. The present provision absolves the unmarried father from the responsibilities of safeguarding and promoting the child's health, development and welfare, of providing direction and guidance to the child, and of maintaining contact with the child. As such the present provision breaches art. 18, frustrates the Scottish Law Commission's aim of abolishing the concept of illegitimacy, and (by absolving men of their responsibilities towards their children) undermines the whole philosophy of this Part of the Act that responsibilities rather than rights are the basic determinant of a parent's relationship with a child.

Subs. (1)

This subsection re-enacts, with insignificant changes in terminology, the provision previously contained in s.2 of the 1986 Act. All mothers will have full parental responsibilities and parental rights in relation to their children; fathers will have such responsibilities and rights only if married to the mother at the time of, or any time after, the child's conception. The truth is out, and this provision is expressly stated to be "notwithstanding s.1(1)" of the 1986 Act, *i.e.* even although that earlier provision says that children of unmarried parents are to be treated the same as children of married parents, the two classes of children are still to be treated differently, for the child of unmarried parents has a lesser legal relationship with her or his father than the child of married parents.

Time of the child's conception. It is always difficult to determine this accurately (for a discussion, see Wilkinson and Norrie, *Parent and Child* (1993, W. Green) at pp. 129–131).

Subs. (2)

Again repeating the provision in s.2 of the 1986 Act, it is provided that the "marriage" which confers parental responsibilities and parental rights on fathers can be valid, voidable or void. It is not stated, but one can assume, that both regular and irregular marriages are covered (though there is always the difficulty in establishing when an irregular marriage occurred: see Clive, *The Law of Husband and Wife in Scotland* (4th ed., 1997, W. Green) at pp. 57–63).

Believed by them . . . to be valid. In one respect the law is tightened up from the 1986 provisions and fewer fathers than previously will be able to rely on this provision to obtain parental responsibilities. A father will have automatic parental responsibilities and parental rights even when his "marriage" to the mother is void, so long as it was believed "by them", *i.e.* by both the father and the mother, to be valid. In other words, the husband in a void marriage will acquire parental responsibilities and parental rights only if both he and his wife are in good faith. Under s.2(2)(b) of the 1986 Act (and the common law before that: see Fraser, *Parent and Child* (3rd ed., 1906, W. Green) at p. 27), the void marriage had to be believed to be valid "by him", that is by the father alone. The fact that the mother knew the marriage was void (say, because she knew she was already married) did not, under the 1986 Act, prevent the father obtaining parental rights; now, however, bad faith on the part of the mother alone will prevent the father from sharing parental responsibilities and parental rights with the mother. As in s.4(1) below, an unmarried father can be disadvantaged by the wrongdoing of the (equally unmarried) mother.

Subs. (3)

It is enacted for the avoidance of doubt that notwithstanding the automatic conferral of parental responsibilities and parental rights under subs. (1) above, the court can make an order which confers such responsibilities and rights on another person, whether under this Act or another Act or any other rule of law. It may be noted here that when a court confers parental responsibilities and parental rights it is not conferring parenthood on the individual, but merely some of the consequences thereof.

Subs. (4)

This is a new provision, making plain what was implicit in the pre-1995 law, namely that the person with parental responsibilities or parental rights cannot exercise them in such a way as is inconsistent with either a court order or a supervision requirement imposed by a children's hearing. In respect of the children's hearing, this provision is important in emphasising that parental responsibilities and parental rights are effectively superseded in so far as the hearing decides by way of a supervision requirement. So for example when a hearing imposes a supervision requirement with a condition of residence, which it may do under s.70(3) below, this supersedes the parent's responsibility and right to determine the child's residence (but only for so long as the supervision requirement lasts).

Subs. (5)

The ultimate legal responsibility for exercising parental responsibilities and parental rights rests with the parent who has these responsibilities and rights, and that responsibility cannot be given up. Parents cannot (without judicial process) "resign" their parenthood. If the child is harmed as a result of the wrongful exercise of parental responsibilities and parental rights, it is the parent with these responsibilities and rights who must bear the blame. A parent may provide for the fulfilment of her responsibilities at a practical level by someone else, by a formal or an informal arrangement, but while the parent has parental responsibilities and parental rights that delegation does not amount to a delegation of liability.

Arrangement. An informal arrangement is envisaged here, and there is no provision, as there is in s.4 below, for the arrangement to be in any specified format or to be registered anywhere.

Subs. (6)

Following on from the previous subsection, this provides that liability for failure to fulfil parental responsibilities rests with the parent who has such responsibilities. So a parent who leaves the exercise of the responsibility and the right of, for example, legal representation to someone else cannot evade liability for any loss to the child's estate caused by the delegate. If the delegation amounts to the fostering of the child within the meaning of the Foster Children (Scotland) Act 1984 (c. 56) (*i.e.* private fostering rather than fostering as an aspect of local authority care) then that Act will govern the responsibilities of the foster carer (without, of course, prejudice to the liability of the parent under the current provision).

Acquisition of parental rights and responsibilities by natural father

4.—(1) Where a child's mother has not been deprived of some or all of the parental responsibilities and parental rights in relation to him and, by virtue of subsection (1)(b) of section 3 of this Act, his father has no parental responsibilities or parental rights in relation to him, the father and mother, whatever age they may be, may by agreement provide that, as from the appropriate date, the father shall have the parental responsibilities and parental rights which (in the absence of any order under section 11 of this Act affecting those responsibilities and rights) he would have if married to the mother.

(2) No agreement under subsection (1) above shall have effect unless—
(a) in a form prescribed by the Secretary of State; and
(b) registered in the Books of Council and Session while the mother still has the parental responsibilities and parental rights which she had when the agreement was made.

(3) The date on which such registration as is mentioned in subsection (2)(b) above takes place shall be the "appropriate date" for the purposes of subsection (1) above.

(4) An agreement which has effect by virtue of subsection (2) above shall, subject only to section 11(11) of this Act, be irrevocable.

DEFINITIONS
"child": s.15(1).
"parental responsibilities": s.1(3).
"parental rights": s.2(4).

GENERAL NOTE
Under the 1986 Act an unmarried father could obtain parental rights only by being appointed guardian by the testamentary deed of the mother in accordance with s.4 thereof or by being conferred parental rights by a court under s.3 thereof. In addition to these means (which are re-enacted in the present Act), this section provides another means by which a father, who is not married to the mother of the child or was not married to her at the time of the child's conception or subsequently, can acquire parental responsibilities and parental rights in relation to the child, and that is by entering into a registered agreement in prescribed form with the mother. For further discussion, see Norrie, 1996 SCOLAG 94.

Subs. (1)
Where a child's mother has not been deprived. It is only mothers who still retain the full gamut of parental responsibilities and parental rights who have power to confer parental responsibilities and parental rights on unmarried fathers, and it follows that if those responsibilities and rights have been taken away from the mother, whether by private law means (an order under s.11 below) or by public law means (an order under s.86 below or under the Adoption (Scotland) Act 1978 (c. 28)) this section is inapplicable. On the other hand, a mother whose child is subject to a supervision requirement with a condition of residence has not "been deprived" of her parental responsibilities and parental rights; rather they have simply been suspended during the currency of the supervision requirement to the extent necessary to give effect to that requirement, and such a mother can enter into an agreement under this section with the father. While the thinking behind this rule is clear and understandable—a mother ought not to be able to confer upon the father that which she does not herself have—it does nevertheless limit the number of fathers who can acquire parental responsibilities and parental rights by this route, without any fault or influence on the part of the father. A mother, by her failure to fulfil her own parental responsibilities, can thereby create a situation in which the father cannot acquire those responsibilities without going to court.

Deprived of some or all. If the mother has been deprived even of only one of the parental responsibilities or parental rights (*e.g.* that of legal representation) the father loses the chance of acquiring any parental responsibilities and parental rights by an agreement under this section. This is because the agreement can confer only the full gamut, as opposed to a selection, of the parental responsibilities and parental rights and, again, the mother should not be able to give what she does not have.

His father. "Father" is not defined, though s.15(1) defines "parent" to mean "genetic father or mother". We may take "father" to mean "genetic father". It is generally only a child's genetic father who can acquire parental responsibilities and parental rights by registering an agreement under this section. It is not open, for example, to the husband or the cohabitant of the mother (or any other relative of the child) to acquire parental responsibilities and parental rights in this way, even when they have alimentary obligations towards the child. It follows that in order for the agreement to be effective, the father will have to establish that he is indeed the father of the child concerning whom the agreement is made. This can be done either by relying on the presumption in s.5(1)(b) of the 1986 Act, the provision deeming paternity under s.28(3) of the Human Fertilisation and Embryology Act 1990 (c. 37) (even though this does not deem genetic paternity), or by proof in court in an action of declarator of paternity under s.7 of the 1986 Act. The registering of an agreement under this section may well operate to create a presumption of fact that the male party to the agreement is the father of the child.

Whatever age they may be. These words give legal capacity to any person old enough to be a parent to enter into such an agreement. It does not, however, confer upon an under-16-year-old parent any capacity to exercise parental responsibilities or parental rights which he does not otherwise have (see note to s.2(1) above for further comment on the child-parent). A child-parent who acquires parental responsibilities and parental rights by an agreement under this section will not be able to exercise any of them until such time as he has capacity to do so, and the effect of these words is limited to preserving the validity of an agreement entered into before either or both of the parties reaches the age of 16.

Agreement. A father cannot force the mother to share parental responsibilities and parental rights with him; it can only be done by agreement. The matter lies in the hands of the mother to allow the father to obtain responsibilities and rights; but she cannot force him to accept them. Nor can the father force the mother to allow him responsibilities and rights, and there is no provision for the dispensing with the mother's agreement (as in, for example, adoption).

As from the appropriate date. The agreement takes effect on the day the agreement is registered in terms of subs. (2) below (subs. (3)).

He would have if married to the mother. The agreement is non-negotiable in the sense that the mother cannot offer some parental responsibilities only or some parental rights only. Again it is to be emphasised that parental rights exist only in order to allow the fulfilment of parental responsibilities and this would be defeated if only rights or only responsibilities could be obtained by such an agreement. Nor is it open to the mother to confer one of the parental responsibilities with its reciprocal parental right. The agreement must confer on the father all the parental responsibilities listed in s.1(1) together with all the parental rights listed in s.2(1).

Subs. (2)

The agreement in terms of subs. (1) above must be in the form prescribed by the Parental Responsibilities and Parental Rights Agreement (Scotland) Regulations 1996 (S.I. 1996 No. 2549), or in a form to the like effect, and to be effective, the agreement has to be registered in the Books of Council and Session at a time when the mother retains her parental responsibilities and parental rights.

Subs. (4)

Once entered into, only the court can revoke the agreement and it can do so only when making an order under s.11(2)(a) or (b) (*i.e.* an order depriving a person of parental responsibilities or parental rights or an order conferring these responsibilities and rights on a person). As the revocation is done under the authority of s.11, the three overarching principles in s.11(7) must be taken into account by the court. The making of an order under s.11(2)(a) or (b) does not automatically revoke an agreement—rather the court must make an express decision to that effect, separate from its decision to make an order under either of these paragraphs. An example from England is provided by *Re P. (Terminating Parental Responsibility)* [1995] 1 F.L.R. 1048. See also *Re G. (Child Care: Parental Involvement* [1996] Fam.L. 459.

S.I.s ISSUED UNDER SECTION
Parental Responsibilities and Parental Rights Agreement (Scotland) Regulations 1996 (S.I. 1996 No. 2549).

Care or control of child by person without parental responsibilities or parental rights

5.—(1) Subject to subsection (2) below, it shall be the responsibility of a person who has attained the age of sixteen years and who has care or control of a child under that age, but in relation to him either has no parental responsibilities or parental rights or does not have the parental responsibility mentioned in section 1(1)(a) of this Act, to do what is reasonable in all the circumstances to safeguard the child's health, development and welfare; and in fulfilling his responsibility under this section the person may in particular, even though he does not have the parental right mentioned in section 2(1)(d) of this Act, give consent to any surgical, medical or dental treatment or procedure where—

(a) the child is not able to give such consent on his own behalf; and

(b) it is not within the knowledge of the person that a parent of the child would refuse to give the consent in question.

(2) Nothing in this section shall apply to a person in so far as he has care or control of a child in a school ("school" having the meaning given by section 135(1) of the Education (Scotland) Act 1980).

Children (Scotland) Act 1995

DEFINITIONS
"child": s.15(1).
"parental responsibilities": s.1(3).
"parental rights": s.2(4).
"person": s.15(4).
"school": Education (Scotland) Act 1980, s.135(1).

GENERAL NOTE

See Scot. Law Com. No. 135, para. 2.59.

The law as it stood before the making of this provision was very unclear as to the powers of persons who had the care and control of a child but no parental rights in relation to the child. The concept of a person acting *in loco parentis* was undeveloped in Scots law and is a description of fact rather than a distinct legal institution. Yet it frequently happens that a child falls into the care and control of such a person. For example, a neighbour may be looking after a child while a parent is in hospital, or a relative may be taking the child on holiday, or a baby sitter may be watching over a child for an evening, or a child-minder may be caring for the child during the day, or a foster carer may be caring for the child on an emergency and short-term basis; in addition, an unmarried father who lives in family with his child and the mother will often adopt a parenting role even when the law encourages him to shirk his responsibilities. This provision imposes a measure of responsibility on any such person. It is implicit, though surprisingly not stated, that the power or right to act in such a way as is necessary to fulfil the responsibility is also conferred. It is expressly provided that a person with care or control of a child can consent to the child's medical treatment. What, in essence, is contemplated by this provision is a safeguarding power rather than an upbringing role. The House of Lords has held, in relation to the equivalent English provision (Children Act 1989, s.3(5)) that the power granted does not give the holder the ability to change the child's habitual residence merely by taking the child out of the jurisdiction: *Re S. (A Minor)* [1997] 4 All E.R. 251.

Subs. (1)

A person who has care or control of a child under 16 has the responsibility to safeguard the child's health, development and welfare, even though she or he does not have that responsibility by way of parental responsibility or right. The responsibility expressly includes the power to consent to medical treatment when the child cannot give personal consent and when the person is unaware of any parental objection thereto.

Has attained the age of 16 years. This provision does not apply to persons under 16, such as, for example, a 15 year old baby sitter (thus avoiding problems relating to the legal capacity of such a person). Notwithstanding a contrary assumption in the House of Lords debates on this clause (see *Hansard*, H.L., Vol. 564, col. 53) the provision does not require that all babysitters be over the age of 16 years, but merely provides a rule for those who are.

Care or control. Whether a child is in the care or control of another person is a question of fact, to be determined by all the circumstances, and these factual circumstances can change rapidly. Physical possession of and proximity to the child are clearly significant but not determining. It will cover informal temporary arrangements, such as weekends with grand-parents or friends (but not, because of subs. (2) below, school trips), as well as longer term arrangements such as when an unmarried father cares for his child, or the child is being looked after by foster carers; and it is clearly wide enough also to cover the kidnapper.

Do what is reasonable. The responsibility to safeguard the child's health, development and welfare is not absolute and is merely one to use reasonable care. What is reasonable will depend on all the circumstances. A person with long-term care or control will have more extensive responsibilities towards the child's development than a person with care and control for a weekend.

Consent to any surgical, medical or dental treatment or procedure. This phrase reflects that used in s.2(4) of the Age of Legal Capacity (Scotland) Act 1991 (c. 50) and is to be given a wide interpretation. The power to give medical consent under this provision is, however, limited by its protective context. It will not include treatment designed for the benefit of others, such as circumcision or organ donation, nor elective treatment such as contraception or abortion (unless this can be shown to be necessary to safeguard the child's welfare). It may not cover cosmetic surgery (unless this is therapeutic). Experimental treatment for research cannot be consented to under this provision. Power to consent includes power to refuse, because "consent" is simply a shorthand way of expressing the power of medical decision-making (see notes to s.90 below). The reference to s.2(1)(d) (the right of legal representation) indicates that the exercise of the power of consent is an exercise of the right of legal representation rather than the responsibility to safeguard the child's health (this has importance for the purposes of how long the right to represent the child lasts: see the notes to s.15(5) below). If this is so (and it was

18

assumed to be so in Scot. Law Com. No. 135 at para. 2.22) then the acquisition by the child of capacity to consent denies anyone else the right to consent on her or his behalf: this is made explicit by s.15(5) below.

The child is not able to give such consent. A child may not be able to give consent on her or his own behalf for practical reasons (*e.g.* unconsciousness after an accident) or legal reasons (*i.e.* incapacity). A child's capacity to consent to or to refuse medical treatment is governed by s.2(4) of the Age of Legal Capacity (Scotland) Act 1991 (c. 50) (see discussion in Wilkinson and Norrie, *Parent and Child* (1993, W. Green) at pp. 182–187).

Not within the knowledge. The onus of proof lies on the person claiming that it is within the knowledge of the person with care or control of the child that the parent would refuse to give consent.

Would refuse. To deny the person with care or control the power to consent to medical treatment, it has to be shown that the parent would refuse consent, and not simply that the parent is likely to refuse consent. This is a high standard of proof and will only be satisfied in cases in which there is positive and unequivocal evidence, apparent before the need for consent arose, that the parent would not consent, for example if the parent, to the knowledge of the person with care or control of the child, had consistently refused to have the child inoculated.

Subs. (2)

The powers of teachers and school administrators are contained in the Education (Scotland) Act 1980 (c. 44), and are not enlarged by this section.

Views of children

6.—(1) A person shall, in reaching any major decision which involves—

(a) his fulfilling a parental responsibility or the responsibility mentioned in section 5(1) of this Act; or

(b) his exercising a parental right or giving consent by virtue of that section,

have regard so far as practicable to the views (if he wishes to express them) of the child concerned, taking account of the child's age and maturity, and to those of any other person who has parental responsibilities or parental rights in relation to the child (and wishes to express those views); and without prejudice to the generality of this subsection a child twelve years of age or more shall be presumed to be of sufficient age and maturity to form a view.

(2) A transaction entered into in good faith by a third party and a person acting as legal representative of a child shall not be challengeable on the ground only that the child, or a person with parental responsibilities or parental rights in relation to the child, was not consulted or that due regard was not given to his views before the transaction was entered into.

DEFINITIONS

"child": s.15(1).
"legal representative": s.15(5).
"parental responsibilities": s.1(3).
"parental rights": s.2(4).
"person": s.15(4).
"transaction": s.15(1); s.9 of the Age of Legal Capacity (Scotland) Act 1991.

GENERAL NOTE

Article 12 of the UN Convention on the Rights of the Child provides as follows:

"States parties shall assure to the child who is capable of forming his or her own views the right to express those views freely in all matters affecting the child, the views of the child being given due weight in accordance with the age and maturity of the child. For this purpose, the child shall in particular be provided the opportunity to be heard in any judicial and administrative proceedings affecting the child, either directly, or through a representative or an appropriate body, in a manner consistent with the procedural rules of national law."

The duty on courts and children's hearings making decisions in connection with children to take account of the views of children is dealt with in ss.11(7) and 16(2) respectively below. The present provision, following Scot. Law Com. No. 135 at paras 2.60–2.66, attempts to give effect to Art. 12 UN by directing that parents and others exercising parental responsibilities and parental rights are also to have regard to the views of the child and others with parental responsibilities and parental rights in making decisions which will affect the child. The difficulty lies in identifying how this provision can be enforced, or identifying what sanction could follow a failure to fulfil the obligation. In relation to decisions of the court or the children's hearing, the obligation to take account of the child's views can be enforced through the appeal mechanisms; but there is no judicial review of parental decisions and any decision made in the absence of consultation with the child or other person with parental responsibilities and parental rights will be given effect to. This is made explicit in relation to the entering into of transactions; other decisions too will remain effective. So, for example, a parental decision to send a 13-year-old child to one school rather than another will be an effective and valid exercise of a parental responsibility and parental right even although the child or other person has not been consulted.

Subs. (1)

A person fulfilling a parental responsibility or exercising a parental right or otherwise fulfilling a responsibility to safeguard the child's health, development and welfare will frequently have to make decisions which affect the child. In doing so the person is obliged by this provision to have regard to the child's views, taking account of her or his age and maturity. The child is not obliged to express views, but the wording suggests that the person making the decision is obliged to seek out, or at the very least to give the child the opportunity to express, her or his views. A child aged 12 or more is (rebuttably) presumed to be of sufficient age and maturity to form a view. In addition, the decision-maker must take account of the views of any other person with parental responsibilities and parental rights, though the fact that under s.2(2) above each person with parental rights can exercise these rights without the consent of the other renders the obligation of consultation one of symbolic and educative importance only.

Any major decision. Clearly not all decisions affecting a child will fall within this category. Decisions concerning what clothes the child is to wear, when she or he is to be home at night, or what she or he is to eat, are not major decisions. A decision by the parents to move house, which involves moving the child to another school is likely to be considered major, and sending the child to stay long term with a relative certainly is. To change the child's nationality is a major decision, as is a change in her or his domicile or habitual residence, for all these will affect the laws to which the child is subject. The appointment of a guardian is expressly made a major decision: s.7(6) below. Due to the unenforceability of s.6 as a whole, it is unlikely that there will be court proceedings on the question of what is or is not a major decision.

Have regard. The parent must have regard to the views of the child and other person with parental responsibilities and parental rights, but need not follow them. All the provision requires is that the parent seeks out and gives active consideration to any expressed views. These views are not determining, for other considerations, such as costs and practicality and the child's welfare may predominate. A child may desperately wish to attend a fee-paying school, but these wishes are meaningless if the parent cannot afford the fees.

So far as practicable. It may not be practicable to obtain the views of a child or other person on a particular matter and, if so, the obligation under this provision is not breached by a failure to do so. Indeed in circumstances in which it would not be practicable to give effect to any view expressed by the child, the obligation to have regard to such a view is so meaningless as to be non-existent.

If he wishes to express them. A child has no obligation to give views on matters relating to major decisions, and there will indeed be circumstances in which a child's welfare demands that she or he is not disturbed by being asked to make serious choices. It is cruel, for example, for separating parents to ask their young child to choose between them. Pressure should not be put on a child to express views which are difficult to form and awkward to express.

A child 12 years of age or more. Under the adoption legislation a child 12 years of age or over must consent to the adoption before an adoption order can be made (Adoption (Scotland) Act 1978 (c. 28), s.12(8)) and under the Age of Legal Capacity (Scotland) Act 1991 (c. 50), s.2(3), legal capacity to give or withhold that consent is granted at that age. This provision is similar, but not identical. There is a rebuttable presumption that the child of 12 or more is able to form (and express) a view on the matter at issue, but the provision does not give the child a veto, as is the case with adoption. The obligation is as effective for younger children who in fact can form and express a view; and if an older child cannot in fact form a view on the particular matter at issue then there is no obligation under this provision to seek out and have regard to her or his views.

Subs. (2)

This subsection protects the interests of third parties acting in good faith who transact with a person acting as a child's legal representative. If the legal representative has not consulted with, or had regard to the views of, the child or other person with parental responsibilities and parental rights in relation to the transaction, the transaction remains valid (unless it can be challenged on some other ground).

Child. A child for this purpose is a person under 16, otherwise she or he will not have a legal representative who is entitled to act because the child is incapable of so acting (see s.15(5) below).

Guardianship

Appointment of guardians

7.—(1) A child's parent may appoint a person to be guardian of the child in the event of the parent's death; but—
   (a) such appointment shall be of no effect unless—
       (i) in writing and signed by the parent; and
       (ii) the parent, at the time of death, was entitled to act as legal representative of the child (or would have been so entitled if he had survived until after the birth of the child); and
   (b) any parental responsibilities or parental rights (or the right to appoint a further guardian under this section) which a surviving parent has in relation to the child shall subsist with those which, by, under or by virtue of this Part of this Act, the appointee so has.

(2) A guardian of a child may appoint a person to take his place as guardian in the event of the guardian's death; but such appointment shall be of no effect unless in writing and signed by the person making it.

(3) An appointment as guardian shall not take effect until accepted, either expressly or impliedly by acts which are not consistent with any other intention.

(4) If two or more persons are appointed as guardians, any one or more of them shall, unless the appointment expressly provides otherwise, be entitled to accept office even if both or all of them do not accept office.

(5) Subject to any order under section 11 or 86 of this Act, a person appointed as a child's guardian under this section shall have, in respect of the child, the responsibilities imposed, and the rights conferred, on a parent by sections 1 and 2 of this Act respectively; and sections 1 and 2 of this Act shall apply in relation to a guardian as they apply in relation to a parent.

(6) Without prejudice to the generality of subsection (1) of section 6 of this Act, a decision as to the appointment of a guardian under subsection (1) or (2) above shall be regarded for the purposes of that section (or of that section as applied by subsection (5) above) as a major decision which involves exercising a parental right.

DEFINITIONS
   "child": s.15(1).
   "legal representative": s.15(5).
   "parent": s.15(1).
   "parental responsibilities": s.1(3).
   "parental rights": s.2(4).
   "person": s.15(4).

GENERAL NOTE
   See Scot. Law Com. No. 135, paras 3.1.–3.15.
   Until the coming into force of the Age of Legal Capacity (Scotland) Act 1991 (c. 50), the word "guardian" was not a term of art with a uniform recognised meaning in Scots law, notwithstanding that it appeared in numerous statutes (each with its own, peculiar, definition). Since 1991 it has been clear that the primary (but not the only) meaning of the word "guardian" (as used, for example, in the 1986 Act) is "legal representative", in the way that tutor was prior to the Age of Legal Capacity (Scotland) Act 1991. However, ambiguity remained, and it was common to refer to parents as guardians when they were exercising the guardianship role, that is acting as the child's legal representative. Under s.4 of the 1986 Act, a parent could appoint a guardian to a child, but this was an appointment only of a legal representative and did not amount to the conferring of the right of, say, custody. Yet sometimes the word "guardian" was used to mean much more than legal representative, and in the common phrase "parent or guardian", the meaning is clearly understood to be parent on the one hand or parent-substitute

with all the rights and duties of a parent on the other hand. The present Act, though nowhere defining "guardian", clarifies the position, and this section provides that "guardian", as appointed under the provisions of the Act, is a parent-substitute, with all the parental responsibilities and parental rights, and not only the responsibility and right of legal representation. The parent will never act as "guardian", but may act as "legal representative". It should be noted, however, that a guardian is a parent-substitute only for the purposes of parental responsibilities and parental rights as defined in ss.1 and 2 above, and not, for example, for the purposes of succession or the law of incest or the forbidden degrees of marriage. Guardians are no longer to be treated as trustees for the purposes of the Trusts Acts (Sched. 4, para. 6 and Sched. 5), but any person acting as a child's legal representative will be subject to trust-like obligations.

This section deals with the powers of, and testamentary appointment of, guardians, while s.8 below deals with revocation and termination of guardianship, and s.11(2)(h) below deals with court appointment and removal of guardians.

Subs. (1)

This provision re-enacts, with some modification, the rules previously contained in s.4 of the 1986 Act, to the effect that a parent may appoint a person to act as guardian of the child by testamentary deed, and that the appointment does not affect the responsibilities and rights of the other parent.

A child's parent. Subs. (1) applies only to the genetic parent of the child who has the parental responsibility and the parental right of legal representation.

A person. Though the singular is used, normal principles of statutory interpretation (Interpretation Act 1978 (c. 30), s.6(c)) indicate that the singular can include the plural, and it follows that a parent can appoint more than one person to be the child's guardian. This is given further support by subs. (4) below, which would be meaningless if "a person" were interpreted as being restricted to the singular.

To be guardian. The equivalent provision under the 1986 Act (s.4) limited the appointee to the parental right of legal representation, but under the new provision the notion of "guardian" is significantly extended by subs. (5) below and the appointment of a person to be guardian has the effect of conferring all the parental responsibilities and parental rights on the appointee: the appointment of a person to be guardian is an appointment of a person to be parent-substitute of the child.

In the event of the parent's death. The appointment is testamentary in nature, in that it can only take effect as from the date of death of the parent. A parent cannot appoint a guardian to act during that parent's lifetime. The appointment can be made in a will or codicil thereto, or in a separate deed.

Entitled to act as legal representative. These words show a lingering confusion as to whether a guardian is a parent-substitute or a legal representative. Only a parent who has the responsibility and right of legal representation can appoint a guardian, but the appointment, according to subs. (5) below, will confer all the parental responsibilities and rights and not just that of legal representation. If a parent has only the responsibility and right of legal representation and has been denied the others then an appointment would seem to confer upon the appointee more power than the appointer her or himself has (*cf.* s.4(1) above, where a mother who has been denied any one of her parental responsibilities or parental rights is prohibited from agreeing to share parental responsibilities and parental rights with the father, because he would thereby acquire from her more than she had to give). However, the terms of subs. (5) below are clear and unambiguous, with the result that a parent who has the right of legal representation but not the right, say, to have the child living with him can appoint a guardian who will have both the right of legal representation and the right to determine the child's residence. This position is odd but, on the clear wording of the statute, unavoidable.

Survived until after the birth. A person may make such a testamentary appointment even although she or he dies before the birth of the child (following the old common law rule in relation to appointment of tutors: *Murray v. Merschall* (1555) Mor. 16226). However, it should be noted that the child must be conceived and in the womb before the death of the father making the appointment, otherwise the genetic father is not the father in legal terms: Human Fertilisation and Embryology Act 1990, s.28(6)(b).

A surviving parent. The surviving parent who has parental responsibilities and parental rights retains these responsibilities and rights notwithstanding the acquisition of responsibilities and rights by the appointee. There was no such provision in the 1986 Act, though it was certainly assumed to be the law. This provision is included, therefore, for the avoidance of doubt. Section 2(2) above is to be recalled, which allows any person with parental responsibilities or parental rights to exercise them without reference to any other person with the same responsibilities or rights.

Subs. (2)

This is a new provision. One of the flaws in the 1986 Act was that while it allowed parents to appoint guardians, it did not allow guardians to appoint guardians, and so if a child was unfortunate enough to lose a parent, who had appointed a guardian, and then to lose that guardian, the only way a further guardian could be appointed to such a child was by petition to the court. This flaw has now been remedied, in a way consistent with the whole format of this section, which is to give guardians all the parental responsibilities and parental rights of a parent. One of these rights is to appoint a guardian by testamentary deed, and a guardian, whether so appointed or appointed by the court, is now expressly given that right in this subsection.

A guardian. The office of guardianship must be subsisting in the guardian at the date of her or his death.

A person. As with subs. (1) above, the singular includes the plural.

Subs. (3)

Again, this is a new provision added for the avoidance of doubt. The office of guardian can be onerous and is not to be imposed on a person unwilling to accept the responsibilities of a parent-substitute. The appointment, therefore, only takes effect once it has been accepted by the nominee. (The rule may well be different with court appointments under s.11(2)(h), for there is no requirement under that section for the consent of any person before any parental responsibility or parental right be imposed upon them.)

Accepted . . . impliedly. Cases involving implied acceptance of the office of trusteeship may prove of use here: see Wilson and Duncan, *Trusts, Trustees and Executors* (2nd ed., 1995, W. Green) at pp. 297–300.

Subs. (4)

The appointment of more than one guardian is joint and several and any nominee can accept without affecting the nomination of the others. This provision reflects the law as it already stands (see Wilkinson and Norrie, *Parent and Child* (1993, W. Green) at pp. 385–387), but puts it on a statutory basis and is for the avoidance of doubt, as recommended by the Scottish Law Commission (Scot. Law Com. No. 135, para. 3.9).

Subs. (5)

This important provision has the effect of showing that the "guardian" in today's law is a "parent-substitute". Once appointed, the guardian acquires all the parental responsibilities and parental rights that the parent is given under ss.1 and 2 of the present Act. The guardian is no longer simply the legal representative or, as she or he was known at common law, the tutor of the child, but has the full powers, duties, liabilities, responsibilities and rights, of a parent. The guardian steps into the shoes of the parent (for the purposes of parental responsibilities and parental rights as defined in ss.1 and 2 above). The parent making the appointment cannot confer only some of the parental responsibilities or parental rights on the appointee.

Appointed under this section. These words suggest that the rule contained in this subsection applies only when the guardian is appointed by testamentary deed. But the same effect is achieved with court-appointed guardians (see the General Note to s.11(2)(h) below).

Subs. (6)

The effect of this provision is that the views of the child and any other person with parental responsibilities and parental rights must be sought and regard given to them according to the principles in s.6 above in relation to the appointment of a guardian. In other words, when a parent or guardian is drawing up a testamentary deed in which a guardian is to be appointed, she must have regard so far as practicable to the views (if she or he wishes to express them) of the other parent and of the child over whom a guardian is to be appointed, taking account of the child's age and maturity. As with the generality of s.6, this provision is more a pious hope than a legally enforceable obligation. If the child's or other parent's views are not sought, or ignored, then this will not be a ground for challenging the appointment. Section 6(2) saves the validity of "transactions" entered into by legal representatives, but that would not save the appointment of a guardian, which only with some difficulty could be described as an act of legal representation. The absence of a provision similar to that in s.6(2) might indicate that the appointment is not saved. However, it is likely that if Parliament intended that the child's or other parent's consent were a requirement for an appointment as guardian it would have made express provision for this, just as express provision is made for the child's consent to adoption (Adoption (Scotland) Act 1978, s.12(8)). Consent is not a condition precedent, and nor is consultation with the child. It is a hope and an expectation, but in legal terms nothing more. A child or parent who objects to the appointment will be able to apply to the court under s.11 below for the termination of the appointment or for the appointment of someone else. Such an application would only be successful, of course, if the court is persuaded that it is in the child's interests, but it will usually be against a child's interests (particularly when the child is older) to be given a guardian (that is a parent-substitute) to whom she or he objects.

Revocation and other termination of appointment

8.—(1) An appointment made under section 7(1) or (2) of this Act revokes an earlier such appointment (including one made in an unrevoked will or codicil) made by the same person in respect of the same child, unless it is clear (whether as a result of an express provision in the later appointment or by any necessary implication) that the purpose of the later appointment is to appoint an additional guardian.

(2) Subject to subsections (3) and (4) below, the revocation of an appointment made under section 7(1) or (2) of this Act (including one made in an unrevoked will or codicil) shall not take effect unless the revocation is in writing and is signed by the person making the revocation.

(3) An appointment under section 7(1) or (2) of this Act (other than one made in a will or codicil) is revoked if, with the intention of revoking the appointment, the person who made it—

(a) destroys the document by which it was made; or

(b) has some other person destroy that document in his presence.

(4) For the avoidance of doubt, an appointment made under section 7(1) or (2) of this Act in a will or codicil is revoked if the will or codicil is revoked.

(5) Once an appointment of a guardian has taken effect under section 7 of this Act, then, unless the terms of the appointment provide for earlier termination, it shall terminate only by virtue of—

(a) the child concerned attaining the age of eighteen years;

(b) the death of the child or the guardian; or

(c) the termination of the appointment by a court order under section 11 of this Act.

DEFINITIONS
"child": s.15(1).
"parent": s.15(1).

GENERAL NOTE
See Scot. Law Com. No. 135, para. 3.16.

The 1986 Act did not deal expressly with revocation and termination of guardianship, and the law on this point, rather untidily, was mostly to be found in the Trusts (Scotland) Act 1921 (c. 58), since guardians were trustees for the purposes of that Act, and the other Trusts Acts. Scheds 4 and 5 to the present Act remove guardianship from the Trusts Acts and this section aims to provide a complete code of when and how guardianship comes to an end (other than by court termination, which is dealt with under s.11(2)(h) below).

Subs. (1)

This introduces a presumption that a subsequent appointment will supersede a previously made appointment. The appointment, of course, does not take effect until the death of the appointer, and it would have been more apt to talk here of nomination rather than appointment. The nomination that takes effect is the latest in time and a new nomination has the effect of revoking an earlier nomination. It is, however, possible to appoint more than one person to be guardian, and this may be done in consecutive deeds. So it is provided that, so long as this is made clear, a subsequent deed can be interpreted as nominating an additional guardian rather than superseding the previous nomination.

Express provision . . . or by any necessary implication. If the intent is to nominate an additional guardian then it would be better if this were done expressly, but the provision allows such an intent to be indicated by necessary implication. The word "necessary" is likely to receive a strict interpretation. Interpretation of deeds is governed by the intent of the maker of the deed, and not by the welfare of the child (see for example *Spencer's Trs v. Ruggles*, 1982 S.L.T. 165).

24

Subss. (2) and (3)

The nomination must be in writing and signed by the person making it (s.7(1)(a) and (2) above); likewise the revocation of the nomination must be in writing and signed by the person who made it. This is the only stated method by which a nomination contained in a will or codicil to a will can be revoked. Alternatively, if the nomination does not appear in a will or codicil, it can be revoked by intentional destruction, either at the hands of the appointer or at the hands of someone else at the instigation of and in the presence of the appointer.

Subs. (4)

It is assumed that when a will that contains an appointment is revoked, the appointment too is revoked. If the appointer does not intend that result, she or he must make a new appointment at the revocation of the will, or revoke the will in such a way that the appointment is preserved (*e.g.* by revoking the individual legacies in the will rather than the will itself).

Subs. (5)

An appointment, once it takes effect, is irrevocable: neither parents nor parent-substitutes can escape from their parental responsibilities and parental rights and the office of guardian (like the role of parent) is not one from which a person can resign. This clarifies the position from the old law, in which it was at least arguable that a guardian could resign by using the power of resignation contained in the Trusts (Scotland) Act 1921 (see Wilkinson and Norrie, *Parent and Child* (1993, W. Green) at pp. 395–397).

Unless the terms of the appointment provide for earlier termination. These words suggest that, notwithstanding the fact that a testamentary appointment will confer upon the appointee all the responsibilities and rights of a parent (s.7(5) above), the appointment itself may allow the parent-substitute to escape from these responsibilities and rights earlier than a parent could, either by providing a power to resign or by specifying for how long the appointment is to last. Such a provision should, it is submitted, be interpreted very strictly since it will seldom be in the interests of the child to allow a person to escape her or his responsibilities towards the child. In the case of a court appointment it would only be in highly exceptional circumstances that the decree appointing a person as guardian would allow the person to relinquish the parental responsibilities and rights undertaken. In the absence of any such term, the appointment as guardian will terminate only when the child grows up, or when the child or guardian dies, or when the court orders termination under s.11 below.

Has taken effect. This will normally be on the moment of death, since the appointment is testamentary in nature. It might, however, be at some time after death if the acceptance of the office of guardian has not occurred before then (see s.7(3) above).

Eighteen years. This again shows that the appointment is as a parent-substitute and not simply as legal representative, because the parental responsibility and parental right of legal representation lasts only until the child is 16. Indeed, all that remains after the child's 16th birthday is the responsibility of providing guidance to the child and the guardian shall have no other legal responsibility than that.

Administration of child's property

Safeguarding of child's property

9.—(1) Subject to section 13 of this Act, this section applies where—
  (a) property is owned by or due to a child;
  (b) the property is held by a person other than a parent or guardian of the child; and
  (c) but for this section, the property would be required to be transferred to a parent having parental responsibilities in relation to the child or to a guardian for administration by that parent or guardian on behalf of the child.

(2) Subject to subsection (4) below, where this section applies and the person holding the property is an executor or trustee, then—
  (a) if the value of the property exceeds £20,000, he shall; or
  (b) if that value is not less than £5,000 and does not exceed £20,000, he may, apply to the Accountant of Court for a direction as to the administration of the property.

(3) Subject to subsection (4) below, where this section applies and the person holding the property is a person other than an executor or trustee,

then, if the value of the property is not less than £5,000, that person may apply to the Accountant of Court for a direction as to the administration of the property.

(4) Where the parent or guardian mentioned in subsection (1)(c) above has been appointed a trustee under a trust deed to administer the property concerned, subsections (2) and (3) above shall not apply, and the person holding the property shall transfer it to the parent or guardian.

(5) On receipt of an application under subsection (2) or (3) above, the Accountant of Court may do one, or (in so far as the context admits) more than one, of the following—

(a) apply to the court for the appointment of a judicial factor (whether or not the parent or guardian mentioned in subsection (1)(c) above) to administer all or part of the property concerned and in the event of the court making such an appointment shall direct that the property, or as the case may be part, concerned be transferred to the factor;

(b) direct that all or part of the property concerned be transferred to himself;

(c) direct that all or, in a case where the parent or guardian so mentioned has not been appointed by virtue of paragraph (a) above, part of the property concerned be transferred to the parent or guardian, to be administered on behalf of the child.

(6) A direction under subsection (5)(c) above may include such conditions as the Accountant of Court considers appropriate, including in particular a condition—

(a) that in relation to the property concerned no capital expenditure shall be incurred without his approval; or

(b) that there shall be exhibited annually to him the securities and bank books which represent the capital of the estate.

(7) A person who has applied under subsection (2) or (3) above for a direction shall not thereafter transfer the property concerned except in accordance with a direction under subsection (5) above.

(8) The Secretary of State may from time to time prescribe a variation in any sum referred to in subsections (2) and (3) above.

(9) In this section "child" means a person under the age of sixteen years who is habitually resident in Scotland.

DEFINITIONS
"child": s.9(9).
"parent": s.15(1).
"parental responsibilities": s.1(3).

GENERAL NOTE
It can sometimes happen that substantial amounts of property fall into the ownership or entitlement of a child, and before the enactment of this provision the child's parent, exercising the right of guardianship, or the child's guardian, had the right to administer that property on behalf of the child. That administration was, however, subject to the provisions of the Judicial Factors Act 1849 (c. 51), with the result that a parent or guardian who received property on behalf of the child was under the supervision of the Accountant of Court, and was obliged to lodge an inventory and to submit annual accounts (1849 Act, ss.3 and 4). Clearly this was frequently ignored, particularly when the sums involved were modest, and the Scottish Law Commission (Scot. Law Com. No. 135 at para. 4.17) suggested a scheme whereby the law impose the obligations of judicial factors on parents and guardians in only some appropriate cases. Their proposals are given effect to in this section. In summary, directions may (and sometimes must) be sought from the Accountant of Court as to the administration of the property that is due to be paid to the parent or guardian on behalf of the child. The Accountant of Court has various options and can make orders and attach conditions thereto, which must be followed by the person who sought the directions. For a further discussion of this provision, see Robertson, "Children as Inheritors of Property" (1997) 42 J.L.S.S. 23.

Subs. (1)

The section applies in any situation in which property which is owned by, or due to, a child is held by a person other than a parent or guardian and would be (but for this section) required to be transferred to a parent or guardian having the right to administer the property on the child's behalf. The most common situations in which this arises is with inheritance, awards of damages (dealt with in s.13 below) and awards under the Criminal Injuries Compensation Scheme, though the section is not limited to these situations. Gretton points out that it is difficult to imagine a situation in which property is owed by or due to a child and at the same time would be required to be transferred to a parent or guardian: (1997) 42 J.L.S.S. 308. The section really only makes sense if each paragraph is an alternative.

A parent or guardian. The word "parent" in subs. (1)(b) refers to a parent with parental responsibilities and parental rights rather than to all genetic parents since the requirement is that the property be held by someone other than a person with parental responsibilities and parental rights.

Required to be transferred. The section applies only when the holder of property is required to pay it over to a parent with parental responsibilities or to a guardian. Not all property due to a child is required to be transferred to a parent or guardian for administration on behalf of the child. A child who earns money is normally entitled to have her or his earnings paid direct (though it would be unusual for the child to earn more than £5,000). Indeed a child who has legal capacity to grant a discharge to any person holding property on her or his behalf can be paid directly, and s.13 below, for example, is certainly based on the assumption that a discharge may sometimes be granted even before the age of 16.

Transferred to a parent ... or to a guardian. If the property is required to be transferred to someone other than a parent or guardian then this provision does not apply. In particular, the obligation may be to transfer the property to a trustee, for which, see subs. (4) below.

Subs. (2)

Under the previous law parents and guardians were treated as judicial factors no matter how modest the sums involved were, and the law was clearly frequently ignored with parents seldom submitting annual accounts. Indeed, when one considers the values of most children's property holding, the expense of fulfilling such an obligation was likely to be disproportionate and therefore against the child's economic welfare. The aim of s.9, therefore, is to ensure that the Accountant of Court becomes involved only when large amounts of money are involved. It is therefore provided that an executor or trustee holding property due to a child *must* apply to the Accountant of Court for directions when the amount exceeds £20,000 in value, and she or he *may* (but is not obliged to) apply for directions when the amount is less than £20,000 but exceeds £5,000. Though not stated, a necessary implication is that it would be incompetent to apply for directions when the sum involved is less than £5,000.

Subs. (3)

It is likely that most cases of a child becoming due amounts in excess of £5,000 will be as a result of inheritance, but there will sometimes be other situations, such as payments under the Criminal Injuries Compensation Scheme, or by gift. In any case other than that of an executor or trustee, if the amount due exceeds £5,000 the person holding the property has the discretion of applying to the Accountant of Court for directions. It is likely to be considered appropriate to seek directions if the sum involved is considerably in excess of £5,000, and while the person holding the property is not a legal representative and therefore not subject to the obligations contained in s.10 below, any person holding property on behalf of another is to some extent subject to the rules of trust law: it follows that the holder of the property is obliged to act as a reasonable and prudent trustee would act, and if loss is caused by a failure to seek directions the holder of the property may be liable to the child.

Subs. (4)

The obligation or discretion to make an application for directions to the Accountant of Court does not apply when the property holder is obliged to transfer the property to a parent or guardian who is a trustee under a trust deed to administer the property concerned. The property holder in that case must pay the property over directly to such a parent or guardian. This is because the child's interest in the property will be sufficiently protected by its being transferred into a trust and thereby subject to the rules of trust law.

Subs. (5)

If an application is made to the Accountant of Court he may either apply to the court for the appointment of a judicial factor, direct that the property be transferred to himself, or direct that the property be transferred to the parent or guardian; in each case so that it can be properly administered on behalf of the child.

May do one. The terms of the statute do not here admit of a discretion on the part of the Accountant of Court to do none of the listed acts. He may do one or he may do another or he may do more than one, but he must respond in one of the listed ways.

Apply to the court for the appointment of a judicial factor. If the Accountant of Court makes the application for such an appointment, the court is not obliged to grant it, nor to grant it in the terms in which the Accountant asks. If the court does make an appointment of a judicial factor then it must direct that the appropriate property be transferred to the factor. The factor will be subject, of course, to the rules in the Judicial Factors Act 1849.

The property concerned be transferred to himself. If the Accountant of Court directs that the property or part thereof be transferred to himself, then it shall be up to him to invest, administer or otherwise deal with the property on behalf of the child.

The property concerned be transferred to the parent or guardian. If the Accountant of Court directs that the property be transferred to the parent or guardian, then the parent or guardian must administer it on behalf of the child by exercising the responsibility and right of legal representation.

Subs. (6)

If the Accountant of Court has directed that all or part of the property concerned be transferred to the parent or guardian to be administered on behalf of the child, then he may include in that direction such conditions as he considers appropriate. The provision is wide in its terms, and paras (a) and (b) give examples of the sorts of condition that might, in appropriate cases, be included.

Subs. (7)

If an application for directions has been made to the Accountant of Court, the person making the application must follow these directions in transferring the property. If he transfers the property otherwise than in accordance with the directions, say by paying direct to a parent or guardian instead of, as instructed, to the Accountant of Court, and loss is caused to the child thereby, that person may be called upon to pay again out of his own pocket the value of the property in accordance with the directions. This liability is not spelt out in the statute, but is analogous to the liability of a trustee who pays out to a wrong beneficiary to pay again to the correct beneficiary. See Wilson and Duncan, *Trusts, Trustees and Executors* (2nd ed., 1995, W. Green) at pp. 438–444.

Subs. (8)

The figures of £5,000 and £20,000 may be varied by the Secretary of State.

Subs. (9)

Child. The protections provided by this section are not required for persons who are able to administer their own property for themselves, and since the coming into effect of the Age of Legal Capacity (Scotland) Act 1991, this has been at age 16 at the latest and, sometimes, earlier. The responsibility and the right of legal representation lasts only until the child is 16 in any case (ss.1(2) and 2(7) above) or sometimes ends sooner (s.15(5) below).

Habitually resident. For the meaning of this phrase, see notes to s.14(1) below.

Obligations and rights of person administering child's property

10.—(1) A person acting as a child's legal representative in relation to the administration of the child's property—

    (a) shall be required to act as a reasonable and prudent person would act on his own behalf; and

    (b) subject to any order made under section 11 of this Act, shall be entitled to do anything which the child, if of full age and capacity, could do in relation to that property;

and subject to subsection (2) below, on ceasing to act as legal representative, shall be liable to account to the child for his intromissions with the child's property.

    (2) No liability shall be incurred by virtue of subsection (1) above in respect of funds which have been used in the proper discharge of the person's responsibility to safeguard and promote the child's health, development and welfare.

DEFINITION
  "legal representative": s.15(5).

GENERAL NOTE
  The previous law imposed a duty on all parents or guardians who administered the estate of a child to account to the child for their intromissions with the funds. The Scottish Law Commission felt that it was inappropriate to impose this duty on everyone, given that most parents and guardians will at some time have to manage very small sums on behalf of their children (see Scot. Law Com. No. 135 at para. 4.22). This present section attempts to balance the need to ensure that parents and guardians can be called to account in appropriate cases with the reality that most parents will control funds for the benefit of the child which are so small that the obligation to account is next to meaningless. It does so by imposing an obligation, similar to the obligation on trustees in managing trust funds for the benefit of beneficiaries, to act as a reasonable and prudent person would act on her or his own behalf, and to subject the parent or guardian to liability for failing so to act. In addition, it obliges the parent or guardian to account for intromissions, but exempts the parent or guardian from liability for using the child's funds for the promotion of the child's welfare.

Subs. (1)
  The obligation imposed in para. (a) is to achieve the standard of the reasonable and prudent person acting as she or he would on her or his own behalf. This is an objective test, as it is in trust law (see Norrie and Scobbie, *Trusts* (1991, W. Green) at p. 141), and it is no defence for the legal representatives who have failed in this obligation to show that they acted as they would act on their own behalf: the question is not how they themselves would act in their own affairs, but how the reasonable and prudent person would act in her or his own affairs.
  Paragraph (b) confers on the legal representative the right to do anything which the child would be able to do with her or his own property, had she or he been of full age and capacity. This has the effect of distancing the position of the legal representative both from the guardian of the previous law and from the trustee (Sched. 5 below removes the position of guardian from the operation of the Trusts Acts). Previously, a guardian had a primarily preservative function, particularly in relation to heritage, and this had the effect that property owned by the child could not be disposed of by the guardian, even when this was in the interests of the child. In trust law, trustees are subject to the same limitations, and they can be avoided only by going to the expense of petitioning the court. Now the rule for children is that their legal representatives can do all that the children could do if they were of full age and capacity.
  Acting as a child's legal representative. This could be a parent with the parental responsibility and parental right of legal representation, or a guardian with such responsibility and right. Legal representation lasts, at most, until the child is 16 years old, for only before then is the child incapable of acting on her or his own behalf.

Subs. (2)
  If the legal representative has used funds in the proper discharge of her or his responsibilities to safeguard and promote the child's health, development and welfare, that is the parental responsibility contained in s.1(1)(a), then the legal representative has no liability to account for such funds.
  Proper discharge. The key word in this subsection is "proper", and non-liability to account only arises if the parental responsibility has been discharged properly. If it has not then the legal representative will be under the obligation to account contained in subs. (1) above. So, for example, a parent who expends a child's money on private health care of that child will not be called to account if the expenditure is designed to safeguard and promote the child's health and welfare, but will be called to account if the expenditure is wasteful and harmful such as, for example, some forms of cosmetic surgery. Likewise a parent can expend the child's money on private schooling because this promotes the child's development, without being called to account (though if the expenditure is great, the reasonable and prudent person is likely to keep proper accounts). In practical terms the onus will be on the person alleging improper use of funds to show this.

Court orders

Court orders relating to parental responsibilities etc.

11.—(1) In the relevant circumstances in proceedings in the Court of Session or sheriff court, whether those proceedings are or are not independent of any other action, an order may be made under this subsection in relation to—

   (a) parental responsibilities;
   (b) parental rights;
   (c) guardianship; or
   (d) subject to section 14(1) and (2) of this Act, the administration of a child's property.

(2) The court may make such order under subsection (1) above as it thinks fit; and without prejudice to the generality of that subsection may in particular so make any of the following orders—

   (a) an order depriving a person of some or all of his parental responsibilities or parental rights in relation to a child;
   (b) an order—
      (i) imposing upon a person (provided he is at least sixteen years of age or is a parent of the child) such responsibilities; and
      (ii) giving that person such rights;
   (c) an order regulating the arrangements as to—
      (i) with whom; or
      (ii) if with different persons alternately or periodically, with whom during what periods,
     a child under the age of sixteen years is to live (any such order being known as a "residence order");
   (d) an order regulating the arrangements for maintaining personal relations and direct contact between a child under that age and a person with whom the child is not, or will not be, living (any such order being known as a "contact order");
   (e) an order regulating any specific question which has arisen, or may arise, in connection with any of the matters mentioned in paragraphs (a) to (d) of subsection (1) of this section (any such order being known as a "specific issue order");
   (f) an interdict prohibiting the taking of any step of a kind specified in the interdict in the fulfilment of parental responsibilities or the exercise of parental rights relating to a child or in the administration of a child's property;
   (g) an order appointing a judicial factor to manage a child's property or remitting the matter to the Accountant of Court to report on suitable arrangements for the future management of the property; or
   (h) an order appointing or removing a person as guardian of the child.

(3) The relevant circumstances mentioned in subsection (1) above are—

   (a) that application for an order under that subsection is made by a person who—
      (i) not having, and never having had, parental responsibilities or parental rights in relation to the child, claims an interest;
      (ii) has parental responsibilities or parental rights in relation to the child;
      (iii) has had, but for a reason other than is mentioned in subsection (4) below no longer has, parental responsibilities or parental rights in relation to the child; or
   (b) that although no such application has been made, the court (even if it declines to make any other order) considers it should make such an order.

(4) The reasons referred to in subsection (3)(a)(iii) above are that the parental responsibilities or parental rights have been–

   (a) extinguished on the making of an adoption order;
   (b) transferred to an adoption agency on the making of an order declaring the child free for adoption;
   (c) extinguished by virtue of subsection (9) of section 30 of the Human Fertilisation and Embryology Act 1990 (provision for enactments about adoption to have effect with modifications) on the making of a parental order under subsection (1) of that section; or

(d) transferred to a local authority by a parental responsibilities order.

(5) In subsection (3)(a) above "person" includes (without prejudice to the generality of that subsection) the child concerned; but it does not include a local authority.

(6) In subsection (4) above—

"adoption agency" and "adoption order" have the same meanings as they are given, in section 18 of the Adoption (Scotland) Act 1978, by section 65(1) of that Act; and

"parental responsibilities order" has the meaning given by section 86(1) of this Act.

(7) Subject to subsection (8) below, in considering whether or not to make an order under subsection (1) above and what order to make, the court—

(a) shall regard the welfare of the child concerned as its paramount consideration and shall not make any such order unless it considers that it would be better for the child that the order be made than that none should be made at all; and

(b) taking account of the child's age and maturity, shall so far as practicable—

(i) give him an opportunity to indicate whether he wishes to express his views;

(ii) if he does so wish, give him an opportunity to express them; and

(iii) have regard to such views as he may express.

(8) The court shall, notwithstanding subsection (7) above, endeavour to ensure that any order which it makes, or any determination by it not to make an order, does not adversely affect the position of a person who has, in good faith and for value, acquired any property of the child concerned, or any right or interest in such property.

(9) Nothing in paragraph (b) of subsection (7) above requires a child to be legally represented, if he does not wish to be, in proceedings in the course of which the court implements that paragraph.

(10) Without prejudice to the generality of paragraph (b) of subsection (7) above, a child twelve years of age or more shall be presumed to be of sufficient age and maturity to form a view for the purposes both of that paragraph and of subsection (9) above.

(11) An order under subsection (1) above shall have the effect of depriving a person of a parental responsibility or parental right only in so far as the order expressly so provides and only to the extent necessary to give effect to the order; but in making any such order as is mentioned in paragraph (a) or (b) of subsection (2) above the court may revoke any agreement which, in relation to the child concerned, has effect by virtue of section 4(2) of this Act.

(12) Where the court makes a residence order which requires that a child live with a person who, immediately before the order is made does not have in relation to the child all the parental responsibilities mentioned in paragraphs (a), (b) and (d) of section 1(1), and the parental rights mentioned in paragraphs (b) and (d) of section 2(1), of this Act (those which he does not so have being in this subsection referred to as the "relevant responsibilities and rights") that person shall, subject to the provisions of the order or of any other order made under subsection (1) above, have the relevant responsibilities and rights while the residence order remains in force.

(13) Any reference in this section to an order includes a reference to an interim order or to an order varying or discharging an order.

DEFINITIONS

"adoption agency": Adoption (Scotland) Act 1978, s.65(1).

"adoption order": Adoption (Scotland) Act 1978, s.65(1).

"child": ss.2(7), 15(1).

"contact order": s.11(2)(d).

"parental responsibilities": s.1(3).
"parental responsibilities order": s.86(1).
"parental rights": s.2(4).
"person": ss.11(5), 15(4).
"residence order": s.11(2)(c).

GENERAL NOTE
See Scot. Law Com. No. 135, Part V.

In many respects this is the fundamental section of this Part, replacing the very much shorter s.3 of the 1986 Act (which similarly played a central role there). The old s.3 had much value, in its terseness and wideness, but its drawback was that it relied to a very great extent on the common law telling us what parental rights were, how they were to be exercised and how the court should resolve disputes. The present provision attempts to put all questions of parental responsibilities and parental rights on to a statutory basis. The court's powers to make orders are clearly spelt out, together with various supplementary rules relating to their effect. Issues of title, which had generated much case law under the 1986 Act, are dealt with similarly.

The major change effected by this section is the replacement of custody and access orders with the new concepts of residence and contact orders. This terminology follows that introduced in England by the Children Act 1989 (c. 41) and has important symbolic as well as practical significance. The whole ethos of Part I is to move away from the common understanding that parents have a right to keep and to control their children and towards an understanding that mothers and good fathers have a responsibility to protect and guide their children and to maintain contact with them. Parental responsibilities and parental rights are governed by ss.1–6 above and this section allows the court to make orders regulating any issue in connection therewith, or in connection with guardianship (governed by ss.6–8 above), or the administration of children's property (ss.9–10 above).

Though the theoretical basis of the law has been changed, much of the old law will remain since the factors previously relevant to the determination of custody disputes will be those that are relevant to the determination of an application for a residence order, and the factors previously relevant to access will be those that are relevant to contact orders. The familiar welfare principle remains paramount, but further guidance is given to the court as to how it should come to its decisions. Applications for all s.11 orders are governed by O.C.R. 1993, rr. 33.60–33.65 and R.C. 1994, rr. 49.58–49.63.

Subs. (1)

In any proceedings in which the issue arises, the court can make an order relating to parental responsibilities or parental rights, guardianship, or administration of children's property. Any of the orders specified in subs. (2) below can be made whether the action is raised under this section or by any other means. So the court can make an order under this section when the issue before the court is primarily something other than whether an order relating to the child should be made. Typically this will be in a divorce action, but the terms of the section are wide and the court can make an order in any action, so long as the "relevant circumstances", set out in subs. (3) below, exist.

Subs. (2)

Under the old s.3(1) of the 1986 Act, the court was empowered to make any order relating to parental rights it thought fit; the present provision similarly empowers the court to make any order it thinks fit in relation to parental responsibilities and parental rights, guardianship, or administration of children's property and, without limiting that wide discretion, it lists a number of particular orders that can be made. Other orders, relating to these matters, which do not precisely fit into one or other of the stated orders, can be made. Any order can only be made in the "relevant circumstances" as defined in subs. (3) below and the court is obliged, in coming to its decision, to have regard to the three "overarching principles" listed in subs. (7) below.

Paragraph (a) allows the court to make an order depriving a person who has parental responsibilities or parental rights of some or all of these rights. The order will have to be explicit as to which responsibilities and rights are being removed, and this provision is to be read with subs. (11) below. That subsection creates an important change in the law. The old custody orders were assumed, unless joint custody was awarded (which was rare), to remove any rights of custody which existed in the person who was not awarded custody, even when this was not made plain in the court decree. Indeed, this was often their sole effect: when custody was awarded to one of the divorcing parents, it was giving that parent what she or he already had and taking away the right from the other parent. It is now required that for that result to follow the court must make a specific decision to that effect (taking account of the overarching principles in subs. (7) below) and the effect must be spelt out in the decree.

Paragraph (b), conversely, allows the court to impose parental responsibilities or confer parental rights on any person, and again the court must be explicit that this is what has been determined to be best for the child. It should be noted here that an order conferring parental responsibilities and parental rights does not confer the status of parenthood (for the purposes, for example, of succession or the obligations of aliment and child support) but merely imposes some of the consequences. The order can impose merely some of the parental responsibilities and rights on a person rather than them all: the generality of s.11(1) clearly allows for this and the competence of doing so is confirmed by s.103(1) below. If all the parental responsibilities and parental rights are to be conferred on a person who is not a parent, then the person is probably being appointed as a guardian, *i.e.* a parent-substitute, and as such the order is more properly one under para. (h) below than this one. This paragraph will be more appropriate when only a limited number of specific parental responsibilities or parental rights are being imposed or conferred.

The court can confer responsibilities and rights only on a person who is aged 16 years or more except in one situation; that is when the person under 16 is the child's parent (*i.e.* father, since mothers of whatever age have parental responsibilities and parental rights automatically under s.3(1)(a) above). The section is no authority, however, for giving an under-16-year-old parent legal capacity he does not otherwise have, and it will not be in the interests of any child to give the responsibility and right of legal representation in relation to a child to a boy-parent who lacks the capacity to act as such. Indeed it is difficult to imagine a situation in which it would ever be in the child's interests to confer any parental responsibility or parental right on a father under the age of 16: though there is no age limit on a mother automatically acquiring those rights, that acquisition is an inevitable legal consequence to which the child's welfare is irrelevant.

Paragraph (c) allows the court to make what is termed a "residence order", which is an order regulating the arrangements as to with whom the child is to live. The terminology of the paragraph should be noted. Residence orders will not be made "in favour of" one parent or the other, for it is to be remembered that mothers and good fathers will already have the right (from s.2(1)(a) above) to have their children living with them in any case: the order will not be made simply to confer upon a parent that which she or he already has (for that would offend the "minimum interference principle" in subs. (7) below). Rather, the order will regulate, for the benefit of the child, the arrangements under which parents can exercise their rights. The paragraph is designed to give the court maximum flexibility in regulating these arrangements, and subparagraph (ii) permits residence orders to make arrangements whereby the child lives periodically with more than one person. If the parents both have parental responsibilities and parental rights the order under s.11(2)(c) will do no more than "regulate" the arrangements; if the applicant does not have parental responsibilities and parental rights (but only in that case) then making a residence order in the applicant's favour will confer upon her or him all the relevant parental responsibilities and parental rights (subs. (12) below). It follows, as was pointed out by Sheriff Kelbie in *McBain v. McIntyre*, 1997 S.C.L.R. 181 (Notes), that a "residence order" should be made in favour of a person only when a child is to "live" with that person and that while the present provision permits the order to arrange for the child to live periodically with more than one person, this should be done only when the child truly "lives" with both. Overnight contact stays with a parent do not amount to a child living with that parent. However, it is possible, depending upon the circumstances in each particular case, for a child to live with both parents periodically, if for example she or he has a room in both establishments, keeps clothes, toys, school work, etc., at both. See, for example, *McKiver v. McKiver*, 1995 S.L.T. 790. In these circumstances it might be appropriate to make a residence order in favour of the parent who has no parental responsibilities and parental rights even when he has the child staying only for two nights every week. But in doing so the court must bear in mind that full parental responsibilities and parental rights are carried with a residence order in such circumstances, and it will be appropriate, therefore, only when that result is in the interests of the child.

Unless parental responsibilities and parental rights have been removed from one parent, the effect of any such arrangement will be very different from an award of custody to one parent with residential access, say at weekends, being given to the other parent. Under that arrangement (common in the old law) the parent with custody had full rights in relation to the care and upbringing of the child, and the parent with access had minimal rights. Joint custody orders, though competent, were not favoured. This often left the parent with regular access in a very awkward position and the practice, for example, of many schools and medical practitioners was to refuse to divulge information about the child to the parent with access without the permission of the parent with custody. This inhibited the parent with access from playing a full role in the child's life. That role is now to be encouraged and the regulation of a child's residence will not in itself have the effect of minimising one parent's rights. If one parent wishes to be in sole control of the child's upbringing with sole decision-making powers, then she or he must apply for the removal of the other's parental responsibilities and parental rights under para. (a) above rather than through the arrangements regulating where the child is to live under this paragraph. The onus will be on the applicant, not to show why she or he should be in sole charge of the child's upbringing, but why the other should be denied responsibilities and rights (see also subs. (11) below).

Paragraph (d) concerns what used to be called access and an order under this paragraph is to be termed a "contact order". The careful wording of this paragraph is designed to move away from the notion that parents have a right of access and to reiterate the idea that parents have a responsibility to maintain personal relations and direct contact with the child (s.1(1)(c) above). That responsibility is not removed by a residence order under para. (c) above in favour of someone else and what this paragraph does is to allow the court to make an order regulating the fulfilment of that responsibility; in addition it can regulate the contact the child is to have with any other person who does not have the responsibility and right to maintain relations and contact with the child. Inevitably, previous decisions relating to access applications will remain of relevance in identifying the sorts of considerations the courts are likely to take into account in determining how best to regulate contact between the child and another person. As under the pre-1995 law (see *D v. Strathclyde Regional Council*, 1985 S.L.T. 114), a court order regulating contact will be inoperative during the subsistence of an inconsistent supervision requirement made under s.70 below. The discretion of a children's hearing to regulate contact (indeed their obligation to consider whether to do so under s.70(2) below) is not inhibited by a court order regulating contact, just as their power to impose a condition of residence is not inhibited by the granting by a court of a residence order.

Paragraph (e) allows the court to make an order regulating "any specific question" which has arisen in relation to parental responsibilities or rights, or guardianship, or the administration of a child's property. This is very wide and reflects the (implicit) position in the old s.3(1) of the 1986 Act. This provision could be used to allow the court to determine wherein the child's welfare lies in any situation in which there is dispute, for example in relation to medical treatment, schooling, religious upbringing, or any aspect of the child's lifestyle. Of course an order under this paragraph, as under all the others, is subject to the minimum intervention principle in subs. (7) below (one of the three "overarching principles"), and there are some situations in which this principle will be very useful. For example it will seldom be better for a child that a court regulates her or his religious upbringing than that the matter be left to be worked out between the child and the person with whom the child lives. On the other hand, there are some situations, such as consent to medical treatment, in which the court might have a very important role to play, and there have been many cases in England in which the courts were faced with difficult questions to resolve in that field: see for example, *B (A Minor) (Wardship: Sterilization), Re* [1988] A.C. 199 and *E (A Minor) (Medical Treatment), Re* [1991] 2 F.L.R. 585 (sterilisation); *B (A Minor), Re* [1981] 1 W.L.R. 1421, *C (A Minor) (Wardship: Medical Treatment), Re* [1989] 2 All E.R. 782 and *J (A Minor) (Wardship, Medical Treatment), Re* [1990] 3 All E.R. 930 (life-saving or life-prolonging treatment); *R (A Minor) (Wardship: Medical Treatment), Re* [1991] 4 All E.R. 177 and *W (A Minor) (Medical Treatment: Court's Jurisdiction), Re* [1992] 4 All E.R. 627 (child refusing treatment).

Paragraph (f) allows the court to interdict the exercise of a parental responsibility or a parental right which it determines is against the welfare of the child. So, for example, the court could interdict a parent from consenting to, and doctors from performing, the sterilisation of a mildly mentally retarded child (see *D (A Minor) (Wardship: Sterilization), Re* [1976] 1 All E.R. 326). Or the court could interdict the legal representative from selling or dissipating a child's property, or putting it to improper purposes. It should be noted, however, that the court is exhorted to "endeavour to ensure that any order that it makes, or any determination by it not to make an order, does not adversely affect the position of a person who has, in good faith and for value, acquired any property of the child concerned, or any right or interest in such property" (subs. (8) below). So, for example, a parent who has improperly leased the child's property to a third party can be interdicted from doing so again or from continuing to do so, but the order must attempt to preserve the position of the bona fide third party (the lessee).

Paragraph (g) deals with a different situation from either s.9 above or s.13 below, though both provide the court with similar powers. Here the situation envisaged is that of a child who already owns and possesses property, and it is in the interests of the child that some appropriate person be appointed to manage that property on the child's behalf.

Paragraph (h) allows the court to appoint or remove a person as guardian of the child.

Before the coming into force of this Act, s.5(2) of the Age of Legal Capacity (Scotland) Act 1991 (c. 50) provided that the only two ways in which a guardian could be appointed were by court order under s.3 of the 1986 Act or by testamentary deed under s.4 thereof. Schedule 4 to the present Act amends s.5(2) of the 1991 Act to read that the only way in which a guardian can be appointed is by testamentary deed under s.7 of the present Act. The omission of a reference to the present paragraph is surprising, but not fatal, and there is no doubt that court appointments are valid and the new wording of s.5(2) is inept. A person appointed guardian under this section will have all the parental responsibilities and parental rights conferred on a parent by ss.1 and 2 above, and will become, therefore, a parent-substitute. This is made plain in s.7(5) above in relation to appointment of guardians under that section, but is not stated in so many words here. However, there is nothing in the Act to indicate that the powers, duties, liabilities and role of guardian are different depending upon whether the person comes into that office by means of a court order under s.11 or by testamentary appointment under s.7, and had Parliament intended to change the law in that respect it would surely have done so expressly. The court can, of course, make the appointment of guardian subject to such conditions as it thinks fit.

Subs. (3)

Under the old law an order relating to parental rights could be sought by "any person claiming interest" (1986 Act, s.3(1)). This phrase gave rise to much dispute, both academic and judicial (see *AB* v. *M*, 1988 S.L.T. 652; *F.* v. *F.*, 1991 S.L.T. 357; *D.* v. *Grampian Regional Council*, 1995 S.L.T. 519; *Osborne* v. *Matthan*, May 12, 1998 (First Division)), and the case law was being developed both during and after the parliamentary passage of the Bill that became the present Act. The Bill was amended from a form very similar in effect to that in the 1986 Act to its present structure as a result of the House of Lords decision in *D* v. *Grampian Regional Council*, which was decided on March 9, 1995 while the Bill was being considered by the Special Standing Committee in the House of Commons. Subsections (3) and (4) are designed to give statutory effect to the decision in *D* v. *Grampian Regional Council* and to clarify other related issues that it raised.

An order under s.11 can be made by the court if an application for such an order has been made by a person falling within one of three separate classes, which will cover any person except those specified in subss (4) and (5) below. (It should be noted that it makes no practical difference which class the applicant comes within, so long as she or he is not in one of the excluded classes in subss (4) or (5) below.) In addition, it is made clear that an order under s.11 can be made in any other action in which such an application has not been made but in which the court considers it appropriate (taking account of the overarching principles in subs. (7) below) to make the order.

A person. Excluded from the definition of "person" are local authorities (subs. (5) below), but nowhere are other non-natural persons excluded from title (*cf.* the terms of s.15(4) below under which only natural persons can have parental responsibilities and parental rights). While the typical applicant will be a natural person there is nothing to prevent an application by a corporate body which claims an interest. So, for example, an NHS Trust might seek a specific issues order to regulate the child's medical treatment over which some argument has arisen. But an NHS trust cannot, because of the terms of s.15(4), be appointed guardian, or seek to exercise any parental responsibility or parental right.

Who ... claims an interest. As in the pre-1995 law, title to seek an order is not subject to artificial limitations (see Wilkinson, 1976 S.L.T. (News) 221 and 237) and technical issues of title tend to be subsumed into the substantive issue of the child's welfare (see Wilkinson and Norrie, *Parent and Child* (1993, W. Green) at pp. 202–204). Title inheres under this subparagraph in unmarried fathers, grandparents, step-parents, siblings, other relatives and anyone else with a connection to or legitimate concern for the welfare of the child, such as foster carers (see *M.* v. *Lothian Regional Council*, 1990 S.L.T. 116, *F.* v. *F.*, 1991 S.L.T. 357 and *Sanderson* v. *McManus*, 1997 S.L.T. 629, 1997 Fam.L.R. 36). "A person who ... claims an interest" includes the child her or himself (subs. (5) below.) Excluded from this paragraph are those who currently have parental responsibilities and parental rights, and those who used to, but no longer, have parental responsibilities and parental rights.

Has parental responsibilities or parental rights. This category includes any person who has such responsibilities and rights automatically, or has acquired them by any means whatsoever. (It does not include a local authority who has acquired parental responsibilities by means of a parental responsibilities order in its favour: subs. (5) below). The use of the word "or" suggests that this category includes a person who has one particular responsibility or right but not all of them, such as the responsibility or right to maintain contact with the child.

Has had, but ... no longer has. This category includes persons whose responsibilities and rights have been lost by private law means, such as a court order under the present section. So a person who is deprived of all parental responsibilities and parental rights under s.11(2)(a) above retains title to seek their restoration or to seek any other s.11 order. Excluded from this category are those who lose their parental responsibilities and parental rights by some public law process, specified in subs. (4) below.

Although no such application has been made. If the court is not dealing with an application under the present section but nevertheless considers that an order should be made it may make such an order. In certain actions, specified in s.12(1) below, the court is obliged to consider whether to make a s.11 order. In any other action the court may consider the question without any request to do so and may make any s.11 order that it considers should be made. This allows the court to act *ex proprio motu* or on the motion of any party in, for example, an action for divorce, judicial separation, declarator of marriage, nullity of marriage, parentage or non-parentage or any other action. This expands the jurisdiction of the Court of Session, which prior to the coming into force of this Act could deal with parental rights only in certain specified actions (Court of Session Act 1988 (c. 36), s.20, repealed in Sched. 5 below).

Subs. (4)

In *Beagley v. Beagley*, 1984 S.C.(HL) 69 the House of Lords held that a person who had lost parental rights by means of a resolution under s.16 of the 1968 Act vesting parental rights and powers in a local authority had no title to seek their restoration by way of a custody application; and in *Borders Regional Council v. M*, 1986 S.C. 63 the Inner House came to the same conclusion when parental rights were removed by an order freeing a child for adoption. These decisions pre-dated the 1986 Act, s.3(1) of which conferred title to seek an order relating to parental rights under that Act on "any person claiming interest". In *D v. Grampian Regional Council*, 1994 S.L.T. 1038 the Inner House (by a majority) took the view that this overturned the earlier decisions and that "any person" meant precisely that and therefore included a mother whose parental rights had been removed by an order freeing the child for adoption. The House of Lords overruled this (1995 S.L.T. 519), holding that the phrase "any person" as it appeared in the 1986 Act could not be interpreted literally. They held that the removal of parental rights by an adoption order or by an order freeing a child for adoption under the Adoption (Scotland) Act 1978 removed title to seek an order relating to parental rights under the 1986 Act. There were, however, some difficulties with that decision, primarily that it was based very firmly on an analysis of the law of adoption, which rendered it unclear whether the same result would be reached in other situations in which parental rights had been removed by public law process (such as in particular by a parental rights resolution under s.16 of the Social Work (Scotland) Act 1968 (c. 49)). It is the purpose of this subsection (together with subs. (3) above) to give statutory effect to the House of Lords decision and to clarify the doubts that it raised.

The subsection sets out four categories of natural person who cannot seek a s.11 order. There are no others and the terms of subs. (3) above are wide enough to ensure that title inheres in any other person except either those mentioned here, or local authorities (subs. (5) below). The categories are persons whose parental responsibilities and parental rights have been removed by: (i) s.12(3) of the Adoption (Scotland) Act 1978 on the making of an adoption order, (ii) s.18(5) of the 1978 Act on the making of an order freeing a child for adoption, (iii) s.30(9) of the Human Fertilisation and Embryology Act 1990 on the making of a parental order after a surrogacy arrangement, and (iv) s.86(1) below on the making of a parental responsibilities order transferring those rights and responsibilities to a local authority. It may appear at first sight a little odd that a person whose parental responsibilities and parental rights are removed under s.11(2)(a) above can seek their restoration under s.11 while a person whose responsibilities and rights have been removed under s.86 below cannot, but there is a clear distinction to be drawn between the public law and the private law processes. It would lead to confusion and delay which would inevitably be detrimental to the child if both processes could be utilised, and the Act is sensible in separating them out so clearly.

There may be very exceptional circumstances in which this rule seems to work harshly. For example, an adopted child may in fact maintain a relationship of affection with her or his natural mother; if the adoptive parents die or otherwise become unable to look after the child the natural mother would be unable to seek a s.11 order. However, this harshness can be mitigated by other means. The natural mother is not prevented from adopting the child; the child her or himself can seek an order under s.11 conferring parental responsibilities and parental rights on the natural mother, as can any other person who claims an interest. For it is to be remembered that subss (3) and (4) merely deny title, but they do not prevent the court from making any order at all in favour of any person whose title is denied.

Subs. (5)

The child concerned. The "person" who can raise an action under subs. (1) above is stated here to include the child concerning whom the application is made. The terms of the old s.3 of the 1986 Act were clearly wide enough to include the child, but the matter was occasionally doubted and this provision is enacted for the avoidance of that doubt. A child can seek an order, for example, removing the parental responsibilities and rights from her or his own parent or guardian, or an order regulating a specific question such as medical treatment. The provision does not, however, grant to a child any legal capacity to raise (or defend) an action that she or he would not otherwise have, and that capacity remains to be determined by the Age of Legal

Capacity (Scotland) Act 1991. Section 2(4A) of that Act provides that a person under the age of 16 years shall have legal capacity to instruct a solicitor in connection with any civil matter where that person has a general understanding of what it means to do so, and s.2(4B) provides that a person under 16 with that capacity has also capacity to sue or to defend in any civil proceedings. A person aged 12 years or more is presumed to be of sufficient age and maturity to have such an understanding. A child with legal capacity to sue or defend in civil proceedings can nevertheless consent to be represented in these proceedings by a person who would be their legal representative if they did not have such capacity: see s.15(6) below.

A local authority. Excluded from the definition of "a person who ... claims an interest" in subs. (3) above are local authorities. Part I of the present Act deals exclusively with private law matters, in respect of which local authorities have no standing. Local authorities' rights, duties, powers and interests are governed exclusively by Part II, which is the limit of their interest and role. It must follow from this, though it is not expressly stated, that the decision in *M v. Dumfries and Galloway Regional Authority*, 1991 S.C.L.R. 481 (Sh.Ct) is no longer good law (if it ever was). In that case a local authority was held to be entitled to rely upon s.3(2) of the 1986 Act to defend an action for delivery of a child whom they were keeping under no statutory authority. This was, however, expressly departed from by Sheriff Principal Nicholson in *City of Edinburgh District Council v. M*, 1996 S.L.T. (Sh.Ct) 112. The local authority cannot raise an action under Part I and nor, it is submitted, can they rely on any rule or principle in Part I to achieve that which they cannot achieve by other means. Nor can local authorities become involved in a child's upbringing under a s.11 order by means of a condition attached to such an order made in favour of someone else. So, for example, a contact order cannot require that contact take place only under the supervision of a local authority. Section 12 of the Matrimonial Proceedings (Children) Act 1958 and s.11 of the Guardianship Act 1973, permitting the court to place a child under the supervision of a local authority, have been repealed (Sched. 5) and are not re-enacted. Notwithstanding the apparent breadth of the words in s.11(2): "The court may make such order ... as it thinks fit", it was a matter of agreement between counsel in *Osborne v. Matthan*, May 12, 1998 (which the First Division accepted without comment) that it would be incompetent for a sheriff to subject a child to local authority supervision. Local authority involvement in children's lives is limited to and governed by Pt II of the present Act.

Subs. (7)

In making any decision about whether or not to make any order under this section, the court is obliged by this subsection to have regard to three quite distinct principles, which have been referred to above as the overarching principles.

Welfare of the child. The first overarching principle is that the welfare of the child concerned is to be the court's paramount consideration. (For the statute to require the court to regard welfare as "its paramount consideration" neatly sidesteps the rather sterile argument that arose in the negotiations before the adoption of the UN Convention on the Rights of the Child about whether welfare should be "a paramount consideration" or "the paramount consideration".) This welfare test is familiar and no different from that required under the old law contained in s.3(2) of the 1986 Act (on the application of the welfare test in custody disputes, see Wilkinson and Norrie, *Parent and Child* (1993, W. Green) at pp. 206–225).

Shall not make any such order. The second overarching principle is that the court is prohibited from making any order unless it considers that making an order would be better for the child than making none (see Scot. Law Com. No. 135 at paras 5.16–5.18). This is what might be called the "minimum intervention principle", under which it is assumed that matters are best left without court interference and that the onus is on the party seeking an order to persuade the court that it satisfies the welfare test (see *Porchetta v. Porchetta*, 1986 S.L.T. 105 and *Sanderson v. McManus*, 1997 S.L.T. 629). This was probably the position under the old law in any case (a good example is to be found in the judgment of Lord Gill in *Clayton v. Clayton*, April 21, 1995, where he refused to make one of the orders sought in relation to the child's upbringing because he was not persuaded that the party who sought the order had proved it was "necessary"), but the current provision makes it absolutely plain. And it is a particularly important break on unnecessary orders, given the extension of the court's powers to make orders even when not asked to do so (subs. (3)(b) above). The application of the principle is general. It applies both when it is sought to regulate the exercise of pre-existing parental responsibilities and rights and when an applicant seeks to have parental responsibilities and rights conferred for the first time. The principle will prevent a residence order being made in favour of a person who already has parental responsibilities and parental rights, such as a mother, because such an order will give her nothing she does not already have. If the aim of the application is to deny parental responsibilities and parental rights to the father then this must be done by means of an order under s.11(2)(a) rather than a residence order under s.11(2)(c) in favour of the mother (see subs. (11) below). This is an important practical difference from the old law when it was common to grant custody to a person who already had the legal right of custody as a means of denying custody to someone else.

One consequence of the minimum intervention principle which is not altogether satisfactory is that any particular decision may be made according to how the question comes before the court, rather than according to its merits in the abstract. For example, a person may seek an interdict against a child attending the services of some quasi-religious sect, and the court, adopting the principle of minimum intervention, may well refuse to grant the interdict (allowing the child to continue attending). If, on the other hand, the child raises the action seeking an interdict against the parents' attempts to prevent the attendance at the services of the sect the court may well again apply the principle of minimum intervention to refuse the interdict (effectively allowing the parents to continue to prevent the child attending). If the onus of satisfying the welfare test cannot be satisfied then the unregulated position, whichever that is, will govern.

Shall ... have regard ... to the views ... of the child. The third overarching principle is that the court should give the child the opportunity to express views on the matter the court is being asked to determine, and should have appropriate regard to any view expressed. This provision has been enacted in order to bring Scots law into line with Art. 12 of the UN Convention on the Rights of the Child (the terms of which are set out in the General Note to s.6 above), and is similar in its terms to s.6 of the Adoption (Scotland) Act 1978 (which is amended later in the current statute). The important change in the law here is that the child's views are to be taken into account in all actions before the court in which a s.11 order is being considered, with the result that for the first time in Scots law there is a requirement on the court to take account of the views of the child in determining whether to regulate residence and contact, and how to do so. Further, the court is prohibited by the Rules from making any order in relation to a child who has indicated a wish to express views unless due weight has been given to these views: see O.C.R. 1993, r.33.19 and R.C. 1994, r. 49.20. There is no age limit, though it is provided by subs. (10) below that a child aged 12 or over is presumed capable of forming a view. This has the effect that the court should not take account of the views of a child over 12 only when persuaded (and the issue is a matter of fact) that the child is not of sufficient age and maturity to form a view. This certainly does not prevent the court taking account of the views of children under 12 and there have been cases in which the court has considered it proper to have regard to the expressed views of even very young children (see for example *Pow v. Pow*, 1931 S.L.T. 485, which involved children of 10 and eight, and *Russell v. Russell*, 1991 S.C.L.R. 429, which involved a five-year-old). On the procedure to be followed in the sheriff court where a child wishes to express views, see the Ordinary Cause Rules 1993 (S.I. 1993 No. 1956), rr. 33.19–33.20.

Similar, but not identical, provisions are to be found in s.6 above, which obliges a parent exercising a parental responsibility or parental right to have regard to the views of the child, and in s.95 below, which amends s.6 of the Adoption (Scotland) Act 1978, to oblige the court making an adoption order to have regard to the views of the child. The difference in s.6 above is that the parent must also have regard to the views of the other parent (which is not the case here) and the difference in s.95 is that there the court is obliged also to have regard to the child's racial origins and cultural and linguistic background (which is not the case here).

If he wishes to express them. There is no obligation on the child to express a view. The court should seek the child's opinion but must also be careful not to burden a child with undue pressure to make a decision and, in general, care ought also to be taken to ensure that the child understands that her or his views, if expressed, will help the judge decide but will not themselves decide the issue. No child should ever be made to feel, for example, that she or he has the burden of deciding which parent to live with. The child may speak directly to the judge (see subs. (9) below).

Subs. (8)
See the notes to subs. (2)(f) above.

Subs. (9)
In fulfilling his obligation to have regard to the views of the child concerned, the judge may speak directly to the child, who is not obliged (but is permitted) to speak through a legal representative with a right of audience to the court.

Subs. (10)
See the notes to subs. (7) above.

Subs. (11)
Parental responsibilities and parental rights continue in existence, once acquired, subject only to their express removal by the court acting under subs. (2)(a) or (h) above. Such removal is only to the extent specified by the court. So, for example, if a court denies a parent the right to regulate the child's residence (the right under s.(2)(1)(a) above) and nothing more, that parent

remains subject to all the responsibilities listed in s.1 above and possessed of all the other rights listed in s.2 above. In addition, it is provided here that in making an order depriving a person of parental responsibilities or rights or imposing and conferring parental responsibilities and rights, the court can revoke an agreement under s.4 above giving an unmarried father parental responsibilities and rights: examples from England include *Re P. (Terminating Parental Responsibility)* [1995] 1 F.L.R. 1048 and Re G. (Child Case: Parental Involvement) [1996] Fam.L. 459.

Subs. (12)
See the notes to subs. (2)(c) above.

Subs. (13)
The court can make an interim order or can vary or discharge an order in the same circumstances as it can make a final order, and in particular the same overarching principles listed in subs. (7) above must be applied.

Restrictions on decrees for divorce, separation or annulment affecting children

12.—(1) In any action for divorce, judicial separation or declarator of nullity of marriage, the court shall, where this section applies, consider (in the light of such information as is before the court as to the arrangements which have been, or are proposed to be, made for the upbringing of each child by virtue of which it applies) whether to exercise with respect to him the powers conferred by section 11 or 54 of this Act.

(2) Where, in any case to which this section applies, the court is of the opinion that—

(a) the circumstances of the case require, or are likely to require, it to exercise any power under section 11 or 54 of this Act with respect to the child concerned;

(b) it is not in a position to exercise that power without giving further consideration to the case; and

(c) there are exceptional circumstances which make it desirable in the interests of that child that it should not grant decree in the action until it is in a position to exercise such a power,

it shall postpone its decision on the granting of decree in the action until it is in such a position.

(3) This section applies where a child of the family has not reached the age of sixteen years at the date when the question first arises as to whether the court should give such consideration as is mentioned in subsection (1) above.

(4) In this section "child of the family", in relation to the parties to a marriage, means—

(a) a child of both of them; or

(b) any other child, not being a child who is placed with them as foster parents by a local authority or voluntary organisation, who has been treated by both of them as a child of their family.

DEFINITIONS
"child": s.15(1).
"foster parent": Fostering of Children (Scotland) Regulations 1996 (S.I. 1996 No. 3263).
"local authority": Local Government etc. (Scotland) Act 1994 (c. 39), s.2.

GENERAL NOTE
Under the Matrimonial Proceedings (Children) Act 1958 (c. 40) the court was obliged in actions for divorce, nullity of marriage or separation to consider the arrangements for the care and upbringing of the children involved (1958 Act, s.8), and it could commit the child to the care of an individual other than the parent or to the care of a local authority (1958 Act s.10). These sections are now repealed (Sched. 5 below) and the current provision requires the court, in any matrimonial proceeding concerning a family in which there is a child, to consider whether to grant any of the s.11 orders and whether to refer the case of the child to the reporter under s.54.

Subs. (1)

In considering whether to make a s.11 order, account must be taken of the overarching principles in s.11(7) above; in addition, referring the child to the reporter is appropriate only when the court considers that one of the grounds of referral listed in s.52(2) below exists.

Subs. (2)

If the court believes that an order under s.11 or a reference under s.54 is required, or is likely to be required, but it is not in the position to make such an order without further consideration, and there are exceptional circumstances requiring the court to postpone granting decree for divorce, separation or nullity, then the court shall so postpone granting decree until it is able to decide whether and how to exercise a power under s.11 or s.54. This provision replaces s.8 of the Matrimonial Proceedings (Children) Act 1958, though the emphasis is significantly different. Under the 1958 Act the court was duty bound to refuse the matrimonial decree unless satisfied as to the arrangements for the care and upbringing of the child; under the present provision it may postpone its decision only in "exceptional circumstances".

Exceptional circumstances. These words suggest that the norm will be that the matrimonial decree will be granted even although the court is not in a position to exercise its powers in relation to the child. The circumstances must relate to the welfare of the child.

Subss. (3) and (4)

The court must consider whether to make a s.11 order or to make a referral to the reporter under s.54, or postpone deciding whether to grant a matrimonial decree only when a child, of the family concerning which the decree is being sought, has not reached the age of 16 at the date when the question first arises. "Child of the family" is defined to mean either a child of both parties to the marriage which is the subject of the action, or any other child who has been treated by both the parties as a child of their family.

A child of both of them. This covers the genetic child of both, the adopted child of both, the genetic child of one who is the adopted child of the other, and the child over whom both have a parental order under s.30 of the Human Fertilisation and Embryology Act 1990.

Any other child. There is no requirement (as there was, for example, in the unamended Family Law Act 1986: *Bradley v. Bradley*, 1987 S.C.L.R. 62) that the child be related to one or other of the parties to the marriage. Children being boarded with the family under the Fostering of Children (Scotland) Regulations 1996 (S.I. 1996 No. 3263) are excluded from these provisions.

Treated by both of them as a child of their family. The pre-1995 legislation talked of a child being "accepted" rather than "treated" as a child of the family, and that word gave rise to much judicial discussion in England (see Wilkinson and Norrie, *Parent and Child* (1993, W. Green) at p. 240). Most of the legislation in which that phrase appeared is amended in Sched. 4 so that the word used is now "treated". (The most notable exception is the Family Law (Scotland) Act 1985.) "Treated" requires, as acceptance did not, some positive act or course of action by the parties to the marriage, directed towards the child, indicating that she or he is regarded by the parties as a child of their family. The parties to the marriage must act in some way consistent with them having adopted a parenting role and accepting all the parental responsibilities and parental rights. The test is objective: see *Teeling v. Teeling* [1984] F.L.R. 808 and *Re A. (Child of the Family)* [1998] 1 F.L.R. 347.

Awards of damages to children

13.—(1) Where in any court proceedings a sum of money becomes payable to, or for the benefit of, a child under the age of sixteen years, the court may make such order relating to the payment and management of the sum for the benefit of the child as it thinks fit.

(2) Without prejudice to the generality of subsection (1) above, the court may in an order under this section—

(a) appoint a judicial factor to invest, apply or otherwise deal with the money for the benefit of the child concerned;

(b) order the money to be paid—
    (i) to the sheriff clerk or the Accountant of Court; or
    (ii) to a parent or guardian of that child,
    to be invested, applied or otherwise dealt with, under directions of the court, for the benefit of that child; or

(c) order the money to be paid directly to that child.

(3) Where payment is made to a person in accordance with an order under this section, a receipt given by him shall be a sufficient discharge of the obligation to make the payment.

DEFINITIONS
"child": s.15(1).
"parent": s.15(1).

GENERAL NOTE
An issue concerning a child may be before the court not only in matrimonial proceedings but also in proceedings in which a sum of money becomes payable to or for the benefit of the child, typically in an action for damages in which the child is the successful pursuer. Before the coming into force of this provision, there were rules allowing the Court of Session to appoint a judicial factor and allowing the sheriff court to direct payment of awards into court to be administered on behalf of the child. There was little reason for the procedures to be different depending upon which court was involved, and the Scottish Law Commission (Scot. Law Com. No. 135, para. 4.7) recommended that there should be common rules and that these rules should be contained in primary legislation. These recommendations are given effect to in this section, which confers wide discretionary powers on the Court of Session and the sheriff court, and makes provision for the granting of a discharge of the obligation to make payment. It is to be noted that the three overarching principles in s.11(7) do not apply here. While the minimum intervention principle is obviously inappropriate it is, perhaps, surprising that there is no requirement to have regard to the views of the child nor any reference to the interests of the child. Inevitably, however, the court in making decisions under this section that "it thinks fit" will regard the child's interests as, at the very least, always relevant.

Subs. (1)
The provision is in the widest possible terms, covering any court proceedings in which, by any means, a sum of money becomes payable to or for the benefit of a person under the age of 16 years. The court is empowered to make any such order relating to the payment and management of the sum as it sees fit, so long as this is for the benefit of the person under 16.

Subs. (2)
This provision lists the sorts of orders that the court can make, though the list is not exhaustive and the court can make any order under subs. (1) above that it considers will be for the benefit of the child. There are three basic sorts of order: (i) the appointment of a judicial factor, (ii) an order to pay the money to the sheriff clerk or the Accountant of Court or to a parent or guardian of the under-16-year old, or (iii) an order to pay the money direct to the person under the age of 16. The second form of order may contain directions by the court how to invest, apply or otherwise deal with the property, and the person who is paid the property must follow these directions.

To be invested. Investments made in terms of this provision are not governed by the terms of the Trustee Investments Act 1961 (c. 62). The 1961 Act no longer defines "trustee" to include "guardian" (Sched. 5), and there is, quite deliberately (Scot. Law Com. No. 135, para. 4.8), no provision in the current statute subjecting the powers of investment in this section to the 1961 Act.

Parent. Section 15(1) defines this word to mean "genetic father or mother", and it is nowhere limited for the purposes of the present section to parents with parental responsibilities or parental rights. The generality of s.13 requires that the court has the power to order payment to a parent, such as an unmarried father, who has no responsibility or right of legal representation, and any other interpretation of "parent" would render the definition in s.15 meaningless since this provision is the only one in Part I in a context other than parental responsibilities and parental rights (where the definition is inept since the genetic but unmarried father is excluded). However, it will seldom be in the interests of the child for this to be done unless such a parent were also given that responsibility and right, but extreme cases are not beyond the bounds of imagination and such an order would not be incompetent. In any case directions as to the investment or application of the money would be given, which the parent would have to follow, and the authority to do so would be the order under this section itself.

Order the money to be paid directly to that person. The court can order that a sum of money falling due in the court proceedings to a person under the age of 16 can be paid directly to that child. It is likely that the court would only consider this appropriate when the sum involved is relatively modest; and though there is no express limitation on the court's discretion, there is the practical limitation that a discharge of the obligation to make payment will have to be given (see subs. (3) below) and the person under 16 would need to have capacity to grant that discharge: it follows that a court ought not to order money to be paid direct to a person who has no legal capacity to grant a discharge for the payment.

Subs. (3)

Once payment has been made to a person (including the child) in terms of subs. (1) above, a receipt for that payment given by the person who receives it will be sufficient discharge. The only problematic case would be if the court ordered the money to be paid direct to the child, for this provision merely states the effect of the discharge and does not itself give capacity to grant a discharge. Section 2(1) of the Age of Legal Capacity (Scotland) Act 1991 grants capacity to a person under 16 to do that which is commonly done by persons of her or his age and circumstances and on terms which are not unreasonable. A discharge in the face of a court order for payment is unlikely to be considered unreasonable, and it might be an act commonly done by children who are the recipients of awards of damages. The terms of this subsection necessarily imply that a child under 16 could have capacity to grant the discharge, otherwise subs. (2)(c) above would be meaningless and could never be applied.

Jurisdiction and choice of law

Jurisdiction and choice of law in relation to certain matters

14.—(1) The Court of Session shall have jurisdiction to entertain an application for an order relating to the administration of a child's property if the child is habitually resident in, or the property is situated in, Scotland.

(2) A sheriff shall have jurisdiction to entertain such an application if the child is habitually resident in, or the property is situated in, the sheriffdom.

(3) Subject to subsection (4) below, any question arising under this Part of this Act—

(a) concerning—
   (i) parental responsibilities or parental rights; or
   (ii) the responsibilities or rights of a guardian,
   in relation to a child shall, in so far as it is not also a question such as is mentioned in paragraph (b) below, be determined by the law of the place of the child's habitual residence at the time when the question arises;

(b) concerning the immediate protection of a child shall be determined by the law of the place where the child is when the question arises; and

(c) as to whether a person is validly appointed or constituted guardian of a child shall be determined by the law of the place of the child's habitual residence on the date when the appointment was made (the date of death of the testator being taken to be the date of appointment where an appointment was made by will), or the event constituting the guardianship occurred.

(4) Nothing in any provision of law in accordance with which, under subsection (3) above, a question which arises in relation to an application for, or the making of, an order under subsection (1) of section 11 of this Act falls to be determined, shall affect the application of subsection (7) of that section.

DEFINITIONS
"child": ss.9(9), 15(1).
"parental responsibilities": s.1(3).
"parental rights": s.2(4).

GENERAL NOTE
Jurisdiction in relation to many of the issues governed by Part I, in particular parental responsibilities and parental rights, remains governed by the Family Law Act 1986 (as amended to take account of the present statute). That Act does not, however, cover the administration of children's property and this section provides the rules for that issue in relation to both jurisdiction and choice of law. In addition it provides choice of law rules for various other issues.

Subs. (1)

In questions concerning the administration of a child's property, the Court of Session will have jurisdiction either if the child is habitually resident in Scotland, or if the property concerned is situated in Scotland. The property can be either heritable and moveable property. As an issue of administration, "child" is limited to a person under the age of 16 years (s.9(9) above).

Habitual residence. For the meaning of this concept, see Anton and Beaumont, *Private International Law* (2nd ed., 1990, W. Green) at pp. 150–152. The concept has been discussed recently in a number of cases arising out of the Hague Convention on International Child Abduction: see *Dickson v. Dickson*, 1990 S.C.L.R. 692, *J (A Minor) (Abduction), Re* [1990] 2 A.C. 562, *S (Minors), Re* [1994] 2 W.L.R. 228, *Findlay v. Findlay*, 1994 S.L.T. 709; *Cameron v. Cameron*, 1996 S.L.T. 306; *Moran v. Moran* 1997 Fam.L.R. 6; *Re FM (A Minor) (Habitual Residence)* [1996] 2 F.C.R. 333. And see Crawford " 'Habitual Residence of the Child' as a Connecting Factor in Child Abduction Cases", 1992 J.R. 177; Clive, "The Concept of Habitual Residence", 1997 J.R. 137.

Subs. (2)

In questions concerning the administration of a child's property, the sheriff will have jurisdiction either if the child is habitually resident in the sheriffdom, or if the property concerned is situated in the sheriffdom.

Subss. (3) and (4)

These subsections deal with choice of law, that is the question of which legal system is to apply to the determination of particular matters. The matters dealt with are the responsibilities and rights of parents and guardians, the immediate protection of the child, and the appointment of guardians.

In any question concerning the responsibilities and rights of parents or guardians, the court is obliged to apply the law of the child's habitual residence, which is determined at the time when the question arises. However, this rule must be read in the light of subs. (4) below which requires that the three overarching principles in s.11(7) above be given effect: the result is that no matter which law the Scottish court is applying, it must regard the child's welfare as its paramount consideration, must not make any order unless it considers that making that order is better for the child than making none and must give the child the opportunity to express views on the matter at issue, taking appropriate account of any views expressed.

In any question concerning the immediate protection of the child, the law to be applied is the law of the place where the child actually is when the question arises. If a question of the child's immediate protection comes before the Scottish court then most likely the child will be in Scotland and Scots law will apply. It is however possible to envisage a situation in which a child is furth of Scotland and an issue concerning its immediate protection is brought before the Scottish court (though practically speaking the need for speedy enforcing of any protection will demand that the applicant take the case to the court of the place where the child actually is). "Child" here is defined in s.15(1) to mean a person under the age of 18 years.

In any question concerning the appointment or constitution of guardianship, the matter will be determined by the law of the child's habitual residence on the date when the appointment was made or event constituting the guardianship occurred. In Scots law a person can become guardian only by appointment, either by the parent or guardian (s.7 above) or by the court (s.11(2)(h) above) and in no other way (see the General Note to s.11(2)(h) above), but other systems may allow guardianship to be imposed upon an individual by facts and circumstances, rather as the law imposes a trust on constructive trustees. If an appointment as guardian is made by a parent or guardian in a will, the date of death shall be taken to be the date of appointment and the date, therefore, at which the child's habitual residence is determined for the purposes of choice of law.

Interpretation

Interpretation of Part I

15.—(1) In this Part of this Act—

"child" means, where the expression is not otherwise defined, a person under the age of eighteen years;

"contact order" has the meaning given by section 11(2)(d) of this Act;

"parent", in relation to any person, means, subject to Part IV of the Adoption (Scotland) Act 1978 and sections 27 to 30 of the Human Fertilisation and Embryology Act 1990 and any regulations made under subsection (9) of the said section 30, someone, of whatever age, who is that person's genetic father or mother;

"parental responsibilities" has the meaning given by section 1(3) of this Act;

"parental rights" has the meaning given by section 2(4) of this Act;

"residence order" has the meaning given by section 11(2)(c) of this Act;

"specific issue order" has the meaning given by section 11(2)(e) of this Act; and

"transaction" has the meaning given by section 9 of the Age of Legal Capacity (Scotland) Act 1991 (except that, for the purposes of subsection (5)(b) below, paragraph (d) of the definition in question shall be disregarded).

(2) No provision in this Part of this Act shall affect any legal proceedings commenced, or any application made to a court, before that provision comes into effect; except that where, before section 11 of this Act comes into force, there has been final decree in a cause in which, as respects a child, an order for custody or access, or an order which is analogous to any such order as is mentioned in subsection (2) of that section, has been made, any application on or after the date on which the section does come into force for variation or recall of the order shall proceed as if the order had been made under that section.

(3) In subsection (2) above, the reference to final decree is to a decree or interlocutor which, taken by itself or along with previous interlocutors, disposes of the whole subject matter of the cause.

(4) Any reference in this Part of this Act to a person—

(a) having parental rights or responsibilities;

(b) acting as a legal representative; or

(c) being appointed a guardian,

is to a natural person only.

(5) Any reference in this Part of this Act to a person acting as the legal representative of a child is a reference to that person, in the interests of the child—

(a) administering any property belonging to the child; and

(b) acting in, or giving consent to, any transaction where the child is incapable of so acting or consenting on his own behalf.

(6) Where a child has legal capacity to sue, or to defend, in any civil proceedings, he may nevertheless consent to be represented in those proceedings by any person who, had the child lacked that capacity, would have had the responsibility to act as his legal representative.

GENERAL NOTE

This is the interpretation section, and is largely self-explanatory. To be noted, however, are the definitions of "child" and "parent".

Subs. (1)

Child. The definition of "child" is not helpful since each provision in Part I either defines the word itself or adopts by necessary implication a definition from another provision. So s.1 defines child as a person under the age of 16 years except in relation to the parental responsibility of providing guidance (when the age is 18); s.2 defines child as a person under the age of 16 years for all the parental rights; ss.3, 4, 6, 7 and 8 adopt by necessary implication these definitions; ss.5 and 9 expressly limit child to person under the age of 16; s.10, referring to the responsibility and right of legal representation, is implicitly limited to age 16; s.11 adopts by necessary implication the ages appropriate to the particular issue; ss.12 and 13 expressly limit child to persons under 16; and s.14 adopts by necessary implication the ages appropriate to the issue, with the sole exception of immediate protection under s.14(3)(b). That is the only provision with which the definition of "child" contained in s.15(1) is applicable.

Parent. This word is stated to mean, in cases other than those in which parenthood is determined by the Adoption (Scotland) Act 1978 or the Human Fertilisation and Embryology Act 1990, "genetic father or mother". This of course must be read subject to s.3(1)(b), which provides that the "father" (*i.e.* the genetic father) is not to have parental responsibilities and rights automatically. Whenever the word parent is used in circumstances other than in relation to parental responsibilities and parental rights the word refers to all mothers and fathers and not just those with these responsibilities and rights. The word is used in this way only in s.13(2). To be noted are the words "of whatever age", which provide recognition that a person under the age of 16 can be a parent. The position of such a child-parent, and her ability to exercise responsibilities and rights, is discussed in the notes to s.2(1), s.4(1) and s.11(2)(b) above.

Subss. (2) and (3)

If proceedings are commenced before the coming into force of Part I they shall continue to be governed by the previous law. However, an application after the coming into force of Part I to vary or recall a custody or access order contained in a final decree granted before its coming into force will be governed by the new law. Final decrees are decrees disposing of all the issues.

Subs. (4)

This provision emphasises the point discussed in the note to s.11(5) above, that is that Part I concerns private law and cannot be used in any way by local authorities. It is provided here that any reference in Part I of the Act to a person having parental responsibilities or parental rights or acting as legal representative or being appointed a guardian is to a natural person only. A local authority or corporate body cannot be appointed a child's guardian, and cannot be granted any parental responsibilities or rights. Though not expressed, it can be assumed that a local authority cannot be required (under Part I) to administer a child's property, for that is an act of legal representation.

Subs. (5)

This is an important provision, clarifying a doubt created in 1991. Under the Age of Legal Capacity (Scotland) Act 1991 a child under the age of 16 is given legal capacity to enter into transactions of a kind that are not uncommon and on terms that are not unreasonable (1991 Act, s.2(1)). That Act did not affect the right of the parent to act as the child's legal representative, and the position seemed to be that a child could exercise a legal capacity (*e.g.* to purchase clothes with her or his own money) and the parent at the same time had the right to use the child's money to enter into transactions such as the purchase of clothes on the child's behalf. It is now made plain, however, that a person may act as a child's legal representative only when the child is incapable of acting on her or his own behalf. It follows that when a child acquires capacity under the 1991 Act before the age of 16, the parent or guardian who is the child's legal representative loses the right to act in relation to the particular transaction which the child has capacity to enter into her or himself. This applies not only to the entering into of contracts but other legal transactions such as the giving or withholding of consent to medical treatment (assumed to be an issue of legal representation in s.5(1) above). A child under 16 can acquire capacity to consent in terms of s.2(4) of the 1991 Act and when she or he does so, the effect of this provision is to deny the parent or guardian any power or capacity to consent on the child's behalf. The exclusion in the definition of "transaction" (subs. (1) above) of the giving of consent having legal effect does not exclude medical consent from this provision: it merely prevents the tautology that would be inherent if it were included in para. (b) ("giving consent to [the giving by a person of any consent having legal effect]").

Subs. (6)

A child's capacity to sue or defend in civil proceedings is governed by the 1991 Act and the effect of subs. (5) above is that the child's legal representative loses the right to sue or defend actions on behalf of the child when the child acquires capacity under that Act. This provision allows a child who has capacity to act for her or himself to consent to be represented in civil proceedings by a person who was her or his legal representative. This is limited to civil proceedings and cannot be relied upon by a child wishing someone to act on her or his behalf in some other transaction such as, for example, a contract (though the law of agency is available to a mature child). Nor can this provision be relied upon for the giving of consent to medical treatment, and that act must be performed by the child her or himself.

PART II

PROMOTION OF CHILDREN'S WELFARE BY LOCAL AUTHORITIES AND BY CHILDREN'S HEARINGS ETC.

CHAPTER 1

SUPPORT FOR CHILDREN AND THEIR FAMILIES

Introductory

Welfare of child and consideration of his views

16.—(1) Where under or by virtue of this Part of this Act, a children's hearing decide, or a court determines, any matter with respect to a child the welfare of that child throughout his childhood shall be their or its paramount consideration.

(2) In the circumstances mentioned in subsection (4) below, a children's hearing or as the case may be the sheriff, taking account of the age and maturity of the child concerned, shall so far as practicable—

   (a) give him an opportunity to indicate whether he wishes to express his views;

   (b) if he does so wish, give him an opportunity to express them; and

   (c) have regard to such views as he may express;

and without prejudice to the generality of this subsection a child twelve years of age or more shall be presumed to be of sufficient age and maturity to form a view.

(3) In the circumstances mentioned in subsection (4)(a)(i) or (ii) or (b) of this section, no requirement or order so mentioned shall be made with respect to the child concerned unless the children's hearing consider, or as the case may be the sheriff considers, that it would be better for the child that the requirement or order be made than that none should be made at all.

(4) The circumstances to which subsection (2) above refers are that—

   (a) the children's hearing—

      (i) are considering whether to make, or are reviewing, a supervision requirement;

      (ii) are considering whether to grant a warrant under subsection (1) of section 66, or subsection (4) or (7) of section 69, of this Act or to provide under subsection (5) of the said section 66 for the continuation of a warrant;

      (iii) are engaged in providing advice under section 60(10) of this Act; or

      (iv) are drawing up a report under section 73(13) of this Act;

   (b) the sheriff is considering—

      (i) whether to make, vary or discharge a parental responsibilities order, a child assessment order or an exclusion order;

      (ii) whether to vary or discharge a child protection order;

      (iii) whether to grant a warrant under section 67 of this Act; or

      (iv) on appeal, whether to make such substitution as is mentioned in section 51(5)(c)(iii) of this Act; or

   (c) the sheriff is otherwise disposing of an appeal against a decision of a children's hearing.

(5) If, for the purpose of protecting members of the public from serious harm (whether or not physical harm)—

   (a) a children's hearing consider it necessary to make a decision under or by virtue of this Part of this Act which (but for this paragraph) would not be consistent with their affording paramountcy to the consideration mentioned in subsection (1) above, they may make that decision; or

(b) a court considers it necessary to make a determination under or by virtue of Chapters 1 to 3 of this Part of this Act which (but for this paragraph) would not be consistent with its affording such paramountcy, it may make that determination.

DEFINITIONS
"child": s.93(2)(a).
"child assessment order": ss.55(1), 93(1).
"child protection order": ss.57(1), 93(1).
"children's hearing": s.93(1).
"exclusion order": ss.76(12), 93(1).
"parental responsibilities order": ss.86(1), 93(1).
"supervision requirement": ss.70(1), 93(1).

GENERAL NOTE
The court, when deciding whether to make any Part I order under s.11 above, is obliged to have regard to the three overarching principles listed in s.11(7). The same three principles are applied by this section to the matters governed by Part II of the Act. An important difference, however, is that in Part II only the welfare principle applies to all matters, and the other two principles apply only in certain (differently) specified circumstances.

The overarching principles listed in this section apply in terms only to decisions and determinations of courts and children's hearings, notwithstanding that Part II allows other persons and bodies to make decisions that might significantly affect individual children. Local authorities are subject to similar principles under s.17 below; reporters on the other hand, who have various decision-making powers under Chapters 2 and 3 of Part II, are not governed by the overarching principles, though inevitably any decision they make will be strongly influenced by their views of the welfare of the child concerned.

Subs. (1)
The paramount consideration of a court or a children's hearing in determining or deciding any matter under Part II is the child's welfare. This does not mean to say that all other considerations are irrelevant, nor even that the decision must always be to favour the child's interests above those of all other persons. This is made plain in subs. (5) below. Rather, it simply means that the child's welfare is always the most important consideration and is likely, in most cases, to determine the issue to be resolved.

Any matter. These words are not to be read literally. The only matters that can be determined taking account of the child's welfare are the discretionary decisions that a court or a children's hearing may be called upon to make, such as whether to impose or to terminate a supervision requirement or whether to make or vary a parental responsibilities order or to grant a child protection order. Decisions of fact which a court has to make are not to be influenced by the child's welfare. So, for example, on an application before a sheriff under s.68 to determine whether or not a ground of referral has been established, the welfare of the child is irrelevant to that determination (though it is, of course, the paramount consideration in determining what steps a hearing should take in response to a finding that the grounds are established). A sheriff could not hold something in the order of the following: "the evidence is too finely balanced for me to determine whether or not the ground of referral has been made out, but the child's interests clearly demand that compulsory measures of supervision be imposed, and so I hold that this is enough to tip the balance towards a finding that the ground is established". Similarly, the welfare of the child will not determine whether the conditions for granting a child protection order, laid down in s.57 below, are satisfied, but will determine whether the order ought to be made or not.

Throughout his childhood. These words are to be compared with those in s.11(7) above in which the welfare test is made the paramount consideration in relation to parental responsibilities and parental rights but no limitation in terms of time is laid down, and with s.95, which amends s.6 of the Adoption (Scotland) Act 1978 to ensure that welfare, expressly "throughout the child's life", is the paramount consideration in the adoption process. For the purposes of the present section, childhood ends when the person reaches the age of 18 years (see the definition of "child" in s.93(2)(a) below) and the person's welfare until then must be taken into account. Even when the child reaches the age of 18, welfare is to be given broad scope and is not to be looked at as a short-term consideration. That of course is often little more than a pious hope. A children's hearing or a court can seldom predict how a child's life is going to develop beyond the immediate or, at best, medium term future, and they are not to be criticised if, in the long term and with hindsight, it is obvious that some other decision would have been preferable.

Subs. (2)

In some of their decisions or determinations, listed in subs. (4) below, the court or children's hearing must give the child the opportunity to express her or his views on the matter under consideration, and must take account of any views expressed in coming to these decisions or determinations. As with s.6 and s.11(7) above, this provision is designed to bring Scots law into line with Art. 12 of the UN Convention on the Rights of the Child (quoted in the notes to s.6 above). There is little significant alteration to the law in relation to children's hearings, the whole point of which has always been to afford the child the opportunity to express views, and the important change lies in the application of this rule to the sheriff. As with s.11(7), there is no age limit, though it is similarly provided that a child aged 12 years or more is presumed capable of forming a view. This has the effect that the court or children's hearing need not take into account the views of a child over the age of 12 only when they are persuaded as a matter of fact that the child is not of sufficient maturity to form a view, and it certainly does not prevent the court or children's hearing taking account of the views of children under 12 when in fact the child under that age is capable of forming and expressing a view. The capacity of each child is to be judged individually. Both the sheriff and the hearing are prohibited from making any order or decision before having regard to the child's views whenever the child must be given the opportunity to express views and has indicated a desire to do so: 1996 Rules, r. 15(3)(b) and A.S. 1997, r. 3.5(1)(b).

Subs. (3)

This is the "minimum intervention principle", reflecting that contained in s.11(7)(a) above in relation to Part I. It applies to all those matters in which the child's views must be taken into account under subs. (2) above, except in relation to a children's hearing either providing advice to a sheriff as to whether a child protection order should be continued or drawing up a report in relation to certain orders that are proposed, and in relation to the disposal by the sheriff of most appeals from decisions of children's hearings. The only time this principle applies on appeal is when the sheriff is exercising his power under s.51(5)(c)(iii) below to substitute his own disposal for that of the hearing: so both the children's hearing and the sheriff must apply this principle in deciding upon the appropriate disposal of a case. The minimum intervention principle amounts to a presumption that matters are best left as they are, and the practical effect of that is that the onus lies with the person seeking intervention by court order or decision of the children's hearing to justify why intervention is necessary: that justification will nearly always lie in the protection or enhancement of the child's welfare.

Subs. (5)

While the welfare of the child is the paramount consideration for both the children's hearing and the court, this must not be allowed to deny necessary protection to others, and this subsection permits the children's hearing or the court to make a decision or determination which will protect members of the public (implicitly, from the child concerned), even when the decision is not in the best interests of the child. It will, for example, often not be in a child's best interests to be kept in secure accommodation, but a decision to this effect might be necessary in order to protect others. This provision is to be read with s.70(10) below, the notes to which reference should be made.

Serious harm (whether or not physical harm). The harm to which members of the public are to be protected from can be physical harm to person or to property, or emotional or psychological harm: in any case it must be serious harm. Serious harm is harm that is not trivial. The phrase ought to be interpreted strictly and this subsection should not be used lightly by either the children's hearing or the sheriff.

Duty of local authority to child looked after by them

17.—(1) Where a child is looked after by a local authority they shall, in such manner as the Secretary of State may prescribe—

(a) safeguard and promote his welfare (which shall, in the exercise of their duty to him be their paramount concern);

(b) make such use of services available for children cared for by their own parents as appear to the authority reasonable in his case; and

(c) take such steps to promote, on a regular basis, personal relations and direct contact between the child and any person with parental responsibilities in relation to him as appear to them to be, having regard to their duty to him under paragraph (a) above, both practicable and appropriate.

(2) The duty under paragraph (a) of subsection (1) above includes, without prejudice to that paragraph's generality, the duty of providing advice and assistance with a view to preparing the child for when he is no longer looked after by a local authority.

(3) Before making any decision with respect to a child whom they are looking after, or proposing to look after, a local authority shall, so far as is reasonably practicable, ascertain the views of—

(a) the child;

(b) his parents;

(c) any person who is not a parent of his but who has parental rights in relation to him; and

(d) any other person whose views the authority consider to be relevant, regarding the matter to be decided.

(4) In making any such decision a local authority shall have regard so far as practicable—

(a) to the views (if he wishes to express them) of the child concerned, taking account of his age and maturity;

(b) to such views of any person mentioned in subsection (3)(b) to (d) above as they have been able to ascertain; and

(c) to the child's religious persuasion, racial origin and cultural and linguistic background.

(5) If, for the purpose of protecting members of the public from serious harm (whether or not physical harm) a local authority consider it necessary to exercise, in a manner which (but for this paragraph) would not be consistent with their duties under this section, their powers with respect to a child whom they are looking after, they may do so.

(6) Any reference in this Chapter of this Part to a child who is "looked after" by a local authority, is to a child—

(a) for whom they are providing accommodation under section 25 of this Act;

(b) who is subject to a supervision requirement and in respect of whom they are the relevant local authority;

(c) who is subject to an order made, or authorisation or warrant granted, by virtue of Chapter 2, 3 or 4 of this Part of this Act, being an order, authorisation or warrant in accordance with which they have responsibilities as respects the child; or

(d) who is subject to an order in accordance with which, by virtue of regulations made under section 33(1) of this Act, they have such responsibilities.

(7) Regulations made by the Secretary of State under subsection (1) above may, without prejudice to the generality of that subsection, include—

(a) provision as to the circumstances in which the child may be cared for by the child's own parents; and

(b) procedures which shall be followed in the event of the child's death.

DEFINITIONS

"accommodation": s.25(8).

"child": s.93(2)(a).

"local authority": Local Government etc. (Scotland) Act 1994, s.2.

"parental responsibilities": ss.1(3), 93(1).

"parental rights": ss.2(4), 93(1).

"relevant local authority": s.93(1).

"supervision requirement": ss.70(1), 93(1).

GENERAL NOTE

The notion of "children in care" under the 1968 Act disappeared with the current legislation, and children are now "looked after" by local authorities rather than in their "care". Replacing the much shorter s.20 of the 1968 Act, this section sets out, in general terms, the duties that local authorities have in relation to children who are being looked after by them, and how they are to go about fulfilling these duties. In addition, it defines the circumstances in which a child is being "looked after" for the purposes of the legislation. The drafting of the section is, in places, unhelpful, with terms remaining undefined (such as "parent"), with some provisions referring to persons with parental responsibilities while other provisions refer to persons with parental rights. Also unhelpful is the fact that there are shades of the three overarching principles listed in s.16 to guide local authorities, but they are not, for no apparent reason, identical in either wording or effect to those in s.16 which guide courts and children's hearings.

Subss. (1) and (2)
The local authority is obliged to perform the listed duties in relation to children who are being looked after by them, in the manner prescribed in regulations. The basic duty is to safeguard and promote the child's welfare (*cf.* the parental responsibility in s.1(1) above to safeguard and promote the child's health, development and welfare), and that promotion includes, under subs. (2), the duty to advise and assist the child in preparing for the time when she or he is no longer being looked after by the local authority.
Looked after. A child is considered as being looked after by a local authority in the circumstances listed in subs. (6) below.
Direct contact between the child and any person with parental responsibilities. The duty here is to encourage the person with the parental responsibility under s.1(1)(c) to maintain personal relations and direct contact with the child to fulfil that responsibility. That person will have the right to do so under s.2(1)(c), with the result that the local authority is not permitted to inhibit the exercise of that right. "Promote" means encourage, but the duty to encourage contact is made subject to the paramount duty to safeguard and promote the child's welfare.

Subs. (3)
Local authorities will have to make a variety of different decisions in relation to children whom they look after, and before coming to their decision they must ascertain the views of the listed individuals on the matter being considered.
So far as reasonably practicable. A local authority must act reasonably in attempting to ascertain the views of the individual, but an inability to ascertain these views does not nullify the decision made. It would not be practicable to ascertain the views of a parent when that person was unknown, or when the individual's whereabouts were unknown, or when the individual was unable, for whatever reason, to express a view.
His parents. There is no definition in this Part of the Act of "parent", and there is no limitation to parents with parental responsibilities or parental rights. An unmarried father is often considered by the law to be a parent (for example in relation to succession and aliment and child support): there is no reason to apply any other meaning to the word "parent" than the normal meaning of either mother or father irrespective of that person's marital status. "Parent" will, of course, include adoptive parent, person deemed parent by an order under ss.27, 28 or 30 of the Human Fertilisation and Embryology Act 1990, and parent presumed under s.5 or declared under s.7 of the 1986 Act.
Parental rights. It is surprising that the reference in para. (c) is not to parental responsibilities and parental rights, but the sloppy draftsmanship has no effect since a person who is not a parent cannot acquire parental rights in relation to a child unless she or he also acquires parental responsibilities.
Any other person. The local authority must act reasonably in determining whose views are relevant, and invariably any person who ordinarily has charge of or control over the child ought to be considered relevant. This would include any relative with whom the child is living, or any foster carer.

Subs. (4)
Having obtained the views they are obliged to obtain under subs. (3) above, the local authority must go on to make the decision concerning the child, and in doing so must have regard, so far as practicable, to the listed matters, including the views of the child.
Shall have regard. The obligation is to take account of the matters listed rather than necessarily follow any views expressed. The decision must be made regarding the child's welfare as the authority's paramount concern (subs. (1) above).
The views ... of the child concerned. This may be compared to s.16(2) above, under which sheriffs and children's hearings must have regard to the views of the child concerned. The terms of the provisions are not identical, however, in that there is no presumption here concerning the ability to express a view after the age of 12, as there is in s.16(2) (and, indeed, as there is in s.25(5) in relation to the local authority's powers to provide accommodation). This omission is unlikely to be a deliberate attempt to distinguish this situation from those others and it simply means that local authorities must exercise some care in determining whether any child is of sufficient age and maturity to express views.

The child's religious persuasion. It is the child's religious persuasion that is important here and not the persuasion of any parent or guardian of the child. The provision is inapplicable to children who are too young to be persuaded.

Racial origin and cultural and linguistic background. These matters are never determining of any decision that has to be made by a local authority looking after a child, but are always relevant.

Subs. (5)

This provision ensures that a local authority is not inhibited from taking necessary protective steps by any obligation contained in this section (such as the obligation to regard the child's welfare as paramount or the obligation to take account of the child's or other person's views). These obligations are qualified, but only to the extent necessary for protecting members of the public from "serious" harm. See the General Note to s.16(5) above.

Subs. (6)

This subsection defines the child who is being "looked after" by a local authority. It represents a substantial improvement from the 1968 Act, under which the child "in care" was defined as such by a number of different provisions. In all the circumstances described in each of the following paragraphs a child will be regarded as being "looked after" by a local authority, and the local authority will have all the duties and responsibilities in relation to the child listed in this Chapter of Part II.

Para. (a). A local authority may provide accommodation to a child under s.25 below when (i) no-one has parental responsibility for her or him; or (ii) when she or he is lost or abandoned; or (iii) when the person caring for the child is unable to provide suitable accommodation; or (iv) when the local authority consider that it would safeguard or promote the child's welfare for them to provide accommodation.

Para. (b). A child who is the subject of a supervision requirement, whether that requirement has a condition of residence with the local authority or not, is being "looked after" by the local authority.

Para. (c). A child who is the subject of a place of safety order, child protection order, parental responsibilities order, a warrant to apprehend or keep in a place of safety, under which the local authority have responsibilities in relation to the child, is being "looked after" by the local authority.

Para. (d). When a local authority has responsibilities over a child as a result of an order made by a court in another part of the United Kingdom and which has effect in Scotland as a result of regulations made under s.33, that child is being "looked after" by the local authority.

Subs. (7)

A child being looked after by a local authority may in fact remain in the care of her or his parents: regulations may provide for the circumstances in which this can occur. In addition, these regulations may prescribe the procedures to be followed in the event of the child's death: this was a matter previously governed by s.28 of the 1968 Act.

S.I.s ISSUED UNDER SECTION

Children's Hearings (Transmission of Information etc.) (Scotland) Regulations 1996 (S.I. 1996 No. 3260).

Arrangements to Look After Children (Scotland) Regulations 1996 (S.I. 1996 No. 3262).

Children (Scotland) Act 1995 etc. (Revocations and Savings) (Scotland) Regulations 1997 (S.I. 1997 No. 691).

Duty of persons with parental responsibilities to notify change of address to local authority looking after child

18.—(1) Where a child is being looked after by a local authority, each natural person who has parental responsibilities in relation to the child shall, without unreasonable delay, inform that authority whenever the person changes his address.

(2) A person who knowingly fails to comply with the requirement imposed by subsection (1) above shall be liable on summary conviction to a fine of level 1 on the standard scale; but in any proceedings under this section it shall be a defence that—

    (a) the change was to the same address as that to which another person who at that time had parental responsibilities in relation to the child was changing; and

(b) the accused had reasonable cause to believe that the other person had informed the authority of the change of address of them both.

DEFINITIONS
"child": s.93(2)(a).
"local authority": Local Government etc. (Scotland) Act 1994, s.2.
"parental responsibilities": ss.1(3), 93(1).

GENERAL NOTE
It is part of the local authority's duties, when they are looking after a child, to promote personal relations and direct contact between the child and anyone with parental responsibilities on a regular basis. They can do so effectively only when they know the address of the person with parental responsibilities. This section imposes upon a person with parental responsibilities the obligation to inform the local authority looking after the child of any change of address that she or he makes. Breach of that obligation is a criminal offence, but there is a defence if the accused was flitting with another person who also has parental responsibilities and the accused had reasonable cause to believe that the other person had informed the local authority of the change of address.
Looked after by a local authority. A child is "looked after" by a local authority in the circumstances described in s.17(6) above.

Provision of services

Local authority plans for services for children

19.—(1) Within such period after the coming into force of this section as the Secretary of State may direct, each local authority shall prepare and publish a plan for the provision of relevant services for or in respect of children in their area.

(2) References to "relevant services" in this section are to services provided by a local authority under or by virtue of—
(a) this Part of this Act; or
(b) any of the enactments mentioned in section 5(1B)(a) to (o) of the Social Work (Scotland) Act 1968 (enactments in respect of which Secretary of State may issue directions to local authorities as to the exercise of their functions).

(3) A local authority shall from time to time review the plan prepared by them under subsection (1) above (as modified, or last substituted, under this subsection) and may, having regard to that review, prepare and publish—
(a) modifications (or as the case may be further modifications) to the plan reviewed; or
(b) a plan in substitution for that plan.

(4) The Secretary of State may, subject to subsection (5) below, issue directions as to the carrying out by a local authority of their functions under subsection (3) above.

(5) In preparing any plan, or carrying out any review, under this section a local authority shall consult—
(a) every Health Board and National Health Service trust providing services under the National Health Service (Scotland) Act 1978 in the area of the authority;
(b) such voluntary organisations as appear to the authority—
   (i) to represent the interests of persons who use or are likely to use relevant services in that area; or
   (ii) to provide services in that area which, were they to be provided by the authority, might be categorised as relevant services;
(c) the Principal Reporter appointed under section 127 of the Local Government etc. (Scotland) Act 1994;
(d) the chairman of the children's panel for that area;
(e) such housing associations, voluntary housing agencies and other bodies as appear to the authority to provide housing in that area; and
(f) such other persons as the Secretary of State may direct.

DEFINITIONS
"local authority": Local Government etc. (Scotland) Act 1994, s.2.
"Principal Reporter": s.93(1).

GENERAL NOTE
Local authorities have the obligation, introduced by this section, to prepare and publish and keep under review plans for their provision of services to children in their area.

Subs. (1)
The obligation is absolute: each local authority must draw up, in consultation with the persons and bodies mentioned in subs. (5) below, plans setting out how they intend to provide those services towards children that they are legally obliged to provide. The plan concerns general policy rather than plans in relation to individual children.
Relevant services. See subs. (2) below.
Children in their area. This means children who are physically present in the local authority area. The domicile or habitual residence of the child is not relevant. "Children" means persons under the age of 18 years.

Subs. (2)
This subsection indicates the services upon which plans must be prepared and published. These include services provided under this Part of this Act, such as services for disabled children provided under ss.23 and 24, the provision of accommodation to children under s.25, the provision of day care under s.27, and after care and training under ss.29 and 30.

Subs. (3)
In addition to drawing up and publishing plans, local authorities are obliged to keep these plans under constant review and may make modifications to or substitutions for them. The Act does not require that reviews be at any stated period but merely that they be held "from time to time". Local authorities must act reasonably in interpreting that phrase. There is nothing to prevent local authorities reviewing some parts of their plans more frequently than other parts.

Subs. (4)
The Secretary of State may direct how reviews are to be carried out, and when, but may not absolve the local authority from consulting those whom they are obliged to consult under subs. (5) below.

Subs. (5)
This lists the bodies and persons whom the local authority are obliged to consult in drawing up their plans or in reviewing them. It is hoped that this duty of consultation will allow local authorities readily to identify gaps in their provision of services to children. There is no requirement that each body or person specified has to be consulted on every aspect of the plan. For example a National Health Service trust providing very limited services (say, dental services) need not be consulted in respect of that part of the plan relating to the provision of accommodation for children.

Publication of information about services for children

20.—(1) A local authority shall, within such period after the coming into force of this section as the Secretary of State may direct, and thereafter from time to time, prepare and publish information—

(a) about relevant services which are provided by them for or in respect of children (including, without prejudice to that generality, services for or in respect of disabled children or children otherwise affected by disability) in their area or by any other local authority for those children; and

(b) where they consider it appropriate, about services which are provided by voluntary organisations and by other persons for those children, being services which the authority have power to provide and which, were they to do so, they would provide as relevant services.

(2) In subsection (1) above, "relevant services" has the same meaning as in section 19 of this Act.

DEFINITIONS
"local authority": Local Government etc. (Scotland) Act 1994, s.2.
"relevant services": s.19(2).

GENERAL NOTE

In addition to the obligation to prepare and publish plans under s.19 above, local authorities are also obliged to prepare and publish information about services which they provide as "relevant services" (*i.e.* those described in s.19(2) above) for children in their area or which are provided for these children by other local authorities. Local authorities may also, where they consider it appropriate, publish information about services provided by voluntary organisations, such as Children First (the RSPCC), Shelter (Scotland), adoption societies and churches when these services are such that, were the local authority to provide them, they would be "relevant services".

Information. What must be provided are details about how the relevant services are provided and how access to these services can be obtained.

Co-operation between authorities

21.—(1) Where it appears to a local authority that an appropriate person could, by doing certain things, help in the exercise of any of their functions under this Part of this Act, they may, specifying what those things are, request the help of that person.

(2) For the purposes of subsection (1) above, persons who are appropriate are—

(a) any other local authority;

(b) a health board constituted under section 2 of the National Health Service (Scotland) Act 1978;

(c) a national health service trust established under section 12A of that Act; and

(d) any person authorised by the Secretary of State for the purposes of this section;

and an appropriate person receiving such a request shall comply with it provided that it is compatible with their own statutory or other duties and obligations and (in the case of a person not a natural person) does not unduly prejudice the discharge of any of their functions.

DEFINITION
"local authorities": Local Government etc. (Scotland) Act 1994, s.2.

GENERAL NOTE

This section permits the local authority to request help in the exercise of any function that they have under this Part of this Act from any of the persons specified in subs. (2). It also imposes an obligation on the person requested to provide help: that obligation is absolute unless the provision of the help is not compatible with the requested person's own statutory or other duties.

Promotion of welfare of children in need

22.—(1) A local authority shall—

(a) safeguard and promote the welfare of children in their area who are in need; and

(b) so far as is consistent with that duty, promote the upbringing of such children by their families,

by providing a range and level of services appropriate to the children's needs.

(2) In providing services under subsection (1) above, a local authority shall have regard so far as practicable to each child's religious persuasion, racial origin and cultural and linguistic background.

(3) Without prejudice to the generality of subsection (1) above—

(a) a service may be provided under that subsection—

(i) for a particular child;

(ii) if provided with a view to safeguarding or promoting his welfare, for his family; or

    (iii) if provided with such a view, for any other member of his family; and

(b) the services mentioned in that subsection may include giving assistance in kind or, in exceptional circumstances, in cash.

(4) Assistance such as is mentioned in subsection (3)(b) above may be given unconditionally or subject to conditions as to the repayment, in whole or in part, of it or of its value; but before giving it, or imposing such conditions, the local authority shall have regard to the means of the child concerned and of his parents and no condition shall require repayment by a person at any time when in receipt of—

(a) income support or family credit payable under the Social Security Contributions and Benefits Act 1992; or

(b) an income-based jobseeker's allowance payable under the Jobseekers Act 1995.

DEFINITIONS
    "child": s.93(2)(a).
    "family": s.93(1).
    "local authority": Local Government etc. (Scotland) Act 1994, s.2.

GENERAL NOTE
    This section imposes upon local authorities an obligation to promote the welfare of children in need by providing a range and level of services appropriate to the children's needs. It is left to local authorities to determine how and to what extent these services are to be provided, but certain guidance is given here.

Subs. (1)
    Section 1(1) above imposes upon mothers and good fathers the obligation to safeguard and promote the welfare of their children, and this provision imposes upon local authorities a similar obligation in relation to children in their area who are in need, to provide services appropriate to that need and to promote the upbringing of these children by their families.
    Children... who are in need. This phrase is defined in s.93(4)(a) below. "Need" refers to being in need of care and attention because the child is unlikely to achieve or maintain a reasonable standard of health or development without the provision of local authority services; or because her or his health or development is likely to be impaired without such services; or because she or he is disabled within the meaning of s.23(2) below; or because some other member of her or his family is disabled and that disability will adversely affect the child.
    Promote the upbringing... by their families. It is considered that a child's needs are best met by being brought up by her or his family (that is to say, by the person who has parental responsibility for the child and any other person with whom the child has been living: s.93(1) below) and local authorities must therefore provide such services as will promote, that is to say encourage and allow in practical terms, the child's family to bring up the child. The obligation to encourage is not an obligation to ensure, and the local authority may promote the upbringing of children by their families only in so far as this is consistent with their duty to safeguard and promote the welfare of children. This amounts to a presumption that in providing services for children these services are best directed towards the maintaining of the child at home, together with a recognition that sometimes a child's welfare can be safeguarded and promoted only by removing the child from her or his home in accordance with later provisions in this Act.

Subs. (2)
    A local authority must be sensitive to the child's religious persuasion, racial origin and cultural and linguistic background and must take these matters into account in determining what services to provide in order to fulfil their obligations under subs. (1) above. The obligation, like that in s.17(4) above, is not absolute and a local authority need not, for example, provide social workers with the ability to speak all the languages native to all the children they provide services to. This subsection must not be used to provide either a greater or a lesser level of service for those of minority persuasions, origins or backgrounds than is provided to those of the majority in Scotland today.

Subs. (3)
    The services that can be provided under subs. (1) above include services provided directly to children in need, or to the family as a whole of a child in need or to an individual member of the family of a child in need.

Assistance in kind. Goods may be provided, such as for example cooking equipment provided to the parent of a child in need.

In exceptional circumstances, in cash. There is no indication as to what circumstances would amount to exceptional but is likely to include circumstances in which the child's needs can be practically met in no other way.

Subs. (4)
This provision is designed to give the local authority maximum flexibility in the provision of assistance in kind or in cash, and it imposes upon the local authority the obligation to take account of the needs of the child and her or his parents in determining the conditions upon which assistance is given. The persons mentioned are not to be required to repay any assistance given, but there is no absolute obligation to give such assistance to such persons.

Parents. There is no limitation on this word to parents with parental responsibilities within the meaning of Part I of the Act. Both parents have legal obligations to maintain their child, and their means can be taken into account here whether or not they live with the child or have responsibilities towards the child under Part I.

Children affected by disability

23.—(1) Without prejudice to the generality of subsection (1) of section 22 of this Act, services provided by a local authority under that subsection shall be designed—

  (a) to minimise the effect on any—
     (i) disabled child who is within the authority's area, of his disability; and
     (ii) child who is within that area and is affected adversely by the disability of any other person in his family, of that other person's disability; and
  (b) to give those children the opportunity to lead lives which are as normal as possible.

(2) For the purposes of this Chapter of this Part a person is disabled if he is chronically sick or disabled or suffers from mental disorder (within the meaning of the Mental Health (Scotland) Act 1984).

(3) Where requested to do so by a child's parent or guardian a local authority shall, for the purpose of facilitating the discharge of such duties as the authority may have under section 22(1) of this Act (whether or not by virtue of subsection (1) above) as respects the child, carry out an assessment of the child, or of any other person in the child's family, to determine the needs of the child in so far as attributable to his disability or to that of the other person.

DEFINITIONS
    "child": s.93(2)(a).
    "family": s.93(1).
    "local authority": Local Government etc. (Scotland) Act 1994, s.2.

GENERAL NOTE
    See White Paper, *Scotland's Children: Proposals for Child Care Policy and Law* (Cm. 2286, August 1993) paras 4.1–4.10.
    The aim of this section is to ensure that, in carrying out their obligation to provide services to safeguard and promote the welfare of children in their area, local authorities take account of, and provide for the needs of, disabled children in their area. The nature of the service to be provided will, of course, depend upon the nature of the disability, but it must aim both to minimise the effect of the disability on the child, whether it is the child or a member of the child's family who has the disability, and to allow the child the opportunity to lead as normal a life as possible.

Subss. (1) and (2)
    Disabled child. A person is disabled if she or he is chronically sick or disabled or suffers from mental disorder within the meaning of the Mental Health (Scotland) Act 1984. "Chronic" means long term and continuously. "Sick or disabled" is to be given broad scope.

Subs. (3)

An assessment of the child's needs created by the disability of the child or the member of her or his family must be carried out by the local authority, if requested to do so. The aim of this assessment will be for the local authority to identify the appropriate services that they have to provide to the child to fulfil their obligations under this Chapter in relation to the particular disabled child.

Parent or guardian. Neither of these words is defined in this Part of the Act but they should be interpreted in the light of the reference to the child's family in subs. (1) above. "Parent" is not to be limited to parent with parental responsibilities or parental rights; "guardian" means a person appointed as parent-substitute to the child under s.7 or s.11 of the present Act.

Assessment of ability of carers to provide care for disabled children

24.—(1) Subject to subsection (2) below, in any case where—

(a) a local authority carry out under section 23(3) of this Act an assessment to determine the needs of a disabled child, and

(b) a person (in this section referred to as the "carer") provides or intends to provide a substantial amount of care on a regular basis for that child,

the carer may request the local authority, before they make a decision as to the discharge of any duty they may have under section 2(1) of the Chronically Sick and Disabled Persons Act 1970 or under section 22(1) of this Act as respects the child, to carry out an assessment of the carer's ability to continue to provide, or as the case may be to provide, care for that child; and if the carer makes such a request, the local authority shall carry out such an assessment and shall have regard to the results of it in making any such decision.

(2) No request may be made under subsection (1) above by a person who provides or will provide the care in question—

(a) under or by virtue of a contract of employment or other contract; or

(b) as a volunteer for a voluntary organisation.

(3) Where an assessment of a carer's ability to continue to provide, or as the case may be to provide, care for a child is carried out under subsection (1) above, there shall, as respects the child, be no requirement under section 8 of the Disabled Persons (Services, Consultation and Representation) Act 1986 (carer's ability to continue to provide care to be considered in any decision as respects provision of certain services for disabled persons) to have regard to that ability.

(4) In this section "person" means a natural person.

DEFINITIONS

"child": s.93(2)(a).
"disabled child": s.23(2).
"local authority": Local Government etc. (Scotland) Act 1994, s.2.

GENERAL NOTE

Local authorities have obligations under s.22 above to provide services to children appropriate to their needs, and these needs will be affected both by the nature of any disabilities they suffer from and by the care that is provided to them by other persons. Provision was made under s.23(3) above for the assessment of the child's disability; this section provides for the assessment of the care that the child is receiving. It requires the local authority—if requested to do so—to make an assessment as to the ability to provide care for disabled children of those (natural) persons who care for these children on a regular basis and requires the local authority to have regard to that assessment, once it has been carried out, in making their decisions as to how to fulfil their duties to provide services to disabled children in their area.

Subss. (1) and (2)

A person who provides a substantial amount of care on a regular basis to a disabled child, otherwise than by virtue of a contract or as a volunteer for a voluntary organisation, may request the local authority to assess her or his ability to provide that care. The local authority is then obliged to carry out that assessment and is further obliged to have regard to its results in determining how to provide services to the child under s.22 above.

Substantial amount of care on a regular basis. It is envisaged that the carer under this section is the main, or one of the main, carers of the child, without whose care the development or welfare of the child would be prejudiced.

Subs. (3)

Once they have carried out an assessment under subs. (1) above, the local authority is absolved from the obligation to take it into account in making decisions under the Disabled Persons (Services, Consultation and Representation) Act 1986 (c. 33) as to whether to provide any of its welfare services under that or any other enactment. Though not so obliged, it remains open to the local authority to take the assessment into account if they think fit.

Provision of accommodation for children, etc.

25.—(1) A local authority shall provide accommodation for any child who, residing or having been found within their area, appears to them to require such provision because—

(a) no-one has parental responsibility for him;

(b) he is lost or abandoned; or

(c) the person who has been caring for him is prevented, whether or not permanently and for whatever reason, from providing him with suitable accommodation or care.

(2) Without prejudice to subsection (1) above, a local authority may provide accommodation for any child within their area if they consider that to do so would safeguard or promote his welfare.

(3) A local authority may provide accommodation for any person within their area who is at least eighteen years of age but not yet twenty-one, if they consider that to do so would safeguard or promote his welfare.

(4) A local authority providing accommodation under subsection (1) above for a child who is ordinarily resident in the area of another local authority shall notify the other authority, in writing, that such provision is being made; and the other authority may at any time take over the provision of accommodation for the child.

(5) Before providing a child with accommodation under this section, a local authority shall have regard, so far as practicable, to his views (if he wishes to express them), taking account of his age and maturity; and without prejudice to the generality of this subsection a child twelve years of age or more shall be presumed to be of sufficient age and maturity to form a view.

(6) Subject to subsection (7) below—

(a) a local authority shall not provide accommodation under this section for a child if any person who—

(i) has parental responsibilities in relation to him and the parental rights mentioned in section 2(1)(a) and (b) of this Act; and

(ii) is willing and able either to provide, or to arrange to have provided, accommodation for him,

objects; and

(b) any such person may at any time remove the child from accommodation which has been provided by the local authority under this section.

(7) Paragraph (a) of subsection (6) above does not apply—

(a) as respects any child who, being at least sixteen years of age, agrees to be provided with accommodation under this section; or

(b) where a residence order has been made in favour of one or more persons and that person has, or as the case may be those persons have, agreed that the child should be looked after in accommodation provided by, or on behalf of, the local authority;

and paragraph (b) of that subsection does not apply where accommodation has been provided for a continuous period of at least six months (whether by a single local authority or, by virtue of subsection (4) above, by more than one local authority), unless the person removing the child has given the local authority for the time being making such provision at least fourteen days' notice in writing of his intention to remove the child.

(8) In this Part of this Act, accommodation means, except where the context otherwise requires, accommodation provided for a continuous period of more than twenty-four hours.

DEFINITIONS

"child": s.93(2)(a).
"local authority": Local Government etc. (Scotland) Act 1994, s.2.
"parental responsibilities": ss.1(3), 93(1).
"parental rights": ss.2(4), 93(1).
"residence order": ss.11(2)(c), 93(1).

GENERAL NOTE

This section replaces s.15 of the 1968 Act, and makes some substantial alterations to the law contained therein. In particular, the notion of a duty to "receive children into care" has been removed from the law, and replaced with the idea that local authorities must "look after" certain children and provide them with accommodation. The duties that local authorities have in looking after children are spelt out in s.17 above; one class of children to whom these duties are owed is that for whom the local authority provides accommodation for a continuous period of more than 24 hours. This section imposes upon local authorities a duty, and in some cases a power, to provide such accommodation for children in their area. The connection between the old s.15 and the old s.16 has been broken, with the result that parental responsibilities orders under s.86 below (replacing parental rights resolutions under the old s.16) are no longer dependent on the child being "in care" or "looked after" by the local authority: accommodation is provided to children who need accommodation, and parental responsibilities orders are granted in relation to children who need such orders.

The old s.15 had always been awkwardly worded, and had become more so over the years as amendments and insertions were made and the present section simplifies the rules greatly.

Subs. (1)

This subsection imposes upon local authorities the duty (and subs. (2) below in some cases confers upon them the power) to provide accommodation to children in their area. If accommodation is provided by a local authority, whether as a result of fulfilling their duty or exercising their power, then the local authority becomes subject to the obligations specified in s.17 above. Reflecting, without substantive change, s.15(1) of the 1968 Act (except for the change from "receiving into care" to "providing accommodation"), subs. (1) obliges the local authority to provide accommodation in the stated circumstances. The subsection is designed to deal with cases in which there is no-one able or willing to look after and provide appropriate care and accommodation for the child. It is in these circumstances that a duty, as opposed to the power in subs. (2) below, arises. If the duty is not fulfilled, a remedy is available in terms of a petition to the Court of Session under s.91 of the Court of Session Act 1868 to ordain the local authority to perform their statutory duty.

Accommodation. This is defined in subs. (8) below to mean accommodation provided for a continuous period of more than 24 hours: in other words, it necessarily includes the provision of a place to sleep.

Child. A child for these purposes is a person under the age of 18 years.

Residing or having been found within their area. Mere physical presence of the child in the local authority area is sufficient to impose the duty or confer the power and the child's nationality, domicile or habitual residence is irrelevant, except that the provision of accommodation for a child ordinarily resident in the area of another local authority can be taken over by that other local authority under subs. (4) below.

Appears to them to require. The obligation to provide accommodation arises only when it appears to the local authority that one or more of the specified circumstances exists. It follows that a bona fide decision by the local authority as to whether these circumstances exist cannot be challenged except by way of judicial review.

Lost or abandoned. A child has been abandoned when she or he has been left to her or his fate. "Lost" means lost to the parent or guardian, who one can assume will be searching for the child, and does not mean lost in the sense that no-one can find the child.

Prevented ... for whatever reason. It is a matter of fact whether the person previously caring for the child is now prevented from providing suitable accommodation and the reason for that prevention is entirely irrelevant to the question of whether the fact exists. A parent may be imprisoned, or made homeless, or fall ill, or be no longer able to cope with the child: if she or he is "prevented", that is to say in fact cannot (in the view of the local authority), provide suitable accommodation or care, then the obligation under subs. (1) arises.

Subs. (2)

As well as the obligation to provide accommodation under subs. (1) the local authority has the power to provide accommodation under subs. (2) whenever they consider that to do so would safeguard or promote the welfare of the child. This will allow a local authority to provide, for example, respite care when a parent remains able to provide accommodation but it is in the interests of the child to spend some time away from home. The local authority may not exercise this power when the parent objects (subs. (6) below).

Subs. (3)

A local authority similarly has the power, but not the obligation, to provide accommodation to persons who are over the age of 18, but are not yet 21, when such provision would promote the young person's welfare. This allows local authorities to accommodate, for example, homeless young persons (though it does not oblige them to do so). Such a person is not a child, with the result that the local authority is not subject to the s.17 duties when they provide accommodation to such a person.

Subs. (4)

Reflecting and simplifying s.15(4) of the 1968 Act, this subsection allows the provision of accommodation for a child to be taken over by the local authority in whose area the child is ordinarily resident from the authority which has provided accommodation on the basis that the child was found within their area. Section 86 of the 1968 Act, which deals with disputes as to the child's residence for this purpose, remains in force.

Subs. (5)

This provision reflects that contained in s.6 above, in relation to parents fulfilling parental responsibilities or exercising parental rights, and reference to the notes to that section should again be made. This is an important addition to the law in this context, for under s.15 of the 1968 Act there was no such provision. It does not give the child a veto, but a voice which will be a heavy consideration in determining her or his welfare.

Subs. (6)

The provision of accommodation under this section is voluntary in the sense that the section does not permit such provision to be made against the wishes of a person with the responsibility and right to provide accommodation for the child. Consequently it is provided here, reflecting the rules contained in s.15(3) of the 1968 Act, that the local authority may not provide accommodation when a person who has parental responsibilities for the child is willing and able to take over the provision of that accommodation and objects to the local authority providing the accommodation. Such a person may (subject to the immediately following subsection) remove the child from accommodation at any time and the local authority cannot prevent that removal under this section.

Shall not provide. It would appear from these words that the local authority is prohibited from providing accommodation if the stated circumstances present themselves. That however is qualified by the words "under this section", and a local authority may provide accommodation under some other provision in the Act, even when a person with parental responsibilities towards the child objects (such as, for example, providing residential accommodation under a supervision requirement granted under s.70(3) below). If the local authority believes that the child's welfare would be threatened by being returned to a person with parental responsibilities, it will have to rely on the compulsory or emergency measures later in the Act to ensure the child's welfare.

Subs. (7)

The prohibition on providing accommodation to a child when the child's parent objects (para. (a) of subs. (6) above) does not apply when the child is at least 16 years old and she or he agrees to be provided with accommodation or when a person in whose favour a residence order has been made under s.11 above so agrees. It is, perhaps, unfortunate that the statute adopts an absolute age limit rather than some formula similar to that contained in the Age of Legal Capacity (Scotland) Act 1991, which recognises that some children below the age of 16 are mature enough to make their own decisions in many matters, but this approach does avoid disputes concerning whether the child is mature enough to make such a decision.

The power of a person with parental responsibilities, who is willing and able to provide accommodation, to remove the child from local authority accommodation (para. (b) of subs. (6)

above) is qualified when the child has been provided with accommodation by one or more local authorities for a continuous period of six months: in that situation the person with parental responsibilities can remove the child only after having given the local authority at least 14 days written notice of their intention to remove the child. It is, at first sight, odd that para. (a) of subs. (6) above is not similarly qualified. That paragraph states that the local authority "shall not" provide accommodation when a person with parental responsibilities who is able and willing to provide accommodation objects, and since this is not qualified they seem to be prohibited from providing accommodation to the child during the 14-day period of notice. However, it is submitted that when a child has been in local authority accommodation for more than six months, the person with parental responsibilities is not "able" to provide accommodation during the 14-day period, with the result that all the conditions in para. (a) of subs. (6) are not satisfied, thus maintaining the local authority's obligation to provide accommodation. "Able" in that subsection means lack of legal constraint as well as practical ability.

Manner of provision of accommodation to child looked after by local authority

26.—(1) A local authority may provide accommodation for a child looked after by them by—
  (a) placing him with—
      (i) a family (other than such family as is mentioned in paragraph (a) or (b) of the definition of that expression in section 93(1) of this Act);
      (ii) a relative of his; or
      (iii) any other suitable person,
      on such terms as to payment, by the authority or otherwise, as the authority may determine;
  (b) maintaining him in a residential establishment; or
  (c) making such other arrangements as appear to them to be appropriate, including (without prejudice to the generality of this paragraph) making use of such services as are referred to in section 17(1)(b) of this Act.

(2) A local authority may arrange for a child whom they are looking after—
  (a) to be placed, under subsection (1)(a) above, with a person in England and Wales or in Northern Ireland; or
  (b) to be maintained in any accommodation in which—
      (i) a local authority in England and Wales could maintain him by virtue of section 23(2)(b) to (e) of the Children Act 1989; or
      (ii) an authority within the meaning of the Children (Northern Ireland) Order 1995 could maintain him by virtue of Article 27(2)(b) to (c) of that Order.

DEFINITIONS
  "accommodation": s.25(8).
  "child": s.93(2)(a).
  "family": s.93(1).
  "local authority": Local Government etc. (Scotland) Act 1994, s.2.
  "residential establishment": s.93(1).

GENERAL NOTE
  Under s.25 above local authorities have duties and sometimes powers to provide accommodation for children in need. This section sets out the different forms which that provision may take, and the aim of the section is to give as wide a range of options to the local authority as is possible.

Subs. (1)
  The local authority may fulfil their obligation or exercise their right to provide accommodation by placing the child in a domestic familial situation (that is to say with foster carers), or with a relative of the child (that is to say someone with whom the child has a relationship of blood or affinity), or with any other suitable person (that is suitable to look after and provide accommodation for a child of the age and circumstances of the particular child). In addition the

local authority may place the child in a residential establishment, or may make any other appropriate arrangements. These arrangements might well include allowing the parents of the child to provide accommodation for the child.

Subs. (2)

The person with whom the child is placed, or the accommodation provided, may be in England or Wales or in Northern Ireland.

Day care for pre-school and other children

27.—(1) Each local authority shall provide such day care for children in need within their area who—

(a) are aged five or under; and

(b) have not yet commenced attendance at a school,

as is appropriate; and they may provide such day care for children within their area who satisfy the conditions mentioned in paragraphs (a) and (b) but are not in need.

(2) A local authority may provide facilities (including training, advice, guidance and counselling) for those—

(a) caring for children in day care; or

(b) who at any time accompany such children while they are in day care.

(3) Each local authority shall provide for children in need within their area who are in attendance at a school such care—

(a) outside school hours; or

(b) during school holidays,

as is appropriate; and they may provide such care for children within their area who are in such attendance but are not in need.

(4) In this section—

"day care" means any form of care provided for children during the day, whether or not it is provided on a regular basis; and

"school" has the meaning given by section 135(1) of the Education (Scotland) Act 1980.

DEFINITIONS

"children": s.93(2)(a).

"local authority": Local Government etc. (Scotland) Act 1994, s.2.

"school": Education (Scotland) Act 1980, s.135(1).

GENERAL NOTE

This section governs the local authority's duty and power to provide day care for pre-school children.

Subs. (1)

Each local authority has a duty to provide day care for pre-school children in their area who are in need; in addition they have the power to provide day care for pre-school children who are not in need. "Need" is defined in s.93(4)(a) below; "day care" is defined in subs. (4) below. The regulation of day care found in Part X of the Children Act 1989 does not apply to local authority provision of day care.

Subs. (2)

The local authorities are empowered to provide facilities for those adults who care for children on a day care basis or who accompany them at day care.

Subs. (3)

The local authorities are obliged to provide appropriate care outside school hours and during school holidays to school children in need ("need" again being defined in s.93(4)(a) below), and they are empowered to provide such care to school children who are not in need.

Removal of power to arrange for emigration of children

28. Section 23 of the Social Work (Scotland) Act 1968 (which provides a power for local authorities and voluntary associations, with the consent of the Secretary of State, to make arrangements for the emigration of children in their care) shall cease to have effect.

GENERAL NOTE
The power contained in s.23 of the 1968 Act to arrange for the emigration of a child in care had for many years been outdated and the exercise of the power was almost unknown. Local authorities can no longer deal with children in their care by removing them from the United Kingdom, but must continue to look after them according to their duties under this Act. Schedule 5 below contains many other repeals from the 1968 Act and other Acts.

Advice and assistance for young persons formerly looked after by local authorities

After-care

29.—(1) A local authority shall, unless they are satisfied that his welfare does not require it, advise, guide and assist any person in their area over school age but not yet nineteen years of age who, at the time when he ceased to be of school age or at any subsequent time was, but who is no longer, looked after by a local authority.

(2) If a person within the area of a local authority is at least nineteen, but is less than twenty-one years of age and is otherwise a person such as is described in subsection (1) above, he may by application to the authority request that they provide him with advice, guidance and assistance; and they may, unless they are satisfied that his welfare does not require it, grant that application.

(3) Assistance given under subsection (1) or (2) above may include assistance in kind or in cash.

(4) Where a person—

(a) over school age ceases to be looked after by a local authority; or

(b) described in subsection (1) above is being provided with advice, guidance or assistance by a local authority,

they shall, if he proposes to reside in the area of another local authority, inform that other local authority accordingly provided that he consents to their doing so.

DEFINITIONS
"local authority": Local Government etc. (Scotland) Act 1994, s.2.
"school age": Education (Scotland) Act 1980, s.31.

GENERAL NOTE
See White Paper: *Scotland's Children: Proposals for Child Care Policy and Law* (Cm. 2286, August 1993) at paras. 3.36–3.40.

Children brought up by their parents can usually turn to them for advice, guidance and assistance, even after they reach full adulthood, but this is often not possible for persons who, while they were children, were looked after by local authorities. This section, in an important addition to the law, gives power to local authorities to continue to provide advice, guidance and assistance to young persons whom they looked after as children.

Subs. (1)
Local authorities are obliged to provide advice, guidance and assistance to any person under the age of 19 years but over school age who were, but are no longer, looked after by the local authority. This obligation is qualified in cases in which the person's welfare does not require such advice, guidance and assistance. It does not apply to children who were, but had ceased to be, looked after by a local authority before they ceased to be of school age, with the result that it might benefit a child about to cease to be of school age to continue to be looked after until that time: this might well be a relevant consideration for children's hearings deciding whether to terminate a supervision requirement under s.73(9) below.

Looked after. The definition of children who are or were "looked after" by a local authority is found in s.17(6) above.

Subs. (2)

In addition to the obligation under subs. (1) above, local authorities also have the power to provide advice, guidance and assistance to persons over the age of 19 years and under the age of 21 years who are no longer looked after by the local authority. That power can be exercised whenever application has been made to the local authority by the person seeking advice, guidance and assistance. The matter is entirely within the discretion of the local authority to grant or withhold what has been applied for, except that they have no power to provide it when satisfied that the person's welfare does not require it.

Subs. (3)

The assistance, whether given under the local authority's duty or power, may be goods or services or cash. Again, the matter is in the discretion of the local authority.

Subs. (4)

Where the local authority has a duty to provide advice, guidance and assistance under subs. (1) above, and the person to whom it is provided moves to another local authority area, the providing local authority must inform the new local authority, so long as the person consents to this being done.

Financial assistance towards expenses of education or training and removal of power to guarantee indentures etc.

30.—(1) Without prejudice to section 12 of the Social Work (Scotland) Act 1968 (general social welfare services of local authorities), a local authority may make—

(a) grants to any relevant person in their area to enable him to meet expenses connected with his receiving education or training; and

(b) contributions to the accommodation and maintenance of any such person in any place near where he may be—

(i) employed, or seeking employment; or

(ii) receiving education or training.

(2) Subject to subsection (3) below, a person is a relevant person for the purposes of subsection (1) above if—

(a) he is over school age but not yet twenty-one years of age; and

(b) at the time when he ceased to be of school age or at any subsequent time he was, but he is no longer, looked after by a local authority.

(3) A local authority making grants under paragraph (a), or contributions under paragraph (b)(ii), of subsection (1) above to a person may continue to make them, though he has in the meantime attained the age of twenty-one years, until he completes the course of education or training in question; but if, after he has attained that age, the course is interrupted by any circumstances they may only so continue if he resumes the course as soon as is practicable.

(4) Section 25 of the Social Work (Scotland) Act 1968 (which empowers a local authority to undertake obligations by way of guarantee under any indentures or other deed of apprenticeship or articles of clerkship entered into by a person in their care or under supplemental deeds or articles) shall cease to have effect.

DEFINITIONS

"local authority": Local Government etc. (Scotland) Act 1994, s.2.

"school age": Education (Scotland) Act 1980, s.31.

GENERAL NOTE

Local authorities have the power (to be exercised at their discretion) to make grants towards the expenses of education or training or to make contributions towards the accommodation and maintenance of "relevant persons" who are employed or seeking employment or are receiving education or training. "Relevant person" is defined in subs. (2) to be a person who is over school age but under the age of 21 years, and who was, but no longer is, being "looked after" by the local authority. Persons "looked after" by local authorities are defined in s.17(6) above. Grants and contributions can be continued after the person reaches 21 years until the relevant education or training is completed; but any interruption of that education or training after the person's 21st birthday will take away the local authority's power to make grants and contributions unless the course is recommenced as soon as practicable.

Local authorities will no longer have express power to guarantee indentures or apprenticeships or articles of clerkship in relation to young persons who are or were in their care. This repeals s.25 of the 1968 Act, though the power contained in that section is now subsumed into the more general power in this section.

Miscellaneous and General

Review of case of child looked after by local authority

31.—(1) Without prejudice to their duty under section 17(1)(a) of this Act, it shall be the duty of a local authority who are looking after a child to review his case at such intervals as may be prescribed by the Secretary of State.

(2) The Secretary of State may prescribe—
  (a) different intervals in respect of the first such review and in respect of subsequent reviews;
  (b) the manner in which cases are to be reviewed under this section;
  (c) the considerations to which the local authority are to have regard in reviewing cases under this section.

DEFINITIONS
  "child": s.93(2)(a).
  "local authority": Local Government etc. (Scotland) Act 1994, s.2.

GENERAL NOTE
  A local authority which is looking after a child must periodically review the child's case in order to determine whether the method adopted for the looking after of the child remains appropriate and whether any changes require to be made in the way the child is being looked after or the legislative provisions under which the child is being looked after. The intervals at which such reviews must be held, the manner in which reviews are to be conducted and the considerations to be taken into account in these reviews are specified in the undernoted Regulations, as are various other issues.

S.I.s ISSUED UNDER SECTION
  Arrangements to Look After Children (Scotland) Regulations 1996 (S.I. 1996 No. 3262).
  Children (Scotland) Act 1995 etc. (Revocations and Savings) (Scotland) Regulations 1997 (S.I. 1997 No. 691).

Removal of child from residential establishment

32. A local authority, notwithstanding any agreement made in connection with the placing of a child in a residential establishment under this Chapter, or Chapter 4, of this Part of this Act by them—
  (a) may, at any time; and
  (b) shall, if requested to do so by the person responsible for the establishment,
remove a child so placed.

DEFINITIONS
  "child": s.93(2)(a).
  "local authority": Local Government etc. (Scotland) Act 1994, s.2.
  "residential establishment": s.93(1).

GENERAL NOTE
  The local authority which has provided accommodation for a child in a residential establishment must remove the child from the establishment if requested to do so by the manager of the establishment, and has the power to remove the child at any other time (if, presumably, they consider that to do so is in the child's best interests or in the interests of other persons in the establishment).

Effect of orders etc. made in different parts of the United Kingdom

33.—(1) The Secretary of State may make regulations providing for a prescribed order which is made by a court in England and Wales or in Northern Ireland, if that order appears to him to correspond generally to an order of a kind which may be made under this Part of this Act or to a supervision requirement, to have effect in prescribed circumstances and for prescribed purposes of the law of Scotland as if it were an order of that kind or, as the case may be, as if it were a supervision requirement.

(2) The Secretary of State may make regulations providing—

   (a) for a prescribed order made under this Part of this Act by a court in Scotland; or

   (b) for a supervision requirement,

if that order or requirement appears to him to correspond generally to an order of a kind which may be made under any provision of law in force in England and Wales or in Northern Ireland, to have effect in prescribed circumstances and for prescribed purposes of the law of England and Wales, or as the case may be of Northern Ireland, as if it were an order of that kind.

(3) Regulations under subsection (1) or (2)(a) above may provide for the order given effect for prescribed purposes to cease to have effect for those purposes, or for the purposes of the law of the place where the order was made, if prescribed conditions are satisfied.

(4) Where a child who is subject to a supervision requirement is lawfully taken to live in England and Wales or in Northern Ireland, the requirement shall cease to have effect if prescribed conditions are satisfied.

(5) Regulations under this section may modify any provision of—

   (a) the Social Work (Scotland) Act 1968 or this Act in any application which the Acts may respectively have, by virtue of the regulations, in relation to an order made otherwise than in Scotland;

   (b) the Children Act 1989 or the Children and Young Persons Act 1969 in any application which those Acts may respectively have, by virtue of the regulations, in relation to an order prescribed under subsection (2)(a) above or to a supervision requirement; or

   (c) the Children (Northern Ireland) Order 1995 or the Children and Young Persons Act (Northern Ireland) 1968 in any application which they may respectively have, by virtue of the regulations, in relation to an order so prescribed or to a supervision requirement.

DEFINITION
"supervision requirement": ss.70(1), 93(1).

S.I.s ISSUED UNDER SECTION
   Children (Reciprocal Enforcement of Prescribed Orders etc.) (England and Wales and Northern Ireland) (Scotland) Regulations 1996 (S.I. 1996 No. 3267).
   Children (Scotland) Act 1995 etc. (Revocations and Savings) (Scotland) Regulations 1997 (S.I. 1997 No. 691).

Registration and inspection of certain residential grant-aided and independent schools etc.

34.—(1) Part IV of the Social Work (Scotland) Act 1968 (which makes provision as regards residential and other establishments) shall be amended in accordance with this section.

(2) [*Amends s.61 of the 1968 Act.*]
(3) [*Substitutes s.61A of the 1968 Act.*]
(4) [*Inserts new s.62A into the 1968 Act.*]
(5) [*Amends s.65 of the 1968 Act.*]
(6) [*Substitutes s.67 of the 1968 Act.*]

Welfare of children in accommodation provided for purposes of school attendance

35. *[Inserts new s.125A into the Education (Scotland) Act 1980 (c.44).]*

Welfare of certain children in hospitals and nursing homes etc.

36.—(1) Where a child is provided with residential accommodation by a person mentioned in subsection (3) below and it appears to the person that the child either—

(a) has had no parental contact for a continuous period of three months or more; or

(b) is likely to have no parental contact for a period which, taken with any immediately preceding period in which the child has had no such contact, will constitute a continuous period of three months or more,

the person shall (whether or not the child has been, or will be, so accommodated throughout the continuous period) so notify the local authority in whose area the accommodation is provided.

(2) A local authority receiving notification under subsection (1) above shall—

(a) take such steps as are reasonably practicable to enable them to determine whether the child's welfare is adequately safeguarded and promoted while he is so accommodated; and

(b) consider the extent to which (if at all) they should exercise any of their functions under this Act with respect to the child.

(3) The persons are—

(a) any health board constituted under section 2 of the National Health Service (Scotland) Act 1978;

(b) any national health service trust established under section 12A of that Act;

(c) any person carrying on—

(i) a private hospital registered under Part IV of the Mental Health (Scotland) Act 1984; or

(ii) a nursing home in respect of which either he is registered under section 1(3) of the Nursing Homes Registration (Scotland) Act 1938 or exemption has been granted under section 6 or 7 of that Act.

(4) For the purposes of subsection (1) above, a child has parental contact only when in the presence of a person having parental responsibilities in relation to him.

(5) A person duly authorised by a local authority may in the area of that authority, at all reasonable times, enter for the purposes of subsection (2) above or of determining whether there has been compliance with subsection (1) above any such place as is mentioned in sub-paragraph (i) or (ii) of subsection (3)(c) above and may for those purposes inspect any records or registers relating to that place; and subsections (2A) to (2D) and (4) of section 6 of the Social Work (Scotland) Act 1968 (exercise of powers of entry and inspection) shall apply in respect of a person so authorised as they apply in respect of a person duly authorised under subsection (1) of that section.

DEFINITIONS

"accommodation": s.25(8).

"child": s.93(2)(a).

"local authority": Local Government etc. (Scotland) Act 1994, s.2.

"parental responsibilities": ss.1(3), 93(1).

GENERAL NOTE

Whenever a child is being accommodated, that is to say provided with accommodation for longer than 24 hours, by a health board, a national health service trust, a private hospital, or a nursing home, and the person providing that accommodation concludes that the child has not been visited personally by any person with parental responsibilities for the child for a period of more than three months, that person must inform the local authority of that fact. The local authority must then determine whether the child's welfare is adequately safeguarded and whether they ought to exercise any of their functions under the Act. This might include, for example, providing accommodation to the child under s.25 above, or giving information to the reporter under s.53 below. The local authority also has the power to enter certain premises to ensure that the obligation to inform them under this section is being properly carried out. In addition, such a failure to visit a child might amount to a ground of referral to the children's hearing on the basis of lack of parental care: see *M v. McGregor*, 1982 S.L.T. 41.

Modification of provisions of Children Act 1989 regarding disqualification from registration as child minder etc.

37. In paragraph 2 of Schedule 9 to the Children Act 1989 (which provides for regulations disqualifying certain persons from registration as a child minder or as a provider of day care for young children), at the end of sub-paragraph (1) there shall be added "unless he has—
(a) disclosed the fact to the appropriate local authority; and
(b) obtained their written consent.".

GENERAL NOTE
   This addition to a part of the Children Act 1989 that applies to Scotland allows a person to be registered as a child minder when she or he would otherwise be disqualified, so long as both the stated conditions are satisfied.

Short-term refuges for children at risk of harm

38.—(1) Where a child appears—
(a) to a local authority to be at risk of harm, they may at the child's request—
   (i) provide him with refuge in a residential establishment both controlled or managed by them and designated by them for the purposes of this paragraph; or
   (ii) arrange for a person whose household is approved by virtue of section 5(3)(b) of the Social Work (Scotland) Act 1968 (provision for securing that persons are not placed in any household unless the household has prescribed approval) and is designated by them for the purposes of this paragraph to provide him with refuge in that household,
   for a period which does not exceed the relevant period;
(b) to a person who carries on a residential establishment in respect of which the person is for the time being registered (as mentioned in section 61(2) of that Act), or to any person for the time being employed in the management of that establishment, to be at risk of harm, the person to whom the child so appears may at the child's request provide him with refuge, for a period which does not exceed the relevant period, in the establishment but shall do so only if and to the extent that the local authority within whose area the establishment is situated have given their approval to the use of the establishment (or a part of the establishment) for the purposes of this paragraph.
(2) The Secretary of State may by regulations make provision as to—
(a) designation, for the purposes of paragraph (a) of subsection (1) above, of establishments and households;
(b) application for, the giving of and the withdrawal of, approval under paragraph (b) of subsection (1) above;
(c) requirements (if any) which must be complied with while any such approval remains in force;
(d) the performance by a person mentioned in the said paragraph (b) of anything to be done by him under that paragraph;

   (e) the performance by a local authority of their functions under this section; and

   (f) the giving, to such persons or classes of person as may be specified in the regulations, of notice as to the whereabouts of a child provided with refuge under this section,

and regulations made under this subsection may include such incidental and supplementary provisions as he thinks fit.

(3) While a child is being provided with refuge under, and in accordance with regulations made under, this section, none of the enactments mentioned in subsection (4) below shall apply in relation to him unless the commencement of the period of refuge has followed within two days of the termination of a prior period of refuge so provided to him by any person.

(4) The enactments are—

   (a) section 89 of this Act and, so far as it applies in relation to anything done in Scotland, section 83 of this Act; and

   (b) section 32(3) of the Children and Young Persons Act 1969 (compelling, persuading, inciting or assisting any person to be absent from detention etc.), so far as it applies in relation to anything done in Scotland.

(5) References in this section to the relevant period shall be construed as references either to a period which does not exceed seven days or, in such exceptional circumstances as the Secretary of State may prescribe, to a period which does not exceed fourteen days.

(6) A child who is provided with refuge for a period by virtue of such arrangements as are mentioned in subsection (1)(a) above shall not be regarded as a foster child for the purposes of the Foster Children (Scotland) Act 1984 by reason only of such provision.

DEFINITIONS
   "child": s.93(2)(a).
   "local authority": Local Government etc. (Scotland) Act 1994, s.2.
   "residential establishment": s.93(1).

GENERAL NOTE
   See White Paper: *Scotland's Children: Proposals for Child Care Policy and Law* (Cm. 2286, August 1993) paras 5.21–5.22.
   Local authorities and persons who carry on residential establishments may provide short-term refuge (*i.e.* for a period not exceeding seven, or exceptionally 14, days) to children who appear to be at risk of harm and who themselves request to be provided with such refuge. A child provided with such a refuge will not be regarded as a foster child for statutory purposes, and, in a significant alteration to the law, the person who provides such a refuge will not be subject to certain specified offences, including that under s.83 of the present Act (harbouring). The Secretary of State may make regulations providing for various matters in connection with such short-term refuges. There is no limitation on the source of the harm, nor its duration, nor its nature and it is likely, therefore, to be given wide scope. The only limitation is that the child her or himself requests refuge and this section does not, therefore, apply to children who are too young themselves to seek refuge, or who do not want to go to the relevant residential establishment.
   A local authority which does provide such a refuge will frequently, if not invariably, be obliged to pass information concerning the child to the reporter in terms of s.53 below.

S.I.s ISSUED UNDER SECTION
   Refuges for Children (Scotland) Regulations 1996 (S.I. 1996 No. 3259).
   Children (Scotland) Act 1995 etc. (Revocations and Savings) (Scotland) Regulations 1997 (S.I. 1997 No. 691).

CHAPTER 2

CHILDREN'S HEARINGS

Constitution of children's hearings

Formation of children's panel and children's hearings

39.—(1) For every local government area there shall be a children's panel for the purposes of this Act, and any other enactment conferring powers on a children's hearing (or on such a panel).

(2) Schedule 1 to this Act shall have effect with respect to the recruitment, appointment, training and expenses of members of a children's panel and the establishment of Children's Panel Advisory Committees and joint advisory committees.

(3) Sittings of members of the children's panel (to be known as "children's hearings") shall be constituted from the panel in accordance with subsection (5) below.

(4) A children's hearing shall be constituted for the performance of the functions given to such a hearing by or by virtue of—

(a) this Act; or

(b) any other enactment conferring powers on a children's hearing.

(5) A children's hearing shall consist of three members, one of whom shall act as chairman; and shall not consist solely of male, or solely of female, members.

DEFINITIONS

"children's hearing": s.93(1).

"local government area": Local Government etc. (Scotland) Act 1994, s.2.

GENERAL NOTE

This section replaces much of ss.33 and 34 of the Social Work (Scotland) Act 1968 with little substantive alteration, except that the role of the local authority is minimised due to the system being administered on a national, rather than a regional, level. The section provides that in every local government area there shall be a children's panel, which is a panel of individuals recruited, appointed and trained in accordance with Sched. 1, and from whose numbers shall be constituted children's hearings to deal with the cases of individual children. These hearings consist of three panel members, at least one of whom must be a woman and at least one of whom must be a man.

Qualifications, employment and duties of reporters

Qualification and employment of reporters

40.—(1) The qualifications of a reporter shall be such as the Secretary of State may prescribe.

(2) A reporter shall not, without the consent of the Scottish Children's Reporter Administration, be employed by a local authority.

(3) The Secretary of State may make regulations in relation to the functions of any reporter under this Act and the Criminal Procedure (Scotland) Act 1975.

(4) The Secretary of State and the Lord Advocate may—

(a) by regulations empower a reporter, whether or not he is an advocate or solicitor, to conduct before a sheriff any proceedings which under this Chapter or Chapter 3 of this Part of this Act are heard by the sheriff;

(b) prescribe such requirements as they think fit as to qualifications, training or experience necessary for a reporter to be so empowered.

(5) In this section, "reporter" means—
(a) the Principal Reporter; or
(b) any officer of the Scottish Children's Reporter Administration to whom there is delegated, under section 131(1) of the Local Government etc. (Scotland) Act 1994, any of the functions which the Principal Reporter has under this or any other enactment.

This section replaces ss.36 and 36A of the 1968 Act. It deals with the qualifications and employment of children's reporters, taking account of the reorganisation of the reporters' service in the Local Government etc. (Scotland) Act 1994 (c. 39), but making little substantive change in the law. The service, to be known as the Scottish Children's Reporter Administration, is now run on a national basis, rather than being tied in to regional council areas, and the chief officer of the service is the Principal Reporter.

Subs. (1)
As under s.36(2) of the 1968 Act, the Secretary of State for Scotland is empowered to prescribe the qualifications of reporters.

Subs. (2)
This provision has its origins in s.36(5) of the 1968 Act, which prohibited reporters from being employed by local authorities in any capacity other than as reporter. Reporters are now employed by the Scottish Children's Reporter Administration and are prohibited from being employed in any capacity at all by local authorities. That prohibition could under the 1968 Act be removed in individual cases with the consent of the Secretary of State; under the present provision the consent of the Scottish Children's Reporter Administration is required.

Subs. (4)
See Reporters (Conduct of Proceedings before the Sheriff) (Scotland) Regulations 1997 (S.I. 1997 No. 714) as amended by the Reporters (Conduct of Proceedings before the Sheriff) (Amendment) Regulations 1997 (S.I. 1997 No. 1084).

Subs. (5)
The term "reporter" means the Principal Reporter and any officer to whom he has delegated any of his functions under s.131(1) of the Local Government etc. (Scotland) Act 1994. Throughout the remainder of the Act the term "Principal Reporter" is used, but that is defined in s.93(1) in the same way as "reporter" is defined here. For the sake of simplicity, these annotations will refer only to "the reporter".

S.I.s ISSUED UNDER SECTION
Children's Hearings (Transmission of Information etc.) (Scotland) Regulations 1996 (S.I. 1996 No. 3260).
Reporters (Conduct of Proceedings before the Sheriff) (Scotland) Regulations 1997 (S.I. 1997 No. 714).
Reporters (Conduct of Proceedings before the Sheriff) (Amendment) Regulations 1997 (S.I. 1997 No. 1084).

Safeguards for children

Safeguarding child's interests in proceedings

41.—(1) Subject to subsection (2) below, in any proceedings under this Chapter or Chapter 3 of this Part of this Act either at a children's hearing or before the sheriff, the hearing or, as the case may be, the sheriff—
(a) shall consider if it is necessary to appoint a person to safeguard the interests of the child in the proceedings; and
(b) if they, or he, so consider, shall make such an appointment, on such terms and conditions as appear appropriate.
(2) Subsection (1) above shall not apply in relation to proceedings under section 57 of this Act.

(3) Where a children's hearing make an appointment under subsection (1)(b) above, they shall state the reasons for their decision to make that appointment.

(4) The expenses of a person appointed under subsection (1) above shall—

(a) in so far as reasonably incurred by him in safeguarding the interests of the child in the proceedings, and

(b) except in so far as otherwise defrayed in terms of regulations made under section 101 of this Act,

be borne by the local authority—

(i) for whose area the children's panel from which the relevant children's hearing has been constituted is formed;

(ii) where there is no relevant children's hearing, within whose area the child resides.

(5) For the purposes of subsection (4) above, "relevant children's hearing" means, in the case of proceedings—

(a) at a children's hearing, that hearing;

(b) under section 68 of this Act, the children's hearing who have directed the application;

(c) on an appeal under section 51 of this Act, the children's hearing whose decision is being appealed against.

DEFINITIONS
"child": s.93(2)(b).
"children's hearing": s.93(1).
"local authority": Local Government etc. (Scotland) Act 1994, s.2.

GENERAL NOTE
Safeguarders were introduced into the children's hearing system by s.66 of the Children Act 1975, coming into effect on June 30, 1985, with the insertion into the 1968 Act of a new s.34A. The present provision replaces the old s.34A, making some important alterations to the law, which are designed both to clarify and to strengthen the role of the safeguarder. The ground upon which a safeguarder can be appointed is substantially widened. Rule 14 of the 1996 Rules governs the role of the safeguarder appointed by the hearing. The equivalent rules for sheriff court appointees are found in rr. 3.6–3.10 of A.S. 1997.

Subs. (1)
In any proceedings conducted under either Chapter 2 or Chapter 3 of Part II of the Act, the sheriff or the children's hearing must consider whether the interests of the child make it necessary to appoint a safeguarder and, if it is considered necessary, must make such an appointment. Under s.34A(1)(c)(i) of the 1968 Act, appointment was permitted when there was, or might have been, a conflict of interest between the child and the parent. The present provision does not specify why the appointment of a safeguarder is necessary, except that it must be in the interests of the child, and the appointment can now be made whenever and for whatever reason the child's interests will be served by such an appointment. This might be because, for example, there is a conflict of interests between the parent and the child, or because there is a conflict of views between the family and the Social Work Department, or because this is the best way of giving the child a voice in the hearing.

Any proceedings. Except in relation to child protection orders (for which see subs. (2) below), the appointment of a safeguarder can be made in any proceedings before the sheriff or the children's hearing which are governed by Chapters 2 or 3. These words are, however, subject to the (unspoken) qualification that the outcome of the proceedings must not be a dispositive decision: it would, it is submitted, be incompetent to appoint a safeguarder in proceedings in which the sheriff or the children's hearing dispose of the case. For example, in proceedings before the sheriff under s.68 below to establish the grounds of referral a safeguarder could be appointed, but not if the sheriff discharges the referral under s.68(9); similarly if the hearing decides to discharge the referral under s.69(12) or to make a supervision requirement under s.70(1) or to terminate a supervision requirement under s.73(9), no safeguarder can be appointed. This is because the only function of the safeguarder is to provide the sheriff or hearing with information upon which to make a dispositive decision. The role of the safeguarder comes to an end when a dispositive decision is made (and consequently she or he needs to be reappointed for the purposes of a review hearing, if that is necessary: see *Catto v. Pearson*, 1990 S.L.T. (Sh. Ct) 77).

The hearing. Under the 1968 Act, the decision whether to appoint a safeguarder lay solely in the discretion of the chairman of the children's hearing (see the old s.34A(1)(c)). This was one of the very few decisions that was made by the chairman alone rather than by the hearing as a whole though there was no good reason why that should have been so, and (sensibly) this has now been changed so that under the present provision the matter is one for the hearing to decide. As always in relation to decisions of a children's hearing, a majority decision is sufficient. The decision is governed by the welfare principle in s.16(1) above, but not the other two overarching principles in s.16(2) or (3). Nevertheless in the context of a children's hearing, it will often be appropriate to discuss the possible appointment of a safeguarder with a child.

Subs. (2)

A safeguarder cannot be appointed in proceedings before a sheriff in which a child protection order is sought. This reflects the fact that such proceedings are emergency proceedings which are required to be concluded as quickly as possible. The exclusion of the power to appoint safeguarders is, however, limited to proceedings under s.57 and it probably follows that safeguarders can be appointed in subsequent child protection order proceedings under later sections, such as at the initial hearing under s.59 or during an application to the sheriff to set aside or vary an order under s.60(7). The delay inherent in a shrieval appointment of a safeguarder suggests that it will rarely be appropriate for a sheriff to make the appointment; an appointment by the initial hearing will seldom achieve much since the eighth-working-day hearing (see s.65(2) below) will have the power to make one, and will invariably be continued in any case.

Subs. (3)

A children's hearing is required under the rules to state the reasons for any decision that they make. This subsection, together with r.14(1) of the 1996 Rules, ensures that, in addition to stating why they have, for example, continued the hearing, they also state why they felt it necessary in the interests of the child to appoint a safeguarder. This was not necessary under the old law since there was only one reason why a safeguarder was appointed in any case, namely that there was a conflict of interest between parent and child. Now there are many possible reasons (see notes to subs. (1) above), and a statement of the hearing's reason not only consists with their general duty to state reasons for their decisions but will in addition serve the useful purpose of indicating to the safeguarder the issues that she or he ought to address.

Subs. (4)

This replaces the old s.34A(3) under which expenses were paid by the local authority of the area from which the children's hearing was formed. This will generally continue to be the case, but there may now be no relevant children's hearing or at least not yet, before a safeguarder is appointed. One of the new powers granted to sheriffs by the present Act is to refer the case of a child to a children's hearing under s.54 below. At that point there will be no relevant children's hearing, and if the sheriff appoints a safeguarder in such proceedings it is the local authority within whose area the child lives which must bear the expenses of the safeguarder.

Subs. (5)

This replaces the old s.34A(4) and makes no substantive changes. It specifies the children's hearing which has appointed a safeguarder to any particular child in order to identify which local authority must bear the safeguarder's expenses.

Conduct of proceedings at and in connection with children's hearing

Power of Secretary of State to make rules governing procedure at children's hearing etc.

42.—(1) Subject to the following provisions of this Act, the Secretary of State may make rules for constituting and arranging children's hearings and other meetings of members of the children's panel and for regulating their procedure.

(2) Without prejudice to the generality of subsection (1) above, rules under that subsection may make provision with respect to—

    (a) the conduct of, and matters which shall or may be determined by, a business meeting arranged under section 64 of this Act;

    (b) notification of the time and place of a children's hearing to the child and any relevant person in relation to the child and to such other persons as may be prescribed;

   (c) how the grounds for referring the case to a children's hearing under section 65(1) of this Act are to be stated, and the right of the child and any such relevant person to dispute those grounds;
   (d) the making available by the Principal Reporter, subject to such conditions as may be specified in the rules, of reports or information received by him to—
      (i) members of the children's hearing;
      (ii) the child concerned;
      (iii) any relevant person; and
      (iv) any other person or class of persons so specified;
   (e) the procedure in relation to the disposal of matters arising under section 41(1) of this Act;
   (f) the functions of any person appointed by a children's hearing under section 41(1) of this Act and any right of that person to information relating to the proceedings in question;
   (g) the recording in writing of any statement given under section 41(3) of this Act;
   (h) the right to appeal to the sheriff under section 51(1)(a) of this Act against a decision of the children's hearing and notification to such persons as may be prescribed of the proceedings before him;
   (i) the right of the child and of any such relevant person to be represented at a children's hearing;
   (j) the entitlement of the child, of any such relevant person and of any person who acts as the representative of the child or of any such relevant person to the refund of such expenses, incurred by the child or as the case may be the person or representative, as may be prescribed in connection with a children's hearing and with any proceedings arising from the hearing;
   (k) persons whose presence shall be permitted at a children's hearing.

S.I.s ISSUED UNDER SECTION

Children's Hearing (Transmission of Information etc.) (Scotland) Regulations 1996 (S.I. 1996 No. 3260).

Children's Hearings (Scotland) Rules 1996 (S.I. 1996 No. 3261).

Children's Hearings (Scotland) Rules 1986 etc. (Revocations) (Scotland) Rules 1997.

Privacy of proceedings at and right to attend children's hearing

43.—(1) Subject to subsection (3) below, a children's hearing shall be conducted in private, and, subject to any rules made under section 42 of this Act, no person other than a person whose presence is necessary for the proper consideration of the case which is being heard, or whose presence is permitted by the chairman, shall be present.

(2) The chairman shall take all reasonable steps to ensure that the number of persons present at a children's hearing at any one time is kept to a minimum.

(3) The following persons have the right to attend a children's hearing—

   (a) a member of the Council on Tribunals, or of the Scottish Committee of that Council, in his capacity as such; and
   (b) subject to subsection (4) below, a bona fide representative of a newspaper or news agency.

(4) A children's hearing may exclude a person described in subsection (3)(b) above from any part or parts of the hearing where, and for so long as, they are satisfied that—

   (a) it is necessary to do so, in the interests of the child, in order to obtain the child's views in relation to the case before the hearing; or

(b) the presence of that person is causing, or is likely to cause, significant distress to the child.

(5) Where a children's hearing have exercised the power conferred by subsection (4) above to exclude a person, the chairman may, after that exclusion has ended, explain to the person the substance of what has taken place in his absence.

DEFINITIONS
"child": s.93(2)(b).
"children's hearing": s.93(1).

GENERAL NOTE
Subsections (1)–(3) of this section replace without substantive alteration the first three subsections of s.35 of the 1968 Act, and aim to ensure that there are as few people as possible present at a children's hearing. The significant change in the law is contained in subss (4) and (5), under which the children's hearing are given the power to exclude from the hearing journalists, who otherwise have an absolute right to attend.

Subs. (1)
A children's hearing is to be conducted in private, and members of the public are not permitted to attend. The only persons normally present will be those who are necessary for a proper consideration of the child's case, though exceptionally the chairman may permit the presence of other persons. Other classes of person permitted to attend are listed in rr. 12 and 13 of the 1996 Rules.
Necessary for the proper consideration of the case. The presence of those who have an obligation to attend is normally, but not always, necessary for the proper consideration of the case. In addition, social workers, safeguarders, interpreters if required, representatives, and anyone who can speak to reports on the child may well be considered necessary.
Permitted by the chairman. The discretion to permit the presence of individuals who have no statutory right to attend a children's hearing rests solely with the chairman, who is guided in her or his decision by subs. (2) below. Any decision made by the chairman cannot be challenged (see notes to s.51(1) below).

Subs. (2)
The chairman is obliged to keep the number of persons present at a children's hearing at any one time to a minimum. This does not entitle the chairman to exclude any person who has a right to attend, except for the reasons specified in any statutory provision which permits such exclusion (as in subs. (4) below or s.46 below); and this subsection does no more than exhort the chairman to minimise the number of those persons whose presence can be admitted under subs. (1) above on a discretionary basis. These will be, for the most part, observers rather than active participants, but individuals such as foster carers, unmarried fathers who are not "relevant persons", or other relatives may well have some role to play in helping the consideration of the case.
At any one time. The chairman can sanction an arrangement whereby parts only of the hearing take place in the presence of particular individuals.

Subs. (3)
This subsection lists the persons who have a right to attend a children's hearing and who cannot, therefore, be excluded. Paragraph (b) deals with journalists, but their right to attend is subject to subs. (4) below.

Subs. (4)
A journalist who would otherwise have the right to attend a hearing under subs. (3) above may be excluded from part or all of the hearing if the journalist's presence either (a) inhibits the child from expressing her or his views, or (b) is causing or is likely to cause significant distress to the child.
A children's hearing may. The decision to exclude a journalist lies with the whole hearing and not solely with the chairman. It is governed by the welfare principle in s.16(1) above.
It is necessary to do so. The exclusion under para. (a) is justified only when it is likely that the child will not express her or his views while the journalist is present. This may arise if the child is inhibited due to the large number of people present at the hearing, or if the child is afraid that the journalist will report her or his views, or if the matters being discussed are of a particularly personal nature.

Significant distress. A preference on the part of the child that the journalist be absent is not sufficient to justify exclusion under para. (b). The presence must cause or be likely to cause "significant" distress, though there is probably no requirement that that distress be of a long lasting nature, so long as it is severe at the moment.

Subs. (5)
If a journalist has been excluded from a hearing under the terms of subs. (4) above, the substance of what has taken place may be explained to the journalist by the chairman.

The chairman may. The right to explain rests with the chairman and there is no obligation on the chairman to do so. If, for example, the matters discussed were particularly personal the chairman may take the view that they should not be revealed to the journalist. If the journalist has been excluded because she or he has deliberately distressed the child, the chairman might properly take the view that the journalist has forfeited the right to an explanation. The decision whether to reveal to a journalist the substance of what occurred is to be determined by having regard only to the welfare of the child and should not be influenced by considerations of "freedom of the press" or "the public's right to know".

After that exclusion has ended. If the journalist has been excluded for the whole of the hearing, the explanation, if the chairman decides to give one, will be after the hearing's decision has been made and the rights of the family have been explained to them. Since the parent and child have a right to attend all parts of the hearing, the explanation to the excluded journalist should be made in their presence.

Prohibition of publication of proceedings at children's hearing

44.—(1) No person shall publish any matter in respect of proceedings at a children's hearing, or before a sheriff on an application under section 57, section 60(7), section 65(7) or (9), section 76(1) or section 85(1) of this Act, or on any appeal under this Part of this Act, which is intended to, or is likely to, identify—
(a) any child concerned in the proceedings or appeal; or
(b) an address or school as being that of any such child.

(2) Any person who contravenes subsection (1) above shall be guilty of an offence and shall be liable on summary conviction to a fine not exceeding level 4 on the standard scale in respect of each such contravention.

(3) It shall be a defence in proceedings for an offence under this section for the accused to prove that he did not know, and had no reason to suspect, that the published matter was intended, or was likely, to identify the child or, as the case may be, the address or school.

(4) In this section "to publish" includes, without prejudice to the generality of that expression,—
(a) to publish matter in a programme service, as defined by section 201 of the Broadcasting Act 1990 (definition of programme service); and
(b) to cause matter to be published.

(5) The requirements of subsection (1) above may, in the interests of justice, be dispensed with by—
(a) the sheriff in any proceedings before him;
(b) the Court of Session in any appeal under section 51(11) of this Act; or
(c) the Secretary of State in relation to any proceedings at a children's hearing,
to such extent as the sheriff, the Court or the Secretary of State as the case may be considers appropriate.

DEFINITIONS
"child": s.93(2)(b).
"children's hearing": s.93(1).

GENERAL NOTE
This section replaces, in rather stronger terms, s.58 of the 1968 Act, and it prohibits the publication of any matter either intended to or likely to identify any child, or her or his address or school, who is subject to proceedings at a children's hearing or before a sheriff in relation to child protection orders, exclusion orders, referrals from a children's hearing, rehearing of evidence, or an appeal. The omission of a reference to child assessment orders granted under

s.55 is odd, and publication of the identity of the child in proceedings for such an order would appear not to be a criminal offence.

The prohibition is more extensive than that contained in the 1968 Act, and the section applies in England and Wales and in Northern Ireland (s.105(8) below).

Subs. (1)

Subject to subs. (3) below, the prohibition is absolute, and the offence created by this section is committed if the prohibited matter is intended to, or is likely to, identify the child, or her or his address or school. It may well follow from this that nothing at all can be published in relation to children from small country or island communities where there is only one school, while similar matters could be published in relation to children from urban communities.

No person. These words are to be given broad scope. The section is not limited to representatives of the media but includes individuals such as reporters, social workers, panel members, parents and relatives. Also covered will be publishers and distributors of material containing the information.

Publish. Subs. (4) below indicates some forms of publication covered by the prohibition, but the prohibition is wider. For one person to inform another person is not to "publish", which requires a more general communication, though it is not necessary that the communication be to a large number of individuals. The word ought to be interpreted in the light of its clear aim, which is to protect the privacy of children. This again is wider than the prohibition contained in the 1968 Act.

Any child concerned. This is not limited to the child referred to the children's hearing, but might include, for example, another child giving evidence or a child in the same household as the referred child and victim of a Sched. 1 offence: *McArdle v. Orr*, 1994 S.L.T. 463.

Subs. (2)

Each such contravention. Every time prohibited material is published by an accused a new offence is committed which will attract the stated penalty. A single publication can constitute many offences if different people are involved in its production and distribution.

Subs. (3)

This defence did not exist in the 1968 Act, but it is necessary now since the prohibition has been extended to cover any person and can be used, for example, by a distributor of a newspaper which, unknown to him, carries the prohibited material. Those responsible for the contents of the material, such as newspaper editors, are unlikely to be able to rely on the defence in this subsection. The onus is on the accused to prove his own ignorance.

Subs. (5)

Under s.58(3) of the 1968 Act the Secretary of State could permit publication if it were in the interests of justice to do so. The present provision permits the sheriff to do so in relation to proceedings before him, the Court of Session to do so in relation to appeal proceedings before them, and the Secretary of State to do so in relation to proceedings at a children's hearing. The children's hearing themselves have no power to grant such a dispensation.

In the interests of justice. Dispensation can be given only in the interests of justice. In making their decision, however, sheriffs and the Court of Session must regard the child's welfare as their paramount consideration (s.16(1) above applies here as to any other decision affecting the child), and this has the result, it is submitted, that the publication ban can be lifted only when this is in the interests of justice *to the child*; circumstances in which this will be so are difficult to visualise but might, for example, cover the case of a child who wishes publicly to clear her or his name from an allegation made in a previous, unauthorised, publication. The Secretary of State is not governed by s.16, but the welfare of the child will in any case be a heavy consideration in his balancing of the interests of justice. If he does decide to lift the publication ban, this should be only in the most exceptional circumstances and only to the extent that is absolutely necessary to achieve the particular interests of justice that have been identified. The interests of persons other than the child may well be taken into account by the Secretary of State, but again it is difficult to visualise circumstances in which this would be appropriate. No dispensation was ever given by the Secretary of State under the equivalent provision in the 1968 Act (according to the Earl of Lindsay, speaking for the Government in the House of Lords Committee of the Whole House, June 7, 1995, col. 95).

S.I. ISSUED UNDER SECTION

Children (Scotland) Act 1995 etc. (Revocations and Savings) (Scotland) Regulations 1997 (S.I. 1997 No. 691).

Attendance of child and relevant person at children's hearing

45.—(1) Where a child has been notified in accordance with rules made under subsection (1) of section 42 of this Act by virtue of subsection (2)(b) of that section that his case has been referred to a children's hearing, he shall—
(a) have the right to attend at all stages of the hearing; and
(b) subject to subsection (2) below, be under an obligation to attend those stages in accordance with the notice.

(2) Without prejudice to subsection (1)(a) above and section 65(4) of this Act, where a children's hearing are satisfied—
[1] (a) in a case concerned with an offence mentioned in Schedule 1 to the Criminal Procedure (Scotland) Act 1995, that the attendance of the child is not necessary for the just hearing of that case; or
(b) in any case, that it would be detrimental to the interests of the child for him to be present at the hearing of his case,
they may release the child from the obligation imposed by subsection (1)(b) above.

(3) Subject to subsection (2) above, the Principal Reporter shall be responsible for securing the attendance of the child at the hearing of his case by a children's hearing (and at any subsequent hearing to which the case is continued under section 69(1)(a) of this Act).

(4) On the application of the Principal Reporter, a children's hearing, if satisfied on cause shown that it is necessary for them to do so, may issue, for the purposes of subsection (3) above, a warrant under this subsection to find the child, to keep him in a place of safety and to bring him before a children's hearing.

(5) Where a child has failed to attend a children's hearing in accordance with such notice as is mentioned in subsection (1) above, they may, either on the application of the Principal Reporter or of their own motion, issue a warrant under this subsection, which shall have the same effect as a warrant under subsection (4) above.

(6) A child who has been taken to a place of safety under a warrant granted under this section shall not be kept there after whichever is the earlier of—
(a) the expiry of seven days beginning on the day he was first so taken there; or
(b) the day on which a children's hearing first sit to consider his case in accordance with subsection (7) below.

(7) Where a child has been found in pursuance of a warrant under this section and he cannot immediately be brought before a children's hearing, the Principal Reporter shall, wherever practicable, arrange a children's hearing to sit on the first working day after the child was so found.

(8) Subject to section 46 of this Act, a person who is a relevant person as respects a child shall, where a children's hearing are considering the case of the child—
(a) have the right to attend at all stages of the hearing; and
(b) be obliged to attend at all stages of the hearing unless the hearing are satisfied that it would be unreasonable to require his attendance or that his attendance is unnecessary for the proper consideration of the case.

(9) Any person who fails to attend a hearing which, under subsection (8)(b) above, he is obliged to attend shall be guilty of an offence and shall be liable on summary conviction to a fine not exceeding level 3 on the standard scale.

NOTE
1. As amended by the Criminal Procedure (Consequential Provisions) (Scotland) Act 1995, c. 40, s.3 and Sched. 3, para. 97.

DEFINITIONS
  "child": s.93(2)(b).
  "children's hearing": s.93(1).
  "place of safety": s.93(1).
  "Principal Reporter": s.93(1).
  "relevant person": s.93(2)(b).
  "working day": s.93(1).

GENERAL NOTE
  This section replaces, with important alterations in substance, parts of s.40 and all of s.41 of the 1968 Act. It obliges the child and the parent to attend the children's hearing, makes it a criminal offence for the parent to fail to do so, and allows for the issuing of warrants to find, keep and bring the child before a children's hearing.

Subs. (1)
  The child who has been notified of the fact that a children's hearing has been arranged, whether to put grounds of referral to her or him, or to discuss established grounds, or for a review of an existing supervision requirement, is granted the right and subjected to the obligation to attend all stages of the hearing, together with any continuations thereof. Granting the child the right to attend is an important improvement on the 1968 Act, which nowhere expressly granted to the child the right to attend her or his own hearing (though as Sheriff Kelbie pointed out in *Sloan v. B*, 1991 S.L.T. 530 at p. 535A, the obligation to attend implicitly carried with it the right of the child to attend the hearing). Paragraph (a) of the present subsection puts the matter beyond any doubt, and additionally has the symbolic importance of emphasising that the hearing is the child's hearing.
  Notified. A child is notified under r.6 of the 1996 Rules when a notification in relevant form has been sent to her or his address. It is not notification to send it to any address at which the reporter is aware the child is not living (*Sloan v. B*, 1991 S.L.T. 530, *per* Lord President Hope at p. 540I).
  The right to attend. If the child insists on attending, she or he cannot be excluded from any part of the hearing and that includes those parts from which she or he may not be obliged to attend in terms of subs. (2) below. The reporter must, therefore, always give the child the opportunity to attend, by inviting that attendance in the notice given, even when the child has been excused attendance: 1996 Rules, r. 6(3).
  At all stages. This includes the stages at which the grounds are to be put, the case is considered, and the decision is made, together will all continuations and reviews. It does not, however, include business meetings arranged under s.64 below.
  Under an obligation. If the child fails or is likely to fail to attend a hearing in circumstances in which she or he has not been relieved of that obligation under subs. (2) below, a warrant can be issued under the terms of subs. (4) or subs. (5) below.

Subs. (2)
  Notwithstanding the child's obligation to attend all stages of the children's hearing considering her or his case, the children's hearing may conduct all or any part of the proceedings in the absence of the child, if the child chooses not to exercise her or his right to attend and the hearing decides to release the child from the obligation to attend.
  Without prejudice to subs. (1) above. The power to proceed in the absence of the child is expressly "without prejudice" to the child's right to attend, with the result that the children's hearing can do so only when the child has agreed not to be present (either expressly or impliedly): it is important to note that all this provision does is release the child from the obligation to attend and it does *not* deny the child the right to attend. The hearing cannot "exclude" the child in the way that they can "exclude" a journalist under s.43(4) above or a parent under s.46(1) below.
  Without prejudice to . . . s.65(4). The releasing of the child from the obligation to attend does not release the chairman from the obligation in s.65(4) below to explain the grounds to the child. It follows that it will seldom be appropriate to allow the child not to attend at that stage of the hearing at which grounds are to be put; and if this is done the hearing will be unable to proceed to a consideration of the case because there will have been no acceptance of the grounds on the part of the child. This resolves the difficulties created under the 1968 Act by the First Division's decision in *Sloan v. B.*, 1991 S.L.T. 530 (see Norrie, "Excluding Children from Children's Hearings" 1993 S.L.T. (News) 67; Wilkinson and Norrie, *Parent and Child* (1993, W. Green) at pp. 464–467) which held that children could competently be excluded from that part of the hearing whenever a referral to the sheriff would be necessary in any case. The new wording allows the hearing to proceed in the absence of the child, but still requires an explanation of the

grounds to be given to the child, with the result that the only time it would be appropriate to permit non-attendance from the part of the hearing at which grounds are to be put is when the child will be too young to understand and reference to the sheriff will be required in any case under s.65(9)(a) below.

Just hearing of that case. Under para. (a) the child can be permitted not to attend when her or his attendance is not necessary for a just consideration of the case. These words suggest that the major aim of this provision is to avoid the possibility of the child being inhibited or influenced in what she or he says by the presence of another person, though a secondary aim is probably the avoidance of distress to the child. It might also be used when the child is too young to make any meaningful contribution to the consideration of the case.

Detrimental to the interests of the child. Under para. (b) it would appear that the primary aim is to avoid distress to the child, but since it would clearly be detrimental to her or his interests to be influenced by the presence of another person that too must be an important factor.

May release the child. The decision to allow the child not to attend her or his hearing is governed by s.16(1) and the paramount consideration of the children's hearing must therefore be the child's welfare. The decision cannot be appealed (see the General Note to s.51(1) below).

Subs. (3)

It is the reporter who is responsible for ensuring that the child is properly notified and attends the hearing, whether an initial hearing or a review hearing. To a large extent, however, the reporter is dependent upon the parent or social worker bringing the child to the hearing, and if there is reason to believe that this will not happen, for whatever reason, the reporter will be obliged to utilise the provisions of subs. (4) below.

Subs. (4)

This replaces s.40(4) of the 1968 Act and deals with the situation when the reporter believes that for some reason the child is unlikely to attend the hearing. In these circumstances, in order to allow her or him to fulfil the obligation under subs. (3) above, the reporter may apply to a children's hearing to issue a warrant to find the child, keep her or him in a place of safety, and bring her or him to a hearing. (Subs. (5) below deals with the situation in which the child has actually failed to attend the hearing.)

A children's hearing. This will not be the children's hearing arranged to consider the child's case, otherwise subs. (5) below would be the appropriate authority under which the warrant is issued. A children's hearing arranged for some other purpose, or solely for this purpose, may issue the warrant under this subsection.

On cause shown. The reporter must have reason to believe that the child will not attend, or will be prevented from attending, the hearing without the utilisation of this provision, and must explain that reason to the children's hearing. The cause might be that the child has a history of non-attendance at hearings, or a belief that the child is at risk of being spirited away before the hearing.

It is necessary for them to do so. The reporter must persuade the children's hearing that it is necessary for a warrant to be issued, but necessity is to be interpreted in light of the purposes of the warrant, which is to allow the reporter to fulfil her or his obligation under subs. (3) above to ensure the child's attendance. A warrant under this section is not available to protect the child's interest or to ensure her or his safety in circumstances in which there is no suggestion of the child failing to attend.

Subs. (5)

If a hearing has been arranged but the child has failed to attend, then the children's hearing which had been arranged to consider the child's case are empowered to issue a warrant to find the child, keep her or him in a place of safety, and bring her or him to a hearing. Under the 1968 Act power to issue a warrant in these circumstances was contained in s.40(4), together with the power now governed by subs. (4) above. The present Act separates the two circumstances. Subsection (4) above applies when there is reason to believe that the child is unlikely to attend the hearing, while the present subsection applies when the child has in fact failed to attend the hearing. The practical difference is that the hearing under this subsection, but not under subs. (4) above, can issue the warrant on their own motion, as well as on the application of the reporter. The effect of the warrant, however, is the same under both subsections.

Subs. (6)

If a warrant has been issued by a children's hearing under either subs. (4) or subs. (5) above and the child has been taken to a place of safety, that warrant will last for only a limited period of time, and will terminate at the earlier of (a) the expiry of seven days from the day the child was first taken to the place of safety, or (b) the day on which a children's hearing first sit to consider the child's case.

The expiry of seven days. The seven days begin to run on the day the child is taken to a place of safety, and expire on midnight of the seventh day. So for example if a child is taken to a place of safety on a Monday, the period expires at midnight on the following Sunday.

Consider his case. In most cases in which a child has been taken to a place of safety under a warrant issued under this section, the cessation of the authority to detain will come about by the sitting of a children's hearing arranged in accordance with subs. (7) below, for seldom will seven days elapse before it is practicable to arrange a hearing.

Subs. (7)

It may be impossible to bring a child before a children's hearing immediately because of the lateness of the hour, because it is not a working day, or because there is no time to prepare any reports that will be necessary. Whatever the reason why the child is not brought to a hearing immediately after being found (notice, not taken to a place of safety, but found) a children's hearing must be arranged for the first working day thereafter. Due to the requirement in the Rules that the hearing members have three days notice of the hearing, in order to allow them time to give proper consideration to any reports submitted, a children's hearing arranged under this subsection will normally have to be continued under s.69(2) below. The hearing under this subsection brings any warrant issued under this section to an end (subs. (6) above), but that does not prevent the hearing deciding to grant a warrant under s.69(7) below.

Wherever practicable. A hearing is not incompetent just because it has been arranged more than one working day after the child was found, for it may not have been practicable to arrange a hearing. The reason may be, for example, because there is no reporter available to deal with the case or because parents or other relevant persons have to travel some distance.

First working day. "Working day" is defined in s.93(1) below. If the child is found on a Tuesday, she or he must, wherever practicable, be brought before a children's hearing on the following Wednesday; if found on a Friday she or he must, wherever practicable, be brought before a children's hearing on the following Monday.

Subss. (8) and (9)

These two subsections replace, with little substantive alteration, the provisions in s.41 of the 1968 Act. The "relevant person" has a right to attend the children's hearing and is indeed obliged so to attend. Failure to attend in breach of this obligation is a criminal offence for which the penalties are listed in subs. (9). The obligation does not, however, apply if the children's hearing are satisfied that it would be unreasonable to require the attendance of the relevant person or that such attendance is not necessary for the proper consideration of the case.

Relevant person. The definition of relevant person is found in s.93(2)(b) below, and it has a similar but not identical effect to the position under the 1968 Act. Under s.41 of that Act the parent of the child was obliged to attend the children's hearing, but "parent" was defined to include "guardian", which itself was defined to include any person who, *in the opinion of the court or children's hearing having cognisance of the case,* had for the time being custody or charge of or control over the child. Section 93(2)(b) below, on the other hand, defines "relevant person" to mean any person with parental responsibilities or parental rights, however obtained, and any person who appears to have charge of or control over the child. The significant difference is that in the present Act it is not specified to whom it must appear that a person has charge of or control over the child, with the result that any person or body that deals with a "relevant person" must decide whether a particular individual comes within the definition. The practical effect of this is, it is submitted, that the reporter must notify any person who appears *to the reporter* to be a relevant person and is no longer entitled to wait for recognition by a children's hearing of a status that gives a right to attend. Any person who appears to a criminal court dealing with an offence under subs. (9) to have charge of or control over the child may be found guilty of non-attendance even when the children's hearing have not yet recognised the person as a relevant person.

At all stages. The right and obligation to attend the children's hearing extends to all stages of the hearing, that is to say the explanation of the grounds, the consideration of the case, and the making of the decision by the hearing, as well as any other part of the procedure, whether at an initial hearing or at a review hearing. There is, however, no right to attend a business meeting arranged under s.64 below.

Unless the hearing are satisfied. The hearing can determine that the attendance of the parent is unreasonable or unnecessary either when the parent does not show up or when the parent asks to be excused. Since failure to attend without this dispensation is a criminal offence (subs. (9)), the hearing ought to make a positive (and recorded) decision to this effect and ought not simply to proceed in the absence of the relevant person. A decision to proceed in the absence of the relevant person does no more than take away the legal obligation to attend: it does not take away the right to do so (unless a decision under s.46 below has been made) and a relevant person can still attend if she or he wishes even after the hearing have decided to proceed in her or his absence: see 1996 Rules, r. 7(2).

Power to exclude relevant person from children's hearing

46.—(1) Where a children's hearing are considering the case of a child in respect of whom a person is a relevant person, they may exclude that person, or that person and any representative of his, or any such representative, from any part or parts of the hearing for so long as is necessary in the interests of the child, where they are satisfied that—

(a) they must do so in order to obtain the views of the child in relation to the case before the hearing; or

(b) the presence of the person or persons in question is causing, or is likely to cause, significant distress to the child.

(2) Where a children's hearing exercise the power conferred by subsection (1) above, the chairman of the hearing shall, after that exclusion has ended, explain to any person who was so excluded the substance of what has taken place in his absence.

DEFINITIONS
"child": s.93(2)(b).
"children's hearing": s.93(1).

GENERAL NOTE
This provision grants a wholly new power to the children's hearing, with nothing analogous appearing in the 1968 Act. For some time it had been felt that the child's interests, and her or his right to speak freely, were not sufficiently protected. Sometimes the child and parent ought not to be in the same room, and sometimes a child's ability to voice opinions is inhibited by the parent's presence. Under the 1968 Act, while it was always open to the hearing to request a parent to withdraw from the hearing for a short period, such a request could not be enforced and these problems could be dealt with only by excluding the child from her or his own hearing. This new provision entitles the hearing to exclude the parent or her or his representative for stated reasons. The representative's right to attend, and role, is dealt with in r. 11 of the 1996 Rules.

Subs. (1)
Are considering. A children's hearing cannot proceed to a consideration of the child's case until the grounds of referral have been accepted or established (see wording of s.69(1) below) and it follows that the power to exclude a relevant person under this section is limited to that stage of the proceedings at which the case is being considered and *not* from the putting of the grounds. The need for a relevant person's acceptance of the grounds cannot, therefore, be avoided by excluding that person before the grounds are put.

They may exclude. The children's hearing are not obliged to exclude a person even when one of the grounds for exclusion exists. It is a matter in their discretion. The power to exclude rests with the hearing as a whole and not solely with the chairman. As usual decisions are made on a majority basis and the paramount consideration in making the decision is the welfare of the child (s.16(1) above).

In order to obtain the views of the child. It may frequently happen that a child is likely to speak more openly in the absence of a parent. This may be because there is a conflict of interest between the parent and the child, or because the child is embarrassed to talk about certain personal matters in front of a parent. This ground might also be used if the parent is disrupting the hearing or, due to the parent insisting on answering for the child, the child is being deprived of the chance to speak for her or himself.

Significant distress. The presence of both parent and child in the same room may sometimes cause the child significant distress. This will commonly be because the parent has abused the child and the child is afraid of the parent, but it might also be, for example, when the child is settled in an environment away from the parent and the security of that settlement would be disturbed by contact with the parent. Under the old law this could only be resolved by excluding the child; this section gives the children's hearing an option which will often be more appropriate.

Subs. (2)
This provision is to be compared with that in s.43(5), under which if a journalist has been excluded the chairman may explain to the journalist what took place in his absence. If, on the other hand, a parent or representative is excluded under subs. (1) above, the chairman has no option but is obliged to explain to such a person the substance of what took place in her or his absence. There will usually be little point in excluding a parent solely in order to allow a child to

speak freely on matters she or he does not want her or his parents to know about and it should be made plain to both parent and child that the substance of what takes place must be revealed. It is not possible, therefore, to use the exclusion as a means of protecting the child's confidentiality against a parent.

Presumption and determination of age

47.—(1) Where a children's hearing has been arranged in respect of any person, the hearing—

(a) shall, at the commencement of the proceedings, make inquiry as to his age and shall proceed with the hearing only if he declares that he is a child or they so determine; and

(b) may, at any time before the conclusion of the proceedings, accept a declaration by the child, or make a fresh determination, as to his age.

(2) The age declared to, or determined by, a children's hearing to be the age of a person brought before them shall, for the purposes of this Part of this Act, be deemed to be the true age of that person.

(3) No decision reached, order continued, warrant granted or requirement imposed by a children's hearing shall be invalidated by any subsequent proof that the age of a person brought before them had not been correctly declared to the hearing or determined by them.

DEFINITIONS
   "child": s.93(2)(b).
   "children's hearing": s.93(1).

GENERAL NOTE
   This provision replaces s.55 of the 1968 Act and makes no substantive alteration to the law contained therein.

Subs. (1)
   The hearing (normally the chairman) opens the proceedings by asking the child or parent to state the child's age. The children's hearing have jurisdiction only over "children" and are permitted to proceed either to put grounds or to consider the case only when satisfied that the person is indeed a child. Their determination on this matter can change in the course of the hearing, though if it is subsequently determined that the person is not a child, this brings the proceedings to an automatic end.
   That he is a child. A "child" for the purposes of chapters 2 and 3 of this Part of the Act is defined in s.93(2) below as (i) a child who has not attained the age of 16 years; (ii) a child over the age of 16 years but under the age of 18 years in respect of whom a supervision requirement is in force; (iii) a child whose case has been referred to a children's hearing from another part of the U.K. (where childhood lasts until the age of 18); and (iv) in relation to a child referred on the ground of school non-attendance, a child over the age of 16 who is not yet over school age.

Subs. (2)
   If the hearing have determined that the child is a "child" within the terms of Part II then the age so determined shall be deemed to be the true age of the child until the hearing make a fresh determination of the child's age under subs. (1)(b) above.

Subs. (3)
   Following on from subs. (2) above, under which a determination of age is treated as the child's true age whether it is or not, any decision, order, warrant or requirement made under Part II is not challengeable on the ground that the age determined by the hearing is not the child's true age.

Transfer etc. of cases

Transfer of case to another children's hearing

48.—(1) Where a children's hearing are satisfied, in relation to a case which they are hearing, that it could be better considered by a children's hearing constituted from a children's panel for a different local government area, they may at any time during the course of the hearing request the Principal Reporter to arrange for such other children's hearing to dispose of the case.

(2) Where a case has been transferred in pursuance of subsection (1) above, the grounds of referral accepted or established for the case shall not require to be further accepted or established for the purposes of the children's hearing to which the case has been transferred.

GENERAL NOTE
This provision replaces, with no substantive alteration, s.54 of the 1968 Act. It provides that when a children's hearing considers that the case would be better dealt with by a children's hearing in another local government area, they may request the reporter to arrange for the case to be transferred to that other area. Accepted or established grounds remain accepted or established before the new hearing.

Referral or remission to children's hearing where child guilty of an offence

49. *[Repealed by the Criminal Procedure (Consequential Provisions) (Scotland) Act 1995 (c. 40), s.6 and Sched. 5.]*

NOTE
1. Replaced by s.49 of the Criminal Procedure (Scotland) Act 1995. For details, see Norrie, *Children's Hearings In Scotland* (1997) at pp. 125–130.

Treatment of child's case on remission by court

[1] **50.**—(1) Where a court has, under section 49 of the Criminal Procedure (Scotland) Act 1995, remitted a case to a children's hearing for disposal, a certificate signed by the clerk of the court stating that the child or person concerned has pled guilty to, or has been found guilty of, the offence to which the remit relates shall be conclusive evidence for the purposes of the remit that the offence has been committed by the child or person.

(2) Where a court has under subsection (7) of the said section 49 remitted a case to a children's hearing for disposal, the provisions of this Act shall apply to the person concerned as if he were a child.

NOTE
1. As amended by the Criminal Procedure (Consequential Provisions) (Scotland) Act 1995, c. 40, s.3 and Sched. 3, para. 97.

GENERAL NOTE
Replacing, with no substantive alteration in the law, ss.56 and 57 of the 1968 Act, this section ensures that when a court remits a case to a children's hearing under the provisions in s.49 of the Criminal Procedure (Scotland) Act 1995, the ground of referral (being that the child has committed an offence: s.52(2)(i)) shall be treated as having been established. It follows that a children's hearing which is empowered by the remit to dispose of the case can move straight onto a consideration of the case and disposal thereof without having to put the ground to the child and parent for acceptance under s.65(3) below.

Subsection (2) is required since a person over 16 who is not currently under supervision (but who might be put under supervision by s.49(7) of the 1995 Act) is not a "child" for the purposes of the children's hearing provisions in the present Act. Such a person is to be treated as a child for these purposes if s.49(7) applies.

Appeals

Appeal against decision of children's hearing or sheriff

51.—(1) Subject to subsection (15) below, a child or a relevant person (or relevant persons) or both (or all)—

(a) may, within a period of three weeks beginning with the date of any decision of a children's hearing, appeal to the sheriff against that decision; and

(b) where such an appeal is made, shall be heard by the sheriff.

(2) The Principal Reporter shall, in respect of any appeal under subsection (1) above, ensure that all reports and statements available to the hearing, along with the reports of their proceedings and the reasons for the decision, are lodged with the sheriff clerk.

(3) The sheriff may, on appeal under subsection (1) above, hear evidence from, or on behalf of, the parties in relation to the decision; and, without prejudice to that generality, the sheriff may—

(a) examine the Principal Reporter;

(b) examine the authors or compilers of any reports or statements; and

(c) call for any further report which he considers may assist him in deciding the appeal.

(4) Where the sheriff decides that an appeal under this section has failed, he shall confirm the decision of the children's hearing.

(5) Where the sheriff is satisfied that the decision of the children's hearing is not justified in all the circumstances of the case he shall allow the appeal, and—

(a) where the appeal is against a warrant to find and keep or, as the case may be, to keep a child in a place of safety, he shall recall the warrant;

(b) where the child is subject to a supervision requirement containing a condition imposed under section 70(9) of this Act, he shall direct that the condition shall cease to have effect; and

(c) in any case, he may, as he thinks fit—

    (i) remit the case with reasons for his decision to the children's hearing for reconsideration of their decision; or

    (ii) discharge the child from any further hearing or other proceedings in relation to the grounds for the referral of the case; or

    (iii) substitute for the disposal by the children's hearing any requirement which could be imposed by them under section 70 of this Act.

(6) Where a sheriff imposes a requirement under subsection (5)(c)(iii) above, that requirement shall for the purposes of this Act, except of this section, be treated as a disposal by the children's hearing.

(7) Where the sheriff is satisfied that an appeal under subsection (1) above against the decision of a children's hearing arranged under section 73(8) of this Act is frivolous, he may order that no subsequent appeal against a decision to continue (whether with or without any variation) the supervision requirement in question shall lie until the expiration of twelve months beginning with the date of the order.

(8) An appeal under subsection (1) above in respect of the issue of a warrant by a children's hearing shall be disposed of within three days of the lodging of the appeal; and failing such disposal the warrant shall cease to have effect at the end of that period.

(9) Where a child or a relevant person appeals under subsection (1) above against a decision of a children's hearing in relation to a supervision requirement, the child or the relevant person may make application to a children's hearing for the suspension of the requirement appealed against.

(10) It shall be the duty of the Principal Reporter forthwith to arrange a children's hearing to consider the application under subsection (9) above, and that hearing may grant or refuse the application.

(11) Subject to subsections (13) and (15) below, an appeal shall lie by way

of stated case either on a point of law or in respect of any irregularity in the conduct of the case—
  (a) to the sheriff principal from any decision of the sheriff—
      (i) on an appeal under subsection (1) of this section;
      (ii) on an application made under section 65(7) or (9) of this Act; or
      (iii) on an application made under section 85(1) of this Act; and
  (b) to the Court of Session from any decision of the sheriff such as is mentioned in sub-paragraphs (i) to (iii) of paragraph (a) above and, with leave of the sheriff principal, from any decision of the sheriff principal on an appeal under that paragraph; and the decision of the Court of Session in the matter shall be final.
  (12) An appeal under subsection (11) above may be made at the instance of—
  (a) the child or any relevant person, either alone or together; or
  (b) the Principal Reporter on behalf of the children's hearing.
  (13) An application to the sheriff, or as the case may be the sheriff principal, to state a case for the purposes of an appeal under subsection (11)(a) or (b) above shall be made within a period of twenty-eight days beginning with the date of the decision appealed against.
  (14) On deciding an appeal under subsection (11) above the sheriff principal or as the case may be the Court of Session shall remit the case to the sheriff for disposal in accordance with such directions as the court may give.
  (15) No appeal shall lie under this section in respect of—
  (a) a decision of the sheriff on an application under section 57 of this Act; or
  (b) a decision of a children's hearing continuing a child protection order under section 59(4) of this Act.

DEFINITIONS
  "child": s.93(2)(b).
  "children's hearing": s.93(1).
  "principal reporter": s.93(1).
  "relevant person": s.93(2)(b).
  "supervision requirement": ss.70(1), 93(1).

GENERAL NOTE
  Decisions of the children's hearing can be appealed against by the child or the parent, as can decisions of the sheriff. This section governs appeals and replaces, with some important alterations in the law, ss.49 and 50 of the 1968 Act. The basic principle remains that any decision of the children's hearing can be appealed to the sheriff, and any decision of the sheriff, whether on an application for finding established a ground of referral or in dealing with an appeal from the hearing's decision, can be appealed to the Court of Session on a point of law or in respect of procedural irregularity. The two major changes are (i) the introduction of a new level of appeal to the sheriff principal, and (ii) the conferring upon the sheriff of a power, on appeal from a decision of the children's hearing, to substitute his own disposal for that of a hearing with whom he disagrees.
  As under the old law, there is no appeal from the Court of Session to the House of Lords, and there are some decisions of the children's hearing which are not open to appeal at all. The power of the Secretary of State to terminate a supervision requirement, previously contained in s.52 of the 1968 Act, has not been re-enacted. Procedure is governed by A.S. 1997, rr. 3.53–3.61.

Subs. (1)
  Within three weeks of a decision of the children's hearing, either the child or the relevant person, or both, can appeal against that decision to the sheriff, and the sheriff is obliged to hear the appellants. The reporter, of course, has no title or interest in appealing a decision of the hearing, but is the contradictor in any appeal made to the sheriff.
  Relevant person. This is the person who has the right and obligation to attend the children's hearing and to dispute the grounds of referral. The right of appeal inheres in this person even when she or he did not attend the hearing. Because the definition in s.93(2) is a factual one, susceptible to change, a person may move out of the category of "relevant person" after the hearing and also lose the right of appeal: *S v. Lynch*, 1997 S.L.T. 1377. Presumably a person may also move into this category.

Within a period of three weeks. The appeal must be made within 21 days of the date of the hearing's decision, the day of the decision being the first day (*S, Appellants,* 1979 S.L.T. (Sh.Ct.) 37). So if a children's hearing make a decision on Wednesday, August 1, the appeal must be lodged on or before Tuesday, August 21.

Any decision. It is not, in fact, any decision that a hearing reaches that can be appealed against. Under subs. (15) below no appeal can be had against a decision of the hearing to continue a child protection order under s.59(4) below. In addition to this, however, it had been established by the case law under the 1968 Act (in which the same words appeared) that appeals can be had only against dispositive decisions of the children's hearing or decisions on the granting or renewing of warrants. Decisions which are merely procedural steps in the process towards the making of a dispositive decision, such as decisions to direct the reporter to apply to the sheriff for a finding as to whether the grounds of referral are established, are not appealable (*H. v. McGregor,* 1973 S.C. 95, *Sloan v. B,* 1991 S.L.T. 530 at p. 545L), and confirmation that this remains the law can be found in subs. (5)(c)(iii) below which allows a sheriff to substitute his own disposal for that of the hearing—but that disposal must be one governed by s.70, which deals only with final dispositive decisions. Into the category of unappealable decisions will also fall decisions to exclude journalists or parents or representatives from part or all of the hearing, decisions to excuse the child from her or his obligation to attend, and decisions to continue the case to a subsequent hearing under s.69(1)(a) below. A decision to appoint a safeguarder under s.41 above is likely to be considered unappealable.

"Any decision" does include a dispositive decision of a children's hearing arranged to reconsider their decision after a sheriff has found that decision not justified, and the special rules for appeals in that case under s.51 of the 1968 Act have not been re-enacted.

Appeal to the sheriff. The old s.49 specified that the appeal would be to the sheriff in chambers, and this rule is now contained in s.93(5) below.

Subs. (2)

It is the responsibility of the reporter to ensure that there are lodged with the sheriff clerk all the appropriate documents relevant to the appeal, which includes all reports available to the hearing, reports of the proceedings at all the hearings, and the reasons for the decision which have been made or been caused to have been made by the chairman under r.10(5) of the 1996 Rules.

Subs. (3)

In hearing an appeal from a decision of the children's hearing the sheriff is permitted to hear evidence only from or on behalf of the parties to the appeal (that is the child and the relevant persons and the reporter) and in addition he may examine the reporter and the compilers of any reports he has received. This includes the chairman of the hearing who has drawn up the reasons for the decision. It is in the discretion of the sheriff whom he wants to examine and he may call for further reports, such as an updated social background report, educational report, medical report, or safeguarder's report.

Subs. (4)

If the appeal fails, the decision of the hearing is confirmed without variation. Any suspension of a supervision requirement granted under subs. (9) below will (though the Act does not tell us so) be lifted on the rejection of the appeal.

Subs. (5)

The grounds of appeal to the sheriff are not specified in the Act (as they were not in the 1968 Act) except for the rule in this subsection that the sheriff shall allow the appeal if the decision of the children's hearing is "not justified in all the circumstances of the case". These words (taken from s.49(5) of the 1968 Act) do not permit the sheriff to allow the appeal merely because he has a difference of opinion with the hearing as to the correct disposal of the case. It is perfectly conceivable that two different, even opposing, disposals are justifiable in the circumstances of a single case. Rather, the sheriff must be satisfied either that there was a procedural irregularity in the conduct of the case before the hearing, or that the hearing failed to give proper consideration to some factor in the case.

Once the sheriff has decided that the appeal is to be allowed, he must proceed according to one of the three options listed in para. (c). In addition, if the successful appeal is against a warrant to find or keep a child in a place of safety, the sheriff is obliged to recall the warrant. And if the supervision requirement contained an authorisation under s.70(9) to keep the child in secure accommodation, he is obliged to direct that that authorisation shall cease to have effect (though he will be entitled to grant such authorisation himself under para. (c)(iii), which allows him to do anything that the hearing can do under s.70). The three options open to the sheriff are:

(i) To remit the case back to the hearing for reconsideration. When the sheriff does this, he must give reasons for his decision, but he is not entitled to give any directions as to how the hearing should proceed with the case or dispose of it, for that would be to usurp the role of the children's hearing. His statement of reasons must be limited to a statement of why he has found the decision appealed against to be not justified in all the circumstances of the case: *Kennedy v. A*, 1986 S.L.T. 358.

(ii) To discharge the child from any further hearing or proceedings in respect of the grounds which led to the hearing whose decision is being appealed against. Any supervision requirement imposed in respect of these grounds will be terminated, together with any order attached thereto.

(iii) To make a supervision requirement in terms of s.70 below on whatever terms and conditions permitted by that section the sheriff considers appropriate. The overwhelming majority of appeals will govern cases in which a supervision requirement has been imposed or continued in any case, and the disposal of the sheriff under this subparagraph will therefore normally amount to a variation of its terms (for example removing a requirement that the child resides at a specified place, or varying a direction regulating contact between the child and another person). Appeals against discharge of a referral or termination of a supervision requirement are not incompetent, and on such appeals the sheriff can impose a supervision requirement on such terms and conditions as are available to the hearing under s.70. Though technically all the disposals open to the children's hearing are open to the sheriff, he will in practice be unable to adopt the very disposal previously adopted by the children's hearing themselves, for that would amount to an acceptance by the sheriff that that disposal was justifiable—in which case he must reject the appeal and allow the hearing's decision to stand.

Prior to the enactment of this provision the sheriff's role on allowing an appeal was limited to ordering the children's hearing to reconsider the case or to terminate the supervision requirement. It is unclear how sheriffs are to come to their conclusions as to what disposal is appropriate, for there is no provision in the Act permitting the sheriff to conduct a sort of shrieval children's hearing. In *Children's Hearings in Scotland* (W. Green, 1997) at p. 188 the present writer made the following suggestion: "Since the children's hearing is always the most appropriate forum for determining what compulsory measures of supervision will best meet the child's needs and since it is in every child's interests to have their case determined by the most appropriate forum, it is suggested that sheriffs should use their power under this provision only when it is clear that there is only one possible option which will serve the child's interests and when, therefore, it would be a procedural waste of time to send the matter back to the children's hearing for disposal."

Subs. (6)

A supervision requirement substituted by the sheriff under subs. (5) above will be treated as a disposal of the children's hearing in relation to effect, duration, review and termination. Its date of making will be the date of the sheriff's decision.

Subs. (7)

Where a sheriff has rejected an appeal against a decision of the children's hearing at a review of a supervision requirement and he is satisfied that the appeal was "frivolous", he may prohibit for a period of 12 months any subsequent appeal against a subsequent decision to continue (with or without variation) the supervision requirement in respect of which the appeal was made. In other words, if the supervision requirement continued by a decision frivolously appealed against is reviewed at any time within 12 months of the sheriff's order, any decision at that review is not appealable until these 12 months have elapsed. An order under this subsection will prevent an appeal by anyone, even by those who did not join in the frivolous appeal.

An appeal ... against a decision ... under s.73(8). An order under this subsection can be made only in the context of an appeal from a decision of a hearing reviewing a supervision requirement and not from the decision which initially imposes it.

Frivolous. The Act does not define what a frivolous appeal is, but the aim of the provision is clear: it is to ensure that the courts are not cluttered by appeals which have no chance of success or which seek review when no change whatsoever has occurred in the child's circumstances since the last review and which are being brought by the child or parent simply in order to prolong the procedure.

Subs. (8)

If the appeal is against the hearing's issuing of a warrant, whether under s.45 above, s.66 below, or under any other provision in the Act permitting a children's hearing to grant a warrant, that appeal must be heard and disposed of within three days of its lodging and if it is not so disposed of the warrant shall cease to have effect.

At the end of that period. The first day is the day after which the appeal is lodged (*B v. Kennedy*, 1992 S.L.T. 870), and the end of the period of three days is the end of the third day. So if an appeal is lodged on a Monday it must be disposed of by the following Thursday, otherwise the warrant shall cease to have effect at midnight on that day. Notice that the days here are not "working days", as is the case in, for example, s.60(8).

Subss. (9) and (10)

As under s.49(8) of the 1968 Act, the child or parent who appeals against a decision of the children's hearing imposing, continuing or varying a supervision requirement can apply to the hearing for the suspension of the requirement until the appeal has been heard. The application can be made immediately the appeal is lodged, but not before. It is the responsibility of the reporter to arrange a hearing to consider the application for suspension, and that hearing may grant or refuse the application. There is no indication as to what criteria the hearing should use to determine such an application, but the decision is clearly one governed by the welfare of the child as the paramount consideration (s.16(1) above). Though s.16(2) does not apply, good practice will be for the hearing to take account of any views expressed by the child in appropriate circumstances.

Forthwith. This means as soon as practically possible, rather than immediately (see *Viola v. Viola*, 1988 S.L.T. 7 on the meaning of "forthwith" in the context of the Child Abduction and Custody Act 1985).

Subs. (11)

Replacing s.50 of the 1968 Act, this subsection allows for appeals from decisions of the sheriff, both in determining an appeal from a decision of the children's hearing and in determining whether grounds of referral have been established (whether on the initial application or at a review of the evidence). Title to appeal inheres in the child, all relevant persons, and the reporter. The reporter may appeal against a finding that the grounds of referral have not been established, but has no interest in appealing against a decision that the grounds are established; since she or he appeals "on behalf of the children's hearing" (subs. (12)(b) below), she or he can appeal against the sheriff's finding that the hearing's decision was not justified, but not against a confirmation of the hearing's decision.

In a significant change from the 1968 Act (not, incidentally, wholeheartedly supported by Lord Hope of Craighead in his maiden speech in the House of Lords: see *Hansard*, H.L. Vol. 564, col. 41), a new level of appeal is added, from the sheriff to the sheriff principal. This is an additional rather than an alternative appeal, and appeal can be had from the sheriff's decision to the sheriff principal and then from the sheriff principal (with his consent) to the Court of Session, or direct from the sheriff to the Court of Session. The first appeal to the sheriff principal was *D. G. v. Templeton*, 1998 S.C.L.R. 180. Procedure is governed by A.S. 1997 rr. 3.59–3.61. It is to be expected that appeals direct to the Court of Session will occur when the point of law is particularly difficult or contentious, or raises an important matter of principle. Appeal, whether to the sheriff principal or to the Court of Session, is by way of stated case and is on a point of law or in respect of any irregularity in the conduct of the case. There is no appeal from the Court of Session to the House of Lords.

Subject to subsections (13) and (15). The right of appeal is lost if not exercised within 28 days (subs. (13) below); there are certain decisions which are unappealable (subs. (15) below).

To the sheriff principal. Appeal is to the sheriff principal of the sheriffdom in which the sheriff, from whose decision the appeal is being taken, sits.

Any decision. This is subject to subs. (15) which states that decisions of the sheriff granting child protection orders are not appealable.

To the Court of Session ... with leave of the sheriff principal. Leave is not required to appeal from the sheriff to the sheriff principal nor direct from the sheriff to the Court of Session, but if an appeal has already been made from the sheriff to the sheriff principal a further appeal to the Court of Session will require the leave of the sheriff principal. No guidance is given to the sheriff principal as to the circumstances in which it would be appropriate to grant or to withhold leave, but the aim of the provision (see *Hansard*, H.L. Vol. 565, col. 1152) is to ensure that the new appeal to the sheriff principal is not used simply as a delaying tactic. Leave ought to be refused, it is submitted, when an appeal to the sheriff principal has failed and it is his view that the ground of appeal put forward was not arguable. Leave ought to be granted if appeal to the Court of Session is necessary to resolve a difference which has arisen between sheriff principals.

Subs. (12)

The appeal against the sheriff's decision to either the sheriff principal or the Court of Session, and against the sheriff principal's decision to the Court of Session, can be made at the instance of the child or the relevant person, or by the reporter. The child or parent can appeal against a decision discharging the referral: although this would be unusual, it is competent, and might be appropriate, where the child is seeking the protection of a supervision requirement, or the parent is seeking to exercise parental control with the assistance of a supervision requirement. The reporter appeals on behalf of the children's hearing and so has interest to appeal only against a decision which alters or challenges the hearing's decision: she or he cannot appeal against the sheriff's confirmation of the decision under subs. (4) above. In addition to this provision in the Act, the Rules permit a safeguarder appointed by a children's hearing to sign an appeal on the child's behalf: A.S. 1997, r. 3.53(3). This has long been taken to give the safeguarder title to appeal: see, *e.g. Catto v. Pearson*, 1990 S.L.T. (Sh.Ct) 77.

Subs. (13)
An appeal from a decision of the sheriff or the sheriff principal is by way of stated case (subs. (11) above) and the application to state a case must be made within a period of 28 days from the date of the sheriff's or the sheriff principal's decision, otherwise the right of appeal is lost. The date of the decision is the first day, so if the decision is made on Wednesday, October 1, the application must be made on or before Tuesday, October 28.

Subs. (14)
Once the appeal has been decided the sheriff principal or the Court of Session must remit the case back to the sheriff for disposal.
In accordance with such directions as the court may give. While a sheriff who remits a case back to a children's hearing after a successful appeal (subs. (5)(c)(i) above) cannot give directions to a children's hearing as to how they should dispose of the case, nor the factors they should take into account (*Kennedy v. A*, 1986 S.L.T. 358), an appeal court is, as Kearney points out (*Butterworths Family Law Service* at para. c.2094), in a different position and is able under this provision to give such directions as it thinks fit. While in most cases procedural directions only will be appropriate, the words of the statute are broad and suggest that an appeal court can direct the sheriff to dispose of a case in a particular manner, including whether the supervision requirement should be terminated, or varied, or continued. This power may be taken to reflect, and is therefore consistent with, the power of the sheriff to substitute his own decision on an appeal from a children's hearing, for effectively it gives the appeal court the power to make its own decision. It should be noted that this position is inconsistent with that suggested by the present author when this work was first published and in *Children's Hearings in Scotland* (W. Green, 1997) at p. 194.

Subs. (15)
This section specifies decisions which are not appealable: decisions of the sheriff to make a child protection order, and decisions of the children's hearing to continue a child protection order at an initial hearing arranged under s.59 below. It might be argued that by specifying these decisions the Act is indicating that all other decisions are appealable, including those characterised as unappealable in the notes to subs. (1) above. It is submitted, however, that this argument (*expressio unius est exclusio alterius*) is not good since the same wording is used in subs. (1) above as appeared in the 1968 Act and there is no indication other than the present subsection that the words are to be given a meaning different from that gleaned by the courts since 1968. This subsection lists, it is submitted, decisions which are unappealable in addition to those which have long been regarded as such, and was rendered necessary as a consequence of the creation of the new child protection orders with their own, special, appeal mechanisms.

CHAPTER 3

PROTECTION AND SUPERVISION OF CHILDREN

Children requiring compulsory measures of supervision

Children requiring compulsory measures of supervision

52.—(1) The question of whether compulsory measures of supervision are necessary in respect of a child arises if at least one of the conditions mentioned in subsection (2) below is satisfied with respect to him.

(2) The conditions referred to in subsection (1) above are that the child—
(a) is beyond the control of any relevant person;
(b) is falling into bad associations or is exposed to moral danger;
(c) is likely—
  (i) to suffer unnecessarily; or
  (ii) be impaired seriously in his health or development,
  due to a lack of parental care;
[1] (d) is a child in respect of whom any of the offences mentioned in Schedule 1 to the Criminal Procedure (Scotland) Act 1995 (offences against children to which special provisions apply) has been committed;
(e) is, or is likely to become, a member of the same household as a child in respect of whom any of the offences referred to in paragraph (d) above has been committed;
(f) is, or is likely to become, a member of the same household as a person who has committed any of the offences referred in paragraph (d) above;
[1] (g) is, or is likely to become, a member of the same household as a person in respect of whom an offence under sections 1 to 3 of the Criminal Law (Consolidation) (Scotland) Act 1995 (incest and intercourse with a child by step-parent or person in position of trust) has been committed by a member of that household;
(h) has failed to attend school regularly without reasonable excuse;
(i) has committed an offence;
(j) has misused alcohol or any drug, whether or not a controlled drug within the meaning of the Misuse of Drugs Act 1971;
(k) has misused a volatile substance by deliberately inhaling its vapour, other than for medicinal purposes;
(l) is being provided with accommodation by a local authority under section 25, or is the subject of a parental responsibilities order obtained under section 86, of this Act and, in either case, his behaviour is such that special measures are necessary for his adequate supervision in his interest or the interest of others.
(3) In this Part of this Act, "supervision" in relation to compulsory measures of supervision may include measures taken for the protection, guidance, treatment or control of the child.

NOTE
1. As amended by the Criminal Procedure (Consequential Provisions) (Scotland) Act 1995, (c. 40), s.3 and Sched. 3, para. 97.

DEFINITIONS
"child": s.93(2)(b).
"children's hearing": s.93(1).
"compulsory measures of supervision": s.93(1).
"local authority": Local Government etc. (Scotland) Act 1994, s.2.
"parental responsibilities": ss.1(3), 93(1).
"parental responsibilities order": ss.86(1), 93(1).
"relevant person": s.93(2)(b).

GENERAL NOTE
This important section sets out the grounds upon which a child can be referred to a children's hearing. It replaces s.32 of the 1968 Act, and while there has been some tidying of the wording there is little substantive alteration to the grounds themselves. It is a pity that the opportunity was not taken to simplify the wording to make the grounds more readily understandable to children and to lay people, especially since one of the most important duties of the chairman of the hearing is to explain the grounds to the family (s.65(4) below). The concept, for example, of "relevant person" is unlikely to prove readily understandable to many people unversed in the intricacies of the present Act. There is some confusion possible with this section adopting the

terminology of "conditions" while other parts of the Act refer to "grounds" (see for example ss.65, 68 and 69). There is, however, no difference between conditions and grounds and what are commonly referred to as "the grounds of referral" (as in s.69(1 below) or, sometimes, the "grounds for referral" (as in s.68(8) below) are the conditions listed in subs. (2) of the present section and it is these conditions that must be explained by the chairman at the commencement of the proceedings in accordance with s.65(4) below. The existence of a ground of referral founds the jurisdiction of the children's hearing, which cannot consider the case of a child in order to determine whether compulsory measures of supervision are required unless one or more of them exists.

Subs. (1)

The satisfaction of one or more of the conditions in subs. (2) below or, to put it another way, the existence of one or more of the grounds of referral, will be established either by the child and the parent accepting that they exist (s.65(5) below) or by the sheriff finding that they exist on an application under either s.68 or s.85 below or by a court holding that they exist under s.54 below. The existence of one or more of the grounds of referral is not, however, in itself proof that compulsory measures of supervision are necessary; conversely, however, their absence is conclusive of a lack of any need for such measures. The existence of a ground of referral does no more than raise the question of whether or not compulsory measures of supervision are necessary, and that question can be answered either by the reporter deciding to take no further action (as she or he is permitted to do under s.56(4) below) or by a children's hearing arranged by the reporter under s.65(1) below). If no ground exists the question does not arise, the children's hearing have no jurisdiction, and no compulsory measures of supervision can be imposed; if a ground does exist then the hearing have jurisdiction to embark upon a consideration of the child's case in order to determine whether compulsory measures of supervision are required, and if so what form these measures should take.

Subs. (2)

This central provision lists the grounds of referral, and reflects to a very large degree the grounds that existed in s.32(2) of the 1968 Act. The only substantive alteration to the old law are to be found in para. (g) which extends the old incest ground to include male children and to include offences related to incest, and in para. (j) which introduces a wholly new ground of referral.

Para. (a). A "relevant person" is someone who has parental responsibilities or parental rights in relation to a child (however acquired), or who ordinarily has charge of, or control over, a child (s.93(2)(b) below). Such a person has the responsibility of providing control for the child, and if unable, for whatever reason, to exercise that control the child shall be considered to be beyond the control of such person. "Control" must, it is submitted, be interpreted in a manner appropriate to the particular child: the control required to be provided to a young child is very different from that to be provided to a teenager who is nearing 16.

Para. (b). This is identical to the old ground under s.32(2)(b) of the 1968 Act. Wilkinson and Norrie, *Parent and Child* (1993, W. Green) at p. 450 say of this ground: "Any association which may be harmful to the child's welfare in any, not only in its moral, aspect, may be regarded as bad. Moral danger is commonly equiperated with the risk of sexual corruption, but there is no warrant for restricting it to such cases. The mere commission of an offence does not, but the exposure to circumstances from which a habitual pattern of criminal conduct is likely to follow probably does, indicate moral danger. There are obvious hazards and difficulties in going beyond recognised categories such as sexual corruption and criminality, but a wide scope is clearly intended. Thus, exposure of a child to scenes of habitual drunkenness may involve moral danger or at least indicate that the child is falling into bad associations. Similarly, circumstances in which the child is likely to indulge in solvent abuse or to develop the habit of taking drugs or drinking to excess may be regarded as obnoxious to this condition". It is illegitimate to attempt to avoid the higher standard of proof required to establish that the child has committed a criminal offence by seeking to prove this ground with facts showing that the child has committed an offence: *Constanda v. M.*, 1997 S.L.T. 1396.

Para. (c). This is worded differently from, but has the same effect as, s.32(2)(c) of the 1968 Act. "Parental care" is care provided by any person who has the parental responsibility of safeguarding and promoting the child's health, development and welfare. The reason for the lack of care is irrelevant, and the important point is the likelihood that such lack will cause the child to suffer unnecessarily (that is avoidably) or seriously to impair her or his health or development. On "likelihood" in the context of the offence of wilful neglect of a child, see *H v. Lees, D v. Orr*, 1994 S.L.T. 908; *M. v. Normand*, 1995 S.L.T. 1284.

Children (Scotland) Act 1995

Para. (d). This replaces the first part of s.32(2)(d) of the 1968 Act and concerns children who have been the victim of certain specified offences. In relation to the existence of this ground of referral, it is of no significance who perpetrated the offence, nor where the offence was perpetrated; these matters will, of course, be highly relevant to the final disposal of the child's case. Proof of this ground, though it is proof of a criminal offence, is on the civil standard, and this can be met even in the absence of a conviction: the issue at stake is the harm to the child rather than how it was perpetrated. The offence may be committed in Scotland or elsewhere: *S. v. Kennedy*, 1996 S.L.T. 1087.

Para. (e). This replaces the second part of s.32(2)(d) of the 1968 Act, and provides a ground of referral in relation to a child who is or is likely to become, a member of the same household as a child victim of the offences covered in para. (d) above. So if one child in a household is a victim of, say, physical abuse, all the children in that household can be referred to the children's hearing. This is based on the assumption, borne out by experience, that if one child in a household is threatened by a source of danger, that source is likely to have access to and constitute a threat to the other children in the household. Again it is to be emphasised that the existence of the ground of referral merely raises the question of whether compulsory measures of supervision are necessary and is not conclusive of that necessity. On the meaning of "household" in this context, and in the context of the following two paragraphs, see Norrie "The Meaning of 'Household' in Referrals to Children's Hearings", 1993 S.L.T. (News) 192. See also *Templeton v. Espindola*, 1998 S.C.L.R.

Para. (f). This replaces the old s.32(2)(dd). A child who lives with a Sched. 1 offender may not be in need of compulsory measures of supervision, but the very existence of the offence raises the question. It will normally be essential to establish who the perpetrator is in order to establish that the child is a member of her or his household.

Para. (g). Under the old s.32(2)(e) female children who were members of the same household as female victims of the crime of incest could be referred to the children's hearing if both females were members of the same household as the perpetrator of that crime. This tortuous ground was not needed under the 1968 Act and while it has been slightly tidied up, it is not needed under the current legislation. The ground is expanded to allow it to bring boys as well as girls to a children's hearing, and it is further expanded to cover the offences related to incest which were created by the Incest and Related Offences (Scotland) Act 1986. However, all cases in which this ground would be applicable will be covered by para. (f) above since incest and the related offences are all now Sched. 1 offences and if the child is in the same household as the perpetrator, para. (f) is activated. It is obscure why incest and the related offences are given their own separate (and still opaque) paragraph, and chairmen will still suffer the difficulties of explaining this ludicrous and unnecessary ground to children. It was very seldom used under the 1968 Act. The figures for 1994 were no referrals on this ground out of a total of 14,019 referrals of girls, and for 1995 five referrals out of a total of 14,946: *Statistical Bulletin*, Scottish Office, No. SWK/CH/1997/20.

Para. (h). Before this ground can be made out, the child must, one assumes, be "of school age" (defined in s.93(1) below and s.31 of the Education (Scotland) Act 1980). "Reasonable excuse" is to be proved by the child or parent, and will usually mean a reason for which neither can be held responsible, such as illness. An exclusion order issued due to the child's disruptive behaviour does not constitute a reasonable excuse for not attending school. The fact that the child is being appropriately educated at home is, on the other hand, a reasonable excuse.

Para. (i) This is identical to the ground in s.32(2)(g) of the 1968 Act, and while the consideration and disposal of a case brought on this ground is no different from cases brought on any other ground, the establishment of this ground does raise some specialties. In particular, proof, if an application has been made to the sheriff to establish the ground, is on the criminal rather than the civil standard (see s.68(3)(b) below). The ground is applicable only to children who are above the age of criminal responsibility, which is eight years old (see *Merrin v. S*, 1987 S.L.T. 193). And a child who has pleaded guilty to or been found guilty of an offence in a criminal court can have the case referred by the court to a children's hearing, in which case a certificate of the court will be considered conclusive proof for the purpose of establishing the ground of referral (s.50(1) above).

Para. (j). This is an entirely new ground of referral, and was designed to bring Scots law into line with Art. 33 of the UN Convention on the Rights of the Child. That obliges States to take all appropriate measures to protect children from the illicit use of drugs. Usually under the old law children who misused drugs or alcohol could be referred under another ground in any case, such as being beyond parental control, or falling into bad associations, or lack of parental care. Drug and alcohol abuse is however a significant threat to the well-being of some children and the introduction of this ground serves to strengthen the concern rightly felt about the problem. Also, it may well be clearer as a ground in itself rather than evidence of another ground, and thus easier to establish.

Para. (k). This is the same as the old s.32(2)(gg).

Para. (l). This replaces the old s.32(2)(i) and takes account of the amendments in the law in other parts of the Act. The addition to the old law comes in the words "or the interest of others", but in practical terms this adds little since a child who harms the interests of others is inevitably harming her or his own interests as well.

Subs. (3)

This is, effectively, the same as subs. (3) in the old s.32. The words "may include" allow the children's hearing to dispose of a case by means of a form of supervision that provides only some of these elements.

Preliminary and investigatory measures

Provision of information to the Principal Reporter

53.—(1) Where information is received by a local authority which suggests that compulsory measures of supervision may be necessary in respect of a child, they shall—

(a) cause inquiries to be made into the case unless they are satisfied that such inquiries are unnecessary; and

(b) if it appears to them after such inquiries, or after being satisfied that such inquiries are unnecessary, that such measures may be required in respect of the child, give to the Principal Reporter such information about the child as they have been able to discover.

(2) A person, other than a local authority, who has reasonable cause to believe that compulsory measures of supervision may be necessary in respect of a child—

(a) shall, if he is a constable, give to the Principal Reporter such information about the child as he has been able to discover;

(b) in any other case, may give the Principal Reporter that information.

(3) A constable shall make any report required to be made under paragraph (b) of section 17(1) of the Police (Scotland) Act 1967 (duty to make reports in relation to commission of offences) in relation to a child to the Principal Reporter as well as to the appropriate prosecutor.

(4) Where an application has been made to the sheriff—

(a) by the Principal Reporter in accordance with a direction given by a children's hearing under section 65(7) or (9) of this Act; or

(b) by any person entitled to make an application under section 85 of this Act,

the Principal Reporter may request any prosecutor to supply him with any evidence lawfully obtained in the course of, and held by the prosecutor in connection with, the investigation of a crime or suspected crime, being evidence which may assist the sheriff in determining the application; and, subject to subsection (5) below, it shall be the duty of the prosecutor to comply with such a request.

(5) A prosecutor may refuse to comply with a request issued under subsection (4) above where he reasonably believes that it is necessary to retain the evidence for the purposes of any proceedings in respect of a crime, whether the proceedings have been commenced or are to be commenced by him.

(6) The Lord Advocate may direct that in any specified case or class of cases any evidence lawfully obtained in the course of an investigation of a crime or suspected crime shall be supplied, without the need for a request under subsection (4) above, to the Principal Reporter.

[1] (7) In subsections (3), (4) and (5) above "crime" and "prosecutor" have the same meanings respectively given by section 307 of the Criminal Procedure (Scotland) Act 1995.

Children (Scotland) Act 1995

NOTE

1. As amended by the Criminal Procedure (Consequential Provisions) (Scotland) Act 1995, c. 40, s.3 and Sched. 3, para. 97.

DEFINITIONS

"child": s.93(2)(b).
"children's hearing": s.93(1).
"compulsory measures of supervision": s.93(1).
"constable": s.93(1) and Police (Scotland) Act 1967 (c.77).
"local authority": Local Government etc. (Scotland) Act 1994, s.2.
"principal reporter": s.93(1).
"prosecutor": Criminal Procedure (Scotland) Act 1995, s.307(1).

GENERAL NOTE

The reporter is dependent, for the proper carrying out of her or his functions under the Act, on receiving information concerning children from various sources, including local authorities, schools, welfare agencies and the police. The reporter's duty to respond to information obtained is governed by s.55 below; the present section deals with the rights and obligations of others to furnish the reporter with information which suggests that a child may be in need of compulsory measures of supervision. Subsections (1) and (2) replace, with no substantive alteration to the law, the provisions in s.37(1) and (1A) of the 1968 Act, subs. (3) replaces s.38(2), and the remaining subsections impose new obligations on the prosecuting authorities to pass on information and evidence to the reporter.

Subs. (1)

An obligation is imposed here upon local authorities who receive information concerning children to investigate that information in order to determine whether it suggests that compulsory measures of supervision may be necessary, and to pass to the reporter that information and any other information that their investigations reveal. They may seek a child protection order under s.57(2) below if their investigations are being frustrated by the refusal of parents to allow them access to a child. The reporter will usually carry out an initial investigation too (s.56(1) below) and it is the reporter who decides whether it is necessary to arrange a children's hearing: it follows that the decision the local authority have to make under this provision is restricted to a determination of whether compulsory measures of supervision *may* be necessary, and they have neither power nor ability to determine that such measures are in fact necessary.

Information . . . which suggests. The obligations imposed on the local authority by this section only arise when the information they receive is of a nature which suggests that one or more of the grounds of referral under s.52(2) above exist, for otherwise the question of whether compulsory measures of supervision are necessary does not arise (s.52(1) above).

Received by a local authority. Information is received by a local authority when any of their officers or agencies, or anyone acting on their behalf, comes to hold information of the appropriate nature. This will include social work departments, education departments and local authority medical services, but it is not limited to these agencies and the phrase is to be given wide scope.

Unless . . . satisfied that such inquiries are unnecessary. Inquiries may be unnecessary because the question clearly arises as to whether compulsory measures of supervision are necessary (i.e. the information suggests that one or more of the grounds of referral exists) or because clearly no such question arises from the information (i.e. information does not indicate that any of the grounds of referral exists).

Subs. (2)

This permits any person other than a local authority to give to the reporter such information as she or he has which gives reasonable cause to believe that one or more of the grounds of referral exists in relation to a particular child. There is no limitation on who has the right to pass information to the reporter, and it may be a medical practitioner, law enforcement officer, school teacher, group leader, neighbour, relative, child protection agency or even the child her or himself. If the person with the information is a police officer, the right to give information to the reporter becomes a duty to give that information.

Reasonable cause to believe. The right or duty to give information exists only in so far as the person with the information has reasonable cause to believe that it indicates that one or more of the grounds of referral are made out. This suggests that there is no right to give information when there is no reasonable cause for that belief. It is clearly not the aim of the Act to discourage the passing of information concerning children to the reporter, even when investigations are likely to show that there is no cause for concern (see further *D v. NSPCC* [1977] 1 All E.R. 589), but these words ensure that a person acting maliciously in giving the reporter information is not completely immune to legal redress. In other words, the transmission of information to the reporter is an act which is protected by the defence of qualified privilege in the law of defamation, and in order to establish liability the pursuer would have to show both malice on the part of the defender and want of probable cause (see Norrie, *Defamation and Related Actions in Scots Law* (1995, Butterworths) at pp.123–124).

Subs. (3)

When police officers are required to make reports to prosecutors in connection with the commission of offences, they are also required to make reports to the reporter if the report relates to a child. This replaces, without substantive alteration, s.38(2) of the 1968 Act.

In relation to a child. The child may be the perpetrator of the offence being reported, or the victim thereof.

Subs. (4)

This is a new and highly significant provision. Not only are the police obliged to pass information to the reporter to assist her or him in deciding whether it is necessary to arrange a children's hearing under s.65 below, but the prosecuting authorities are now also obliged to pass on to the reporter evidence they hold when the reporter is trying to establish a ground of referral before the sheriff (whether on an initial application to the sheriff or on a rehearing of the evidence). Previously the sharing of evidence with reporters was a matter of practice rather than statutory obligation on the prosecutor. The obligation of co-operation imposed by this subsection arises only when the evidence is such that it may assist the sheriff in determining whether the ground of referral is made out or not, and when the reporter has made a request to be supplied with such evidence.

Evidence. This might be information or property or evidence of any other nature.

Lawfully obtained. Evidence that has been obtained by the prosecutor unlawfully cannot be made available to the reporter.

A crime or suspected crime. There is no limitation on who the evidence relates to, so long as it is relevant to the existence of a ground of referral in relation to the child. So the evidence can refer to a crime or suspected crime of which the child is either the perpetrator or the victim, or of which the perpetrator or victim is a member of the same household as the child.

Subs. (5)

The obligation to supply the reporter with evidence in subs. (4) above suffers an exception when the prosecutor reasonably believes that he must retain the evidence for use in proceedings that he has commenced or is going to commence. The prosecutor has no obligation to retain the evidence and in many situations will be able to co-operate with the reporter. Refusal to comply with the reporter's request ought only to be made when it is essential in the interests of justice that the evidence be retained by the prosecutor.

Subs. (6)

The Lord Advocate is given the power to specify a case or type of case in which evidence obtained in the course of a criminal investigation will automatically be supplied to the reporter, even without a request. It is expected that evidence suggesting, for example, that a child has committed an offence will automatically be shared with the reporter.

Reference to the Principal Reporter by court

54.—(1) Where in any relevant proceedings it appears to the court that any of the conditions in section 52(2)(a) to (h), (j), (k) or (l) of this Act is satisfied with respect to a child, it may refer the matter to the Principal Reporter, specifying the condition.

(2) In this section "relevant proceedings" means—

(a) an action for divorce or judicial separation or for declarator of marriage, nullity of marriage, parentage or non-parentage;

(b) proceedings relating to parental responsibilities or parental rights within the meaning of Part I of this Act;

(c) proceedings for an adoption order under the Adoption (Scotland) Act 1978 or for an order under section 18 of that Act declaring a child free for adoption; and

(d) proceedings for an offence against section 35 (failure by parent to secure regular attendance by his child at a public school), 41 (failure to comply with attendance order) or 42(3) (failure to permit examination of child) of the Education (Scotland) Act 1980.

(3) Where the court has referred a matter to the Principal Reporter under subsection (1) above, he shall—

(a) make such investigation as he thinks appropriate; and

(b) if he considers that compulsory measures of supervision are necessary,

arrange a children's hearing to consider the case of the child under section 69 of this Act; and subsection (1) of that section shall apply as if the condition specified by the court under subsection (1) above were a ground of referral established in accordance with section 68 of this Act.

DEFINITIONS

"adoption order": Adoption (Scotland) Act 1978, s.65(1).
"children's hearing": s.93(1).
"parental responsibilities": ss.1(3), 93(1).
"parental rights": ss.2(4), 93(1).
"Principal Reporter": s.93(1).

GENERAL NOTE

Though this section does have statutory antecedents, there was no provision analogous to the present section in the 1968 Act. Various statutes had permitted the court in specified circumstances to commit the child to the care of a local authority: see the Matrimonial Proceedings (Children) Act 1958 (c. 40), s.10 (actions of divorce or nullity of marriage or separation), the Guardianship Act 1973 (c. 29), s.11 (custody cases), and the Adoption (Scotland) Act 1978 (c. 28), s.26 (adoption applications). In each situation committal to care was on the basis that it was not appropriate for the child to remain in the care of either of her or his parents. All these provisions are repealed in Sched. 5 below, but a similar though more appropriate effect is achieved here. Instead of committing the child to the care of a local authority, the court is empowered to refer the case of a child to the reporter. The court may do so, not when it considers neither parent to be suitable to have the care of the child, but when during the course of any of the specified proceedings the court comes to be of the view that one of the grounds of referral exists in relation to that child. The committal to care provisions were not used very frequently and the replacement of the concept of care in Chapter 1 of this Part of the Act renders it more appropriate that the court directs its attention to the question of whether the child requires compulsory measures of supervision. The proceedings in which the court may exercise this power are, mostly, family proceedings and they do not include, for example, a criminal trial in which it becomes evident that a child has been the victim of a Sched. 1 offence.

Subs. (1)

It appears to the court. The court, which can be either the sheriff court or the Court of Session must make a positive determination that the ground of referral exists, and it will only be able to do so if there is sufficient evidence to suggest it. An unsubstantiated allegation by one party in the course of divorce proceedings would not, it is submitted, be sufficient. It is to be noted that subs. (3) below provides that if the court refers the matter to the reporter specifying the ground, the ground will be treated as having been established: this suggests that the ground must be established in the relevant proceedings with the sufficiency of evidence required for a sheriff to determine that a ground has been established on application of the reporter under s.68 below. This is, however, very different from the provision in s.50(1) above where a criminal court's certificate is conclusive of a child having committed an offence, since the whole purpose of these criminal proceedings would have been to establish the child's guilt. Courts will have to be very careful here to ensure that there is sufficient opportunity to challenge any evidence suggesting that the appropriate ground of referral exists, since the main purpose of the proceedings is not directed towards that finding.

Any of the conditions in s.52(2)(a) to (h), (j), (k) or (l). The only ground that the court cannot hold to be satisfied is subs. (2)(i), that is to say that the child has committed an offence.

With respect to a child. There is no limitation in relation to which child the court can make such a reference. The typical case will be in an action for divorce in which the parents are arguing about the child's residence and evidence is presented to the court which leads it to believe, for example, that there is a lack of parental care. Information may come to the attention of the court even when the child is not being argued over, such as in a divorce in which residence has already been agreed upon by the parties. It is possible for information to come to the attention of the court concerning a child with no connexion whatsoever with the parties, and the terms of the section are clearly wide enough to cover such a case. For example if during the course of an adoption application in relation to one child it is alleged that the natural parent who is withholding consent abused another child, that child could be referred to the reporter, so long as there is sufficient evidence to satisfy the court. The comment under "It appears to the court" should again be referred to.

May refer. The court has a discretion and is not obliged to refer the matter to the reporter, even when it appears that a ground of referral does exist. It may be appropriate not to refer the matter to the reporter when another option available to the court is likely to be better for the child, such as for example making a residence order under s.11 above in favour of someone other than the parties to the proceedings. The court's decision to refer the case to the reporter is one to which the welfare of the child is paramount under s.16(1), but it is not one to which the other two "overarching principles" in s.16(2) (regard to the child's views) and s.16(3) (the minimum intervention principle) apply: that does not, however, prohibit the court from applying these principles if to do so enhances the child's welfare.

Subs. (2)

The court cannot refer any matter to the reporter in proceedings other than those specified, though of course any person involved in other proceedings (including the judge) may provide the reporter with information under s.53(2) above. (If the reporter receives information under s.53 the immediately following subsection does not come into play.)

Subs. (3)

If the court refers the case of a child to the reporter the reporter is obliged to make such investigations as she or he thinks appropriate and must arrange a children's hearing if she or he considers that compulsory measures of supervision are necessary. The ground specified by the court shall be regarded as being a ground established by the sheriff on an application by the reporter and the hearing will not, therefore, be obliged or entitled to put the ground of referral to the child or parent. The hearing will proceed immediately to a consideration of the child's case, and make a decision and disposal in accordance with ss.69 and 70 below. Note again the comment in subs. (1) above under "It appears to the court".

Child assessment orders

55.—(1) A sheriff may grant an order under this section for an assessment of the state of a child's health or development, or of the way in which he has been treated (to be known as a "child assessment order"), on the application of a local authority if he is satisfied that—
  (a) the local authority have reasonable cause to suspect that the child in respect of whom the order is sought is being so treated (or neglected) that he is suffering, or is likely to suffer, significant harm;
  (b) such assessment of the child is required in order to establish whether or not there is reasonable cause to believe that the child is so treated (or neglected); and
  (c) such assessment is unlikely to be carried out, or be carried out satisfactorily, unless the order is granted.
  (2) Where—
  (a) an application has been made under subsection (1) above; and
  (b) the sheriff considers that the conditions for making a child protection order under section 57 of this Act are satisfied,
he shall make such an order under that section as if the application had been duly made by the local authority under that section rather than this section.
  (3) A child assessment order shall—
  (a) specify the date on which the assessment is to begin;
  (b) have effect for such period as is specified in the order, not exceeding seven days beginning with the date specified by virtue of paragraph (a) above;
  (c) require any person in a position to produce the child to—
      (i) produce him to any authorised person;
      (ii) permit that person or any other authorised person to carry out an assessment in accordance with the order; and

(iii) comply with any other conditions of the order; and
(d) be carried out by an authorised person in accordance with the terms of the order.
(4) A child assessment order may—
(a) where necessary, permit the taking of the child concerned to any place for the purposes of the assessment; and
(b) authorise the child to be kept at that place, or any other place, for such period of time as may be specified in the order.
(5) Where a child assessment order makes provision under subsection (4) above, it shall contain such directions as the sheriff considers appropriate as to the contact which the child shall be allowed to have with any other person while the child is in any place to which he has been taken or in which he is being kept under a child assessment order.
(6) In this section "authorised person" means any officer of the local authority, and any person authorised by the local authority to perform the assessment, or perform any part of it.

DEFINITIONS
"child": s.93(2)(b).
"child protection order": ss.57(1), 93(1).
"local authority": Local Government etc. (Scotland) Act 1994, s.2.

GENERAL NOTE
One of the difficulties facing child care agencies responsible for ensuring the well-being of children is that they may well have suspicions of abuse or neglect but be unable to provide evidence, necessary for the application of many of the care mechanisms in the Act, without a medical examination or other assessment of the child. Medical examination or assessment can be carried out only with the consent of a person who has the right and capacity to provide that consent, though there has long been a suspicion that this requirement is often ignored in practice and children subjected to intimate examination without the appropriate consent being obtained. This section, following the model established by s.43 of the English Children Act 1989, introduces a wholly new form of order available to the court and is designed to allow an assessment to be made of a child's health or development or of the way in which she or he has been treated even in the absence of consent by the parent, and it authorises the removal of the child to the place where the assessment is to be carried out, and the keeping of the child there or elsewhere. For comment on the English legislation, see Lavery, "The Child Assessment Order: A Reassessment" (1996) 8 Ch.Fam. L.Q. 41.
It is not made explicit in the Act what happens when the child her or himself is old enough to consent or refuse consent to medical examination (as it is, for example, when a supervision requirement contains a condition under s.70(5)(a) below that the child submit to medical treatment). Capacity to consent or refuse is governed by s.2(4) of the Age of Legal Capacity (Scotland) Act 1991, and the effect of that provision is expressly preserved by s.90 below. It follows (though it would have been better to express this) that an assessment cannot be carried out upon a child who refuses to submit to it, whenever the child is of sufficient mental maturity to understand the nature and consequences of the proposed procedure. A child assessment order under this section cannot authorise what would otherwise be an assault against the child, for otherwise s.2(4) of the 1991 Act would be compromised, contrary to the express terms of s.90 below. The order, therefore, permits an assessment to be carried out in the absence of parental consent but not in the absence of the capable child's own consent.
Child assessment orders have not proved popular in England, and local authorities there have been much more inclined to seek child protection orders. This may well eventuate in Scotland also. Sheriffs are obliged to make a child protection order when a child assessment order is sought but the conditions for the granting of a child protection order are established, and the difference between the conditions required for each will often be subtle. Under this section a child assessment order will be available when there is reasonable cause for suspecting that the child is at risk; under s.57(1) below a child protection order will be available when there are reasonable grounds for believing that the child is at risk. A local authority with reasonable cause for suspecting will usually have little difficulty in establishing reasonable grounds for believing. Whether the introduction of child assessment orders under this section adds significantly to the armoury of the law of child protection will depend upon how willing local authorities are to seek the less interventionist order: they may well feel that, for no other reason than their own protection, the more interventionist (but still temporary) order under s.57 ought to be sought. In which case the present section will have added little in practical terms. Procedure is governed by A.S. 1997, rr. 3.25–3.28.

Subs. (1)

A sheriff can grant a child assessment order if a local authority have applied for it and he is satisfied that the three specified conditions are made out. Paragraph (a) is satisfied when the local authority have reasonable cause to suspect that the child might be suffering harm; para. (b) is satisfied when an assessment is shown to be necessary to test that suspicion; and para. (c) requires that it be shown that the assessment would not be carried out properly without the order.

A sheriff may grant. Even although the sheriff is satisfied that the three conditions for the granting of the order exist, the matter is still within his discretion. His decision is governed by all three overarching principles in s.16, and so he must regard the welfare of the child as his paramount consideration, must give the child an opportunity to express views and take appropriate account of them, and must not make the order unless he considers that it would be better for the child that the order be made than that it not be made at all.

The state of a child's health or development. The child assessment order may be designed to assess the state of the child's current health or her or his development. Part of that assessment will inevitably include an assessment of what is necessary to ensure that the child attains the state of health or development that she or he should have.

Or of the way in which he has been treated. These words permit the assessment to be used to examine the child to see whether there is any evidence of past abuse or maltreatment, which would justify the utilisation of any of the care procedures in the Act.

On the application of a local authority. Only local authorities have title to apply for child assessment orders.

Reasonable cause to suspect. Each case must be dealt with individually in determining whether the local authority's suspicions are founded on reasonable cause. Since the purpose of the order is to allow a testing of that suspicion, the level of suspicion is unlikely to be required to be high. An allegation of abuse, even when made anonymously, may well give reasonable cause for suspicion (unless clearly spurious) as might, for example, the failure of a very young child to thrive. It is likely that only in cases in which there is no cause whatsoever to suspect that the child is suffering will this provision not be satisfied.

Significant harm. Significant harm is harm that is serious and of a not minor or transient nature. It may be physical or emotional. *Cf.* s.57(1) below where the same phrase is used.

Subs. (2)

The conditions for the granting of a child protection order laid down in s.57 below are stricter than the conditions for the granting of a child assessment order in the sense that it must be shown in that section that there actually are reasonable grounds for believing the child is suffering significant harm, while the present provision requires that it be shown that there are grounds for suspicion and the assessment is necessary to test that suspicion. Nevertheless there may well be cases in which in establishing the grounds for the suspicion the local authority actually establish grounds for believing that the child is suffering significant harm. This subsection therefore provides that if the conditions for a child protection order are shown to be satisfied then an order under s.57 must be made rather than a child assessment order.

He shall make. These words suggest that the sheriff has no discretion but must make the child protection order if the conditions in s.57(1) below are found to be satisfied in an application under s.55(1). This, however, must be read in light of s.57(1) itself, which provides that the sheriff "may make" a child protection order. It is submitted that the words "he shall make" should be interpreted to mean that he must treat an application made under s.55 as if it were an application under s.57, so permitting the sheriff the discretion contained in the latter section. This, admittedly, involves some violence to the actual terms of the statute, but the alternative of giving the sheriff a discretion to make an order under s.57 when the application is made under s.57 but obliging him to make an order under s.57 when the application is made under s.55 is ludicrous, and an interpretation which avoids that result is to be preferred. A factor telling against this proposed interpretation, however, is the wording of s.76(8) below, which in relation to an application for an exclusion order provides a similar rule to that contained in this subsection, except that it is provided that the sheriff "may" rather than "shall" make an order under s.57. The principle behind the rule in both provisions is the same but the fact that different words are used might be taken to indicate a parliamentary intention that the provisions are to have a different effect; a more realistic explanation for the difference is, it is submitted, sloppy draftsmanship. "Shall", for the purposes of this subsection, means "may".

Subs. (3)

The child assessment order will last for a specified period of time, not exceeding seven days, and its effect will commence on a date that must be specified in the order. In addition, it will require any person who can produce the child to do so and to permit the assessment to be carried out as well as to comply with any conditions in the order. And the order will require an officer of the local authority who sought the order, or any person authorised by the local authority, to carry out the assessment in accordance with the terms of the order. That officer or person is referred to in this section as the "authorised person": subs. (6).

Require any person ... to ... comply with any other conditions. The order requires the local authority to carry out the assessment, and it may also require the person in a position to produce the child to do anything specified in the order in addition to producing the child. This might involve, for example, the giving of consent to a particular examination or treatment, though the order itself will normally be sufficient authority to carry out the examination or treatment.

Subss. (4) and (5)

In order to carry out the assessment the child may be taken to any place at which the assessment is to be carried out. The terms of subs. (4) suggest that if this is to happen authority to take the child there must be specified in the order. A child cannot be kept for longer than the order is specified to last (a maximum of seven days). If a child is taken to a place for the carrying out of an assessment the sheriff must consider whether to make directions as to the contact the child is to have with any other person while at the place of assessment. The provision is designed to ensure maximum flexibility: and the sheriff may direct, for example, daily contact when the child is kept for a number of days, or he may direct that the child be accompanied at all times by a parent if, for example, the assessment is likely to last only a matter of hours. The three overarching principles in s.16 govern his decision on this as on other matters relating to child assessment orders.

Where necessary. The order can permit the taking of the child to a place only when the assessment cannot be carried out at the place where the child already is (that is to say, generally speaking, at home).

That place or any other place. The child can be kept in overnight accommodation for a number of days while the assessment itself takes place elsewhere, such as at a hospital.

Initial investigation by the Principal Reporter

56.—(1) Where the Principal Reporter receives information from any source about a case which may require a children's hearing to be arranged he shall, after making such initial investigation as he thinks necessary, proceed with the case in accordance with subsection (4) or (6) below.

(2) For the purposes of making any initial investigation under subsection (1) above, the Principal Reporter may request from the local authority a report on the child and on such circumstances concerning the child as appear to him to be relevant; and the local authority shall supply the report which may contain such information, from any person whomsoever, as the Principal Reporter thinks, or the local authority think, fit.

(3) A report requested under subsection (2) above may contain information additional to that given by the local authority under section 53 of this Act.

(4) The Principal Reporter may decide, after an initial investigation under subsection (1) above, that a children's hearing does not require to be arranged; and where he so decides—

(a) he shall inform the child, any relevant person and the person who brought the case to his notice, or any of those persons, that he has so decided; and

(b) he may, if he considers it appropriate, refer the case to a local authority with a view to their making arrangements for the advice, guidance and assistance of the child and his family in accordance with Chapter 1 of this Part of this Act.

(5) Where the Principal Reporter has decided under subsection (4) above that a children's hearing does not require to be arranged, he shall not at any other time, on the basis solely of the information obtained during the initial investigation referred to in that subsection, arrange a children's hearing under subsection (6) below.

(6) Where it appears to the Principal Reporter that compulsory measures of supervision are necessary in respect of the child, he shall arrange a

children's hearing to which he shall refer the case for consideration and determination.

(7) Where the Principal Reporter has arranged a children's hearing in accordance with subsection (6) above, he—

(a) shall, where he has not previously done so, request a report under subsection (2) above;

(b) may request from the local authority such information, supplementary or additional to a report requested under subsection (2) above, as he thinks fit;

and the local authority shall supply that report, or as the case may be information, and any other information which they consider to be relevant.

DEFINITIONS
"child": s.93(2)(b).
"children's hearing": s.93(1).
"family": s.93(1).
"local authority": Local Government etc. (Scotland) Act 1994, s.2.
"Principal Reporter": s.93(1).
"relevant person": s.93(2)(b).

GENERAL NOTE
This section replaces, with little alteration in content, the provisions previously contained in s.38(1) and s.39 of the 1968 Act. It specifies the actions the reporter must take on receiving information which has come to her or him under s.53 above or by any other means. The reporter must decide whether to make an initial investigation and must thereafter decide whether or not to arrange a children's hearing. These decisions are not governed by the overarching principles in s.16 above (which refers only to decisions made by a court or a children's hearing), but inevitably the reporter will be guided by her or his assessment of the child's welfare. The only change from the 1968 Act is contained in subss. (2) and (3) which permits the reporter to call for a report on the child's circumstances from the local authority in order to assist in the initial investigation in the reporter is making before deciding whether to arrange a children's hearing. It had long been the practice of reporters to call for reports for that reason even before this Act, but the practice is put onto a statutory basis here, and the local authority are now obliged to conform to the reporter's request.

Subs. (1)
May require a children's hearing to be arranged. These words specify the type of information that will trigger the reporter's obligations under this section. A hearing is required to be arranged only if the investigation suggests that one or more of the grounds of referral in s.52 above exists. If the reporter receives information of any other nature her or his response is not governed by this section.
Such initial investigation as he thinks necessary. Having received information from whatever source, the first decision that the reporter must make is whether further investigation is needed. That investigation is to be directed to the question of whether or not a children's hearing requires to be arranged and no investigation is necessary when the reporter is of the view that she or he already has sufficient information to make that decision.

Subss. (2) and (3)
If the reporter decides that an initial investigation is required, then as part of that investigation she or he may request the local authority to draw up a social background report, detailing any circumstances that she or he considers necessary, including information additional to that given to the local authority under the terms of s.53 above. The local authority are obliged to supply this report.

Subs. (4)
Having made such investigation as she or he thinks necessary, the reporter must then make a decision whether a children's hearing requires to be arranged. She or he is obliged by s.65(1) to arrange a hearing when satisfied that at least one of the grounds of referral exist *and* that compulsory measures of supervision are necessary, and she or he may decide that a children's hearing does not require to be arranged only when not satisfied of one or both of these elements. If not so satisfied the reporter's decision not to arrange a children's hearing must be intimated to someone. Just who must be informed, however, is unclear due to the opaque wording in para. (a). As originally drafted, the words "shall inform" appeared as "may inform", and this reflected

the discretionary element in the words "or any of those persons". The latter words remain, suggesting a discretion while the amended words "shall inform" indicate an absolute obligation (s.39(1) of the 1968 Act, which this subsection replaces, qualified the obligation with the words "where he considers this to be the proper course"). The result seems to be an obligation to inform, but a discretion as to who is to be informed. The reporter must inform any one or more of the following persons of the decision that a children's hearing does not require to be arranged: (i) the child, (ii) any person with parental responsibilities or parental rights, or any person who ordinarily has charge of or control over the child, or (iii) the person who supplied the reporter with the information concerning the child in the first place. In addition, the reporter has the power, to be exercised when she or he considers it appropriate, to refer the case to a local authority for the purposes of the authority providing advice, guidance and assistance to the child and family under ss.16–38 above.

Subs. (5)
The effect of this provision is that the decision not to refer the child to a children's hearing cannot be retracted unless new circumstances, which are additional to those discovered in the course of the investigation to determine whether to arrange a hearing, come to the attention of the reporter. These new circumstances might indicate a quite different ground of referral, or they may concern the same—for example, when the decision not to arrange a children's hearing was made on the basis of a lack of evidence which has subsequently come to light. It is unclear when the decision is made and when, therefore, it becomes irrevocable. It is submitted that before the reporter's opinion can properly be characterised as a "decision", some step must be taken consequent upon it or pursuant to it. That step will normally be giving the intimation required under subs. (4) above: in other words the decision not to refer the child to a children's hearing is irrevocable only once the reporter has intimated that decision.

Subs. (6)
This provision is to be compared with, and is probably tautologous in light of, s.65(1) below. The later provision obliges the reporter to arrange a children's hearing when she or he is satisfied that compulsory measures of supervision are necessary *and* when at least one of the grounds of referral exists; the present provision obliges the reporter to arrange a children's hearing when it appears to her or him that compulsory measures of supervision are necessary. The reference to the grounds of referral in s.65(1) is otiose, since the question of whether compulsory measures of supervision are necessary arises only if at least one of these grounds exists (s.52(1) above), with the result that both that provision and this provision amount to exactly the same thing.

Subs. (7)
If a hearing is to be arranged by the reporter, she or he must request a report on the child from the local authority unless she or he has already done so as part of an initial investigation, and she or he may request any supplementary information. The local authority must provide such reports and information, and any other information concerning the child or her or his circumstances that they consider to be necessary. The reporter is not obliged to wait until the children's hearing is arranged before requesting such a report, and it will normally be sensible for her or him to make the request as soon as the decision to arrange a hearing has been made.

Measures for the emergency protection of children

Child protection orders

57.—(1) Where the sheriff, on an application by any person, is satisfied that—
  (a) there are reasonable grounds to believe that a child—
      (i) is being so treated (or neglected) that he is suffering significant harm; or
      (ii) will suffer such harm if he is not removed to and kept in a place of safety, or if he does not remain in the place where he is then being accommodated (whether or not he is resident there); and
  (b) an order under this section is necessary to protect that child from such harm (or such further harm),
he may make an order under this section (to be known as a "child protection order").
  (2) Without prejudice to subsection (1) above, where the sheriff on an application by a local authority is satisfied—

(a) that they have reasonable grounds to suspect that a child is being or will be so treated (or neglected) that he is suffering or will suffer significant harm;

(b) that they are making or causing to be made enquiries to allow them to decide whether they should take any action to safeguard the welfare of the child; and

(c) that those enquiries are being frustrated by access to the child being unreasonably denied, the authority having reasonable cause to believe that such access is required as a matter of urgency,

he may make a child protection order.

(3) Without prejudice to any additional requirement imposed by rules made by virtue of section 91 of this Act, an application for a child protection order shall—

(a) identify—
   (i) the applicant; and
   (ii) in so far as practicable, the child in respect of whom the order is sought;

(b) state the grounds on which the application is made; and

(c) be accompanied by such supporting evidence, whether in documentary form or otherwise, as will enable the sheriff to determine the application.

(4) A child protection order may, subject to such terms and conditions as the sheriff considers appropriate, do any one or more of the following—

(a) require any person in a position to do so to produce the child to the applicant;

(b) authorise the removal of the child by the applicant to a place of safety, and the keeping of the child at that place;

(c) authorise the prevention of the removal of the child from any place where he is being accommodated;

(d) provide that the location of any place of safety in which the child is being kept should not be disclosed to any person or class of person specified in the order.

(5) Notice of the making of a child protection order shall be given forthwith by the applicant to the local authority in whose area the child resides (where that authority is not the applicant) and to the Principal Reporter.

(6) In taking any action required or permitted by a child protection order or by a direction under section 58 of this Act the applicant shall only act where he reasonably believes that to do so is necessary to safeguard or promote the welfare of the child.

(7) Where by virtue of a child protection order a child is removed to a place of safety provided by a local authority, they shall, subject to the terms and conditions of that order and of any direction given under section 58 of this Act, have the like duties in respect of the child as they have under section 17 of this Act in respect of a child looked after by them.

DEFINITIONS
   "child": s.93(2)(b).
   "local authority": Local Government etc. (Scotland) Act 1994, s.2.
   "place of safety": s.93(1).
   "principal reporter": s.93(1).
   "relevant person": s.93(2)(b).

GENERAL NOTE
   Under the 1968 Act a court or justice of the peace could, in the circumstances specified in s.37(2) thereof, authorise the removal of a child to a place of safety, and a constable could take a

child to a place of safety even without such authorisation. A number of criticisms could be made of the law in that provision. For one thing, though the specified circumstances which justified a place of safety order were relatively clear, the Act gave no guidance to the court as to when in any particular case the making of an order was appropriate. It was not, for example, appropriate to remove a child from her or his parent every time the child was a victim of a Sched. 1 offence, though in every such case it would be competent to do so under s.37(2)(a). Another problem, which was illustrated by the Orkney case, was that the mechanisms for appealing against a place of safety order were inextricably linked to the hearing system itself, and the Act did not cater for families who were perfectly willing to attend a children's hearing but wished immediately to challenge the necessity for the removal of children from their homes. Again, the order available under the old s.37 was inflexible in that the only action it authorised was the taking of the child to a place of safety, and it did not authorise the taking of less drastic steps. If removal of the child were considered inappropriate no action could be taken to protect the child until the sitting of a children's hearing. As a result of these, and other, criticisms (see White Paper, *Scotland's Children: Proposals for Child Care Policy and Law* (Cm 2286, August 1993) at paras. 5.8–5.18), the whole procedure for the interim protection of the child has been radically remodelled, with the introduction of a new order, known as a child protection order, which is designed (i) to last for the shortest possible period of time, (ii) to include a speedy review mechanism, (iii) to be more flexible than the old place of safety order, and (iv) to have the conditions for its granting simplified and much more clearly directed towards the immediate need to protect the child from imminent harm. The main provisions are contained in ss.57–60, with supplementary provisions contained in ss.61 and 62. Procedure is governed by A.S. 1997, rr. 3.29–3.33.

Section 57 sets out the grounds upon which a child protection order can be granted, and specifies what actions it may authorise; s.58 deals with the directions that can be attached to a child protection order, and ss.59 and 60 deal with the various means by which the order can be reviewed and brought to an end. There are strict time-limits to be adhered to throughout. In summary, the procedure (assuming the child protection order authorises the removal of a child to a place of safety) is as follows:

STEP 1: A child protection order, once made, must be implemented within 24 hours, and if it is not, it shall *cease to have effect* (s.60(1) below).

STEP 2: Once implemented, the child protection order can be challenged by means of an application to the sheriff within two working days thereafter.

STEP 2A: If STEP 2 is not taken within two working days of the implementation of the child protection order, an initial children's hearing must be convened on the second working day in order to determine whether the child protection order should continue in effect: if no such initial hearing is held, or if the hearing does not continue the child protection order, it shall *cease to have effect* (s.60(6)(a) below).

STEP 2B: If the initial hearing continues the order it can be challenged by means of an application to the sheriff within two working days of the continuation and the same process as below will be followed from STEP 3 to STEP 5.

STEP 3: If the sheriff does not determine that application within three working days of it being made the child protection order shall *cease to have effect* (s.60(2) below).

STEP 4: If the sheriff determines that the conditions for the granting of the child protection order are not satisfied he shall *recall the order* (s.60(13) below); if he determines that the conditions are satisfied he will continue the child protection order until a children's hearing arranged under s.65(2) has commenced (s.60(12)(d) below).

STEP 5: On the commencement of a children's hearing arranged under s.65(2), which must be on the eighth working day after the implementation of the child protection order, the order shall *cease to have effect* (s.60(6)(e) below) and any further protection of the child that is necessary will be provided by the children's hearing system.

Whatever happens, a child protection order must come to an end at the latest on the eighth working day after its implementation. Before then the need for the child protection order will have been reviewed at least once (either by the sheriff or by an initial hearing) and often twice (by an initial hearing and then by the sheriff). Apart from these provisions for review, there is no appeal from the granting or refusal of a child protection order nor its continuation to the sheriff principal or the Court of Session (s.51(15) above); though not expressly excluded there is probably no appeal from the variation of a child protection order either, since the timescale will require the order coming to an end within a very few days of such variation. That consideration does not apply with a sheriff's decision to discharge a child protection order that has already been granted but the only interest in an appeal would lie in those seeking to protect the child and that protection is probably better provided by other means (such as arranging a children's hearing under s.65(1) below); nevertheless it is odd that the right of appeal against discharge of a child protection order is not either expressly excluded or provided for.

Subs. (1)

Any person may apply to the sheriff for him to make a child protection order. If the sheriff is satisfied both that one of the conditions in para. (a) is satisfied and that the making of the order is necessary to protect the child, he may grant such an order.

Any person. The applicant can be a local authority, a parent, a constable, or any other person, but will normally be the local authority.

There are reasonable grounds to believe. The sheriff must be satisfied that there is evidence to show that the child is being or will be harmed and that evidence must give reasonable ground for the belief. If there are grounds for suspicion but they are not themselves sufficient to found a belief then the condition is not satisfied.

Suffering significant harm. The harm that the child must be suffering or threatened with is serious harm of a not minor, transient or superficial nature. It may be physical or emotional. The Act gives little guidance as to how serious this harm need be but it is submitted that, since the aim of the Act is to protect the child's welfare, harm will be significant only when it is clearly more serious than the potential trauma removal from home will almost inevitably cause a child.

Necessary to protect that child. Not only must the ground in para. (a) be satisfied but the sheriff must also be satisfied that the making of a child protection order is necessary to protect the child from the actual or threatened harm there mentioned. It is not assumed, as it was under the old law, that the making of the order is the only way to protect the child. There may be other, equally efficacious, means that are less traumatic for the child (such as the granting of an exclusion order under s.76 below), and the word "necessary" indicates to the court that a child protection order should not be granted unless this is the only, or is the most efficacious, or in the circumstances the most appropriate, means of protecting the child.

May make an order. Even if both paragraphs are satisfied, the sheriff retains a discretion, and he is guided in the exercise of that discretion by s.16(1), under which the welfare of the child must be his paramount consideration. It may well be the case that the making of an order does more harm (perhaps psychological) to the child than good. Welfare, as always, is to be given broad scope and is not limited to the immediate circumstances which would otherwise justify the granting of a child protection order. The other overarching principles in s.16 (*i.e.* having regard to the views of the child and the minimum intervention principle) do not apply to the making of a child protection order though curiously they do apply to the varying and discharging thereof (s.16(4)(b)(ii) above). There is, therefore, no presumption that a child protection order, when sought, ought not to be granted, but there is a presumption that, once granted, it ought not to be varied or discharged.

Subs. (2)

A child protection order can be made under subs. (1) above on the application of anyone so long as there are reasonable grounds to believe that the child is being or will be harmed. In addition, this subsection permits a local authority (but only a local authority) to apply for the granting of a child protection order (which, if granted, can be on the same terms and conditions as one granted under subs. (1) above) when they have reasonable grounds to suspect that the child is being or will be harmed, but the enquiries they are making are being frustrated by the denial to them of access to the child.

Frustrated by access to the child being unreasonably denied. The enquiries must be rendered wholly ineffectual in allowing the local authority to determine whether or not their suspicions are justified, due to the person with control over who has access to the child denying that access for no good cause. Merely hampering or making more difficult these enquiries will not be sufficient. Due to the local authority's various duties in relation to children it would appear that the onus of proving reasonable cause lies with those denying the local authority access (though the onus of proving reasonable grounds for suspicion will lie with the local authority).

Subs. (3)

The application must include information concerning the matters set out here and must be in the form specified in A.S. 1997, r. 3.30 and Forms 47 and 48.

Subs. (4)

A child protection order is much more flexible than the old place of safety order, since it can not only authorise the removal of the child to a place of safety but can also require, authorise or provide any of the other stated actions. This will in appropriate circumstances allow a child to be protected from a source of danger without necessarily removing her or him from her or his home.

Any one or more of the following. The child protection order can do only the things mentioned, and none other. The sheriff can make these subject to appropriate terms and conditions, but he cannot order anything not specified. For example the sheriff cannot, under this provision, exclude a person from the child's home.

Authorise the removal of the child ... [or] authorise the prevention of the removal of the child. It is to be noted that if the child protection order authorises the doing of any of the acts in paras. (b) or (c) then certain other provisions are activated which do not apply when the child protection order authorises only those acts in either para. (a) or para. (d). In particular an initial hearing under s.59 below will have to be held if an application to the sheriff to set aside or vary the order has not already been made, and the reporter has power to release the child from a place of safety under s.60(3) below.

Prevention of the removal of the child. This sort of order is not an order to detain the child against her or his will. The word "removal" suggests that the order prevents someone else from taking the child away, and does not authorise the prevention of the child leaving a place on her or his own instigation.

Subs. (5)
Once made, the applicant must inform the local authority and the reporter of the making of the child protection order. Though not expressed, it can be expected that any person obliged to do anything by the child protection order will also be informed of its making. "Forthwith" means as soon as practicable.

Subs. (6)
A child protection order must not be enforced automatically and unthinkingly, and the applicant is authorised or required to do certain acts only where he reasonably believes that the doing of them is necessary to safeguard or promote the welfare of the child. If the applicant acts without this belief then he is acting without statutory authority and can be subject to liability therefor. Though it is likely to be difficult to establish lack of reasonable belief after a child protection order has been granted, this is not impossible, if for example the original source of danger to the child has died or been imprisoned since the granting of the order.

Subs. (7)
A local authority who "looks after" a child is subject to various obligations under s.17 above. A child removed to a place of safety under subs. (4)(b) above is a child being "looked after" for these purposes (s.17(6)(c)).

Directions in relation to contact and exercise of parental responsibilities and parental rights

58.—(1) When the sheriff makes a child protection order, he shall at that time consider whether it is necessary to give a direction to the applicant for the order as to contact with the child for—

(a) any parent of the child;
(b) any person with parental responsibilities in relation to the child; and
(c) any other specified person or class of persons;

and if he determines that there is such a necessity he may give such a direction.

(2) Without prejudice to the generality of subsection (1) above, a direction under that subsection may—

(a) prohibit contact with the child for any person mentioned in paragraphs (a) to (c) of that subsection;
(b) make contact with the child for any person subject to such conditions as the sheriff considers appropriate to safeguard and promote the welfare of the child.

(3) A direction under subsection (1) above may make different provision in relation to different persons or classes of person.

(4) A person applying for a child protection order under section 57(1) or (2) of this Act may at the same time apply to the sheriff for a direction in relation to the exercise or fulfilment of any parental responsibilities or parental rights in respect of the child concerned, if the person considers such a direction necessary to safeguard or promote the welfare of the child.

(5) Without prejudice to the generality of subsection (4) above, a direction under that subsection may be sought in relation to—

(a) any examination as to the physical or mental state of the child;

107

(b) any other assessment or interview of the child; or
(c) any treatment of the child arising out of such an examination or assessment,

which is to be carried out by any person.

(6) The sheriff may give a direction sought under subsection (4) above where he considers there is a necessity such as is mentioned in that subsection; and such a direction may be granted subject to such conditions, if any, as the sheriff (having regard in particular to the duration of the child protection order to which it relates) considers appropriate.

(7) A direction under this section shall cease to have effect when—
(a) the sheriff, on an application under section 60(7) of this Act, directs that it is cancelled; or
(b) the child protection order to which it is related ceases to have effect.

DEFINITIONS
"child": s.93(2)(b).
"child protection order": ss.57(1), 93(1).
"parental responsibilities": ss.1(3), 93(1).
"parental rights": ss.2(4), 93(1).

GENERAL NOTE
The 1968 Act contained no provisions in relation to the access by a parent or guardian to a child removed to a place of safety and the matter remained in the hands of the local authority, until such time as a children's hearing was convened and made any provision therefor. This was regarded as one of the flaws in the system and this new section therefore imposes upon the sheriff an obligation to consider in all cases in which a child protection order is made the matter of contact between the parent or any other person and the child, and gives him the power to make a direction as to contact. In addition, the sheriff may also make a direction in relation to the exercise of parental responsibilities or parental rights, including directions as to medical examination and treatment of the child. There is no requirement for the sheriff to consider in every case whether this additional type of direction should be given, but the applicant is permitted to request the sheriff to give that matter consideration.

Subs. (1)
This provision imposes an obligation on a sheriff who makes a child protection order to give consideration to the question of whether he should give a direction as to contact, and grants him a discretion to give such an order if he believes that it is necessary. The direction is given to the applicant who, presumably, is then obliged to follow it. Such a direction is not the same as a contact order made under s.11 above and is more in the nature of a direction to one person to allow contact between the child and another person. A direction cannot be given here to a person who is not an applicant and if the applicant is not the person who will be looking after the child then a direction under this section will seldom be appropriate. The applicant will normally be the local authority and the direction under this subsection will be to the effect that, for example, a parent is to be allowed contact with a child who has been removed to a place of safety under s.57(4)(b) above.

Necessary to give a direction. The words "necessary" and "necessity" should be given a strict construction and the direction ought not to be given simply because the sheriff wants everything to remain within judicial control. The philosophy here, as in other parts of the Act, is that the court should get involved in directing children's lives only when not to do so would be against the child's interests. Necessity might arise, for example, when the applicant is minded to grant contact and the sheriff thinks that contact would not be in the child's best interests, or when the applicant cannot come to an agreement with a person who is seeking to have contact with the child.

Subs. (2)
The direction made by the sheriff may arrange contact, or may prohibit it or may subject it to such conditions as the sheriff considers appropriate. So the sheriff may direct that contact always be supervised, or he may direct where it is to take place or how often, or he may direct that any specified person or class of persons is not to have contact at all.

Subs. (3)

The aim of this provision is to ensure maximum flexibility in relation to contact for the benefit of the child. It may be appropriate to direct that contact, say, with a father be prohibited completely and that contact with a mother be supervised at all times.

Subs. (4)

It is important to note that a child protection order does not confer parental responsibilities and parental rights on the applicant and these remain with whomsoever had them before the making of the order. It follows that the direction applied for under this subsection as to the fulfilment of parental responsibilities or the exercise of parental rights will be a direction not to the applicant (unless the applicant otherwise has parental responsibilities or parental rights) as in subs. (1) above but to the person with the parental responsibilities or parental rights, and it will provide directions as to how these responsibilities and rights should be carried out. This subsection merely permits the applicant to request the sheriff to give such a direction, and the sheriff has no power to do so in the absence of such a request. The statute does not indicate the consequences of a failure to follow directions given under this subsection.

Subs. (5)

The applicant may request the sheriff to give any direction in relation to the fulfilment or exercise of parental responsibilities or parental rights and in particular in relation to medical examination and treatment. It is important to be aware of the precise effect of this. The sheriff *cannot* authorise examination or treatment under this provision, nor can he authorise the applicant to carry it out. Rather he can simply direct the parent or guardian to exercise her or his parental responsibilities and parental rights in a particular manner. This may include a direction that the parent, say, consents to medical treatment, but that would be competent only when the parent or guardian has the right to provide such consent. Section 90 below (to which reference should be made) preserves the child's capacity to consent or refuse consent under s.2(4) of the Age of Legal Capacity (Scotland) Act 1991 (c. 50), and s.15(5)(b) above ensures that a person with parental responsibilities and parental rights can consent only when the child cannot consent or refuse on her or his own behalf. It follows that a direction as to medical examination or treatment under the present section would be competent only when the child is too young to consent to that examination or treatment her or himself.

Subs. (6)

A direction to those with parental responsibilities and parental rights as to how they should exercise these responsibilities and rights is to be given only when necessary to safeguard or promote the welfare of the child. Such a direction might be necessary, for example, in order to ensure that a parent maintains beneficial contact with the child, or when a parent refuses to consent to an examination of the physical or mental state of the child and this is considered essential to allow for the proper identification of the child's needs. The sheriff must bear in mind in coming to his decision the duration of the order: a child protection order is designed to last only for the shortest possible period of time, and it follows that directions made in connection with it should not, except in cases of immediate necessity, deal irrevocably with matters of long-term significance. In all cases it will be for the applicant to show the existence of such a necessity.

Subs. (7)

The child protection order . . . ceases to have effect. The direction cannot survive without the child protection order to which it is attached and it will cease to have effect whenever the child protection order ceases to have effect, for whatever reason. So any direction under this section, like the child protection order itself, can last for a maximum of eight working days (see the General Note to s.57 above). For other circumstances in which the order ceases to have effect, see s.60 below.

Initial hearing of case of child subject to child protection order

59.—(1) This section applies where—
(a) a child in respect of whom a child protection order has been made—
(i) has been taken to a place of safety by virtue of section 57(4)(b) of this Act; or

      (ii) is prevented from being removed from any place by virtue of section 57(4)(c) of this Act;

  (b) the Principal Reporter has not exercised his powers under section 60(3) of this Act to discharge the child from the place of safety; and

  (c) the Principal Reporter has not received notice, in accordance with section 60(9) of this Act, of an application under subsection (7) of that section.

(2) Where this section applies, the Principal Reporter shall arrange a children's hearing to conduct an initial hearing of the child's case in order to determine whether they should, in the interests of the child, continue the child protection order under subsection (4) below.

(3) A children's hearing arranged under subsection (2) above shall take place on the second working day after that order is implemented.

(4) Where a children's hearing arranged under subsection (2) above are satisfied that the conditions for the making of a child protection order under section 57 of this Act are established, they may continue the child protection order and any direction given under section 58 of this Act (whether with or without variation of the order or, as the case may be, the direction) until the commencement of a children's hearing in relation to the child arranged in accordance with section 65(2) of this Act.

(5) In subsection (3) above, section 60 and section 65(2) of this Act any reference, in relation to the calculation of any period, to the time at which a child protection order is implemented shall be construed as a reference—

  (a) in relation to such an order made under paragraph (b) of subsection (4) of section 57 of this Act, to the day on which the child was removed to a place of safety in accordance with the order; and

  (b) in relation to such an order made under paragraph (c) of that subsection, to the day on which the order was made,

and "implement" shall be construed accordingly.

DEFINITIONS

  "child": s.93(2)(b).
  "children's hearing": s.93(1).
  "child protection order": s.57(1), 93(1).
  "place of safety": s.93(1).
  "principal reporter": s.93(1).
  "working day": s.93(1).

GENERAL NOTE

  A child protection order may, but will not necessarily, authorise the removal of the child from her or his home and the keeping of the child in a place of safety, or the prevention of the removal of the child from any specified place. Though the child protection order process has been designed to ensure that the order will last for only a short period of time (*i.e.* until the eighth working day after its implementation: s.60(6)(e) below) and that there is an opportunity to challenge the granting of the child protection order even before its termination, it was felt that in addition, if the child has been removed to a place of safety or is being prevented from being removed from a specified place, there should be an automatic review of the order at some time before the children's hearing arranged for the eighth working day. If there is an immediate application to the sheriff to set aside or vary the order then that process provides such a review; in the absence of such an application, this section provides that a review will be undertaken by a children's hearing. It should be noted that it is not the making of a child protection order itself that activates this section, but the removal of a child to a place of safety or the prevention of the child from being removed from a specified place. If an application is made to the sheriff to have the order set aside or varied before this hearing commences, then the need for this initial hearing is obviated and it will not go ahead. The hearing must determine two questions: whether the conditions for the making of a child protection order are established, and, if so, whether the order should be continued in the interests of the child.

Subs. (1)

  This sets out the circumstances in which an initial hearing must be arranged. These are that the child has been removed from her or his home and taken to a place of safety or is being

Children (Scotland) Act 1995

prevented from being removed from any specified place where she or he is being accommodated, *and* that the child remains in the place of safety, *and* that no application to the sheriff to set aside or vary the child protection order has been notified to the reporter.

Subss (2) and (3)
The obligations in these subsections are absolute. An initial hearing must be arranged and it must be held on the second working day after the implementation of the child protection order. It would be incompetent for the hearing to be held on the first working day, even if it were feasible to do so. If the hearing is not arranged or otherwise does not take place when this section applies, then the child protection order cannot be continued under subs. (4) below and it will, therefore, cease to have effect. (The Act does not actually say this, but it is an inevitable result of subs. (4) below permitting only a hearing arranged under subs. (2) to continue the child protection order. *Cf.* s.60(6)(a) in which it is provided that when the initial hearing that has been arranged does not continue the order, it will cease to have effect, and s.60(2) which provides that if the sheriff does not determine an application to review the order within three working days it will cease to have effect.)
A children's hearing. This will be a normal hearing to which all the rules relating to attendance and procedure apply. Its purpose, however, is limited to determining the two questions specified in the General Note above.
Second working day. The day of implementation is what can be called "day zero", the next day is the first working day after the implementation, and the day after that is the second working day. So, for example, if a child protection order is implemented on a Monday, the initial hearing must be convened on the immediately following Wednesday. If the child protection order is implemented on a Friday, the initial hearing must be convened on the immediately following Tuesday (Saturday and Sunday not being "working days": s.93(1) below). "Implementation" is defined in subs. (5) below.

Subs. (4)
The hearing must first decide whether they are satisfied that the conditions for the making of the child protection order, set out in s.57(1) above, exist or not. If they are so satisfied they must then go on to consider whether to continue the order and whether to vary it; if they are not so satisfied they have no authority to continue the order (which brings the order to an end: s.60(6)(a) below).
Conditions ... are established. It is not made clear whether the hearing has to determine that the conditions are established as at the time of the granting of the order, or as at the time they are looking at the matter, though the latter interpretation is probably to be preferred. Given the shortness of time between the making of the order and the initial hearing it is unlikely that there will be any significant change in circumstances, but extreme cases (such as death of the source of danger) are not beyond the realms of possibility.
May continue. Even when the hearing are satisfied that the conditions for the making of the child protection order are established, they need not continue it. They have a discretion, to be exercised by regarding the welfare of the child as paramount (s.16(1) above), in determining whether to continue the order or not. Generally speaking the order should be continued only when there remains a greater risk to the child in its termination than in its continuation. The fact that s.16(2) (requiring regard to be had to the views of the child) is not expressed to apply here does not mean that the hearing should not or cannot seek the child's views, for r. 26 of the 1996 Rules requires the hearing to take steps under r. 15 to obtain the views of the child on what arrangements would be in the best interests of the child. The continuation will be until either the sheriff recalls the child protection order under s.60(13) below or until a full hearing arranged under s.65(2) below has commenced.

Subs. (5)
The children's hearing under this section must meet on the second working day after the implementation of the child protection order which either authorises the removal of and keeping a child in a place of safety, or authorises the prevention of the removal of the child from a specified place. In relation to the former, "implementation" occurs on the day the child is removed, and in relation to the latter, "implementation" is deemed to occur on the day the order is made.

Duration, recall or variation of child protection order

60.—(1) Where, by the end of twenty-four hours of a child protection order being made (other than by virtue of section 57(4)(c) of this Act), the applicant has made no attempt to implement the order it shall cease to have effect.

111

(2) Where an application made under subsection (7) below has not been determined timeously in accordance with subsection (8) below, the order to which the application relates shall cease to have effect.

(3) A child shall not be—

(a) kept in a place of safety under a child protection order;

(b) prevented from being removed from any place by such an order; or

(c) subject to any term or condition contained in such an order or a direction given under section 58 of this Act,

where the Principal Reporter, having regard to the welfare of the child, considers that, whether as a result of a change in the circumstances of the case or of further information relating to the case having been received by the Principal Reporter, the conditions for the making of a child protection order in respect of the child are no longer satisfied or that the term, condition or direction is no longer appropriate and notifies the person who implemented the order that he so considers.

(4) The Principal Reporter shall not give notice under subsection (3) above where—

(a) proceedings before a children's hearing arranged under section 59(2) of this Act in relation to the child who is subject to the child protection order have commenced; or

(b) the hearing of an application made under subsection (7) of this section has begun.

(5) Where the Principal Reporter has given notice under subsection (3) above, he shall also, in such manner as may be prescribed, notify the sheriff who made the order.

(6) A child protection order shall cease to have effect—

(a) where an initial hearing arranged under section 59(2) of this Act does not continue the order under subsection (4) of that section;

(b) where an application is made to the sheriff under subsection (7) below, on the sheriff recalling such order under subsection (13) below;

(c) on the person who implemented the order receiving notice from the Principal Reporter that he has decided not to refer the case of a child who is subject to the order to a children's hearing arranged in accordance with section 65(2) of this Act;

(d) on the Principal Reporter giving notice in accordance with subsection (3) above in relation to the order that he considers that the conditions for the making of it are no longer satisfied; or

(e) where such order is continued under section 59(4) of this Act or subsection (12)(d) below, on the commencement of a children's hearing arranged under section 65(2) of this Act.

(7) An application to the sheriff to set aside or vary a child protection order made under section 57 of this Act or a direction given under section 58 of this Act or such an order or direction continued (whether with or without variation) under section 59(4) of this Act, may be made by or on behalf of—

(a) the child to whom the order or direction relates;

(b) a person having parental rights over the child;

(c) a relevant person;

(d) any person to whom notice of the application for the order was given by virtue of rules; or

(e) the applicant for the order made under section 57 of this Act.

(8) An application under subsection (7) above shall be made—

(a) in relation to a child protection order made under section 57, or a direction given under section 58, of this Act, before the commencement of a children's hearing arranged in accordance with section 59(2) of this Act; and

(b) in relation to such an order or direction continued (whether with or without variation) by virtue of subsection (4) of the said section 59, within two working days of such continuation,

and any such application shall be determined within three working days of being made.

(9) Where an application has been made under subsection (7) above, the applicant shall forthwith give notice, in a manner and form prescribed by rules, to the Principal Reporter.

(10) At any time which is—

(a) after the giving of the notice required by subsection (9) above; but

(b) before the sheriff has determined the application in accordance with subsection (11) below,

the Principal Reporter may arrange a children's hearing the purpose of which shall be to provide any advice they consider appropriate to assist the sheriff in his determination of the application.

(11) The sheriff shall, after hearing the parties to the application and, if he wishes to make representations, the Principal Reporter, determine whether—

(a) the conditions for the making of a child protection order under section 57 of this Act are satisfied; or

(b) where the application relates only to a direction under section 58 of this Act, the direction should be varied or cancelled.

(12) Where the sheriff determines that the conditions referred to in subsection (11)(a) above are satisfied, he may—

(a) confirm or vary the order, or any term or condition on which it was granted;

(b) confirm or vary any direction given, in relation to the order, under section 58 of this Act;

(c) give a new direction under that section; or

(d) continue in force the order and any such direction until the commencement of a children's hearing arranged in accordance with section 65(2) of this Act.

(13) Where the sheriff determines that the conditions referred to in subsection (11)(a) above are not satisfied he shall recall the order and cancel any direction given under section 58 of this Act.

DEFINITIONS
"child": s.93(2)(b).
"child protection order": ss.57(1), 93(1).
"children's hearing": s.93(1).
"parental rights": ss.2(4), 93(1).
"place of safety": s.93(1).
"Principal Reporter": s.93(1).
"relevant person": s.93(2)(b).
"working day": s.93(1).

GENERAL NOTE
As explained more fully in the General Note to s.57, a child protection order is designed to last for as short a period of time as possible, and to give as much opportunity to challenge its implementation as is practicable. This important section sets out the circumstances in which the child protection order will cease to have effect, and prescribes the procedures to be followed in applications to set aside or vary the order. In addition, it permits the reporter to return the child home when her or his interests so require.

Subs. (1)
The child protection order is to be used as an emergency procedure designed to provide immediate protection to the child when this is necessary in her or his welfare. It follows that

when the applicant delays in implementing the order, it can be assumed that the immediate necessity, previously argued for by the applicant, no longer exists, and it therefore ought to fall. The rule is therefore that the child protection order will cease to have effect unless an attempt to implement it is made within 24 hours of making the order.

Has made no attempt. The applicant can be said to make an attempt to implement the order when he takes necessary steps to that end. The nature of the attempt will of course vary with the nature of the order, and this provision specifically does not apply to an order preventing the removal of the child from a place where he is being accommodated. Implementation in that case is deemed to occur on the day the order is made (s.59(5)(b) above). It is difficult to see how the applicant can attempt to implement the keeping secret of the child's whereabouts if no-one attempts to find this out and it is submitted that here too implementation occurs on the obtaining of the order. The attempt might not be successful until after the 24 hours have passed, but that does not bring the order to an end so long as the attempt commences before then. So, for example, if a child protection order authorises the removal of a child to a place of safety the order ceases if the applicant does nothing for more than 24 hours, but it does not cease if the applicant attempts to obtain the child but the attempt is frustrated by the parents of the child spiriting her or him away or the child running away.

Time starts to run in relation to applications to the sheriff, and the arranging of the initial and the full hearings, from the successful implementation of the order.

Shall cease to have effect. If the order ceases to have effect the child is no longer subject to a child protection order with the result that there is no obligation on the reporter to arrange a children's hearing in terms of s.65(2) below. The reporter is still entitled, however, to arrange a hearing under s.65(1) below on the basis of the information obtained as a result of the child protection order though that need not be on the eighth working day after the order was originally implemented. When the order ceases to have effect, any directions to the applicant made under s.58 above also cease to have effect.

Subs. (2)

In order to ensure the speedy resolution of applications to the sheriff to set aside or vary the child protection order, it is provided as an absolute rule that the order will cease to have effect if such an application has not been dealt with within three working days of its being made (subs. (8) below).

Subs. (3)

When a child is kept in a place of safety, or is prevented from being removed from a place, or is subjected to any term or condition, the reporter is obliged to keep a continual eye on the situation, and this subsection ensures that the child protection order will not justify that keeping or prevention or subjection when the reporter considers that the conditions for the granting of the child protection order or the giving of the directions are no longer satisfied. Where the reporter so considers, and notifies the person who implemented the order that she or he so considers, this provision takes away the authority to keep the child or prevent the child's removal and terminates the direction. It follows that the child must be returned home or freed, unless some other statutory authority to keep the child can be invoked. Subsection (6)(d) below provides that in the circumstances described the order shall cease to have effect. This means that there is no obligation on the reporter to arrange a children's hearing in terms of s.65(2) below, but she or he may still do so, in terms of s.65(1) below.

Conditions for the making. This refers to the conditions set out in s.57. The further evidence that comes to the attention of the reporter might suggest that the conditions are no longer satisfied or, implicitly, that they never were, in fact, satisfied. The reporter cannot come to that view unless there has been a change in circumstances or she or he has acquired further information (and she or he cannot, therefore, release a child simply because she or he disagrees with the sheriff who granted the order). Evidence that the child's welfare is suffering due to the implementation of the child protection order will be a persuasive (and usually sufficient) change in circumstances.

And notifies. The authority to keep the child or prevent her or him being removed comes to an end when the reporter's decision is notified to the person who implements the order, and not simply by the reporter making the decision.

Subs. (4)

The effect of this provision almost entirely detracts from the aim of subs. (3) above, which is to allow the reporter to react speedily to sudden changes in circumstances. It provides that the reporter cannot arrange for the return or release of the child after the commencement of any initial hearing that is held under s.59 above or the commencement of any application to the sheriff to set aside or vary the order. This means that the reporter's power to arrange for a release of the child lasts only until the second working day after the implementation of the child protection order and she or he cannot arrange for the child's release thereafter. However, if the reporter decides not to arrange a children's hearing under s.65(2) after the second working day, the child protection order comes to an end and the child must be returned home: subs. (6)(c) below. This does not, however, inhibit the reporter from later arranging a children's hearing under s.65(1).

Subs. (5)

The sheriff who made the child protection order must be informed if the child is to be returned home or released by the reporter's decision under subs. (3) above.

Subs. (6)

The child protection order ceases to have effect (with the result that there is no authority to do any of the acts authorised under the order or an attached direction and the reporter is no longer obliged to arrange a children's hearing in terms of s.65(2) below) immediately on the happening of any of the listed events. Under para. (a) the child protection order ceases either when an initial hearing arranged under s.59 above does not continue the order or (though the statute does not say this) when an initial hearing which ought to have been arranged on the second working day after the implementation of the order did not in fact take place (see comments to s.59(2) above). Paragraph (b) provides that the effect of the sheriff recalling the order is that it shall cease to have effect. Paragraph (c) brings the child protection order to an end when the reporter notifies a decision not to refer the child's case to a children's hearing for consideration and disposal (*i.e.* when she or he has come to the view either that none of the grounds of referral exists or that, even if a ground does exist, compulsory measures of supervision are not necessary). Paragraph (d) brings the order to an end when the reporter notifies the person who implemented the order that the conditions for its making are no longer satisfied. Paragraph (e) ensures that the order ceases as soon as the full children's hearing commences: if the child's welfare requires that she or he be kept in a place of safety thereafter then the provisions in ss.66 and 67 below must be utilised: in other words the matter is in the hands of the children's hearing.

Subs. (7)

The application to the sheriff to set aside or vary a child protection order or an attached direction can be made within two working days of its implementation (*i.e.* before the holding of, and obviating the need for, an initial hearing) or within two working days of its continuation by an initial hearing. That application can be made by or on behalf of only the specified persons (and not, for example, a stranger to the child seeking to clear her or his name of an allegation of abuse against the child).

The child. The child will require the application to be made on her or his behalf when she or he has no capacity (determined by the Age of Legal Capacity (Scotland) Act 1991, s.2(4A) and (4B)) to conduct civil proceedings, or when she or he does not have that capacity but consents to be represented in proceedings by someone who used to be her or his legal representative (s.15(6) above).

A person having parental rights. It is surprising that the reference in para. (b) is not to a person with parental rights or parental responsibilities, for a person with parental responsibilities has as much interest in the child protection order as a person with parental rights. It may be noticed that s.58(1)(b) above (directions as to contact) refers only to a person with parental responsibilities. There is no practical result in this example of sloppy draftsmanship since all such persons come within the category described in the immediately following paragraph (rendering this paragraph entirely otiose).

A relevant person. This is defined to mean a person having parental responsibilities or parental rights or who ordinarily has charge of or control over the child (s.93(2)(b) below).

Subs. (8)

This sets out the strict time-limits within which an application to the sheriff to set aside or vary the child protection order must be made. If it is not made within these times then it is incompetent later to make it. The application must be made *either* before the commencement of an initial hearing (which is to be held on the second working day after implementation of the order in circumstances described in s.59(1) above) *or* if it was not made before then within two workings days of the continuation of the order by the initial hearing. In either situation, the sheriff must determine the application within three working days of its being made (so if the application is made, for example, on a Friday he must determine it by the following Wednesday). If he has not determined the application by then, the child protection order ceases to have effect (subs. (2) above).

Subs. (9)

Notice is necessary since if notice is not given to the reporter of an application to the sheriff to set aside or vary the child protection order within two working days of its implementation, and the order contains an authorisation to remove the child to a place of safety or to keep the child in a place, the reporter is obliged to arrange an initial hearing in terms of s.59 above.

Subs. (10)

This subsection introduces a wholly new type of advice hearing. The reporter is given the discretion to arrange a children's hearing (to which the normal rules of attendance and procedure apply) after an application has been made, but before the sheriff has determined the application, for variation or setting aside of a child protection order, in order that the hearing may provide the sheriff with advice to assist him in his decision. The nature of the advice given is entirely for the children's hearing themselves to decide, but it should, of course, be directed towards the question of whether a child protection order remains in the child's best interests. Any advice the hearing gives must regard the welfare of the child as the paramount consideration (s.16(1) above) and must give the child an opportunity to express views and have regard so far as practicable to these views taking account of the child's age and maturity (s.16(2), as applied to this advice hearing by s.16(4)(a)(iii) above). The statute gives no guidance to the reporter as to how and when to exercise her or his discretion to arrange this advice hearing, and often the matter will be determined by the availability of time: this hearing does not interrupt the running of the three working days within which the sheriff must determine the application. It may well prove impractical in the generality of cases to arrange any advice hearing under this subsection.

Subs. (11)

The application may either request the sheriff to set aside the whole child protection order, which will terminate any directions as to contact or the exercise of parental responsibilities or parental rights given under s.58, or to vary the order, or to vary or cancel any such direction. The sheriff must hear the parties to the application and, if she or he wishes to make representations, the reporter.

The parties to the application. This refers to the parties to the application to set aside or vary the child protection order, which are the applicants themselves (being one of the persons specified in subs. (7) above), and the person who originally sought the child protection order together with any person who opposed its making.

The conditions for the making of a child protection order ... are satisfied. This means, it is submitted, currently satisfied as at the date the sheriff determines the issue rather than the date the child protection order was made. "The conditions" are all the conditions set out in s.57 and not simply the grounds upon which the order was granted set out in s.57(1), otherwise the statute would have limited it to that subsection. So for example the child protection order can be challenged here on the ground that the application was not made in the form specified in s.57(3): adopting the correct form is, it is submitted, one of the conditions for the making of a child protection order set out in s.57.

Subs. (12)

If the conditions for the making of a child protection order are held by the sheriff to be satisfied then he may do any of the acts listed. He is not entitled to do any other act, such as recalling the order. In deciding which option to adopt, the sheriff is governed by the three overarching principles in s.16, that is to say the paramountcy of the child's welfare, the requirement to have regard to the views of the child, and the minimum intervention principle. The last-mentioned amounts in this context to a presumption that the present order is to continue unvaried.

Subs. (13)

A finding that the conditions in s.57 have not been satisfied (*i.e.* all the conditions including but not limited to the grounds in s.57(1): see note to subs. (11) above) seems to oblige the sheriff to recall the order and cancel any directions attached to it. However, the words "shall recall the order" must be read in the light of s.16 above, which provides that the three overarching principles apply when "the sheriff is considering ... whether to ... discharge a child protection order" (s.16(4)(b)(ii): these words have the effect, if they have any effect at all, of conferring a discretion on to the sheriff's decision. If the sheriff finds that the conditions in s.57 have not been satisfied it can be assumed that in the vast majority of cases it will be for the child's welfare to recall the order, but this would not be so if the condition not satisfied were a mere procedural condition (such as that in s.57(3)) and the ground upon which the order was made clearly still exists. In these circumstances the sheriff can, it is submitted, rely on s.16(1) to refuse to recall the order. The views of the child (s.16(2) above) can be taken into account but will never determine the issue and could not, it is submitted, subvert the apparent obligation to recall the order. The minimum intervention principle in s.16(3) amounts to a presumption that no recall will be pronounced unless the sheriff considers that it would be better for the child to pronounce recall than not to do so: this clearly confers a discretion on the sheriff, notwithstanding the words "shall recall the order" as they appear in the present subsection.

Emergency protection of children where child protection order not available

61. (1) Where, on the application of any person, a justice of the peace is satisfied—

(a) both that the conditions laid down for the making of a child protection order in section 57(1) of this Act are satisfied and that it is probable that any such order, if made, would contain an authorisation in terms of paragraph (b) or (c) of subsection (4) of that section; but

(b) that it is not practicable in the circumstances for an application for such an order to be made to the sheriff or for the sheriff to consider such an application,

he may grant to the applicant an authorisation under this section.

(2) Where on the application of a local authority a justice of the peace is satisfied—

(a) both that the conditions laid down for the making of a child protection order in section 57(2) of this Act are satisfied and that it is probable that any such order, if made, would contain an authorisation in terms of paragraph (b) or (c) of subsection (4) of that section; but

(b) that it is not practicable in the circumstances for an application for such an order to be made to the sheriff or for the sheriff to consider such an application,

he may grant an authorisation under this section.

(3) An authorisation under this section may—

(a) require any person in a position to do so to produce the child to the applicant;

(b) prevent any person from removing a child from a place where he is then being accommodated;

(c) authorise the applicant to remove the child to a place of safety and to keep him there until the expiration of the authorisation.

(4) An authorisation under this section shall cease to have effect—

(a) twelve hours after being made, if within that time—

(i) arrangements have not been made to prevent the child's removal from any place specified in the authorisation; or

(ii) he has not been, or is not being, taken to a place of safety; or

(b) where such arrangements have been made or he has been so taken when—

(i) twenty-four hours have expired since it was so given; or

(ii) an application for a child protection order in respect of the child is disposed of,

whichever is the earlier.

(5) Where a constable has reasonable cause to believe that—

(a) the conditions for the making of a child protection order laid down in section 57(1) are satisfied;

(b) that it is not practicable in the circumstances for him to make an application for such an order to the sheriff or for the sheriff to consider such an application; and

(c) that, in order to protect the child from significant harm (or further such harm), it is necessary for him to remove the child to a place of safety,

he may remove the child to such a place and keep him there.

(6) The power conferred by subsection (5) above shall not authorise the

keeping of a child in a place of safety for more than twenty-four hours from the time when the child is so removed.

(7) The authority to keep a child in a place of safety conferred by subsection (5) above shall cease on the disposal of an application in relation to the child for a child protection order.

(8) A child shall not be—

(a) kept in a place of safety; or

(b) prevented from being removed from any place,

under this section where the Principal Reporter considers that the conditions for the grant of an authorisation under subsection (1) or (2) above or the exercise of the power conferred by subsection (5) above are not satisfied, or that it is no longer in the best interests of the child that he should be so kept.

DEFINITIONS

"child": s.93(2)(b).
"child protection order": ss.57(1), 93(1).
"constable": s.93(1).
"local authority": Local Government etc. (Scotland) Act 1994, s.2.
"place of safety": s.93(1).
"principal reporter": s.93(1).

GENERAL NOTE

There may be situations in which either a sheriff is not available to grant a child protection order or it appears that a child's safety can be secured only by her or his immediate and summary removal from a source of danger. In these situations a child protection order, though designed to be granted quickly, might not be available quite quickly enough. This section therefore permits a justice of the peace to grant authorisations to do certain of the acts which could be authorised by a child protection order and permits police officers to remove a child from an immediate source of danger. To a large extent the section has been drafted to mirror the provisions in s.57 above, which sets out the conditions for the making of a child protection order, but this has led to certain anomalies in the present section since the emergency situation is not wholly analogous to the situation governed by s.57. Due to the very limited periods of time the authorisations under this provision can last, there are no provisions for review of or appeal from decisions.

Subs. (1)

When both conditions specified in s.57(1) above for the granting of a child protection order are satisfied, but it is not practicable to obtain such an order from a sheriff, then an authorisation may be granted by a justice of the peace to do any of the acts listed in subs. (3) below, so long as the justice of the peace is satisfied that had a child protection order been granted it is probable that it would have contained an authorisation under s.57(4)(b) (*i.e.* an authorisation to remove the child to a place of safety and to keep the child there) or an authorisation under s.57(4)(c) (*i.e.* an authorisation to prevent the removal of a child from any place where he is being accommodated).

Any person. There is no limitation on who may apply for an authorisation under this subsection, though normally it will be a local authority.

It is probable. This means more likely than not.

Not practicable. The only situation in which it would not be practicable to obtain a child protection order from a sheriff is when no sheriff is, for whatever reason, available in sufficient time to deal with whatever emergency has arisen. This eventuality is unlikely to occur in large urban areas such as Glasgow or Edinburgh in which there are many sheriffs, but it may occur more frequently in rural areas such as the Western or the Northern Isles.

May grant . . . an authorisation. In deciding whether to grant the authorisation the justice of the peace will be governed by the need to regard the welfare of the child as paramount (s.16(1) above) but, not being a sheriff, will not be governed by the requirement to have regard to the views of the child (s.16(2) above) or the minimum intervention principle (s.16(3) above). The grant is not of a child protection order, but merely of an authorisation to do certain acts. It follows that once the authorisation is made the procedures under ss.57–60 are not activated. It is, however, envisaged that a child protection order will be applied for as soon as possible after the granting of the authorisation under this section, and that authorisation comes to an end as soon as an application for a child protection order has been dealt with (subs. (4)(b)(ii) below).

Subs. (2)

This provision reflects that contained in s.57(2) above, whereby a child protection order can be granted if inquiries into the child's wellbeing are being frustrated by a failure to obtain access to the child. In these circumstances, and on the satisfaction of the same conditions as contained in subs. (1) above, a justice of the peace may grant an authorisation to do any of the acts listed in subs. (3) below. As in s.57(2), only a local authority can apply for an authorisation under this subsection. This provision is unlikely to be much used since investigations will seldom require to be carried out with the urgency that this section is designed to deal with.

Subs. (3)

The authorisation under this section may permit the carrying out of any of the listed acts. Paragraph (a) reflects para. (a) in s.57(4), para. (b) reflects para. (c) in s.57(4) and para. (c) reflects para. (b) in s.57(4). The only power in s.57(4) left out is the provision that the location of any place of safety in which the child is being kept should not be disclosed to any person. However, in terms of r. 10 of the Emergency Child Protection Measures (Scotland) Regulations 1996 (S.I. 1996 No. 3258), the applicant may withhold this information if it is necessary to do so in order to safeguard the welfare of the child. It is not easy to understand why the justice of the peace is permitted under this subsection to authorise acts of the same nature as those listed in s.57(4)(a), (b) and (c) but according to subs. (1) above can do so only when he believes that a sheriff would authorise either of the acts in s.57(4)(b) or (c), but this untidiness is unlikely to have much practical effect.

Subs. (4)

This deals with the length of time for which the authorisation survives. Its effect is that the authorisation lasts for a maximum of 24 hours after its granting. If the act authorised is not carried out within 12 hours of being granted it cannot be carried out thereafter; if it is carried out within that time the authorisation for it lapses at the expiry of 24 hours, or on the disposal of an application for a child protection order (if earlier). There is no requirement to seek a child protection order after the obtaining of an authorisation under this section, but that will be the only way in which a child can be kept in a place of safety for longer than the periods provided here.

Subs. (5)

A child can be removed from, or kept away from, a source of immediate danger without any involvement of a sheriff or a justice of the peace by a police officer who has reasonable cause to believe that the conditions for the granting of a child protection order exist but it is not practicable in the circumstances for her or him to obtain a child protection order. However, she or he can only remove or keep a child if this is necessary to protect the child from significant harm. The necessity must be immediate, otherwise the provisions above concerning authorisations by a justice of the peace can be adopted. A police officer can, for example, step in and remove a child to a place of safety if she or he witnesses the child being beaten up by her or his parents, or a child is brought, say, to a female and child unit at a police station in a distressed state, or if the police officer comes across a child who has been expelled from the family home in conditions that create a risk of significant harm. On "significant harm" see the General Note to s.57(1) above.

Subs. (6)

If a child is taken to or kept in a place of safety by a police officer under the terms of subs. (5) above, she or he can be kept there only for a maximum period of 24 hours after first being removed from the source of danger. If the child is to be kept for any longer period than that, a child protection order under s.57 must be sought and obtained. This tightens up the old law under which the time-limits were not so strict (s.37(4) of the 1968 Act was expressed "where practicable").

Subs. (7)

If a child has been taken to or kept in a place of safety by a police officer under the terms of subs. (5) above, the authority to keep her or him there granted by that subsection lapses when a child protection order application has been determined. That determination supersedes subs. (6) above. If the application is successful, the authority to keep the child will be the child protection order; if the application is unsuccessful the child cannot be kept in the place of safety and must be released home forthwith.

Subs. (8)

As in s.60(3) above, the reporter has ultimate control over whether a child is kept in a place of safety, and the child cannot be kept in a place of safety or prevented from being removed from a place by any provision in this section if the reporter is of the view either (i) that it is no longer in the best interests of the child that she or he be kept there, or (ii) in cases of authorisation by a justice of the peace that the conditions for its granting are not satisfied, or (iii) in cases of emergency removal by a constable that the conditions specified in subs. (5) above for the exercise of that power of removal are not satisfied.

Regulations in respect of emergency child protection measures

62.—(1) The Secretary of State may make regulations concerning the duties in respect of a child of any person removing him to, and keeping him in, a place of safety under section 61 above.

(2) Regulations under this section may make provision requiring—

(a) notification of the removal of a child to be given to a person specified in the regulations;

(b) intimation to be given to any person of the place of safety at which a child is being kept;

(c) notification to be given to any person of the ceasing to have effect, under section 61(4)(a) of this Act, of an authorisation.

DEFINITIONS
"child": s.93(2)(b).
"place of safety": s.93(1).

GENERAL NOTE
In addition to the duties imposed by the Emergency Child Protection Measures (Scotland) Regulations 1996 made under this section, a local authority which provides accommodation for a child who is removed to and kept in a place of safety will also be subject to the duties in respect of that child set out in s.17 above: s.17(6)(c).

S.I.s ISSUED UNDER SECTION
Emergency Child Protection Measures (Scotland) Regulations 1996 (S.I. 1996 No. 3258).
Children (Scotland) Act etc. (Revocations and Savings (Scotland) Regulations 1997 (S.I. 1997 No. 691).

Children arrested by the police

Review of case of child arrested by police

[1] **63.**—(1) Where the Principal Reporter has been informed by a constable, in accordance with section 43(5) of the Criminal Procedure (Scotland) Act 1995, that charges are not to be proceeded with against a child who has been detained in a place of safety in accordance with that section, the Principal Reporter shall, unless he considers that compulsory measures of supervision are not required in relation to the child, arrange a children's hearing to which he shall refer the case.

(2) A children's hearing arranged under subsection (1) above shall begin not later than the third day after the Principal Reporter received the information mentioned in that subsection.

(3) Where the Principal Reporter considers that a child of whose detention he has been informed does not require compulsory measures of supervision, he shall direct that the child shall no longer be kept in the place of safety.

(4) Subject to subsection (3) above, a child who has been detained in a place of safety may continue to be kept at that place until the commencement of a children's hearing arranged under subsection (1) above.

(5) Subject to subsection (6) below, a children's hearing arranged under subsection (1) above may—

(a) if they are satisfied that the conditions mentioned in subsection (2) of section 66 of this Act are satisfied, grant a warrant to keep the child in a place of safety; and

(b) direct the Principal Reporter to arrange a children's hearing for the purposes of section 65(1) of this Act, and subsections (3) to (8) of the said section 66 shall apply to a warrant granted under this subsection as they apply to a warrant granted under subsection (1) of the said section 66.

(6) A child shall not be kept in a place of safety in accordance with a warrant granted under subsection (5) above where the Principal Reporter, having regard to the welfare of the child, considers that, whether as a result of a change in the circumstances of the case or of further information relating to the case having been received by the Principal Reporter

   (a) the conditions mentioned in section 66(2) of this Act are no longer satisfied in relation to the child; or

   (b) the child is not in need of compulsory measures of supervision,

and where he does so consider he shall give notice to that effect to the person who is keeping the child in that place in accordance with the warrant.

NOTE
1. As amended by the Criminal Procedure (Consequential Provisions) (Scotland) Act 1995, c. 40, s.3 and Sched. 3, para. 97.

DEFINITIONS
"child": s.93(2)(b).
"children's hearing": s.93(1).
"compulsory measures of supervision": s.93(1).
"constable": s.93(1).
"place of safety": s.93(1).
"principal reporter": s.93(1).

GENERAL NOTE
There was no provision analogous to this section in the 1968 Act, but it does replace those parts of s.296 of the Criminal Procedure (Scotland) Act 1975 (c. 21) (now contained in s.43 of the Criminal Procedure (Scotland) Act 1995 (c. 46)) that are repealed in Sched. 5 below. The aim is clearly to gather together as many as possible of the statutory provisions dealing with the reporter's duties to arrange children's hearings, but this provision significantly alters the rules previously contained in s.296 and produces in their place one of the most peculiar provisions in the present Act. The section was introduced into the Act at a late stage in the parliamentary process (the Report stage in the House of Lords, a fortnight before the Bill received the Royal Assent: see *Hansard*, H.L. Vol. 565, col. 1203) and, like other provisions in that category (see for example the disastrously drafted s.67 below), the lack of proper parliamentary scrutiny is quite apparent.

A child may come to the attention of the reporter as being potentially in need of compulsory measures of supervision not only by the provision of information under s.53 above, but also by being informed that the child is in a place of safety after having been apprehended by the police and detained in a place of safety in terms of s.43(4) of the Criminal Procedure (Scotland) Act 1995. The present section provides that in such circumstances a children's hearing must be arranged to determine whether the child is to continue to be kept in a place of safety and whether the child should be referred to a children's hearing. There are three significant changes to the law. First, the hearing must sit not later than the third day after the reporter receives the relevant information, rather than, as under s.37(4) of the 1968 Act, on the "first lawful day". Secondly, the provision in the old s.296(4)(c) of the 1975 Act permitting the child to be detained for up to seven days has not been re-enacted. And thirdly, the hearing which is held not later than the third day is to determine not only whether to grant a warrant to keep the child in a place of safety (as under the old s.37(4)) but also, bizarrely, whether a children's hearing should be arranged to put grounds of referral to the child and parent. In no other situation does the children's hearing have a role in deciding whether a child's case should be referred to a children's hearing, and that is a matter left entirely within the discretion of the reporter (even when the case is referred to her or him by a court under s.54 above). If this was seriously considered an appropriate role for the children's hearing to play, it is surprising that the role is granted only in the highly unusual circumstances governed by the present section.

Subs. (1)
The police are obliged by s.43(5) of the 1995 Act to inform the reporter whenever a child who has been arrested is detained in a place of safety. On being informed that the child is not to be charged with any offence, the reporter must consider whether, in her or his opinion, compulsory measures of supervision are required and must, subject to what is said below, arrange an initial

children's hearing. That hearing's role is not to consider the child's case in terms of ss.65–70, but to decide whether a warrant needs to be granted and whether a full children's hearing requires to be arranged.

Unless he considers that compulsory measures of supervision are not required. The emphasis is quite deliberately to the effect that there is an obligation on the reporter to arrange an initial children's hearing, unless she or he is persuaded that compulsory measures are not required. In other words, the obligation exists whenever the reporter either believes that compulsory measures of supervision are required or is not convinced that they are not required.

Subs. (2)

The initial children's hearing arranged under this section must commence on or before the third day after the reporter becomes obliged under subs. (1) above to arrange the hearing. So if the reporter receives the appropriate information on a Monday, the first day after that is the Tuesday and the third day after that is the Thursday: the hearing must commence on or before the Thursday.

Shall begin. The reference to a children's hearing "beginning" on a particular day is, in this context, inept. A children's hearing cannot be adjourned overnight (1996 Rules, r.10(4)); rather they can continue a case to another hearing. However, a continuation would not be appropriate in the context of the decisions that the limited hearing under this section must make and would indeed, it is submitted, be incompetent: the hearing that sits no later than the third day must make the two decisions for which the hearing has been arranged. This provision would have been more comprehensible, and more consistent with other provisions in the Act, had it said that the children's hearing will "take place" no later than the third day (*cf.*, for example, s.59(3) above: "A children's hearing ... shall take place on the second working day ...").

Subss. (3) and (4)

If the reporter is of the opinion that the child does not require compulsory measures of supervision, she or he is not obliged to arrange a children's hearing (subs. (1) above), but is obliged to direct that the child no longer be kept in the place of safety to which she or he was taken in pursuance of s.43 of the 1995 Act. If the reporter is of the opinion that the child does or may require compulsory measures of supervision, then the child may be kept in the place of safety until the children's hearing arranged under subs. (1) above commences, that is to say no longer than the third day after the reporter receives the relevant information (see subs. (2) above). If, in breach of the reporter's duty under subs. (1) above, no hearing has been timeously arranged, the child must be released on the third day.

Subs. (5)

This subsection lists the two decisions that the children's hearing arranged under this section must make: they may grant a warrant under para. (a) and they may give a direction under para. (b). Their decision is governed by the welfare principle set out in s.16(1) above. And r. 26 of the 1996 Rules requires steps to be taken to obtain the views of the child. The children's hearing may decide to do neither, or to do both, or to give a direction under para. (b) but not grant a warrant under para. (a); but they cannot, it is submitted, grant a warrant under para. (a) without giving a direction under para. (b).

Grant a warrant. If the hearing are satisfied either (i) that there is reason to believe that the child will not attend any hearing of her or his case or will fail to comply with a requirement to undergo investigation, or (ii) that it is necessary to safeguard or promote her or his welfare that the child be kept in a place of safety, then the hearing may grant a warrant which will have the same effect as one granted under s.66(1) (*i.e.* one granted when the hearing arranged to consider the child's case have directed the reporter to make an application to the sheriff for proof of a ground of referral and the same conditions, in s.66(2), are satisfied).

Subsections (3) to (8) ... shall apply to a warrant granted under this subsection. It is to be noted that the effect of the warrant granted under this subsection is governed only by subss (3) to (8) of s.66, and that its termination does not activate the sheriff's power to grant an additional warrant under s.67, as he may do at the termination of a warrant granted under s.66.

Direct the Principal Reporter. The second decision the children's hearing must make is whether or not to make a direction to the reporter to arrange a children's hearing as under s.65(1) (*i.e.* to put grounds of referral to the child and relevant person). The hearing should so direct the reporter only when satisfied both that one or more of the grounds of referral in s.52 above has been established and that the child is in need of compulsory measures of supervision. The fact that the child has been arrested will indicate that the child may have committed an offence, and it would be appropriate for the hearing not to direct the reporter to arrange a children's hearing only when satisfied that, even if the ground is accepted or established, no compulsory measures of supervision will be required.

While it can be assumed that a reporter directed by a children's hearing to arrange a children's hearing must do so (though the Act does not actually say this), it is left entirely unclear from the terms of the statute whether the children's hearing are permitted expressly to direct the reporter *not* to arrange a children's hearing and whether the reporter can, in the absence of any direction to do so, nevertheless arrange a children's hearing. The discretion of the reporter has long been seen as an important element in the whole system and it is submitted that the terms of this section should be interpreted to limit that discretion only insofar as absolutely necessary to give effect to its wording. It follows (i) that the reporter retains a discretion to arrange a children's hearing even if the hearing arranged under this section do not direct him to do so, and (ii) that the hearing have no power expressly to direct the reporter not to arrange a children's hearing. The hearing's power under this paragraph is limited to directing the reporter to arrange a hearing or leaving the matter to the discretion of the reporter.

Subs. (6)

If, after having arranged an initial hearing in accordance with subs. (1) above, the reporter comes to the conclusion, due to a change in the child's circumstances or because of new information made available to her or him, that the grounds for granting a warrant to detain the child no longer exist *or* that the child is not in need of compulsory measures of supervision, the child cannot be kept in a place of safety and the reporter must give notice to that effect to the person keeping the child.

Business meeting preparatory to children's hearing

Business meeting preparatory to children's hearing

64.—(1) At any time prior to the commencement of proceedings at the children's hearing, the Principal Reporter may arrange a meeting with members of the children's panel from which the children's hearing is to be constituted under section 39(4) of this Act for those proceedings (any such meeting being, in this Part of this Act referred to as a "business meeting").

(2) Where a business meeting is arranged under subsection (1) above, the Principal Reporter shall give notice to the child in respect of whom the proceedings are to be commenced and any relevant person in relation to the child—

   (a) of the arrangement of the meeting and of the matters which may be considered and determined by the meeting;

   (b) of their right to make their views on those matters known to the Principal Reporter; and

   (c) of the duty of the Principal Reporter to present those views to the meeting.

(3) A business meeting, subject to subsection (4) below—

   (a) shall determine such procedural and other matters as may be prescribed by rules under subsection (1) of section 42 of this Act by virtue of subsection (2)(a) of that section; and

   (b) may give such direction or guidance to the Principal Reporter in relation to the performance of his functions in relation to the proceedings as they think appropriate.

(4) Before a business meeting makes such a determination or gives such direction or guidance to the Principal Reporter, the Principal Reporter shall present, and they shall consider, any views expressed to him by virtue of subsection (2)(b) above.

(5) Subject to any rules made under section 42(1) of this Act by virtue of subsection (2)(a) of that section and with the exception of sections 44 and, as regards any determination made by the business meeting under subsection (3)(a) above, 51, the provisions of this Act which relate to a children's hearing shall not apply to a business meeting.

DEFINITIONS

   "child": s.93(2)(b).

   "children's hearing": s.93(1).

   "Principal Reporter": s.93(1).

   "relevant person": s.93(2)(b).

GENERAL NOTE

It had long been the practice in many panel areas for hearings to discuss, and make determinations on, procedural matters relating to a child's case before the meeting of the hearing was properly constituted with the child and family in attendance. Often such a meeting would make a determination that the child's presence at the proper hearing was unnecessary. Under the 1968 Act such meetings had no place in the statutory framework but, when the matter came to the attention of the court in *Sloan v. B*, 1991 S.L.T. 530, their validity received judicial sanction as involving no illegality or unfairness. That sanction was, however, expressly limited to those meetings doing no more than giving guidance to the reporter on such matters as who she or he should invite to the hearing, and the legally efficacious decision on attendance remained to be made and recorded by a properly constituted children's hearing (*per* Lord President Hope at p. 540). The present provision aims to put such meetings on a statutory basis, and to give the child and the parent a chance to express their views. It permits the reporter to arrange what is called a "business meeting" at which procedural and other matters can be discussed and determined before the start of the proper children's hearing and permits the child and the parent to make their views known on the matters to be discussed. Such meetings will be much more formal than the arrangements made in the past, where very often a decision would be made by a hearing concerning a case that was due to be considered the next day, and no notice of the fact that such a decision would be considered was given to anyone. R. 4(2) of the 1996 Rules lists the matters that are open for discussion at a business meeting.

Subs. (1)

The reporter is given a discretion to arrange a business meeting of panel members in order for them to discuss and make decisions upon certain matters relating to the proper running of the full children's hearing when it is convened. These are listed in the note to subs. (3) below.

At any time prior to the commencement of the proceedings. The case of the child must have been referred to a children's hearing under s.65(1) or s.73(8) before a business meeting can be held and it would, it is submitted, be incompetent to hold such a meeting before the reporter has made such a referral.

A meeting with members of the children's panel. The meeting will be between panel members and the reporter. The child and her or his parent or representative will not be present. The panel members who conduct the business meeting need not be the same individuals as those who will constitute the children's hearing when it later meets, but they must be members of the same local authority area panel as that from which those individuals will be chosen. The reporter should always be present, for it is solely in order to guide and direct the reporter that the meeting is being held.

Subs. (2)

Unlike the informal meetings held before the commencement of this Act referred to in the General Note above, business meetings require to be intimated to those who have a right to attend the proper children's hearing. That notice must include intimation of the matters listed here. The implication is, though it is not stated, that failure to adhere to these requirements will invalidate the meeting (though that will have little practical effect since the proper children's hearing will then be able to make those decisions the meeting would otherwise have made).

Subs. (3)

The matters which are open to be discussed and determined by the business meeting are listed in r. 4(2) of the 1996 Rules. These are (i) whether notice of the children's hearing should be given to a person as a relevant person, (ii) whether notice should be given to the child that she or he is released from the obligation to attend the children's hearing, and (iii) whether notice should be given to a relevant person that her or his attendance at the children's hearing is not required or is unnecessary. No dispositive decision will be possible at a business meeting and the purpose will be limited to giving the reporter direction or guidance as to how her or his functions are to be carried out. So, for example, if a business meeting decides to relieve the child of her or his obligation to attend at the proper children's hearing, they can direct the reporter not to arrange for the child to be brought to the hearing (so long as this is done in such a way as protects the child's right to attend if she or he so wishes).

Subs. (4)

If the child or parent has expressed views on the matters they have been informed will be discussed then the reporter must present these views to the meeting.

Subs. (5)

A business meeting is not a children's hearing. It follows that the rules relating to the constitution, conduct and procedure at children's hearings do not apply, subject to the stated exceptions. These are that s.44 above (prohibitions of publications of proceedings) and s.51 (appeals) apply. In relation to appeals it is difficult to see what decisions open to a business meeting could be subject to the appeal provisions in s.51 in any case. Under the 1968 Act there was no appeal from procedural decisions of the children's hearing (see the General Note to s.51(1) above) and the words "any determination made by a business meeting" cannot, it is submitted, grant a right of appeal under s.51 from decisions of such a meeting which, had they been taken by a proper children's hearing, would not be appealable. Probably the only appealable decision of a business meeting is that a person is not (or is) a "relevant person".

The composition of a business meeting is not stated in the Act but r. 4(1) of the 1996 Rules provides that s.39(5), concerning the composition of children's hearings, applies to a business meeting.

Referral to, and disposal of case by, children's hearing

Referral to, and proceedings at, children's hearing

65.—(1) The Principal Reporter shall refer to the children's hearing, for consideration and determination on the merits, the case of any child in respect of whom he is satisfied that—

(a) compulsory measures of supervision are necessary, and

(b) at least one of the grounds specified in section 52(2) of this Act is established;

and he shall state such grounds in accordance with rules made under section 42(1) of this Act by virtue of subsection (2)(c) of that section.

(2) Where a referral is made in respect of a child who is subject to a child protection order made under section 57, and that order is continued under section 59(4) or 60(12)(d), of this Act, the Principal Reporter shall arrange for the children's hearing under subsection (1) above to take place on the eighth working day after the order was implemented.

(3) Where a referral is made in respect of a child who is subject to a supervision requirement, the children's hearing shall, before disposing of the referral in accordance with section 69(1)(b) or (c) of this Act, review that requirement in accordance with subsections (9) to (12) of section 73 of this Act.

(4) Subject to subsections (9) and (10) below, it shall be the duty of the chairman of the children's hearing to whom a child's case has been referred under subsection (1) above to explain to the child and the relevant person, at the opening of proceedings on the referral, the grounds stated by the Principal Reporter for the referral in order to ascertain whether these grounds are accepted in whole or in part by them.

(5) Where the chairman has given the explanation required by subsection (4) above and the child and the relevant person accept the grounds for the referral, the children's hearing shall proceed in accordance with section 69 of this Act.

(6) Where the chairman has given the explanation required by subsection (4) above and the child and the relevant person accept the grounds in part, the children's hearing may, if they consider it appropriate to do so, proceed in accordance with section 69 of this Act with respect to those grounds which are accepted.

(7) Where the chairman has given the explanation required under subsection (4) above and either or both of the child and the relevant person—

(a) do not accept the grounds for the referral; or

(b) accept the grounds in part, but the children's hearing do not consider it appropriate to proceed with the case under subsection (6) above,

the hearing shall either direct the Principal Reporter to make an application to the sheriff for a finding as to whether such grounds for the referral as are not accepted by the child and the relevant person are established or shall discharge the referral.

(8) Subject to subsection (10) below, it shall be the duty of the chairman to explain to the child and to the relevant person the purpose for which the application to the sheriff is being made and to inform the child that he is under an obligation to attend the hearing before the sheriff.

(9) Where a children's hearing are satisfied that the child—

(a) for any reason will not be capable of understanding the explanation of the grounds for the referral required under subsection (4) above; or

(b) has not understood an explanation given under that subsection,

they shall either direct the Principal Reporter to make an application to the sheriff for a finding as to whether any of the grounds of the referral are established or discharge the referral.

(10) The acceptance by the relevant person of the grounds of the referral shall not be a requirement for a children's hearing proceeding under this section to consider a case where that person is not present.

DEFINITIONS

"child": s.93(2)(b).
"child protection order": ss.57(1), 93(1).
"compulsory measures of supervision": s.93(1).
"Principal Reporter": s.93(1).
"relevant person": s.93(2)(b).
"working day": s.93(1).

GENERAL NOTE

Sections 65 to 73 substantially tidy up the provisions they replace in the 1968 Act, though the changes in the law are neither numerous nor fundamental. The rules now contained in the present section were mostly to be found in the old s.42(1), (2), (3), (7) and (8), and the changes here are almost entirely terminological. The section deals with the referral by the reporter of the child's case to a children's hearing and the procedure for establishing whether or not the grounds of referral are accepted.

Subs. (1)

The reporter is obliged under s.56 above to determine, upon receipt of information concerning a child, whether a children's hearing requires to be arranged, and the present subsection obliges her or him to refer the case to a children's hearing when satisfied that compulsory measures of supervision are necessary and that at least one of the grounds of referral exists. The second limb of that test is redundant since the question of whether compulsory measures of supervision are necessary does not arise unless one or more of the grounds of referral exists (s.51(1) above). Nevertheless, the wording of this subsection serves to emphasise that the existence of the ground alone is not sufficient to create an obligation on the reporter to refer the case to a children's hearing. That obligation arises only when, in addition to the existence of the ground, the reporter is satisfied that compulsory measures of supervision are necessary in the interests of the child. The reporter may quite validly take the view that, while a ground exists (*e.g.* an isolated incident of shoplifting, or the kidnapping and abusing of a child of caring parents by a stranger) there is no necessity for the imposition of compulsory measures of supervision: in these circumstances, the reporter must proceed in accordance with s.56(4) and (5) above. If, however, she or he is satisfied that compulsory measures of supervision are necessary, then the grounds must be stated in accordance with r. 17 of the 1996 Rules, and the case referred to a children's hearing.

Subs. (2)

The reporter is also obliged to arrange a children's hearing whenever a child has been made subject to a child protection order under s.57 which is still effective on the eighth working day after its implementation. The nature of the obligation is to act as under subs. (1) above, that is to state grounds in accordance with the rules and to refer the case to a children's hearing. One major difference between this subsection and subs. (1) above is that here there is a strict timetable to be adhered to, and the children's hearing must take place on the eighth working day after the order was implemented.

The eighth working day. It would be incompetent for a children's hearing to take place before the eighth working day, even when this is practicable (though it would be so only when there is no application made to the sheriff to recall the child protection order under s.60(7) above) and any purported decision would be of no legal effect. "Working day" is defined in s.93(1) below to exclude Saturdays and Sundays, and December 25 and 26, and January 1 and 2. It follows that the children's hearing are obliged to sit on a day anything between 10 and 16 days after the implementation of the child protection order, depending upon (i) the day of the week it was implemented, and (ii) whether or not the specified holidays interrupt the running of the eight days.

Implemented. On implementation of a child protection order, see the notes to s.59(5) above.

Subs. (3)

It often happens that the reporter feels obliged to state grounds in respect of a child who is already subject to a supervision requirement, for example because new grounds evidence a deteriorating situation or indicate that the existing measures of supervision are not, or are no longer, appropriate. If that occurred under the 1968 Act then a child could find her or himself subject to two supervision requirements, for there was no provision requiring the original supervision requirement to be reviewed when new grounds were accepted or established and that would only be done if a review were due or had been called by a person able to call for it. This subsection is designed to avoid such untidiness by providing that whenever a children's hearing is arranged to put new grounds of referral to a child who is already subject to compulsory measures of supervision, the existing supervision requirement must be reviewed at the same time.

Before disposing of the referral. The "referral" means referral both in respect of a consideration of the new ground and a review of the current supervision requirement. The review of that requirement can take place at any time before the referral is finally disposed of, and there is no requirement that the review be conducted and determined separately from a consideration of the new grounds. It will normally be best for the children's hearing to look at the child's case as a whole, reviewing the existing supervision requirement as an integral part of their consideration of the new grounds and how to respond to them. The existence of the new grounds may themselves justify the continuation or variation of an existing supervision requirement, and that outcome amounts to a disposal of the combined referral. It would be competent to deal with the review separately from a consideration of the new grounds, but this would be appropriate only when the grounds are to be sent to the sheriff for proof and the existing supervision requirement will lapse before the likely date of the hearing of the application before the sheriff. In that case, if the grounds are held established, the hearing arranged to consider and dispose of the case would appear to be obliged by this subsection to review again the current supervision requirement as part of their consideration of how to dispose of the present referral. Though this appears repetitive, it is perfectly appropriate that the final disposal takes account of the efficacy of the existing supervision requirement.

Subs. (4)

This provision replaces s.42(1) of the 1968 Act, and similarly provides that the chairman of the hearing has the duty of explaining to the child and her or his parent the grounds of referral, in order to ascertain whether these grounds are accepted or not. The wording is, however, a little different from the old s.42(1), presumably in an attempt to clarify some of the problematic issues that were identified by the case of *Sloan v. B*, 1991 S.L.T. 530.

Subject to subsections (9) and (10) below. The obligation to explain to the child does not apply where the children's hearing are satisfied that the child will not be capable of understanding the explanation (see subs. (9) below), and the obligation to explain to the relevant person will not apply where the relevant person has not attended the hearing, in breach of her or his obligation to do so under s.45(8) above (see subs. (10) below).

Explain. The duty of the chairman is not simply to read out the grounds as specified by the reporter, but to explain what these grounds mean. The implicit duty on the chairman is to check that the child and relevant person understand the nature of the grounds. Not only must the statement of facts be explained, but the statutory ground which the facts are alleged to amount to must be explained.

At the opening of the proceedings on the referral. The old s.42(1) obliged the chairman to explain the grounds "at the commencement of the children's hearing and before proceeding to the consideration of the case". The current wording probably creates the same obligation, but rather less clearly than before indicates that the whole proceedings are made up of various different parts: explanation of the grounds (required here), consideration of the case (required in s.69(1) below), and disposal of the referral (dealt with in s.69(2)–(13) and s.70 below). The proceedings still open with an explanation of the grounds and there can be no discussion of the grounds or any other consideration of the child's case until the grounds have been accepted under subs. (5) below or established under s.68(10) below.

In order to ascertain whether the grounds are accepted. The chairman must ask the child and relevant person to indicate whether they accept the grounds stated by the reporter as true or not.

Subs. (5)

The children's hearing can proceed to a consideration of the case under s.69(1) below only if the child and relevant person accept at least part of the stated grounds of referral. If the child does not understand the grounds, the hearing's options are listed in subs. (9) below; there is no provision dealing with the relevant person's lack of understanding but it seems clear that a relevant person who does not understand an explanation cannot give an acceptance of the ground.

The relevant person. Every relevant person who attends the hearing must be asked whether or not they accept the grounds of referral. The "relevant person" is defined in s.93(2)(b) to be any person who has parental responsibilities or parental rights, however acquired, and any person who ordinarily (other than by reason of employment) has charge of or control over the child. Under the 1968 Act a person who had custody or charge of or control over the child similarly had to accept the grounds of referral but, explicitly, had to be recognised by the children's hearing as having such charge or control. The present s.93(2)(b) requires that "it appears" that the person has charge of or control over the child, and in this context this must mean "it appears to the children's hearing". (In other contexts it must so appear to other persons: see notes to s.45(8) above.) For a full discussion of the definition of "relevant person" see Norrie, *Children's Hearings in Scotland* (W. Green, 1997) at pp. 11–13.

Subs. (6)

If the child and the relevant person accept the grounds in part but deny them in part, the children's hearing may proceed with the hearing in respect of the grounds that have been accepted. This might happen either when there are numerous grounds some of which are not accepted, or when the specified ground is accepted subject to alteration (*e.g.* accepting a theft but not of the amount specified, or accepting absence from school but not to the extent specified). So long as there is enough left in the accepted portion to amount to a ground of referral the hearing may proceed.

May proceed. The decision whether to proceed to a consideration of the accepted grounds under s.69, or alternatively to refer the grounds not accepted to the sheriff under subs. (7) below, is to be made by the hearing in the light of the welfare principle contained in s.16(1). It may, for example, be considered detrimental to the child to delay a consideration of her or his case; conversely there are situations in which it would be detrimental to the proper consideration of the child's case not to refer serious grounds to the sheriff.

With respect to those grounds which are accepted. If the children's hearing decide to proceed in respect of the grounds which are accepted, they cannot consider those grounds or portions thereof which have not been accepted in making their dispositive decision. Difficult questions of emphasis may arise if the hearing decide to proceed, for it is permitted to consider the whole of the child's "case", which might well include the fact that allegations have been made but are denied. The proper approach is to hold that any ground or part thereof which is denied and discharged is to be treated as not established fact. For example, a child may be referred to a hearing on the ground that he is beyond parental control and this may be accepted; in addition, there may be a number of offences specified as grounds which the child denies on the basis that while he was present he did not take part in the offences. If the hearing proceeds on the basis that the child is beyond parental control they cannot take into account the fact that offences have been committed, but they can, it is submitted, take into account the fact that the child is associating with persons who lead the child to the attention of the police.

Subs. (7)

This provision replaces the old s.42(2) of the 1968 Act. It provides that where either the child or the relevant person or both deny the grounds, or deny part thereof and the hearing consider that they cannot proceed on that basis, then the hearing have two options: they may either discharge the referral in whole, or they may direct the reporter to apply to the sheriff for a finding as to whether the grounds not accepted are made out. One of the difficulties facing children's hearings is that this decision has to be made only on the basis of the reports already presented to them. No discussion is permitted with the family in order to assist the hearing in determining which option is more appropriate, but the welfare principle in s.16, as always, governs the decision.

Either or both. Before the hearing can proceed in terms of s.69 the child and all the relevant persons must accept the grounds, and if any denies that they exist the hearing cannot proceed. On the "relevant person", see General Note to subs. (5) above.

Subs. (8)

This replaces part of the old s.42(3) of the 1968 Act, though it extends the rule contained therein which, for no good reason, was limited to offence-based cases. If the children's hearing decide to refer grounds to the sheriff for proof, either because they have been denied under subs. (7) above or because they are not understood by the child under subs. (9) below, the chairman of the hearing must explain to the child and the parent the purpose of the sheriff court hearing. It must also be explained to the child that she or he has an obligation (under s.68(4) below) to attend the hearing before the sheriff.

Subs. (9)

This replaces s.42(7) of the 1968 Act, with a change in wording, but little change in effect. Under the old law the wording suggested that the hearing had in every case to examine the child to determine her or his understanding (though this was not how the provision was normally applied in practice). The new provision reflects reality rather more. It is provided that where the children's hearing are satisfied that the child either will not be capable of understanding the explanation of the grounds or has not understood that explanation, they must either discharge the referral or direct the reporter to apply to the sheriff court for proof. That decision is, of course, governed by the welfare principle in s.16(1) above.

Children's hearing are satisfied. Though the obligation to explain the grounds of referral rests with the chairman of the children's hearing, the assessment that the child will not understand or has not understood the explanation is one to be made by the hearing as a whole, and in cases of disagreement amongst the hearing members a majority decision is sufficient. That decision is one of fact and not, therefore, one to which the welfare test in s.16(1) applies. Not being a dispositive decision, it is not appealable under s.51 above.

Will not be capable. In many cases the age of the child will make this quite obvious: a baby or toddler will clearly not understand any explanation. The wording suggests (as the 1968 Act did not) that the chairman is under no obligation to attempt an explanation in these circumstances, and this is confirmed by subs. (4) above (duty to explain) which is expressly made subject to the present subsection. It should be noted that it is not a ground in itself for relieving a child of the obligation to attend under s.45(2) above that the child will not understand the grounds of referral (though this, in addition to some other factor, may well indicate that it would be detrimental to the child's interests to attend): rather, the present provision simply means that the chairman is relieved of the obligation in subs. (4) above to attempt an explanation when the child obviously will not understand.

Has not understood. This provision can be relied upon only when an attempt has been made by the chairman to explain the grounds, but the hearing as a whole are satisfied that the attempt has failed. Whenever an application is made to the sheriff on the basis of this subsection it should be made plain which paragraph the children's hearing are relying upon to justify the application (*cf. Sloan v. B*, 1991 S.L.T. 530).

Subs. (10)

This replaces, with no substantive change, s.42(8) of the 1968 Act, though its wording is possibly not very apt. A children's hearing does not consider the case under this section, but under s.69. Nevertheless the purpose of the provision is clear. Relevant persons have a duty to attend at all stages of a children's hearing and failure to do so can be a criminal offence (see s.45(8) and (9) above). It often happens however that relevant persons do not attend and there is no power under the Act to bring them before a hearing. This subsection allows a hearing to go ahead even in the absence of relevant persons who have breached their obligation to attend, by providing that if they do not attend their acceptance of the grounds of referral specified by the reporter is not required before the hearing can proceed to a consideration of the case. It is to be noted that this subsection is limited in its terms to "the relevant person", and the requirement of the child's acceptance of the grounds is not affected by the absence of the child. If the child is not present there can be no acceptance and the case must either be discharged or referred to the sheriff as under subs. (7) above, or rescheduled to allow for the child's attendance.

Warrant to keep child where children's hearing unable to dispose of case

66.—(1) Without prejudice to any other power enjoyed by them under this Part of this Act and subject to subsection (5) below, a children's hearing—

(a) arranged to consider a child's case under this Part of this Act; and

(b) unable to dispose of the case,

may, if they are satisfied that one of the conditions mentioned in subsection (2) below is met, grant a warrant under this subsection.

(2) The conditions referred to in subsection (1) above are—

(a) that there is reason to believe that the child may—

(i) not attend at any hearing of his case; or

(ii) fail to comply with a requirement under section 69(3) of this Act; or

(b) that it is necessary that the child should be kept in a place of safety in order to safeguard or promote his welfare.

(3) A warrant under subsection (1) above may require any person named in the warrant—

(a) to find and to keep or, as the case may be, to keep the child in a place of safety for a period not exceeding twenty-two days after the warrant is granted;

(b) to bring the child before a children's hearing at such times as may be specified in the warrant.

(4) A warrant under subsection (1) above may contain such conditions as appear to the children's hearing to be necessary or expedient, and without prejudice to that generality may—

(a) subject to section 90 of this Act, require the child to submit to any medical or other examination or treatment; and

(b) regulate the contact with the child of any specified person or class of persons.

(5) Subject to subsection (8) below, at any time prior to its expiry, a warrant granted under this section may, on an application to the children's hearing, on cause shown by the Principal Reporter, be continued in force, whether with or without variation of any condition imposed by virtue of subsection (4) above, by the children's hearing for such further period, not exceeding twenty-two days, as appears to them to be necessary.

(6) Where a children's hearing are satisfied that either of the criteria specified in section 70(10) of this Act are satisfied, they may order that, pending the disposal of his case, the child shall be liable to be placed and kept in secure accommodation within a residential establishment at such times as the person in charge of that establishment, with the agreement of the chief social work officer of the relevant local authority, considers necessary.

(7) Where a children's hearing grant a warrant under subsection (1) above or continue such a warrant under subsection (5) above, they may order that the place of safety at which the child is to be kept shall not be disclosed to any person or class of persons specified in the order.

(8) A child shall not be kept in a place of safety or secure accommodation by virtue of this section for a period exceeding sixty-six days from the day when he was first taken to a place of safety under a warrant granted under subsection (1) above.

DEFINITIONS
"chief social work officer": s.93(1).
"child": s.93(2)(b).
"children's hearing": s.93(1).
"place of safety": s.93(1).
"Principal Reporter": s.93(1).
"relevant local authority": s.93(1).
"residential establishment": s.93(1).
"secure accommodation": s.93(1).

GENERAL NOTE
A child whose case has been referred to a children's hearing has an obligation to attend that hearing (s.45(1) above), and if it appears that the child might not attend (or has failed to attend) a warrant can be issued under s.45(4) (or s.45(5)) to secure her or his attendance. This section allows a warrant to be granted when a children's hearing has been held with the child in attendance but for some other reason no disposal can be made. Such a warrant can be granted either to ensure the attendance of the child at a hearing or to ensure the child's attendance at some investigative clinic or hospital, or to ensure the child's safety in the meantime. The section replaces the provisions in s.40(7)–(8B) of the 1968 Act, and it contains some important tightening and tidying of the old rules. The makeup of this section is confusing and appears to overlap with certain other provisions, and for that reason must be read strictly and in the light of these other provisions. Subsection (1) sets out the circumstances in which the warrant may be granted, subs. (2) lays down the conditions for its granting, subs. (3) describes its effect, subs. (5) permits it to be continued, and subs. (8) limits the total length of time the child can be kept in a place of safety under a warrant granted under this section to 66 days.

Subs. (1)

Where a children's hearing has been arranged but that hearing are unable to dispose of the case, they may grant a warrant, if the conditions specified in subs. (2) below are met, and that warrant will be authority to keep the child in a place of safety and to bring the child to a children's hearing. The hearing may (one assumes – *cf.* s.45(5) where the point is made clear) grant such warrant either *ex proprio motu* or on the motion of the reporter.

Without prejudice to any other power. The existence of a power to grant a warrant under this section does not detract from any power to grant a warrant under any other section in Pt II. Indeed, for reasons which will be explained in the next paragraph, wherever there seems to be a choice of which section to grant a warrant under, the power in this section must give way to the power in that other section.

Unable to dispose of the case. A case is disposed of when the children's hearing makes a dispositive decision, that is to say a decision to impose a supervision requirement or to discharge the referral or, on review, to continue or vary or terminate an existing supervision requirement. If they are unable to make such a decision then they are "unable to dispose of the case" and this section appears to be activated. This can occur when grounds of referral are denied and the hearing decide to direct the reporter to make an application to the sheriff (rather than to discharge the referral) or when the grounds are accepted or established or the case is being reviewed and after a consideration of the case the children's hearing feel that they do not have enough information to make an informed decision. Again, a children's hearing may consider themselves unable to dispose of a case because the child or relevant person breaches her or his obligation to attend and the hearing consider that attendance necessary for a proper consideration of the case. In all these circumstances, the hearing will be unable to dispose of the case and a warrant under this section might appear to be available. However, if the children's hearing are unable to dispose of the case because the child has failed to attend the hearing, a warrant, which can last a maximum of seven days, can be granted under s.45(5) above and it would, it is submitted, be incompetent to grant a warrant under the present provision (which could last initially for 22 days) due to the child's non-attendance. Also, if the children's hearing are unable to dispose of the case because they feel that they do not have enough information and they continue the case under s.69(2) below, a warrant, which can last for a maximum of 22 days, can be granted under s.69(7) below and it would similarly, it is submitted, be incompetent to grant a warrant under the present provision due to the hearing being continued for further investigation. It follows that a warrant under the present section is available not in all cases in which a children's hearing are unable to dispose of the case, but only when they are unable to do so because the grounds have been denied and they direct the reporter to make an application to the sheriff, or because the relevant person does not attend and the hearing consider that they cannot properly consider the case without the relevant person's attendance.

May ... grant a warrant. The hearing is not obliged to grant a warrant under this section even when the conditions for its granting, set out in subs. (2) below, have been satisfied. The decision is one to which all three overarching principles in s.16 apply: the children's hearing must therefore regard the welfare of the child as their paramount consideration (s.16(1) above), they must take appropriate account of the child's views (s.16(2) and s.16(4)(a)(ii) above and 1996 Rules, r. 26), and they must apply the minimum intervention principle (s.16(3) and s.16(4)(a)(ii) above). This last amounts to a presumption that no warrant should be granted, with the result that before granting it the hearing must be persuaded that the warrant is necessary to ensure the child's attendance at the hearing, or at the clinic, hospital or other establishment, or to ensure the child's safety in the meantime.

Subs. (2)

Replacing without substantive change s.40(7) of the 1968 Act, this subsection sets out the conditions, one or other of which must be satisfied before a warrant under subs. (1) above can be granted. These are (a) that the hearing are satisfied that there is reason to believe the child will not attend the next hearing or will fail to comply with a requirement that she or he attend a clinic, hospital, or other establishment for investigation under s.69(3) below, or (b) that it is necessary to safeguard and promote the child's welfare that she or he be kept in a place of safety. A history of non-attendance at children's hearings or at clinics *etc.* for investigation, or a threat by a relevant person to prevent the child attending at the hearing will usually be sufficient to satisfy (a); some other factor, such as the child's continued dangerous behaviour, or a continued threat to the child's wellbeing, will be necessary to satisfy (b).

Subs. (3)

The warrant granted under subs. (1) above may require a person to do one or other or both of the mentioned acts. The time specified in the warrant for the bringing of the child to a children's hearing may be after the 22 days in which she or he was kept in a place of safety, though in practical terms the hearing will usually be arranged during the child's residence in a place of safety.

Twenty-two days after the warrant is granted. If the warrant is granted on Wednesday June 1, the period will end on Thursday June 22. It is to be noted that the 22 days commence when the warrant is granted and not when the child is found or first kept in a place of safety. So if a child is not found until the 21st day after the warrant is granted, she or he can be kept only for one further day (during which time, of course, the warrant may be continued under subs. (5) below).

Subs. (4)

The warrant can contain such conditions as the children's hearing think necessary or expedient. They may require the child to submit to any medical or other examination or treatment, though that examination or treatment cannot be carried out if a child who has capacity to do so under s.2(4) of the Age of Legal Capacity (Scotland) Act 1991 refuses to submit (see s.90 below); and they may regulate the contact that the child is to have with any other person while the child is being kept in the place of safety.

Subs. (5)

A warrant granted by a children's hearing under subs. (1) above allows a child to be kept in a place of safety for a maximum period of 22 days. The present subsection allows that warrant to be continued by the children's hearing, with or without variation, for a further period of 22 days.

Subject to subsection (8) below. Subsection (8) provides that a child can be kept (under this section) for no longer than 66 days, with the result that the children's hearing can continue a warrant granted under this section only twice (or such number of times as does not exceed the limit).

At any time prior to its expiry. A warrant can be continued on any date before the expiry of the original 22 days, and the continuation will last for a maximum of 22 days from the date of continuation.

On cause shown. The reporter has the onus of showing why an application to continue the warrant should be granted by the hearing. This will be satisfied by showing that one of the conditions for its granting (in subs. (2) above) still exists and that it is in the interests of the child to remain in a place of safety; in addition an explanation as to why the case has not advanced ought to be given by the reporter. All three overarching principles in s.16 apply to decisions to continue warrants under this subsection. The views of the child must also be obtained: r. 26 of the 1996 Rules.

Such further period ... as appears to them to be necessary. While the warrant will normally permit the keeping of a child for up to 22 days, there is no reason why the hearing should not specify a shorter period, if this is appropriate in the child's interests.

Subs. (6)

In cases in which a children's hearing are satisfied that the conditions for authorising the child to be kept in secure accommodation (listed in s.70(10) below) are satisfied, the hearing may authorise the child to be kept there. As under s.70(9), the children's hearing do not order that the child be kept in secure accommodation, rather they merely authorise that this can be done if the chief social worker of the relevant local authority considers it necessary. The authorisation under this subsection cannot stand alone and it must be given in connection with a warrant under subs. (1) above: this is implicit from the wording of subs. (8) below which provides that a child may not be kept in a place of safety or in secure accommodation for more than 66 days after being taken to a place of safety under a warrant granted under subs. (1) above.

Subs. (7)

The children's hearing can order that the child's whereabouts not be disclosed to any named person or class of person. This is an important new power, which is also to be found in s.69(10), s.70(6) and s.73(11), and is designed as a protective measure. A children's hearing ought not to make an order under this subsection (or those other subsections) unless they are satisfied that there is a real need for it, that is to say that there is a realistic threat to the child's wellbeing from the named person or class of person.

Subs. (8)

This subsection does not do what it appears, at first sight, to do. It does not provide that a child must be released from a place of safety or secure accommodation having been kept there for a period of 66 days. Rather, all it does is to limit the power of the children's hearing to keep a child in a place of safety to 66 days. The child may be kept there for longer than 66 days if a sheriff at the end of the 66 days grants a warrant under s.67 below: and no limit is expressed on the number of times a warrant can be granted under that section.

Warrant for further detention of child

67.—(1) Where a child is being kept in a place of safety by virtue of a warrant granted under section 66 of this Act or under this subsection, the Principal Reporter at any time prior to the expiry of that warrant may apply to the sheriff for a warrant to keep the child in that place after the warrant granted under the said section 66 or, as the case may be, this subsection has expired.

(2) A warrant under subsection (1) above shall only be granted on cause shown and—

(a) shall specify the date on which it will expire; and

(b) may contain any such requirement or condition as may be contained in a warrant granted under the said section 66.

(3) Where the sheriff grants a warrant under subsection (1) above, he may also make an order under this subsection in such terms as are mentioned in subsection (6) or (7) of the said section 66; and any order under this subsection shall cease to have effect when the warrant expires.

(4) An application under subsection (1) above may be made at the same time as, or during the hearing of, an application which the Principal Reporter has been directed by a children's hearing to make under section 65(7) or (9) of this Act.

DEFINITIONS
"child": s.93(2)(b).
"children's hearing": s.93(1).
"place of safety": s.93(1).
"Principal Reporter": s.93(1).

GENERAL NOTE
This is another provision that was added into the Act at a very late stage (the Report stage in the House of Lords on July 5, 1995: see *Hansard*, H.L. Vol. 565, col. 1206), and like others in that category would have greatly benefited (as very many other provisions did) from further consideration before enactment.

Under the 1968 Act, warrants issued by a children's hearing under s.40(7) could last for 21 days and could be renewed under s.40(8) *once* by the children's hearing for a further 21 days, after which a sheriff could issue a warrant on similar terms under s.40(8A) for a further 21 days, after which the sheriff could renew his warrant *once* under s.40(8B) for a further 21 days: the result was that a child could never be kept in a place of safety under these various provisions for any longer than 84 days. These provisions have been somewhat modified by this and the immediately preceding section. Under s.66 above, a children's hearing can grant a warrant and continue it for such periods as do not exceed 66 days; under this section the sheriff can, on the expiry of the hearing's warrant, grant a warrant whose length we are not told and he can grant a further, unspecified, number of warrants thereafter.

Subs. (1)
If a child has been kept in a place of safety under a warrant granted under s.66 above (that is to say granted when the children's hearing have been unable to dispose of the case because they have directed the reporter to make an application for proof of a ground of referral to the sheriff) and that warrant is about to expire, the reporter can apply to the sheriff for a warrant under this section to keep the child where she or he is after the warrant granted by the children's hearing has expired.

At any time prior to the expiry of that warrant. An application to the sheriff under this section can be made at any time before the warrant granted by the children's hearing has expired, and this will include a time prior to any continuation of a warrant granted by the children's hearing. In other words, the reporter may, a few days after the initial granting of a warrant by a children's hearing under s.66(1) above, apply to the sheriff for a warrant, without again applying to the children's hearing for a continuation of their warrant under s.66(5) above. He must, however, show cause to the sheriff, and there will normally be good cause for bypassing the children's hearing in this manner only when subs. (4) below applies.

By virtue of a warrant granted … under this subsection. A warrant granted under this subsection will expire when the sheriff says it will expire, and these words allow the reporter to apply to the sheriff for another warrant under this subsection whenever a previous warrant granted under this subsection is about to expire. There is a noticeable lack of any provision, such as was contained in s.40(8B) of the 1968 Act, that the sheriff can renew the warrant (or grant another warrant) "on one occasion only", and it would appear from that omission that the sheriff can grant as many warrants as he thinks fit. Reference should, however, be made to s.16(1) above, under which the child's welfare must be the sheriff's paramount consideration—it will seldom be in the child's interests to be kept in a place of safety, waiting to be brought to a children's hearing, for even as long as 66 days. In addition, the other two overarching principles in s.16 also apply to the sheriff's decision whether to grant a warrant under this subsection.

Subs. (2)

On cause shown. The reporter must show to the sheriff cause why a warrant ought to be granted by the sheriff under this section. Though it does not say so, it is submitted that an essential part of that cause must be the continued satisfaction of the conditions listed in s.66(2) for the granting of a warrant under s.66(1) above, for it is only after a warrant granted under that provision has ceased to have effect that this section comes into operation. Because the sheriff is obliged to regard the child's welfare as his paramount consideration (see General Note to subs. (1) above) it must be shown to his satisfaction that it is less detrimental to the child to be kept waiting for this length of time than to be released home. In addition, the reporter is probably also obliged to explain to the sheriff why the case has not advanced sufficiently after 66 days to allow the child to be brought before a children's hearing to consider her or his case.

Shall specify the date on which it will expire. These words appear to give the sheriff an unlimited discretion in specifying how long the warrant he grants under subs. (1) above will last, though because he must specify a date he cannot let it last indefinitely. There is no provision, as there is in s.66(3) above, that the warrant shall authorise the keeping of a child in a place of safety "for a period not exceeding 22 days after the warrant is granted". As such, this provision is unique in the Act, for every other provision in which either a children's hearing or a court can grant a warrant or make an order to detain a child is expressly made subject to strict and very clearly defined time-limits.

May contain any such requirement or condition. Section 66(4) allows a warrant to contain such conditions as appears to be necessary or expedient, and in particular may require the child to submit to medical or other examination or treatment (see notes to s.66(4) above) and may regulate contact between the child and any other person. The sheriff must regard the child's welfare as his paramount consideration when deciding whether to make any such requirement or condition (s.16(1)), he must have regard to any views expressed by the child (s.16(2)), and he must not make any such requirement or condition unless persuaded that it is better for him to do so than not to do so (s.16(3)).

Subs. (3)

If a warrant is granted under this section the sheriff is able to order that the child be liable to be kept in secure accommodation, or that the address of the child be kept secret from any specified person or specified class of person (or, presumably, both). Such orders cease to have effect when the warrant the sheriff grants ceases to have effect.

Subs. (4)

The usual case in which a warrant will be granted by a children's hearing under s.66 above is when they have directed the reporter to apply to the sheriff for proof of a ground of referral. Once that application has been heard by the sheriff the reporter will arrange a children's hearing to consider the child's case, but it might sometimes remain necessary to keep the child in a place of safety after the sheriff's decision until the hearing sits. If that is so, the reporter can apply to the sheriff for a warrant under this section in the same proceedings as those in which the ground of referral is sought to be proved. This is the situation (referred to in the General Note to subs. (1) above) in which it might be appropriate for the reporter to bypass the children's hearing and seek a warrant from a sheriff even before the power of the children's hearing under s.66 above to grant a warrant has been exhausted. A reporter can apply to the sheriff for a warrant under this provision only when the child is currently in a place of safety (for otherwise subs. (1) above does not apply), and it follows that a child who has been at home until the sheriff court hearing cannot be taken to a place of safety thereafter under this provision (the appropriate provision to deal with that situation is s.68(10)(b) below).

Application to sheriff to establish grounds of referral

68.—(1) This section applies to applications under subsections (7) and (9) of section 65 of this Act and a reference in this section (except in subsection (8)) to "an application" is a reference to an application under either of those subsections.

(2) An application shall be heard by the sheriff within twenty-eight days of its being lodged.

(3) Where one of the grounds for the referral to which an application relates is the condition referred to in section 52(2)(i)—

    (a) the application shall be made to the sheriff who would have jurisdiction if the child were being prosecuted for that offence; and

    (b) in hearing the application in relation to that ground, the standard of proof required in criminal proceedings shall apply.

(4) A child shall—

    (a) have the right to attend the hearing of an application; and

    (b) subject to subsection (5) below, be under an obligation to attend such hearing;

and without prejudice to the right of each of them to be legally represented, the child and the relevant person may be represented by a person other than a legally qualified person at any diet fixed by the sheriff for the hearing of the application.

(5) Without prejudice to subsection (4)(a) above, the sheriff may dispense with the obligation imposed by subsection (4)(b) above where he is satisfied—

    (a) in an application in which the ground of referral to be established is a condition mentioned in section 52(2)(d), (e), (f) or (g) of this Act, that the obligation to attend of the child is not necessary for the just hearing of that application; and

    (b) in any application, that it would be detrimental to the interests of the child for him to be present at the hearing of the application.

(6) Where the child fails to attend the hearing of an application at which his attendance has not been dispensed with under subsection (5) above, the sheriff may grant an order to find and keep the child; and any order under this subsection shall be authority for bringing the child before the sheriff and, subject to subsection (7) below, for keeping him in a place of safety until the sheriff can hear the application.

(7) The child shall not be kept in a place of safety by virtue of subsection (6) above after whichever is the earlier of—

    (a) the expiry of fourteen days beginning with the day on which the child is found; or

    (b) the disposal of the application by the sheriff.

(8) Where in the course of the hearing of an application—

    (a) under section 65(7) of this Act, the child and the relevant person accept any of the grounds for referral to which the application relates, the sheriff shall; or

    (b) under section 65(9) of this Act, the relevant person accepts any of the grounds for referral to which the application relates, the sheriff may, if it appears to him reasonable to do so,

dispense with the hearing of evidence relating to that ground and deem the ground to be established for the purposes of the application, unless he is satisfied that, in all the circumstances of the case, the evidence should be heard.

(9) Where a sheriff decides that none of the grounds for referral in respect of which an application has been made are established, he shall dismiss the application, discharge the referral to the children's hearing in respect of

those grounds and recall, discharge or cancel any order, warrant, or direction under this Chapter of this Act which relates to the child in respect of those grounds.

(10) Where the sheriff, after the hearing of any evidence or on acceptance in accordance with subsection (8) above, finds that any of the grounds for the referral to which the application relates is, or should be deemed to be, established—

    (a) he shall remit the case to the Principal Reporter to make arrangements for a children's hearing to consider and determine the case; and

    (b) he may if he is satisfied that—

        (i) keeping the child in a place of safety is necessary in the child's best interests; or

        (ii) there is reason to believe that the child will run away before the children's hearing sit to consider the case,

        issue an order requiring, subject to subsection (12) below, that the child be kept in a place of safety until the children's hearing so sit.

(11) An order issued under subsection (10) above may, if the sheriff is satisfied that either of the criteria mentioned in section 70(10) of this Act is fulfilled, provide that the child shall be liable to be placed and kept in secure accommodation within a residential establishment at such times as the person in charge of the establishment, with the agreement of the chief social work officer of the relevant local authority, considers necessary.

(12) A child shall not be kept in a place of safety by virtue of subsection (10)(b) above after whichever is the earlier of the following—

    (a) the expiry of three days beginning with the day on which he is first so kept; or

    (b) the consideration of his case by the children's hearing arranged under subsection (10)(a) above.

DEFINITIONS

    "chief social work officer": s.93(1).
    "child": s.93(2)(b).
    "children's hearing": s.93(1).
    "place of safety": s.93(1).
    "Principal Reporter": s.93(1).
    "relevant person": s.93(2)(b).

GENERAL NOTE

This section replaces s.42(3)–(6A) of the 1968 Act, with amendments in format but little substantive change. It deals with the procedure for applying to the sheriff for proof of grounds of referral, and with the sheriff's powers in dealing with such applications. See also A.S. 1997, rr. 3.44–3.52.

Subs. (1)

The section deals with applications made by the reporter at the direction of the children's hearing because the grounds of referral explained to the child and parent have not been accepted (s.65(7) above) by one or both, or will not be or have not been understood by the child (s.65(9) above) and the hearing have not considered it appropriate to discharge the referral.

Subs. (2)

The rules provide (A.S. 1997, r. 3.45(1)) that the reporter must lodge an application with the sheriff clerk within seven days of being directed to do so by the children's hearing, and, once lodged, this subsection lays down the time-limit for the hearing of the application by the sheriff. The Act does not specify what happens if the application is not heard within the 28 days, though it is understood that both the application and the referral to the children's hearing will fall in that eventuality.

Shall be heard. All that is required is that the hearing before the sheriff be commenced within 28 days rather than commenced and completed.

By the sheriff. The application will be heard by the sheriff in chambers: s.93(5) below.

Subs. (3)

Cases in which the ground of referral is that the child has committed a criminal offence are treated rather differently in a number of respects from all other cases (see General Note to s.52(2) above). This subsection provides a special jurisdictional rule for such cases, to the effect that the sheriff must hear the case who would have jurisdiction were the child being prosecuted for the offence. In addition, it is provided here that the standard of proof required is proof beyond reasonable doubt (rather than, as with all other grounds, the balance of probabilities). This is the only ground in which this standard applies, notwithstanding that other grounds may involve establishment of the commission of a criminal offence (*McGregor v. D*, 1977 S.L.T. 182; *Harris v. F*, 1991 S.L.T. 242). The reporter may not, however, avoid the higher standard of proof demanded when the child has committed an offence by seeking to show that such commission amounts to another ground of referral: *Constanda v. M.*, 1997 S.L.T. 1396.

Subs. (4)
   A child has both the right and the obligation to attend the hearing before the sheriff, and if that obligation is breached an order may be granted under subs. (6) below for her or his finding and keeping in a place of safety. Both the child and the relevant person can be legally represented, and they may be represented by a person other than a legally qualified person: this gives them an equal right to the reporter, who may have a right of audience even when not legally qualified (see s.40(4) above). Since this section only applies to applications under s.65(7) or s.65(9) (see subs. (1) above) it follows that in applications to review the evidence under s.85 below, the child has neither right nor obligation to attend at the rehearing under that section.

Subs. (5)
   Reflecting the power of the children's hearing to relieve the child of the obligation to attend the hearing under s.45(2) above, this subsection permits the sheriff to relieve the child of the obligation to attend the hearing of the application by the reporter to establish grounds of referral. The notes to s.45(2) should be referred to. But the rules are not quite the same. Para. (a) here specifies the grounds of referral in which it applies, while s.45(2)(a) refers to cases concerning scheduled offences: this makes no difference since the specified grounds all concern scheduled offences. There is, however, a significant difference in that s.45(2) conjoins paras. (a) and (b) with the word "or", while the present provision conjoins the paras. with the word "and". It follows that, in the sheriff court, the child can be relieved of the obligation to attend the hearing of a case involving a scheduled offence only on satisfaction of both paragraphs rather than, as at the children's hearing, on satisfaction of one or the other.
   It is also provided in the sheriff court rules (A.S. 1997, r. 3.47), that the sheriff may exclude the child from any stage of the s.68 proceedings where the nature of the case or of any evidence to be given is such that the sheriff is satisfied that it is in the interests of the child that she or he should not be present; the sheriff may also exclude any person when any child is giving evidence and such exclusion is in the interests of the child and either it is necessary in order to obtain the evidence, or the presence of the person is causing or is likely to cause significant distress to the child.

Subss. (6) and (7)
   If the child breaches her or his obligation to attend the sheriff court hearing, the sheriff may grant an order to find the child and keep her or him in a place of safety until the sheriff can hear the application. The decision to grant such an order is one to which the welfare principle in s.16(1) applies. A child kept in a place of safety under such an order must be released from that place on the earlier of either the expiry of 14 days after being taken there or the disposal of the application by the sheriff. There is no provision for the renewal of this order. This ensures that the hearing of the evidence takes place as soon after the child has been found as possible.
   Expiry of 14 days beginning with the day on which the child is found. The day on which the child is found is the first day, and she or he must be released before the end of the fourteenth day.

Subs. (8)
   This provision replaces s.42(6A) of the 1968 Act. It provides that the sheriff has the power to dispense with the hearing of evidence as to whether the ground is established and, instead of making a finding to that effect from the evidence, he is entitled to deem the ground to be established. Altering the previous law, the sheriff is *obliged* to dispense with hearing evidence where the child and the relevant person, who at the children's hearing denied the grounds of referral, now accept them; and, reflecting the previous law, the sheriff *may* dispense with hearing evidence if the child could not, or did not, understand the explanation of the ground and the relevant person accepts the grounds. In either case he may hear evidence if in all the circumstances of the case he is satisfied that evidence should be heard.
   In the course of the hearing. The sheriff can make his determination to dispense with evidence at any time, whether before any evidence is led or (in cases to which para. (b) applies) while

evidence is being led. A relevant person who denied grounds before the hearing may, for example, accept the grounds when it is explained by the sheriff what it is that is being accepted or when she or he realises that the evidence is incontrovertible.

If it appears to him reasonable to do so. If the child could not, or did not, understand the grounds of referral it may be reasonable to dispense with evidence when all the parties who can accept are accepting and there is no-one denying or disputing the grounds. It might not be reasonable if for some reason it is not in the interests of the child that the evidence remains untested. The decision whether to dispense with evidence or to hear it is a decision governed by the welfare principle in s.16(1).

Subs. (9)

Replacing s.42(5) of the 1968 Act, this subsection provides that when the sheriff finds that none of the grounds is established he must discharge the referral and release the child from any order, warrant or direction she or he is subject to which relates to those grounds. The sheriff has no option in this case and cannot, for example, find that other grounds than those relating to the application have been established. If the evidence suggests the existence of other grounds the reporter may state these new grounds and arrange a children's hearing under s.65(1) above.

Subs. (10)

Where the sheriff has found the grounds, or any of them, established, or has deemed them to be established under the terms of subs. (8) above, he is obliged to remit the case back to the reporter for the arranging of a children's hearing to consider the child's case under s.66 above. In addition, if he is satisfied that the child's best interests require that she or he be kept in a place of safety or that there is reason to believe that the child will run away before the sitting of the children's hearing, the sheriff may issue an order requiring that the child be kept in a place of safety.

Subs. (11)

If the conditions for keeping the child in secure accommodation (listed in s.70(10) below) are satisfied, the sheriff can attach to an order granted under subs. (10) above an authorisation to keep the child in such accommodation. This does not require that the child be kept there, but authorises it if, in addition, the chief social work officer considers it necessary.

Subs. (12)

An order keeping the child in a place of safety issued by the sheriff, and any authorisation to keep the child in secure accommodation, loses effect at the earlier of (a) the expiry of three days or (b) the consideration of the child's case by the children's hearing.

The expiry of three days. It is to be noted that, in distinction from the provisions in the Act dealing with child protection orders, the time is expressed not in "working days" but simply in days. The first day is the day the child is first kept under the order granted in terms of subs. (10) (which will usually be the day that the order is made); the order ceases to have effect on the expiry of the third day. So for example when a child is first kept under this provision on a Monday the order ceases to have effect at the expiry of the immediately following Wednesday. If a child is first kept under this provision on a Friday the order ceases to have effect at the expiry of the immediately following Sunday.

The consideration of his case. The order expires when the children's hearing first consider the case under s.69 below, and not when the hearing disposes of the case. If the children's hearing decide to continue the hearing the order under this provision will have lapsed, and if the hearing decide that the child still requires to be kept in a place of safety they may grant a warrant to this effect under s.69(7) above.

Continuation or disposal of referral by children's hearing

69.—(1) Where the grounds of referral of the child's case stated by the Principal Reporter are accepted or are established in accordance with section 68 or section 85 of this Act, the children's hearing shall consider those grounds, any report obtained under section 56(7) of this Act and any other relevant information available to them and shall—

(a) continue the case to a subsequent hearing in accordance with subsection (2) below;

(b) discharge the referral of the case in accordance with subsection (12) below; or

(c) make a supervision requirement under section 70 of this Act.

(2) The children's hearing may continue the case to a subsequent hearing

under this subsection where they are satisfied that, in order to complete their consideration of the case, it is necessary to have a further investigation of the case.

(3) Where a children's hearing continue the case under subsection (2) above, they may, for the purposes of the investigation mentioned by that subsection, require the child to attend, or reside at, any clinic, hospital or other establishment during a period not exceeding twenty-two days.

(4) Where a child fails to fulfil a requirement made under subsection (3) above, the children's hearing may, either on an application by the Principal Reporter or of their own motion, grant a warrant under this subsection.

(5) A warrant under subsection (4) above shall be authority—
(a) to find the child;
(b) to remove the child to a place of safety and keep him there; and
(c) where the place of safety is not the clinic, hospital or other establishment referred to in the requirement made under subsection (3) above, to take the child from the place of safety to such clinic, hospital or other establishment for the purposes of the investigation mentioned in subsection (2) above.

(6) A warrant under subsection (4) above shall be granted for such period as appears to the children's hearing to be appropriate, provided that no warrant shall permit the keeping of a child in a place of safety after whichever is the earlier of—
(a) the expiry of twenty-two days after the warrant is granted; or
(b) the day on which the subsequent hearing of the child's case by a children's hearing begins.

(7) Where a child's case has been continued under subsection (2) above and the children's hearing are satisfied that
(a) keeping the child in a place of safety is necessary in the interests of safeguarding or promoting the welfare of the child; or
(b) there is reason to believe that the child may not attend the subsequent hearing of his case,
they may grant a warrant requiring that the child be taken to and kept in a place of safety.

(8) A warrant under subsection (7) above shall cease to have effect on whichever is the earlier of
(a) the expiry of twenty-two days after the warrant is granted; or
(b) the day on which the subsequent hearing of the child's case by a children's hearing begins.

(9) A warrant under subsection (4) or (7) above may contain such conditions as appear to the children's hearing to be necessary or expedient, and without prejudice to that generality may—
(a) subject to section 90 of this Act, require the child to submit to any medical or other examination or treatment;
(b) regulate the contact with the child of any specified person or class of persons.

(10) Where a child is to be kept at a place of safety under a warrant granted under this section or is to attend, or reside at, any place in accordance with a requirement made under subsection (3) above, the children's hearing may order that such place shall not be disclosed to any person or class of persons specified in the order.

(11) Where a child is to reside in a residential establishment by virtue of a requirement made or warrant granted under this section, the children's hearing may, if satisfied that either of the criteria mentioned in section 70(10) of this Act is fulfilled, order that while the requirement or warrant remains in effect he shall be liable to be placed in secure accommodation within that establishment at such times as the person in charge of the establishment, with the agreement of the chief social work officer of the relevant local authority, considers necessary.

(12) Where a children's hearing decide not to make a supervision requirement under section 70 of this Act they shall discharge the referral.

(13) On the discharge of the referral of the child's case any order, direction, or warrant under Chapter 2, or this Chapter, of this Act in respect of the child's case shall cease to have effect.

DEFINITIONS
"chief social work officer": s.93(1).
"child": s.93(2)(b).
"children's hearing": s.93(1).
"place of safety": s.93(1).
"Principal Reporter": s.93(1).
"supervision requirement": s.93(1).

GENERAL NOTE
This section deals with matters previously dealt with in s.43 of the 1968 Act. It obliges the children's hearing to consider the case of the child once the grounds of referral have been accepted or established, sets out the options available to the hearing, and governs the procedures to be adopted when the option either of continuing the case or of discharging the referral is chosen.

Subs. (1)
This subsection replaces s.43(1) of the 1968 Act and obliges the children's hearing to consider the child's case once the grounds have been accepted under s.65(5) above, established under s.68(10) above, or established on a review of the evidence under s.85 below. The process of consideration must take into account the grounds of referral, any report and any other relevant information available to the hearing. The test of relevancy of the hearing's consideration is whether the matter is relevant to the question of what course should be taken in the child's best interests and the hearing are not limited to a narrow consideration of the grounds alone (*O v. Rae*, 1993 S.L.T. 570, *per* Lord President Hope at p. 574). The grounds upon which the child has been referred to the hearing are central to the consideration of the case and are always relevant, but there may well be many other additional factors relevant to a determination of what, if any, measures of supervision are in the child's best interests. A child may competently be subject to compulsory measures of supervision which would not be justified simply because of the existence of a ground of referral when there are other significant concerns that do justify them. It is the strength of the system that the existence of a ground of referral merely raises the question of whether compulsory measures of supervision are necessary (s.52(1) above) but does not determine their nature; it is both questions which must be considered by the children's hearing.

Having given consideration to the circumstances of the child's case, the children's hearing must then decide which of the three listed options most appropriately meet the child's needs. These options are as follows. First, the hearing may decide under subs. (2) below to continue the case for further investigation on the basis that they do not have enough information to come to a proper decision. Having chosen this option the hearing can make a requirement under subs. (3) below and enforce it by means of a warrant granted under subs. (4) below; and they can also grant a warrant to ensure the child's safety until the next hearing under subs. (7) below. Secondly, the hearing may decide to discharge the referral under subs. (12) below, in which case any order, direction or warrant issued in respect of the child shall cease to have effect (subs. (13) below). Thirdly the hearing may impose a supervision requirement on the child, in accordance with s.70, considered in detail below.

The decision of which option to choose is one to which all three of the overarching principles in s.16 apply: the children's hearing must regard the child's welfare throughout her or his childhood as paramount, must have regard so far as practicable to the views (if she or he wishes to express them) of the child concerned, and must make no order imposing a supervision requirement or continuing the case or granting a warrant under this section unless they consider that it would be better for the child to do so than to make no order or requirement at all. Decisions are, as always, made on a majority basis, and no decision is made unless it attracts the support of at least two members of the hearing. It is possible that each member of the hearing will decide to do one of the three possibilities listed, in which case no decision has been made. Unless one of the hearing members then wishes to reconsider her or his decision (which is competent if the chairman so permits), the only option is to continue the hearing: there is no provision for the hearing failing to come to a decision and such failure due to the disagreement amounts, it is submitted, to an agreement that the hearing must be continued.

Subs. (2)

This provision, repeated from s.43(3) of the 1968 Act, allows the hearing to continue the case to a subsequent hearing if further investigation is necessary. If, but only if, this option is chosen, subss (3)–(11) below may come into play.

In order to complete their consideration of the case. The hearing's consideration of the case is completed only when they are in a position to make a decision as to what course of action is in the best interests of the child. It follows that a continuation is the proper course when the children's hearing are not in possession of sufficient information, and cannot obtain that information in the course of the current hearing, to make a dispositive decision.

Subs. (3)

Replacing s.43(4) of the 1968 Act, a children's hearing who continue a case under subs. (2) above may require the child to reside in or attend a clinic, hospital or other establishment during a period of not more than 22 days. As explained under subs. (2) above, continuation will be appropriate when further information is required and this subsection can be used only for the gathering of this information. A child may, for example, be required to reside in an assessment centre, or attend an educational psychologist, or even undergo medical examination during the period of continuation. If a requirement is made under this subsection, it may be enforced by means of a warrant granted under subs. (4) below.

During a period not exceeding 22 days. The 22 days start running on the day the investigation commences, which will usually be the day of the hearing which continues the case. If, however, a place at, say, an assessment centre is not available immediately, the 22 days will start running the day the child first attends or resides there.

Subs. (4)

Replacing s.43(5) of the 1968 Act, if a child does not attend or reside for investigation as required under subs. (3) above, a warrant may be granted. The decision is that of the children's hearing, which may make the decision to grant a warrant with or without an application to that effect by the reporter. The warrant under this subsection can, however, only be granted retrospectively, that is after the child has failed to fulfil the requirement, and no warrant can be granted on the basis that the child is likely to fail to fulfil the requirement. The decision is governed by the three overarching principles: s.16 above and r. 26 of the 1996 Rules.

Subs. (5)

This subsection indicates what the warrant granted under subs. (4) above is authority for.

Subs. (6)

There is no limit in time as to how long the warrant can be granted for, though it cannot authorise the keeping of a child in a place of safety for any more than 22 days after the granting of the warrant or after the beginning of the subsequent hearing, whichever is earlier. It is also to be remembered that the requirement to attend or reside at a clinic or hospital cannot exceed 22 days (subs. (3) above), so the warrant to enforce that requirement cannot last beyond the requirement itself.

Subs. (7)

This subsection overlaps the provisions contained in s.66(1) and (2) above, the General Notes to which reference should again be made. Though substantially similar, the main difference between s.66 and the present section is that here the warrant can last a maximum of 22 days and cannot be continued while under s.66 it can, with continuations, last a maximum of 66 days (or even longer if continued by a sheriff under s.67 above). It is therefore important to know under which provision the warrant is granted. As explained in the General Note to s. 66(1) above, that is not immediately clear. Under s.66 a warrant may be granted when the children's hearing are "unable to dispose of the case", while under the present subsection a warrant may be granted when the hearing continue the case under subs. (2) above. The difference lies in the fact that the present provision applies only after a children's hearing have considered the child's case under subs. (1) above and, after that consideration, have determined to continue the case for further investigation under subs. (2) above; s.66, on the other hand, applies when the children's hearing have not yet considered the case (because the grounds are denied or because the parent has not attended). That is not a case of continuation within the terms of subs. (2) above.

The grounds upon which the warrant under this subsection can be granted are specified in paras. (a) and (b): under para. (a) some factor indicating a threat to the child's welfare were she or he not to be kept in a place of safety ought to be shown, and under para. (b) a history of non-attendance will be sufficient as might, for example, a threat by a relevant person not to bring the child back to the continued hearing. The decision is governed by the three overarching principles: s.16 above and r. 26 of the 1996 Rules.

Subs. (8)

The warrant granted under subs. (7) above ceases to have effect either at the end of 22 days after it was granted or on the day a hearing convenes to consider the continued case. There is no provision for the renewal of a warrant granted under subs. (7) (*cf.* s.66(5) above), which is designed to ensure that a continued hearing takes place within a very short period of time. However, the continued hearing may decide again to continue the case on the ground that the investigations are not yet complete, and the granting of another warrant under subs. (7) above would appear to be competent. Indeed there is no limit to the number of times the hearing can continue the case, though clearly it is not in a child's interests to be kept indefinitely in a place of safety without a substantive decision as to her or his future. It is a flaw in the statute that there is no prohibition on multiple warrants being granted under this section beyond the 66-day period that limits warrants under s.66, though perhaps the real flaw lies in the confusing overlap in these provisions.

Subs. (9)

This is in the same terms as s.66(4) above, and the notes to that subsection should again be referred to. The power applies whether the warrant is granted under subs. (4) above or subs. (7) above.

Subs. (10)

This provision gives the same power to the children's hearing granting a warrant under subs. (4) or subs. (7) as is contained in s.66(7) above, and the notes to that provision should again be referred to.

Subs. (11)

This is in similar terms to s.66(6) above, and the General Note to that section should again be referred to. It is to be remembered that this subsection is applicable only when the case has been continued, and the authorisation to keep the child in secure accommodation will not last beyond the commencement of the continued hearing or, if earlier, the cessation of the effect of a warrant or requirement under this section.

Subss. (12) and (13)

A children's hearing can make a supervision requirement under s.70 below only when they are satisfied that compulsory measures of supervision are necessary in the interests of the child. If, after a sufficient consideration of the child's case, taking account of the three overarching principles in s.16 above, they are not so satisfied their decision must be not to make a supervision requirement and they are obliged to discharge the referral. On that discharge all warrants to find and keep the child, orders as to assessments and investigations, directions as to contact, and any other order or requirement made under ss.39–85 in respect of the case based on the referral that is discharged, will cease to have effect.

Disposal of referral by children's hearing: supervision requirements, including residence in secure accommodation

70.—(1) Where the children's hearing to whom a child's case has been referred under section 65(1) of this Act are satisfied that compulsory measures of supervision are necessary in respect of the child they may make a requirement under this section (to be known as a "supervision requirement").

(2) A children's hearing, where they decide to make such a requirement, shall consider whether to impose any condition such as is described in subsection (5)(b) below.

(3) A supervision requirement may require the child—

(a) to reside at any place or places specified in the requirement; and

(b) to comply with any condition contained in the requirement.

(4) The place or, as the case may be, places specified in a requirement under subsection (3)(a) above may, without prejudice to the generality of that subsection, be a place or places in England or Wales; and a supervision requirement shall be authority for the person in charge of such a place to restrict the child's liberty to such extent as that person may consider appropriate, having regard to the terms of the requirement.

(5) A condition imposed under subsection (3)(b) above may, without prejudice to the generality of that subsection—

(a) subject to section 90 of this Act, require the child to submit to any medical or other examination or treatment;

(b) regulate the contact with the child of any specified person or class of persons.

(6) A children's hearing may require, when making a supervision requirement, that any place where the child is to reside in accordance with the supervision requirement shall not be disclosed to any person specified in the requirement under this subsection or class of persons so specified.

(7) A children's hearing who make a supervision requirement may determine that the requirement shall be reviewed at such time during the duration of the requirement as they determine.

(8) A supervision requirement shall be in such form as the Secretary of State may prescribe by rules.

(9) Where a children's hearing are satisfied—

(a) that it is necessary to make a supervision requirement which includes a requirement under subsection (3)(a) above that the child reside in a named residential establishment; and

(b) that any of the criteria specified in subsection (10) below are satisfied,

they may specify in the requirement that the child shall be liable to be placed and kept in secure accommodation in that establishment during such period as the person in charge of that establishment, with the agreement of the chief social work officer of the relevant local authority, considers necessary.

(10) The criteria referred to in subsection (9) above are that the child—

(a) having previously absconded, is likely to abscond unless kept in secure accommodation, and, if he absconds, it is likely that his physical, mental or moral welfare will be at risk; or

(b) is likely to injure himself or some other person unless he is kept in such accommodation.

GENERAL NOTE

Section 69 above deals with the situation where a children's hearing, after considering a child's case, either discharges the referral or continues the case for further investigation. The present section, replacing various parts of ss.44 and 58A of the 1968 Act, deals with the hearing's power, after having considering the child's case, to impose supervision requirements and grant secure accommodation authorisations. A number of important changes to the law have been made. Perhaps the most noticeable, but hardly the most significant in practical effect, is the scrapping of the distinction between supervision requirements imposed under the old s.44(1)(a) and those under the old s.44(1)(b), that is between supervision requirements requiring the child to submit to supervision and supervision requirements requiring the child to reside in a residential establishment. That distinction always was rather artificial, especially in the eyes of children required to live away from home but not in a residential establishment. The present section does not make the distinction, and the children's hearing may now impose a supervision requirement whenever they consider this necessary in the interests of the child, which requirement may or may not contain a condition that the child resides at a specified place, and which specified place may or may not be a residential establishment.

There are a number of other important changes in the law, including new provisions requiring the children's hearing to consider whether a condition in relation to contact should be imposed, allowing the hearing to impose a condition relating to medical examination or treatment, to require that the child's place of residence be kept confidential, and, importantly, to require that a review hearing be arranged within a specified time.

One provision which has not been re-enacted is the unhelpful obligation previously contained in s.44(2) of the 1968 Act, that in making a residential supervision requirement the children's hearing have regard to the religious persuasion of the child. If that matter is important to the child, then it will be a relevant consideration in determining which form of disposal best serves her or his welfare; if it is not important to the child, its importance to any other person is irrelevant.

Subs. (1)

A children's hearing to whom a child's case has been referred under s.65(1) above is obliged to consider that case in accordance with s.69(1) above and if, after that consideration, they come to the view that compulsory measures of supervision are required in respect of that child, they may make a supervision requirement. The wording of this provision is to be noted. If compulsory measures are deemed "necessary", the hearing "may" make a supervision requirement. There are no compulsory measures available to the children's hearing other than a supervision requirement, and the use of the permissive "may" might appear odd at first sight. However, this terminology allows the children's hearing to decide not to impose a supervision requirement in circumstances in which, though such a requirement is considered "necessary" it will not, in fact, succeed (for example in the case of a child nearing 16 who refuses to co-operate with any help offered). The decision whether to make a supervision requirement is one governed by all three overarching principles in s.16, and so while the child's welfare is the hearing's paramount consideration, they must also take into account the child's views, and must make no supervision requirement unless persuaded that it would be better to make the requirement than that none be made at all.

Subs. (2)

Subsection (3) below permits the children's hearing to impose conditions on to a supervision requirement, and this subsection requires the hearing to give consideration to the question of whether a condition relating to contact between the child and any other named person or class of persons should be made. The obligation is *not* to regulate contact in every case in which a supervision requirement is imposed, but simply to give consideration in every case as to whether a condition ought to be attached to the supervision requirement regulating contact.

In its terms the obligation to consider contact is limited to the initial making of a supervision requirement, and there is no express obligation when the children's hearing are considering whether to continue the supervision requirement at a review under s.73. It is submitted that "making" includes "continuing or varying": see Norrie, *Children's Hearings in Scotland* (1997, W. Green), at pp. 143–144.

Subs. (3)

Unlike s.44(1) of the 1968 Act there is now no technical difference in the current provisions between a non-residential supervision requirement and a residential supervision requirement. Instead, this subsection provides that a supervision requirement can require the child to reside at any place or places: this may be in a residential establishment, or with foster carers, or with relatives, or with one parent, or in any other place deemed to be in the best interests of the child. In addition the requirement can oblige the child to comply with any other specified condition. The decision whether to attach a condition to the supervision requirement is one to which all three overarching principles in s.16 apply, even though s. 16(4)(a)(i) refers only to the making or reviewing of supervision requirements, for the terms upon which the supervision requirement is made are, it is submitted, part of the consideration of whether to make it. There is no reason to deny an obligation to have regard to the child's views in relation to conditions when there is such an obligation in relation to the supervision requirement itself; and it is consistent with the principle of minimum intervention to allow the children's hearing to impose conditions only when they consider that that would be better than no conditions. At a review, any conditions are clearly open for consideration and all three of the s.16 principles are to be taken into account.

Specified in the requirement. If the hearing imposes a supervision requirement with a requirement that the child reside somewhere, it must specify that place. The requirement cannot be to the effect that the child is to reside, say, "otherwise than with the parents", or "in an establishment chosen by the local authority", or "with foster carers selected by the local authority". The address of the child must be specified by the hearing, though it may be kept secret from any person under subs. (6) below. It is to be remembered that if a child is to be provided with accommodation by a local authority in a domestic familial context (*i.e.* with foster carers rather than in a residential establishment) the rules contained in the Fostering of Children (Scotland) Regulations 1996 (S.I. 1996 No. 3263) must be adhered to.

Any condition. As under the old law the hearing can impose any condition they consider appropriate on the child, so long as, in their view, this is in the interests of the child. Such a condition may concern one of the matters mentioned in subs. (5) below, but it is not limited to these matters. The only limitation is that the condition must require something of the child. A children's hearing have no power to impose conditions on any other person, such as the parent or the local authority (though the placing of the child under supervision necessarily imposes the duty upon the local authority to "look after" the child in terms of s.17 above and to give effect to the supervision requirement under s.71 below). If the children's hearing decide to impose a condition they must do so expressly and it must be specified in the relevant form: a passage in the statement of reasons issued by the hearing is not a condition attached to the supervision requirement (see *Kennedy v. M*, 1995 S.L.T. 717).

Subs. (4)

This subsection replaces s.44(1A) of the 1968 Act. A supervision requirement that specifies the place of residence of the child may specify a place in England or Wales. If it does specify a place in England or Wales, it shall be authority for the person in charge of that place to restrict the child's liberty to such extent as is appropriate given the terms of the supervision requirement.

Subs. (5)

Under subs. (3) above a supervision requirement can impose any condition that the hearing considers appropriate. The two specified conditions here are, therefore, listed for the avoidance of doubt.

Require the child to submit to any medical or other examination or treatment. The aim of this provision is to ensure that there is legal authority to carry out medical examinations of children when this is necessary to determine what medical treatment she or he might need, and to ensure that such treatment as is necessary is given. This provision *does not* authorise medical examination for the purpose of gaining evidence in order to establish a ground of referral (for which, see s.55 above) nor for the purpose of completing an investigation into the child's needs when a case is continued under s.69(2) above (for which, see s.69(3) above): this requirement is attached to the disposal of the case and is imposed as one of the measures deemed necessary in the interests of the child. In determining whether to attach such a condition to a supervision requirement, the children's hearing must have regard to the three overarching principles in s.16 above; in addition, they should also be aware of s.90 below, to which this paragraph is made subject. Section 90 preserves the child's capacity to consent to or to refuse medical examination or treatment under s.2(4) of the Age of Legal Capacity (Scotland) Act 1991 and expressly provides that any examination or treatment the child is required to receive by a condition under this subsection can only be carried out if the child who has capacity to consent does consent. A children's hearing are not barred from imposing a condition of medical treatment on a refusing child, but such a condition will not provide legal authority for carrying it out. Rather, a child who refuses to submit in the face of such a condition will be treated as having breached that condition, and brought back to a children's hearing for a review under s.73(4)(b) below. A children's hearing ought to give especially careful consideration to the appropriateness of imposing such a requirement when they know that the child is refusing.

Regulate the contact with the child of any specified person. Whenever a supervision requirement is made, the children's hearing are obliged under subs. (2) above to give consideration to the question of whether they should make a condition regulating the contact that the child is to have with any specified person or class of person. If such a condition is to be made then it should be in clear and unambiguous terms. Such a condition will normally be appropriate when the child is required to live away from home and she or he wishes to maintain contact with her or his parents or guardians, but the condition may also be imposed when the child remains at home and the child's interests would be served by some other person, such as an absent unmarried father, or a previous foster carer to whom the child has become attached, having contact. This is, however, a slightly peculiar provision since the condition is in a supervision requirement over the child and it is only the child, in terms of subs. (3) above, who can be required to comply with the condition. The condition imposed by the children's hearing may purport to regulate contact between the child and another person, but steps can be taken to enforce that condition only when it is the child who breaches it. A parent's failure to maintain contact with the child when the children's hearing have considered it to be in the interests of the child will not automatically activate a review under s.73(4)(b) below, but it may well indicate to the local authority that a review should be requested in any case under s.73(4)(a).

Subs. (6)

This provision gives an important new power to the hearing. As part of a supervision requirement, the requirement that the child's residence not be disclosed will be potentially much longer lasting than the similar requirement under s.66(7) and s.69(10) above, though much the same considerations will come into play. A requirement under this subsection would be appropriate when contact between the child and the named person is considered to be harmful to the child, and it is also believed that there is a risk that the named person will attempt to make contact. The statute gives no indication as to when it would be appropriate for the children's hearing to exercise this power and there is nothing to prevent them doing so for the benefit of someone other than the child, such as foster carers. If the person from whom details of the child's residence is to be kept is present at the hearing, care must be taken to ensure that the address is not mentioned and this might require that the person be excluded from part of the hearing (though such a reason for excluding a person does not fit into either of the grounds of exclusion under s.46(1) above). In addition, the person may be entitled to receive a statement of the decision and the grounds for the decision, and care should be taken to ensure that the address is not specified (though it must be specified on the actual supervision requirement).

Subs. (7)
This is another new provision and is a useful addition to the powers of the children's hearing. Under the old law the hearing themselves had no power to specify how long the supervision requirement was to last, and if the case indicated that supervision for a period of less than a year was appropriate, all the hearing could do was to express the hope to the Social Work Department that they would call for a review, or encourage the child and parent to call for a review at some time before the end of the year. Now the hearing may determine that a supervision requirement be reviewed at any time they determine during its currency. As with subs. (2) above, this power inheres in review hearings as well as hearings which originally impose a supervision requirement.

Subss. (9) and (10)
These subsections replace s.58A of the 1968 Act with no substantive alteration, and they provide that the children's hearing can specify that the child be liable to be placed and kept in secure accommodation in a residential establishment during such periods as are considered necessary by the chief social worker. The children's hearing have no power to require that the child be kept in secure accommodation; rather they simply authorise the placing of the child there. Before specifying such an authorisation, the following conditions must be satisfied:
(1) the children's hearing must have made a supervision requirement with a requirement that the child resides in a named residential establishment, *and either*
(2) the child must have absconded from a residential establishment at least once before and is likely to do so again in circumstances in which her or his welfare will be put at risk, *or*
(3) the child is likely to injure either her or himself or some other person unless kept in secure accommodation.
The decision to make the child liable to be kept in secure accommodation is one to which the welfare principle in s.16(1) applies, though that is qualified to a certain extent by s.16(5) above (*cf.* s.1 of the English Children Act 1989 (c. 41), as interpreted by the Court of Appeal in *M (A Minor) (Secure Accommodation), Re* [1995] 2 W.L.R. 302) but not the other overarching principles in s.16(2) and (3). However, it might well be in the interests of the child her or himself to be kept in secure accommodation. See further, Secure Accommodation (Scotland) Regulations 1996 (S.I. 1996 No. 3255).
Injure himself or some other person. This refers to personal injuries, and not economic injuries such as damage to property. However, it can clearly be argued that a child who, for example, steals motor cars is likely to cause himself and others physical injury (since he will not have passed a driving test). A child who commits criminal offences that do not put either himself or other people at risk of physical injury probably does not come within this provision (unless it could be argued that the threat to moral welfare by persistent criminality amounts to an "injury": this is, it is submitted, too wide an interpretation of that word). This provision is to be read with s.16(5) above, which applies "whether or not" the harm threatened is physical.

Duties of local authority with respect to supervision requirements

71.—(1) The relevant local authority shall, as respects a child subject to a supervision requirement, give effect to the requirement.
(2) Where a supervision requirement provides that the child shall reside—
(a) in relevant accommodation; or
(b) in any other accommodation not provided by a local authority,
the relevant local authority shall from time to time investigate whether, while the child is so resident, any conditions imposed by the supervision requirement are being fulfilled; and may take such steps as they consider reasonable if they find that such conditions are not being fulfilled.

(3) In this section, "relevant accommodation" means accommodation provided by the parents or relatives of the child or by any person associated with them or with the child.

DEFINITIONS
"child": s.93(2)(b).
"children's hearing": s.93(1).
"relevant local authority": s.93(1).
"supervision requirement": s.93(1).

GENERAL NOTE

This section replaces s.44(5) of the 1968 Act and provides that a supervision requirement made by a children's hearing must be given effect to by the local authority for whose area the children's hearing sits. The nature of the obligations thereby imposed on the local authority will depend upon the terms of the supervision requirement and the conditions attached thereto. A requirement, for example, that the child reside in a specified residential establishment will oblige the local authority to provide a place in that residential establishment. If there is no requirement that the child resides in a particular place the duty of the local authority is to provide such supervision, guidance and support as the children's hearing have decided is necessary in the child's interests. A failure on the part of the local authority to fulfil their duties under this (or any other) section in the present Act will subject them to liability under s. 91 of the Court of Session Act 1868 (which allows the court to impose such penalty as it thinks fit). In addition an action for judicial review is available (see, for example, *Re J. (Accommodation by Local Authority)* [1995] 1 F.L.R. 159). While local authorities have a certain discretion as to how they are to fulfil their statutory duties they have no discretion as to whether to fulfil them. The House of Lords has recently held that while the resources available to a local authority may be taken into account in determining whether a child is in need, resources (or, more pertinently, lack of them) are irrelevant to the question of how needs, once identified, are to be met: *Re T. (A Minor) 1997*, May 20, 1998, HL. A supervision requirement determines the question of the child's needs; the present section obliges local authorities to meet these needs; and *Re T.* disallows local authorities from taking their resources into account in determining how to meet these needs. Negligence in carrying out their duties will not, however, found liability in delict to those who are injured thereby: *X. v. Bedfordshire County Council* [1995] 3 All E.R. 353.

Subs. (1)

The obligation is absolute. If, for whatever reason, the supervision requirement or any of its conditions cannot be given effect to, the local authority must refer the case to the reporter under s.73(4) below for a review of the supervision requirement by the children's hearing under s.73(8) below.

Subs. (2)

This provision only applies when the supervision requirement requires the child under s.70(3)(a) above to reside in a specified place, but that place is not a residential establishment as defined in s.93(1). In such cases the local authority have an obligation to check that the conditions attached to the supervision requirement are being fulfilled.

Provides that the child shall reside. A supervision requirement that does not contain a requirement under s.70(3)(a) above is not one that provides that the child "shall reside" anywhere and this provision will not, therefore, apply.

Such steps as they consider reasonable. If, on investigation under this section, the local authority discover that any of the conditions attached to the supervision requirement are not being fulfilled, they must either provide such guidance and support as will allow for the fulfilment of the appropriate conditions, or call for a review under s.73(4) below.

Subs. (3)

Parents or relatives. Neither of these words is defined in the Act and both are to be given their natural meaning. "Parent" is not limited to "parent with parental responsibilities"; "relative" means any person with a relationship of blood or affinity with the child.

Any person associated with them or with the child. This phrase is probably to be given broad scope to mean any individual with a legitimate concern with the parents or with the child, such as friends or neighbours to whom the child has some emotional attachment.

Transfer of child subject to supervision requirement in case of necessity

72.—(1) In any case of urgent necessity, where it is in the interests of—

(a) a child who is required by a supervision requirement imposed under section 70(3)(a) of this Act to reside in a specific residential establishment or specific other accommodation; or

(b) other children in that establishment or accommodation,

the chief social work officer of the relevant local authority may direct that, notwithstanding that requirement, the child be transferred to another place.

(2) Any child transferred under subsection (1) above shall have his case reviewed, in accordance with section 73(8) of this Act, by a children's hearing within seven days of his transfer.

DEFINITIONS
"accommodation": s.25(8).
"chief social work officer": s.93(1).
"child": s.93(2)(b).
"children's hearing": s.93(1).
"relevant local authority": s.93(1).
"residential establishment": s.93(1).
"supervision requirement": s.93(1).

GENERAL NOTE
This section replaces s.44(6) and (7) of the 1968 Act, without making any substantive alteration in the law. It deals with the situation of a child who was obliged to reside in a specified place but in her or his interests has had to be transferred to another place immediately.

Subs. (1)
Urgent necessity. In other words, an immediate necessity which cannot wait until a children's hearing has been arranged under s.73(4) in order to decide whether the supervision requirement should be varied to allow the child to be moved to another place.
Residential establishment or specific other accommodation. This section applies to all children who are required under s.70(3)(a) to reside at a specified place as a term of their supervision requirement.
Of ... other children. It may be in the interests of other children at the specified place that the child must be moved if, for example, the child poses a threat to other children residing at the specified place.

Subs. (2)
A review of the child's case, under s.73(8) below, by a children's hearing must be held within seven days of the child's transfer to another place. The purpose will be primarily to examine where the child is to reside in light of the breakdown of the placement previously determined by the children's hearing. It is, however, the whole supervision requirement, or to put it another way, the whole of the child's case, and not only the condition of residence that is to be reviewed.
His case reviewed. It is worthy of note that s.73(8) talks of the supervision requirement being reviewed, while this subsection talks of the child's case being reviewed. The two are, it is submitted, synonymous since the disposals available to the children's hearing conducting the review are identical however the review comes before them. The change in terminology signifies nothing more than sloppy draftsmanship (see further, General Note to s.73(9) below).
Within seven days of his transfer. The day the transfer takes place is the first day and the review hearing must take place on or before the seventh day.

Duration and review of supervision requirement

73.—(1) No child shall continue to be subject to a supervision requirement for any period longer than is necessary in the interests of promoting or safeguarding his welfare.

(2) Subject to any variation or continuation of a supervision requirement under subsection (9) below, no supervision requirement shall remain in force for a period longer than one year.

(3) A supervision requirement shall cease to have effect in respect of a child not later than on his attaining the age of eighteen years.

(4) A relevant local authority shall refer the case of a child who is subject to a supervision requirement to the Principal Reporter where they are satisfied that—

(a) the requirement in respect of the child ought to cease to have effect or be varied;

(b) a condition contained in the requirement is not being complied with; or

(c) the best interests of the child would be served by their—

(i) applying under section 86 of this Act for a parental responsibilities order;

(ii) applying under section 18 of the Adoption (Scotland) Act 1978 for an order freeing the child for adoption; or

(iii) placing the child for adoption,

and they intend to apply for such an order or so place the child.

(5) Where the relevant local authority are aware that an application has been made and is pending, or is about to be made, under section 12 of the said Act of 1978 for an adoption order in respect of a child who is subject to a supervision requirement, they shall forthwith refer his case to the Principal Reporter.

(6) A child or any relevant person may require a review of a supervision requirement in respect of the child at any time at least three months after—

(a) the date on which the requirement is made; or

(b) the date of the most recent continuation, or variation, by virtue of this section of the requirement.

(7) Where a child is subject to a supervision requirement and, otherwise than in accordance with that requirement or with an order under section 11 of this Act, a relevant person proposes to take the child to live outwith Scotland, the person shall, not later than twenty-eight days before so taking the child, give notice of that proposal in writing to the Principal Reporter and to the relevant local authority.

(8) The Principal Reporter shall—

(a) arrange for a children's hearing to review any supervision requirement in respect of a child where—

(i) the case has been referred to him under subsection (4) or (5) above;

(ii) the review has been required under subsection (6) above;

(iii) the review is required by virtue of section 70(7) or section 72(2) of this Act;

(iv) he has received in respect of the child such notice as is mentioned in subsection (7) above; or

(v) in any other case, the supervision requirement will expire within three months; and

(b) make any arrangements incidental to that review.

(9) Where a supervision requirement is reviewed by a children's hearing arranged under subsection (8) above, they may—

(a) where they are satisfied that in order to complete the review of the supervision requirement it is necessary to have a further investigation of the child's case, continue the review to a subsequent hearing;

(b) terminate the requirement;

(c) vary the requirement;

(d) insert in the requirement any requirement which could have been imposed by them under section 70(3) of this Act; or

(e) continue the requirement, with or without such variation or insertion.

(10) Subsections (3) to (10) of section 69 of this Act shall apply to a continuation under paragraph (a) of subsection (9) above of a review of a supervision requirement as they apply to the continuation of a case under subsection (1)(a) of that section.

(11) Where a children's hearing vary or impose a requirement under subsection (9) above which requires the child to reside in any specified place or places, they may order that such place or places shall not be disclosed to any person or class of persons specified in the requirement.

(12) Where a children's hearing is arranged under subsection (8)(a)(v) above, they shall consider whether, if the supervision requirement is not continued, the child still requires supervision or guidance; and where a children's hearing consider such supervision or guidance is necessary, it shall be the duty of the local authority to provide such supervision or guidance as the child is willing to accept.

(13) Where a children's hearing is arranged by virtue of subsection (4)(c) or (5) above, then irrespective of what the hearing do under subsection (9) above they shall draw up a report which shall provide advice in respect of, as the case may be, the proposed application under section 86 of this Act or under section 18 of the said Act of 1978, or the proposed placing for adoption or the application, or prospective application, under section 12 of that Act, for any court which may subsequently require to come to a decision, in relation to the child concerned, such as is mentioned in subsection (14) below.

(14) A court which is considering whether, in relation to a child, to grant an application under section 86 of this Act or under section 18 or 12 of the said Act of 1978 and which, by virtue of subsection (13) above, receives a report as respects that child, shall consider the report before coming to a decision in the matter.

DEFINITIONS
"child": s.93(2)(b).
"children's hearing": s.93(1).
"parental responsibilities order": ss.86(1), 93(1).
"Principal Reporter": s.93(1).
"relevant local authority": s.93(1).
"relevant person": s.93(2)(b).
"supervision requirement": s.93(1).

GENERAL NOTE
A child is subject to compulsory measures of supervision for only a specified period of time which, unless the supervision requirement is renewed, cannot be for more than a year. This section replaces ss.47 and 48 of the 1968 Act and makes some fairly important amendments to the law, as well as tidying it up. It deals with the duration of supervision requirements, their review, and the powers of the children's hearing on review to terminate, vary or continue supervision requirements, and to draw up reports in certain circumstances.

The substantive changes in the law are to be found in subs. (6), under which a review can be required by the child or parent at any time after three months from the making or last review of the requirement, subs. (7), which obliges notice to be given to the reporter if the child is being removed from Scotland, subs. (11), which permits the children's hearing to require that the child's address is kept secret, and subss (13) and (14), which concern the reports that the hearing must draw up in certain circumstances. In addition to the rules relating to termination contained in this section, the court also now has the power under the Adoption (Scotland) Act 1978 (c. 28) to terminate supervision requirements on the making of adoption orders or orders freeing for adoption. However, the Secretary of State no longer has the power himself to terminate supervision requirements (s.51 of the 1968 Act is repealed in Sched. 5 and is not re-enacted). A supervision requirement must also be reviewed (and can be terminated) under s.72 above, s.82 below, r.11 of the Secure Accommodation (Scotland) Regulations 1996, and ss.12(9), 18(9) and 22A of the Adoption (Scotland) Act 1978.

Subs. (1)
A child is to remain subject to a supervision requirement only for so long as her or his interests require that she or he be so subject and this subsection provides that she or he shall not continue to be subject to a supervision requirement when it is no longer necessary in her or his interests. The effect of this provision is *not* to bring the supervision requirement automatically to an end when the child's interests are best served by the termination of the requirement, but rather to indicate to the local authority when they ought to require a review under subs. (4)(a) below, as well as to indicate to the children's hearing the paramount consideration to which they must direct their minds in determining whether or not a supervision requirement should be terminated under subs. (9)(b) below.

Subs. (2)

A supervision requirement, if it has not been reviewed within that time, will remain effective for one year. If no children's hearing has been arranged within that time (contrary to the reporter's obligation to do so under subs. (8)(a)(v) below) the supervision requirement automatically ceases to have effect on the anniversary of its being imposed, and to bring the child back into the system would then require new grounds of referral. If a children's hearing is arranged under any paragraph of subs. (8) below the requirement can be continued for another period of a year (or less if again reviewed before then).

A period longer than a year. A supervision requirement imposed, say, on June 3, will cease to have effect at midnight on June 3 of the following year.

Subs. (3)

A person cannot be subject to a supervision requirement after reaching the age of 18 years, and any subsisting requirement automatically ceases to have effect on the person's 18th birthday, even without the meeting of a hearing to terminate it. The reporter does, however, have an obligation to arrange a review within three months of the expiry of the supervision requirement (subs. (8)(a)(v) below): if this expiry would be effected by this subsection any continuation would last only until the child's 18th birthday. On the attaining of the age of 18 years, see the Age of Legal Capacity (Scotland) Act 1991 (c. 50), s.6.

Subs. (4)

The local authority which are responsible for giving effect to the supervision of the child may call for a review of the requirement by referring the case to the reporter. On such referral, the reporter then has an obligation under subs. (8) below to arrange a review hearing. This subsection replaces s.48(2) of the 1968 Act, but is more specific in that it sets out a number of circumstances in which the local authority are obliged to refer the case to the reporter to arrange a review. Paragraph (a) reflects the old s.47(1) and obliges a referral when the local authority are satisfied that the supervision requirement ought to be varied or terminated (due to some change in the child's circumstances since the supervision requirement was made or last reviewed). Paragraph (b), not expressed in the 1968 Act but reflecting practice, requires a referral when a condition in the supervision requirement is not being fulfilled. It does not matter why the condition is not being fulfilled, whether it is because of non-co-operation by the child, lack of resources by the local authority, or for any other reason. Paragraph (c) is a new provision, requiring a review whenever the local authority intends to do any of the listed acts. These acts are seen as acts which will significantly change the child's circumstances, so making it appropriate that a review of the child's case be held. A children's hearing arranged as a result of a referral under para. (c) must not only review the supervision requirement under subs. (9) below, but must also draw up a report under subs. (13) below.

Subs. (5)

In addition to their duty to refer the case to the reporter in the circumstances listed in subs. (4) above, a local authority also have the duty to refer the case to the reporter when they become aware that an adoption application has been or is about to be made in respect of the child, and the children's hearing will be obliged to draw up a report under subs. (13) below. It is to be remembered that the court that grants an adoption order now has the power to terminate a supervision requirement (see the Adoption (Scotland) Act 1978, s.12(9), as added by Sched. 2 of the present Act).

They shall forthwith. The word "forthwith" does not govern the obligation under subs. (4) above and it serves the function here of indicating that the case should be referred to the reporter as a matter of urgency. "Forthwith" means as soon as practicable.

Subs. (6)

Under the old s.48(4) the child or parent could require a review of the supervision requirement three months after the requirement was made or last varied or six months after it was continued at a review without variation. This new provision allows the child or relevant person to call for a review at any time after three months from the imposition or last continuation of the supervision requirement, whether varied or not.

Relevant person. Defined in s.93(2)(b) below, this is the same person as is obliged under s.45(8) to attend the children's hearing considering the case of the child. See further notes to s.65(9) above. If a child's circumstances have changed since the last review, it is possible that a different person comes within this category. The person who has, for the time being, charge of or control over the child is the person who can call for a review under this provision, whether or not that person was a "relevant person" at the time of the making of the supervision requirement or of its last review.

At least three months after. The months are calendar months and three months after the date on which the requirement was made, continued or varied is the day after the expiry of the three months. For example a supervision requirement made or continued on March 23, can be reviewed at the instance of the child or relevant person on or after June 24. The call for a review can be made at a time before the expiry of the three months, but the children's hearing cannot consider the case until after that expiry.

Subs. (7)
The jurisdiction of the children's hearing extends only to Scotland. This new provision obliges a relevant person who intends to remove a child subject to a supervision requirement from Scotland to notify the reporter at least 28 days before that removal. Notice is required only when the proposal is that the child be taken to live outwith Scotland and not merely for a holiday. Extended holidays may well cause problems here, and the test is probably one of whether the intention is to change the child's habitual residence. On receiving notice under this subsection, the reporter must then arrange a review of the supervision requirement under subs. (8)(iv) below and the children's hearing, by specifying a place of residence for the child within Scotland, may effectively prohibit the child's removal from the jurisdiction (if, as always, they consider that this is necessary in the interests of the child). Again, this provision is designed to ensure that a review takes place whenever there is, or is about to be, a significant change in the child's circumstances.

Subs. (8)
A review of a supervision requirement by the children's hearing must be arranged by the reporter whenever the child's case has been referred to her or him by the local authority under subs. (4) or subs. (5) above, or a review has been requested by the child or parent under subs. (6) above, or the children's hearing have exercised their power under s.70(7) to specify a time at which the requirement must be reviewed, or the child has been moved from specified accommodation to other accommodation under s.72 above, or the reporter has received notice under subs. (7) above that a relevant person intends to remove the child outwith Scotland, or, if none of these circumstances apply, within three months of the expiry of the supervision requirement. In addition to these circumstances in which a children's hearing must be arranged by the reporter for a review, the supervision requirement over a child will also be reviewed whenever a children's hearing has been arranged in order to put new grounds of referral to the child and parent (s.65(3) above); whenever a fugitive child is returned to a place where he or she is required to reside, but the person in charge of that place is unwilling to have the child back (s.82 below); whenever a child has been kept in secure accommodation for three months (Secure Accommodation (Scotland) Regulations 1996 (S.I. 1996 No. 3255 (s.245)), reg. 11); and whenever an adoption society has placed a child for adoption who is subject to a supervision requirement (Adoption (Scotland) Act 1978, s.22A).
The Principal Reporter shall. The reporter is obliged to arrange a review and if the children's hearing is not arranged timeously the supervision requirement will lapse. The reporter, however, is not entitled to decide simply to let the supervision requirement lapse, for that would be usurping the role of the children's hearing as well as constituting a breach of statutory obligation. Once a child is under supervision the reporter has no power to decide that the child is no longer in need of compulsory measures of supervision.
Will expire within three months. A review hearing under para. (a)(v) must be arranged by the reporter not later than three months before the date on which the supervision requirement will cease to have effect, that is to say within three months of the child's 18th birthday or within three months of the anniversary of the imposition or last variation or continuation of the requirement or within three months of the date specified by the children's hearing under s.70(7) for a review.
Make any arrangements incidental to that review. In other words, the reporter must call for reports into the child's circumstances from the Social Work Department of the appropriate local authority, and any other reports in relation to the child that will be relevant to the children's hearing's consideration of the case.

Subs. (9)
Some provisions in the Act refer to the children's hearing considering the child's case (see *e.g.* s.69(2) above), some refer to the review of the child's case (see *e.g.* s.72(2) above), and this subsection requires a review of the supervision requirement. It would be appropriate to refer to a consideration of the child's case when there is no supervision requirement and to refer to a consideration of the supervision requirement when there is such a requirement, but the statute is not consistent in this. There is, however, no difference between a review of the child's case and a review of the supervision requirement, since the supervision requirement cannot properly be reviewed without a consideration of the whole of the child's case. The hearing must direct its

mind to the question of whether the supervision requirement should be terminated, varied, or continued and they can do this only by considering the reports provided before the hearing, the discussion at the hearing, and of all aspects of the case that indicate wherein the child's interests lie. Having considered the child's case, taking account of the effect the supervision requirement in its present form has had so far, and directing their minds to the question of whether it should be terminated, varied or continued without variation, the children's hearing may do one or other of the five options listed in this subsection. It may be noted that there is no requirement on the hearing reviewing a child's case to give any fresh consideration to the original grounds of referral.

The decision which option to adopt at a review is one to which all three overarching principles in s.16 apply: the children's hearing must regard the welfare of the child as their paramount consideration, they must have regard so far as practicable to the views, if she or he wishes to express them, of the child concerned, and they may continue the supervision requirement only when they consider that to do so would be better than having no supervision requirement at all. In addition, the children's hearing at a review must pay regard to the rule in subs. (1) above that no child shall continue to be subject to a supervision requirement for any period longer than is necessary in the interests of promoting or safeguarding her or his welfare.

Subs. (10)

This subsection ensures that if, after having reviewed the child's case, the children's hearing feel that they need more information to make a proper decision and they continue the case to a subsequent hearing, the same powers to require the child to undergo investigative assessment and to be kept in a place of safety apply as when a hearing at which established grounds of referral are being considered is continued. The aim is to ensure that a hearing reviewing a supervision requirement have the same powers as the hearing which decided whether to impose a supervision requirement in the first place.

Subs. (11)

This reflects the power of the children's hearing under s.70(6) above, the General Note to which reference should be made.

Subs. (12)

If the review is arranged because the supervision requirement is about to expire (because it has lasted for a year or because the child is about to attain the age of 18) the children's hearing must consider whether voluntary supervision and guidance is still required for the child. If they do so determine, the local authority must offer such supervision and guidance to the child.

If the supervision requirement is not continued. If the review is other than because the child is about to attain the age of 18 and the children's hearing consider that the child still requires supervision and guidance, then a continuation of the supervision requirement will nearly always be the correct decision.

Subs. (13)

This new provision follows on from the new requirement to arrange a children's hearing under subss (4)(c) or (5) above, that is when the local authority intend to place the child for adoption or to apply for an order freeing the child for adoption or to apply for a parental responsibilities order, or they become aware that someone intends to apply to adopt the child. When a children's hearing is arranged for any of these reasons they are obliged to draw up a report to provide advice to the court in respect of that matter.

Irrespective of what the hearing do under subs. (9). A children's hearing arranged for this reason must review the supervision requirement in respect of the child (subs. (8) above provides that the reporter shall arrange a hearing to review any supervision requirement when a case has been referred to her or him under, *inter alia* subss (4)(c) or (5) above) and it follows that the hearing must make a decision in respect of that requirement in the normal way.

Shall draw up a report. In addition to the decision which the children's hearing make in respect of the supervision requirement the hearing must also draw up a report. This report should be wider than the statement of reasons for the decision, which is limited to justifying the decision made in respect of the supervision requirement. Rather, the report should take the form of the hearing's opinion as to the appropriateness of the order that the court is being asked to make.

Or the proposed placing for adoption. It is not by means of a court order that a child is placed for adoption, and it is not, therefore, for the court that a report is drawn up in these circumstances. In this case there is no obligation under subs. (14) below on any court to consider the report, but it is implicit that the local authority take account of it in deciding whether to go ahead with the placement, otherwise there would be no point in the children's hearing drawing it up. See also s.22A of the Adoption (Scotland) Act 1978. Procedure at any such hearing is governed by r. 22 of the 1996 Rules.

Subs. (14)

The court is obliged to consider the report drawn up by the children's hearing before making a decision as to whether to grant a parental responsibilities order under s.86 below or an order freeing the child for adoption under s.18 of the Adoption (Scotland) Act 1978 or an adoption order under s.12 thereof.

Further provision as respects children subject to supervision requirements

74. The Secretary of State may by regulations provide—

(a) for the transmission of information regarding a child who is subject to a supervision requirement to any person who, by virtue of that requirement, has, or is to have, control over the child;

(b) for the temporary accommodation, where necessary, of a child so subject; and

(c) for the conveyance of a child so subject—

    (i) to any place in which, under the supervision requirement, he is to reside;

    (ii) to any place to which he falls to be taken under subsection (1) or (5) of section 82 of this Act; or

    (iii) to any person to whom he falls to be returned under subsection (3) of that section.

DEFINITIONS

"child": s.93(2)(b).

"supervision requirement": s.93(1).

S.I.s ISSUED UNDER SECTION

Children's Hearings (Transmission of Information etc.) (Scotland) Regulations 1996 (S.I. 1996 No. 3260).

Powers of Secretary of State with respect to secure accommodation

75.—(1) The Secretary of State may by regulations make provision with respect to the placing in secure accommodation of any child—

(a) who is subject to a requirement imposed under section 70(3)(a) of this Act but not subject to a requirement under subsection (9) of that section, or

(b) who is not subject to a supervision requirement but who is being looked after by a local authority in pursuance of such enactments as may be specified in the regulations.

(2) Regulations under subsection (1) above may—

(a) specify the circumstances in which a child may be so placed under the regulations;

(b) make provision to enable a child who has been so placed or any relevant person to require that the child's case be brought before a children's hearing within a shorter period than would apply under regulations made under subsection (3) below; and

(c) specify different circumstances for different cases or classes of case.

(3) Subject to subsection (4) below and without prejudice to subsection (2)(b) above, the Secretary of State may prescribe—

(a) the maximum period during which a child may be kept under this Act in secure accommodation without the authority of a children's hearing or of the sheriff;

(b) the period within which a children's hearing shall be arranged to consider the case of a child placed in secure accommodation by virtue of regulations made under this section (and different periods may be so prescribed in respect of different cases or classes of case).

(4) Subsection (8) of section 66 of this Act shall apply in respect of a child placed in secure accommodation under regulations made under this section as if such placing took place by virtue of that section.

(5) The Secretary of State may by regulations vary the period within which a review of a condition imposed under section 70(9) of this Act shall be reviewed under section 73 of this Act.

(6) The Secretary of State may by regulations make provision for the procedures to be applied in placing children in secure accommodation; and without prejudice to the generality of this subsection, such regulations may—

(a) specify the duties of the Principal Reporter in relation to the placing of children in secure accommodation;

(b) make provision for the referral of cases to a children's hearing for review; and

(c) make provision for any person with parental responsibilities in relation to the child to be informed of the placing of the child in secure accommodation.

DEFINITIONS

"child": s.93(2)(b).
"children's hearing": s.93(1).
"local authority": Local Government etc. (Scotland) Act 1994, s.2.
"parental responsibilities": ss.1(3), 93(1).
"Principal Reporter": s.93(1).
"secure accommodation": s.93(1).
"supervision requirement": s.93(1).

S.I.S ISSUED UNDER SECTION

Secure Accommodation (Scotland) Regulations 1996 (S.I. 1996 No. 3255).
Children (Scotland) Act 1995 etc. (Revocations and Savings) (Scotland) Regulations 1997 (S.I. 1997 No. 691).

Exclusion orders

Exclusion orders

76.—(1) Subject to subsections (3) to (9) below, where on the application of a local authority the sheriff is satisfied, in relation to a child, that the conditions mentioned in subsection (2) below are met, he may grant an order under this section (to be known as "an exclusion order") excluding from the child's family home any person named in the order (in this Part of this Act referred to as the "named person").

(2) The conditions are—

(a) that the child has suffered, is suffering, or is likely to suffer, significant harm as a result of any conduct, or any threatened or reasonably apprehended conduct, of the named person;

(b) that the making of an exclusion order against the named person—

(i) is necessary for the protection of the child, irrespective of whether the child is for the time being residing in the family home; and

(ii) would better safeguard the child's welfare than the removal of the child from the family home; and

(c) that, if an order is made, there will be a person specified in the application who is capable of taking responsibility for the provision of appropriate care for the child and any other member of the family who requires such care and who is, or will be, residing in the family home (in this section, sections 77 to 79 and section 91(3)(f) of this Act referred to as an "appropriate person").

(3) No application under subsection (1) above for an exclusion order shall be finally determined under this section unless—

(a) the named person has been afforded an opportunity of being heard by, or represented before, the sheriff; and

(b) the sheriff has considered any views expressed by any person on whom notice of the application has been served in accordance with rules making such provision as is mentioned in section 91(3)(d) of this Act.

155

(4) Where, on an application under subsection (1) above, the sheriff—

(a) is satisfied as mentioned in that subsection; but

(b) the conditions mentioned in paragraphs (a) and (b) of subsection (3) above for the final determination of the application are not fulfilled,

he may grant an interim order, which shall have effect as an exclusion order pending a hearing by the sheriff under subsection (5) below held within such period as may be specified in rules made by virtue of section 91(3)(e) of this Act.

(5) The sheriff shall conduct a hearing under this subsection within such period as may be specified in rules made by virtue of section 91(3)(e) of this Act, and, if satisfied at that hearing as mentioned in subsection (1) above, he may, before finally determining the application, confirm or vary the interim order, or any term or condition on which it was granted, or may recall such order.

(6) Where the conditions mentioned in paragraphs (a) and (b) of subsection (3) above have been fulfilled, the sheriff may, at any point prior to the final determination of the application, grant an interim order.

(7) An order under subsection (5) or (6) above shall have effect as an exclusion order pending the final determination of the application.

(8) Where—

(a) an application is made under subsection (1) above; and

(b) the sheriff considers that the conditions for making a child protection order under section 57 of this Act are satisfied,

he may make an order under that section as if the application had been duly made by the local authority under that rather than under this section.

(9) The sheriff shall not make an exclusion order if it appears to him that to do so would be unjustifiable or unreasonable, having regard to—

(a) all the circumstances of the case, including without prejudice to the generality of this subsection the matters specified in subsection (10) below; and

(b) any requirement such as is specified in subsection (11) below and the likely consequences in the light of that requirement of the exclusion of the named person from the family home.

(10) The matters referred to in subsection (9)(a) above are—

(a) the conduct of the members of the child's family (whether in relation to each other or otherwise);

(b) the respective needs and financial resources of the members of that family;

(c) the extent (if any) to which—

(i) the family home; and

(ii) any relevant item in that home,

is used in connection with a trade, business or profession by any member of the family.

(11) The requirement referred to in subsection (9)(b) above is a requirement that the named person (whether alone or with any other person) must reside in the family home, where that home—

(a) is or is part of an agricultural holding within the meaning of the Agricultural Holdings (Scotland) Act 1991; or

(b) is let, or is a home in respect of which possession is given, to the named person (whether alone or with any other person) by an employer as an incident of employment.

(12) In this Part of this Act—

"caravan" has the meaning given to it by section 29(1) of the Caravan Sites and Control of Development Act 1960;

"exclusion order", includes an interim order granted under subsection (4) above and such an order confirmed or varied under subsection (5) above and an interim order granted under subsection (6) above; except that in subsection (3) above and in section 79 of this Act, it does not include an interim order granted under subsection (4) above;

"family" has the meaning given in section 93(1) of this Act;
"family home" means any house, caravan, houseboat or other structure which is used as a family residence and in which the child ordinarily resides with any person described in subsection (13) below and the expression includes any garden or other ground or building attached to and usually occupied with, or otherwise required for the amenity or convenience of, the house, caravan, houseboat or other structure.

(13) The description of person referred to in the definition of "family home" in subsection (12) above, is a person who has parental responsibilities in relation to the child, or who ordinarily (and other than by reason only of his employment) has charge of, or control over him.

DEFINITIONS
"child": s.93(2)(b).
"family": s.93(1).
"local authority": Local Government etc. (Scotland) Act 1994, s.2.

GENERAL NOTE
It often happens that the protection of a child can only be achieved by separating that child from the adult who poses a threat to her or his wellbeing. Until the passing of the present Act, if the threatening adult lived in the same household as the child, that separation could only be achieved by removing the child from her or his home, either by means of the emergency provisions (place of safety orders) or by means of more long-term protective measures (supervision requirements with conditions of residence away from the source of danger). It had long been recognised that the removal of a child from her or his home environment would itself in most, if not all, cases, be a traumatic experience for the child and in some cases that trauma could counter or even outweigh any good the removal was designed to achieve. The highlighting of this fact by the Orkney case led it to be seen as a failing in the law that there was no procedure, similar to that contained in the Matrimonial Homes (Family Protection) (Scotland) Act 1981 (c. 59), for the exclusion of an abuser from the child's home (see White Paper *Scotland's Children: Proposals for Child Care Policy and Law* (Cm. 2286, August 1993). Sections 76 to 80 are designed to correct that perceived flaw, by giving sheriffs the right to grant exclusion orders excluding named individuals from the homes of particular children whenever this is necessary for the protection of individual children. Procedure is governed by A.S. 1997, rr. 3.34–3.40.

If a child needs protecting from a particular adult, there is in principle no difference between removing the child from the adult and removing the adult from the child; but in practice the two acts have hugely different consequences. For one thing the removal of the adult may well result in the denial of property rights, which is seldom a consideration with children. Also, removal of an adult may leave the child with no carer in the family home, which would require the child to be taken into care in any case. Again, removal of a child obliges the local authority to provide the child with accommodation whereas removal of an adult does not create any analogous obligation. For these, and other, reasons, the following sections were amongst the most keenly debated and controversial provisions in the whole of the Act. The aim of proponents of exclusion orders, to ensure that children are not disrupted in their lives unduly is, of course, worthy, but it is difficult to see what real benefit the present provisions will bring. There is little possibility of exclusion orders providing emergency protection for children on a short-term basis, for it is likely to be considered "unjustifiable or unreasonable" to exclude a person from her or his own home on the basis of unproven allegations alone, even when such allegations are sufficient to activate the other protection mechanisms in the Act. A child who needs long-term protection from a particular adult will not receive that protection by removing the adult for a period of no more than six months, which is the extent of the exclusion in the present provisions. On the other hand, the exclusion order might well prove of great use to protect a child from an adult who visits the family home regularly and who poses some risk to the child.

The draftsmen have modelled the provisions in ss.76–80 to a large extent on those in the Matrimonial Homes (Family Protection) (Scotland) Act 1981, to which very different considerations apply. As under that Act, interim orders may be made, and the sheriff is obliged to refuse to make an exclusion order in a number of stated circumstances. There is, however, rather more discretion given to sheriffs in the present provisions than in the 1981 Act, and it remains to be seen how willing sheriffs are to utilise their new powers.

Subs. (1)
A local authority can apply to the sheriff for the granting of an exclusion order, which will be granted if the conditions in subs. (2) below are satisfied, and which will have the effect, in terms of s.77(1) below, of excluding from the child's home any named person, preventing that person from entering the home, and suspending during its currency any rights of occupancy in the home that the named person has.

On the application of a local authority. It should be noted that some persons other than local authorities are entitled to seek an exclusion order under the terms of the Matrimonial Homes (Family Protection) Scotland Act 1981, which might be used as a means of protecting a child. The present provision, on the other hand, deals with the power of public authorities to protect children, and it is only a local authority which has title to seek an exclusion order under this Act. This is to be compared with s.57(1) above which entitles "any person" (including a local authority) to apply to the sheriff for a child protection order which will frequently have the effect of removing the child from her or his home. There is no indication given in the Act to local authorities as to when it would be appropriate for them to seek one order rather than the other, but there are at least two considerations which will encourage local authorities to seek a child protection order rather than an exclusion order. First, the burden of proof is rather less under s.57 than under the present section, in that the condition to be established in s.57 is "reasonable grounds for believing" that the child is suffering significant harm while in the present section the condition to be established is that the child is actually suffering significant harm as a matter of fact rather than as a matter of belief. Secondly, there are a number of defences to the granting of exclusion orders (see subss (9)–(11) below) which do not apply to child protection orders, so that even when the conditions for both orders can be satisfied by the applicant local authority, the inclination is likely to be to seek the order which cannot be defended rather than the order which can be.

The sheriff. It is the sheriff within whose sheriffdom the family home is situated who has jurisdiction to make the exclusion order (s.80(2) below).

He may. Even if the local authority establishes the conditions to be satisfied under subs. (2) below (and the defences in subss (9)–(11) below are not satisfied), the sheriff retains a discretion as to whether or not to grant the exclusion order. His decision is governed by all three of the overarching principles set out in s.16: the child's welfare must be his paramount consideration; he must give the child an opportunity to express views and take account of these views; and he must not make the exclusion order unless he considers that it would be better to make the order than that no order be made at all.

The child's family home. The order excludes the named person from the child's family home, that is to say from the place where the child normally lives with a person who has parental responsibilities in relation to the child.

Any person named in the order. The order can exclude any named person from the child's family home, and it is not limited to a relative of the child, nor to someone who is living in the home with the child. The exclusion order may well in practice prove most useful in protecting a child from a regular visitor to the family home, such as an ex-cohabitant of the mother, for it is likely to be easier to show that it is reasonable to exclude a visitor than to show that it is reasonable to exclude a person who lives in the home.

Subs. (2)

All three of the listed conditions must be satisfied, and the onus lies on the local authority to establish them.

Is necessary for the protection of the child. It must be shown by the applicant that the exclusion order is "necessary", but this word is not to be interpreted to mean that the exclusion order can be granted only when no other orders (such as a child protection order) are available to protect the child, for otherwise exclusion orders could never be granted. Rather it must be shown that without this order or any other order the child's welfare is at risk. It is submitted that an exclusion order is "necessary" when it is the most appropriate of the available means of protecting the child from significant harm.

Irrespective of whether the child is ... residing in the family home. An exclusion order may be necessary to allow a child to return home from a short-term refuge to which she or he has fled or been taken.

Would better safeguard the child's welfare. These words require that the sheriff undertakes a balancing of the respective merits and likely success of the different orders available to him (it being remembered that subs. (8) below permits him to make a child protection order even when asked for an exclusion order). An order excluding a regular visitor from the child's home will nearly always be better than removing the child from her or his home; the balance will be less obvious when the local authority's objective is to exclude a resident from the child's home.

There will be a person specified in the application who is capable of taking responsibility. The applicant local authority must name a person who is able to look after the child in the child's own home, and the sheriff must be satisfied that that person is both willing and able to provide that care at that place. An exclusion order will not, therefore, be appropriate in cases in which the threat to the child comes from her or his only carer, nor in cases in which both or all of the carers are alleged to be the source of danger to the child. Having been born out of the Orkney case, it is a nice irony that exclusion orders, had they been in existence then, could not have "protected" the Orkney children.

Subs. (3)

The final determination by the sheriff of the application for an exclusion order cannot be made until such time as the person to be excluded has been given an opportunity to be heard by the sheriff, either personally or through a representative, and the sheriff has given consideration to the views expressed by any person notified of the application under rules to be made. As a consequence, a final exclusion order (as opposed to an interim order made under subs. (4) below) is inappropriate as a means of providing emergency protection for the child. A final exclusion order will last for anything up to six months (see s.79(1) below) and it will, therefore, be appropriate only in those cases in which the child's interests are best served by excluding a person for that length of time. In addition, because exclusion orders are expressly mentioned in s.16(4)(b)(i), the sheriff must give the child an opportunity to express views and have appropriate regard to any views expressed.

Subss. (4), (5) and (6)

A final determination of the application can be made only when both (a) the conditions in subs. (2) above are satisfied and (b) the persons mentioned in subs. (3) above (and the child) have been given an opportunity to express views. This means that the final determination will invariably be too late to use an exclusion order as a means of emergency protection of the child. To deal with this point, the present subsections were introduced to allow immediate exclusion of someone suspected of abusing a child. They provide that where subs. (2) above is satisfied but subs. (3) above is not, an interim exclusion order can be made under subs. (4), and where subs. (3) is satisfied but subs. (2) is not (yet) satisfied an interim exclusion order can be made under subs. (6).

An interim exclusion order, once granted, has the same effect (described in s.77(1) below) as a final order, but its granting under subs. (4) (but not subs. (6)) will require the sheriff to hold a hearing under subs. (5) not later than three working days after the granting of the order (A.S. 1997, r. 3.36). If such a hearing is not timeously held, the interim exclusion order will fall. At that hearing the sheriff must consider whether the conditions for the granting of an exclusion order in subs. (2) above remain satisfied, and if so he may confirm, vary or recall the order. It is not stated but the implication is clear that if not so satisfied he must recall the order. Presumably at this hearing the sheriff may also come to a final determination of the application, but if he does not do so the interim order will remain in effect on the terms laid down until the final determination. An interim order granted under subs. (6) can last up to six months (s.78 below).

Subs. (7)

Any interim order that the sheriff makes under subs. (6) above, or a continuation under subs. (5) above of an interim order made under subs. (4) above shall have the same effect (described in s.77(1) below) as a full exclusion order, and it shall last until the final determination of the application (or until six months after having been made if the application is not finally determined before then).

Subs. (8)

This subsection provides that if the conditions for the granting of a child protection order are established in an application for an exclusion order, the sheriff may treat the application as if it were an application for a child protection order. As pointed out in the notes to subs. (1) above, the conditions listed in subs. (2) above for the granting of an exclusion order are stricter than the conditions for the granting of a child protection order laid down in s.57 above. It follows that in every case in which the conditions in subs. (2) above have been satisfied, the conditions in s.57 will also have been satisfied (for proof that the child has been harmed will invariably include proof that there are reasonable grounds for believing that the child has been harmed) and the sheriff will be entitled to treat the application under this section as if it were an application under that section. In addition, the local authority may fail to satisfy the conditions in this section, but nevertheless succeed in satisfying the conditions in s.57: in that case too the sheriff may treat the application as if it had been made under s.57.

He may. The sheriff has a discretion and he is not obliged to treat the application as one for a child protection order even when the conditions for the granting of such an order have been made out (*cf.* General Note to s.55(2) above). If the conditions for both orders have been satisfied, the sheriff will decide according to which order is most likely to further the welfare of the child. If only the conditions for the granting of a child protection order have been satisfied then he will decide according to whether he considers that order rather than no order is more appropriate to the child's need for protection.

Subs. (9)

Following closely the terms in s.4(3) of the Matrimonial Homes (Family Protection) (Scotland) Act 1981, this and the immediately following two subsections prohibit the sheriff from making an exclusion order in circumstances in which it would be unjustifiable and unreasonable to do so, taking account of certain specified matters.

Unjustifiable or unreasonable. These are clearly the key words in this provision, as they are of the 1981 provision upon which this subsection is based. An exclusion order may well be "necessary" (as required in subs. (2)(b) above) but remain "unjustifiable or unreasonable", because while necessity is to be looked at from the point of view of the child, this provision requires the issue to be looked at from the point of view of the adult whom the local authority want excluded from the child's home. As explained in the General Note to subs. (2) above, an exclusion order may well be "necessary" even when other orders are available for the protection of the child, but the granting of an exclusion order might be considered unjustifiable or unreasonable when some other order is available. This cannot, however, be regarded as an automatic conclusion, otherwise there would always be a defence to an exclusion order under this provision. Rather, what is required from the sheriff is a weighing up of the respective interests of the child and the adult, and the respective effects that the different orders will have on both. If the detriment to the adult is disproportionate to the benefit to the child (bearing in mind, in making that assessment, that the child's welfare is paramount: s.16(1)) then an exclusion order under this section is likely to be considered unjustifiable or unreasonable.

Subs. (10)
The whole circumstances of the case are to be taken into account by the sheriff in determining whether it would be unjustifiable or unreasonable to make an exclusion order, and this subsection lists some of the circumstances that will always be relevant.
The conduct of the members of the child's family. The conduct is to be such as to suggest that an exclusion order should not be granted: it must, therefore, refer to conduct which suggests that members of the child's family are able to protect the child from the risk posed by the person the local authority are seeking to exclude.
Respective needs and financial resources. Every member of a child's family needs accommodation and it will seldom be justifiable or reasonable to exclude a person from her or his home when she or he has nowhere else to go. The reference to financial resources allows the sheriff to take account of the ability of the potentially excluded person to pay for alternative accommodation.

Subs. (11)
In deciding whether an exclusion order would be unjustifiable or unreasonable the sheriff must take account of any requirement (for the reasons listed in this subsection) that the potentially excluded person reside in the child's home and the likelihood of that person losing her or his entitlement to live there if the exclusion order is made.

Subs. (13)
The person with whom the child resides in the family home is defined here in the same way as "the relevant person" is defined throughout the rest of this Part of the Act (except for s.86), except that the reference is to a person with parental responsibilities rather than to a person with parental responsibilities or parental rights. This makes no difference since persons with parental responsibilities have such rights as are necessary to fulfil their responsibilities.

Effect of, and orders etc. ancillary to, exclusion order

77.—(1) An exclusion order shall, in respect of the home to which it relates, have the effect of suspending the named person's rights of occupancy (if any) and shall prevent him from entering the home, except with the express permission of the local authority which applied for the order.

(2) The sheriff, on the application of the local authority, may, if and in so far as he thinks fit, when making an exclusion order do any of the things mentioned in subsection (3) below.

(3) The things referred to in subsection (2) above are—

(a) grant a warrant for the summary ejection of the named person from the home;

(b) grant an interdict prohibiting the named person from entering the home without the express permission of the local authority;

(c) grant an interdict prohibiting the removal by the named person of any relevant item specified in the interdict from the home, except either—

(i) with the written consent of the local authority, or of an appropriate person; or

  (ii) by virtue of a subsequent order of the sheriff;
 (d) grant an interdict prohibiting the named person from entering or remaining in a specified area in the vicinity of the home;
 (e) grant an interdict prohibiting the taking by the named person of any step of a kind specified in the interdict in relation to the child;
 (f) make an order regulating the contact between the child and the named person,
and the sheriff may make any other order which he considers is necessary for the proper enforcement of a remedy granted by virtue of paragraph (a), (b) or (c) of this subsection.

 (4) No warrant, interdict or order (except an interdict granted by virtue of paragraph (b) of subsection (3) above) shall be granted or made under subsection (2) above if the named person satisfies the sheriff that it is unnecessary to do so.

 (5) Where the sheriff grants a warrant of summary ejection under subsection (2) above in the absence of the named person, he may give directions as to the preservation of any of that person's goods and effects which remain in the family home.

 (6) The sheriff may make an order of the kind specified in subsection (3)(f) above irrespective of whether there has been an application for such an order.

 (7) On the application of either the named person or the local authority, the sheriff may make the exclusion order, or any remedy granted under subsection (2) above, subject to such terms and conditions as he considers appropriate.

 (8) In this Part of this Act references to a "relevant item" are references to any item within the home which both—
 (a) is owned or hired by any member of the family concerned or an appropriate person or is being acquired by any such member or person under a hire purchase agreement or conditional sale agreement; and
 (b) is reasonably necessary to enable the home to be used as a family residence,
but does not include any such vehicle, caravan or houseboat or such other structure so used as is mentioned in the definition of "family home" in section 76(12) of this Act.

DEFINITIONS
 "appropriate person": s.76(2)(c).
 "exclusion order": ss.76(12), 93(1).
 "family home": s.76(12).
 "local authority": Local Government etc. (Scotland) Act 1994, s.2.
 "named person": s.76(1).

GENERAL NOTE
 Following on from the section above, this section sets out the effect of an exclusion order and lists various ancillary orders that the sheriff can make in connection with an exclusion order.

Subs. (1)
 The effect of an exclusion order is to prevent the named person from entering the child's home over which the order has been made, and to suspend any right of occupancy that the named person has in that home. Entry into the home is permitted only with the express permission of the local authority.
 Suspending the named person's rights of occupancy (if any). The order granted under s.76 can exclude any person from the child's home, whether or not that person has a right of occupancy. If the person does have a right of occupancy in that home, whether as owner, tenant or otherwise, then this is suspended for the currency of the exclusion order; if she or he has no such right then she or he can be prevented from entering into the home even with the permission of the occupier.

Exclusion order. This means an order granted under s.76(1) above, an interim order granted under s.76(4) above, the continuation granted under s.76(5) of such an interim order, and an interim order granted under s.76(6) above.

Subs. (2)

The sheriff may grant any of the warrants or interdicts or make any of the orders listed in subs. (3) below if he thinks fit. This differs somewhat from the provisions in the Matrimonial Homes (Family Protection) (Scotland) Act 1981, under which the sheriff is obliged to make some of these orders whenever he is requested to do so. Here, the matter lies entirely in the discretion of the sheriff, who must apply the three overarching principles in s.16 above in deciding whether to do any of these things. It is for the local authority which applies for the exclusion order to seek one of these ancillary orders, and to persuade the sheriff that the child's welfare would be advanced by the making of such an order.

Subs. (3)

Paragraphs (a) to (f) list the warrants, interdicts and orders that the sheriff can make ancillary to the making of an exclusion order. In addition, the sheriff can make any other order that is necessary for the proper enforcement of a warrant for summary ejection from the child's home, of an interdict prohibiting the named person entering the child's home, or of an interdict prohibiting the removal of items from the child's home. It is not clear why the statute does not permit orders necessary for the proper enforcement of the other interdicts in the subsection. Powers of arrest may be attached to interdicts granted under this subsection (s.78 below).

Relevant item. This is defined in subs. (8) below.

Vicinity of the home. The interdict can prohibit the named person only from a specified area in the vicinity of the child's home, and not elsewhere, such as, for example, in the vicinity of the child's school. This emphasises the essentially domestic nature of the protection afforded by an exclusion order.

Subs. (4)

The person excluded from the child's home is entitled to seek to persuade the sheriff not to make any of the ancillary orders in subs. (3) above (except one). The onus is on the person to satisfy the sheriff that such an order is unnecessary (unlike with the exclusion order itself, where the onus lies with the applicant to show that it is necessary). Only in relation to an order prohibiting the excluded person from entering the child's home without the local authority's permission is the excluded person not entitled to show that it is unnecessary. This is because such a prohibition is inherent in the exclusion order in any case, which will only have been made if the applicant local authority has established that it is necessary.

Unnecessary. This means unnecessary in light of the threat to the child. An order which is not needed to provide the child with protection is not necessary. So, for example, a warrant for the summary ejection of the excluded person from the child's home will be unnecessary if that person agrees to leave the home voluntarily, or is not in it. It will be unnecessary to grant any of the listed interdicts in situations in which there is no suggestion that the excluded person will perform any of the acts that can be interdicted.

Subs. (5)

Any of the ancillary orders can be made in relation to interim exclusion orders, made before the excluded person has been given the opportunity of being heard by the sheriff. If the ancillary order is one of summary ejection from the child's home, the sheriff may give directions of the nature specified. It is surprising in the light of the terms of subs. (6) below that no express power is given to the sheriff to give directions in the absence of any request to do so, but since the excluded person is *ex hypothesi* absent for the purposes of this subsection, it is unclear who else will make such a request and the implication must be that the sheriff can give directions *ex proprio motu*. There is no requirement that the directions under this subsection be sought by the local authority and any interested party to the exclusion order can, it is submitted, seek directions.

Subs. (6)

The sheriff can make an order regulating the contact between the child and the excluded person even when not requested to do so by the local authority. His determination to do so is governed by the three overarching principles in s.16 above.

Subs. (7)

Once the exclusion order (which includes interim orders and orders continuing interim orders) has been made, either the excluded person or the local authority can request the sheriff to subject that order to such terms and conditions as are appropriate. The sheriff's decision is governed by the three overarching principles in s.16: though s.16(4)(b)(i) refers in its terms only to the making of an exclusion order this includes, it is submitted, the conditions which are to be attached thereto.

Powers of arrest etc. in relation to exclusion order

78.—(1) The sheriff may, whether or not on an application such as is mentioned in subsection (2) below, attach a power of arrest to any interdict granted under section 77(2) of this Act by virtue of subsection (3) of that section.

(2) A local authority may at any time while an exclusion order has effect apply for such attachment of a power of arrest as is mentioned in subsection (1) above.

(3) A power of arrest attached to an interdict by virtue of subsection (1) above shall not have effect until such interdict, together with the attached power of arrest, is served on the named person.

(4) If, by virtue of subsection (1) above, a power of arrest is attached to an interdict, the local authority shall, as soon as possible after the interdict, together with the attached power of arrest, is served on the named person, ensure that there is delivered—

(a) to the chief constable of the police area in which the family home is situated; and

(b) where the interdict was granted by virtue of section 77(3)(e) of this Act, to the chief constable of the area in which the step or conduct which is prevented by the interdict may take place,

a copy of the application for the interdict and of the interlocutor granting the interdict together with a certificate of service of the interdict and, where the application to attach the power of arrest was made after the interdict was granted, a copy of that application and of the interlocutor above granting it and a certificate of service of the interdict together with the attached power of arrest.

(5) Where any interdict to which a power of arrest is attached by virtue of subsection (1) above is varied or recalled, the person who applied for the variation or recall shall ensure that there is delivered to each chief constable specified in subsection (4) above a copy of the application for such variation or recall and of the interlocutor granting the variation or recall.

(6) A constable may arrest without warrant the named person if he has reasonable cause for suspecting that person to be in breach of an interdict to which a power of arrest has been attached by virtue of subsection (1) above.

(7) Where a person has been arrested under subsection (6) above, the constable in charge of a police station may—

(a) if satisfied there is no likelihood of that person further breaching the interdict to which the power of arrest was attached under subsection (1) above, liberate him unconditionally; or

(b) refuse to liberate that person.

(8) Such a refusal to liberate an arrested person as is mentioned in subsection (7)(b) above, and the detention of that person until his appearance in court by virtue of either subsection (11) below, or any provision of the Criminal Procedure (Scotland) Act 1995, shall not subject that constable to any claim whatsoever.

(9) Where a person has been liberated under subsection (7)(a) above, the facts and circumstances which gave rise to the arrest shall be reported to the procurator fiscal forthwith.

(10) Subsections (11) to (13) below apply only where—

(a) the arrested person has not been released under subsection (7)(a) above; and

  (b) the procurator fiscal decides that no criminal proceedings are to be taken in respect of the facts and circumstances which gave rise to the arrest.

[1] (11) A person arrested under subsection (6) above shall, wherever practicable, be brought before the sheriff sitting as a court of summary criminal jurisdiction for the district in which he was arrested not later than in the course of the first day after the arrest, such day not being a Saturday, a Sunday or a court holiday prescribed for that court under section 8 of the said Act of 1995, on which the sheriff is not sitting for the disposal of criminal business.

[1] (12) Subsections (1), (2) and (4) of section 15 of the said Act of 1995 (intimation to a person named by the person arrested) shall apply to a person arrested under subsection (6) above as they apply to a person who has been arrested in respect of an offence.

(13) Where a person is brought before the sheriff under subsection (11) above—

  (a) the procurator fiscal shall present to the court a petition containing—

     (i) a statement of the particulars of the person arrested under subsection (6) above;

    (ii) a statement of the facts and circumstances which gave rise to that arrest; and

   (iii) a request that the person be detained for a further period not exceeding two days;

  (b) the sheriff, if it appears to him that—

     (i) the statement referred to in paragraph (a)(ii) above discloses a *prima facie* breach of interdict by the arrested person;

    (ii) proceedings for breach of interdict will be taken; and

   (iii) there is a substantial risk of violence by the arrested person against any member of the family, or an appropriate person, resident in the family home,

may order the arrested person to be detained for a period not exceeding two days; and

  (c) the sheriff shall, in any case in which paragraph (b) above does not apply, order the release of the arrested person from custody (unless that person is in custody in respect of some other matter);

and in computing the period of two days referred to in paragraphs (a) and (b) above, no account shall be taken of a Saturday, a Sunday or any holiday in the court in which proceedings for breach of interdict will require to be raised.

(14) Where a person—

  (a) is liberated under subsection (7)(a) above; or

  (b) is to be brought before the sheriff under subsection (11) above,

the procurator fiscal shall at the earliest opportunity, and, in the case of a person to whom paragraph (b) above applies, before that person is brought before the sheriff, take all reasonable steps to intimate to—

     (i) the local authority which made the application for the interdict;

    (ii) an appropriate person who will reside in, or who remains in residence in, the family home mentioned in the order; and

   (iii) any solicitor who acted for the appropriate person when the interdict was granted or to any other solicitor who the procurator fiscal has reason to believe acts for the time being for that person,

that he has decided that no criminal proceedings should be taken in respect of the facts and circumstances which gave rise to the arrest of the named person.

NOTE

  1. As amended by the Criminal Procedure (Consequential Provisions) (Scotland) Act 1995, c. 40, s.3 and Sched. 3, para. 97.

GENERAL NOTE
    The sheriff may, at his own hand or on application by the local authority either when the exclusion order is applied for or at any time during its currency, attach a power of arrest to any interdict which has been granted ancillary to the exclusion order itself. This section sets out the applicable circumstances and the consequences of such a power of arrest.

Duration, variation and recall of exclusion order

79.—(1) Subject to subsection (2) below, an exclusion order shall cease to have effect on a date six months after being made.

(2) An exclusion order shall cease to have effect on a date prior to the date mentioned in subsection (1) above where—

(a) the order contains a direction by the sheriff that it shall cease to have effect on that prior date;

(b) the sheriff, on an application under subsection (3) below, recalls the order before the date so mentioned; or

(c) any permission given by a third party to the spouse or partner of the named person, or to an appropriate person, to occupy the home to which the order relates is withdrawn.

(3) The sheriff may, on the application of the local authority, the named person, an appropriate person or the spouse or partner of the named person, if that spouse or partner is not excluded from the family home and is not an appropriate person, vary or recall an exclusion order and any warrant, interdict, order or direction granted or made under section 77 of this Act.

(4) For the purposes of this section, partners are persons who live together in a family home as if they were husband and wife.

GENERAL NOTE
    This section deals with the duration, variation and recall of exclusion orders.

Subs. (1)
    Unless brought to an end earlier in terms of subs. (2) below an exclusion order ceases to have effect six months after it was made. There is nothing to prevent a local authority seeking a new exclusion order immediately on the termination of the old (so long as the conditions in s.76(2) can again be satisfied).
    Exclusion order. What is being referred to here is the final order made on an application under s.76(1) above, an interim order made under s.76(6) and a continuation granted under s.76(5) of an interim order made under s.76(4). The phrase does not include, for this purpose, an interim order made under s.76(4): see s.76(12) above.
    A date six months after being made. It is six calendar months that are being referred to: an order made on February 6 comes to an end at midnight on the immediately following August 5; an order made on September 1 comes to an end at midnight on the immediately following February 28 or 29.

Subs. (2)
    An exclusion order need not last six months if any of the three circumstances listed here applies, that is to say if the sheriff directed on making the order that it should cease on some sooner date, or if the sheriff recalls the order on an application under subs. (3) below, or if the

excluded person's spouse or heterosexual cohabitant (subs. (4) below) or the person looking after the child becomes no longer entitled to occupy the child's home. This last might include, for example, the termination of a lease or the sale of the house during the currency of the exclusion order: it is appropriate to bring the order to an end in these circumstances since the child will no longer practically be able to live in the house the person is excluded from. It is unfortunate that the paragraph was not expressed more clearly in terms of the child's departure rather than the "appropriate person's" right.

Subs. (3)
There is no provision in the Act expressly granting a right of appeal to the sheriff principal or to the Court of Session from a decision of the sheriff to grant (or refuse) an exclusion order, though normal principles of appeal will apply (it is assumed in s.92 below in the legal aid provisions that there is an appeal from the sheriff in relation to exclusion orders). In addition, application can be made under this subsection to the sheriff for the variation or recall of an exclusion order and any order made ancillary to it. The Act gives no direction to the sheriff as to how to deal with such an application, except that the three overarching principles in s.16 above apply. It follows that a sheriff may competently recall an exclusion order if he considers that this is in the interests of the child, even when the conditions for its making remain satisfied. It is unclear why the subsection limits so carefully title to seek a variation or discharge in circumstances in which the child's welfare is paramount. It would have been more consistent with the advancement of the child's welfare to allow any person claiming an interest to make such an application (*cf.* s.11(3) above which entitles "any person who ... claims an interest" to seek a private law order, s.86(5) below which entitles "any person claiming an interest" to seek a variation or discharge of a parental responsibilities order, and s.88(3) below which entitles "any person with an interest" to seek an order as to contact between a child subject to a parental responsibilities order and another person). There would seem to be nothing to prevent an unsuccessful applicant for recall making a fresh application immediately thereafter, and there is no provision, analogous to that contained in s.51(7) above in relation to appeals against decisions of children's hearings, to prevent frivolous applications.

The sheriff. It is the sheriff within whose sheriffdom the family home is situated who has jurisdiction to vary or recall the exclusion order: s.80(2) below.

Exclusion orders: supplementary provisions

80.—(1) The Secretary of State may make regulations with respect to the powers, duties and functions of local authorities in relation to exclusion orders.

(2) An application for an exclusion order, or under section 79(3) of this Act for the variation or recall of such an order or of any thing done under section 77(2) of this Act, shall be made to the sheriff for the sheriffdom within which the family home is situated.

DEFINITIONS
"exclusion order": s.76(12).
"family home": s.76(12).
"local authority": Local Government etc. (Scotland) Act 1995, s.2.

GENERAL NOTE
See A.S. 1997, rr. 3.34–3.40.

Offences in connection with orders etc. for protection of children

Offences in connection with orders etc. for protection of children

81. A person who intentionally obstructs—
(a) any person acting under a child protection order;
(b) any person acting under an authorisation granted under section 61(1) or (2) of this Act; or
(c) a constable acting under section 61(5) of this Act,
shall, subject to section 38(3) and (4) of this Act, be guilty of an offence and shall be liable on summary conviction to a fine not exceeding level 3 on the standard scale.

Children (Scotland) Act 1995

DEFINITION
"child protection order": ss.57(1), 93(1).

GENERAL NOTE
It is an offence, which attracts the stated penalty, intentionally to obstruct any person acting under a child protection order made under s.57 above or under an authorisation granted by a justice of the peace when a sheriff is not available to make a child protection order, or to obstruct a constable removing a child to a place of safety and keeping her or him there.

Fugitive children and harbouring

Recovery of certain fugitive children

82.—(1) A child who absconds—
  (a) from a place of safety in which he is being kept under or by virtue of this Part of this Act;
  (b) from a place (in this section referred to as a "relevant place") which, though not a place of safety such as is mentioned in paragraph (a) above, is a residential establishment in which he is required to reside by virtue of section 70(3)(a) of this Act or a hospital or other institution in which he is temporarily residing while subject to such a requirement; or
  (c) from a person who, by virtue of a supervision requirement or of section 74 of this Act, has control over him while he is being taken to, is awaiting being taken to, or (whether or not by reason of being on leave) is temporarily away from, such place of safety or relevant place,
may be arrested without warrant in any part of the United Kingdom and taken to the place of safety or as the case may be the relevant place; and a court which is satisfied that there are reasonable grounds for believing that the child is within any premises may, where there is such power of arrest, grant a warrant authorising a constable to enter those premises and search for the child using reasonable force if necessary.

(2) Without prejudice to the generality of subsection (1) above, a child who at the end of a period of leave from a place of safety or relevant place fails to return there shall, for the purposes of this section, be taken to have absconded.

(3) A child who absconds from a person who, not being a person mentioned in paragraph (c) of subsection (1) above, is a person who has control over him by virtue of a supervision requirement may, subject to the same provisions as those to which an arrest under that subsection is subject, be arrested as is mentioned in that subsection and returned to that person; and the provision in that subsection for a warrant to be granted shall apply as respects such a child as it applies as respects a child mentioned in that subsection.

(4) If a child—
  (a) is taken under subsection (1) above to a place of safety or relevant place; or
  (b) is returned under subsection (3) above to a person,
but the occupier of that place of safety or of that relevant place, or as the case may be that person, is unwilling or unable to receive him, that circumstance shall be intimated forthwith to the Principal Reporter.

(5) Where intimation is required by subsection (4) above as respects a child, he shall be kept in a place of safety until—
  (a) in a case where he is subject to a supervision requirement, he can be brought before a children's hearing for that requirement to be reviewed; or
  (b) in any other case, the Principal Reporter has, in accordance with section 56(6) of this Act, considered whether compulsory measures of supervision are required in respect of him.

DEFINITIONS
"child": s.93(2)(b).
"children's hearing": s.93(1).
"constable": s.93(1).
"place of safety": s.93(1).
"Principal Reporter": s.93(1).
"residential establishment": s.93(1).
"supervision requirement": ss.70(1), 93(1).

GENERAL NOTE
This section replaces, with only minor amendments, ss.69 and 70 of the 1968 Act, and provides that a child who has absconded from a place of safety or residential establishment or from a person can be arrested without a warrant and returned to where she or he absconded from.

Subss. (1) and (2)
As well as permitting the child to be arrested without a warrant, subs. (1) also permits the court to grant a warrant authorising a police officer to enter premises and search for the child. There are two changes from the 1968 Act: the present provision permits the child's arrest anywhere in the U.K. rather than, as previously, in the U.K. or the Channel Islands (though the reference to the Channel Islands may be restored: see s.105(10) below); and the authorisation to enter premises expressly permits the police officer to use reasonable force.
A child who absconds. A child absconds when she or he removes her or himself from the relevant place. It expressly includes the child who fails to return to a place after a period of leave, and it is likely to include also the child who absents her or himself to prevent being taken in the first place to the relevant place.

Subs. (3)
The same provisions apply in relation to a child who absconds from the control of a person who has that control by virtue of a supervision requirement. This might be, for example, a foster carer or a relative. It would not apply to a child who is required to reside with a person who otherwise than under the supervision requirement has parental responsibilities or parental rights over her or him.

Subss. (4) and (5)
These provisions replace s.69(3) and (4) of the 1968 Act and have much the same effect. If the child cannot be returned to the place or person from whom she or he absconded due to unwillingness to receive the child back, the reporter must be informed and the child kept in a place of safety until a children's hearing has been arranged (if currently subject to a supervision requirement) or the reporter has considered whether compulsory measures of supervision are required (in any other case). One alteration from the 1968 provisions, the reason for which is not apparent, is the removal of the requirement to hold the children's hearing within seven days. The current wording suggests that a hearing should be arranged as soon as practicable, but it does not, unlike most other provisions of the Act, specify when that hearing should be arranged. The provision cannot be interpreted to permit a child to be kept in a place of safety indefinitely.

Harbouring

83. A person who—
(a) knowingly assists or induces a child to abscond in circumstances which render the child liable to arrest under subsection (1) or (3) of section 82 of this Act;
(b) knowingly and persistently attempts to induce a child so to abscond;
(c) knowingly harbours or conceals a child who has so absconded; or
(d) knowingly prevents a child from returning—
    (i) to a place mentioned in paragraph (a) or (b) of the said subsection (1);
    (ii) to a person mentioned in paragraph (c) of that subsection, or in the said subsection (3),
shall, subject to section 38(3) and (4) of this Act, to section 51(5) and (6) of the Children Act 1989 and to Article 70(5) and (6) of the Children (Northern Ireland) Order 1995 (analogous provision for England and Wales and for Northern Ireland), be guilty of an offence and liable on summary conviction

to a fine not exceeding level 5 on the standard scale or to imprisonment for a term not exceeding six months or to both such fine and such imprisonment.

DEFINITION
"child": s.93(2)(b).

GENERAL NOTE
This section replaces s.71 of the 1968 Act, with no substantive change. It is a crime with the stated penalty to do any of the listed acts. This is qualified by s.38 above, under which local authorities can provide short-term refuges for children at risk of harm who seek such refuge.

Implementation of authorisations etc.

Implementation of authorisations etc.

84. Where an order, authorisation or warrant under this Chapter or Chapter 2 of this Part of this Act grants power to find a child and to keep him in a place of safety, such order, authorisation or warrant may be implemented as if it were a warrant for the apprehension of an accused person issued by a court of summary jurisdiction; and any enactment or rule of law applying to such a warrant shall, subject to the provisions of this Act, apply in like manner to the order, authorisation or warrant.

DEFINITIONS
"child": s.93(2)(b).
"place of safety": s.93(1).

GENERAL NOTE
This section specifies the effect of orders, authorisations and warrants granted under ss.39–85 of the present Act.

New evidence: review of establishment of grounds of referral

Application for review of establishment of grounds of referral

85.—(1) Subject to subsections (3) and (4) below, where subsection (2) below applies an application may be made to the sheriff for a review of a finding such as is mentioned in section 68(10) of this Act.

(2) This subsection applies where the sheriff, on an application made by virtue of subsection (7) or (9) of section 65 of this Act (in this section referred to as the "original application"), finds that any of the grounds of referral is established.

(3) An application under subsection (1) above may only be made where the applicant claims—

(a) to have evidence which was not considered by the sheriff on the original application, being evidence the existence or significance of which might materially have affected the determination of the original application;

(b) that such evidence—
  (i) is likely to be credible and reliable; and
  (ii) would have been admissible in relation to the ground of referral which was found to be established on the original application; and

(c) that there is a reasonable explanation for the failure to lead such evidence on the original application.

(4) An application under subsection (1) above may only be made by—
(a) the child in respect of whom the ground of referral was found to be established; or
(b) any person who is a relevant person in relation to that child.

(5) Where the sheriff on an application under subsection (1) above is not satisfied that any of the claims made in the application are established he shall dismiss the application.

(6) Where the sheriff is satisfied on an application under subsection (1) above that the claims made in the application are established, he shall consider the evidence and if, having considered it, he is satisfied that—

    (a) none of the grounds of referral in the original application to which the application relates is established, he shall allow the application, discharge the referral to the children's hearing in respect of those grounds and proceed in accordance with subsection (7) below in relation to any supervision requirement made in respect of the child (whether or not varied under section 73 of this Act) in so far as it relates to any such ground; or

    (b) any ground of referral in the original application to which the application relates is established, he may proceed in accordance with section 68(10) of this Act.

(7) Where the sheriff is satisfied as is mentioned in subsection (6)(a) above, he may—

    (a) order that any supervision requirement so mentioned shall terminate—

        (i) immediately; or

        (ii) on such date as he may specify; or

    (b) if he is satisfied that there is evidence sufficient to establish any ground of referral, being a ground which was not stated in the original application, find such ground established and proceed in accordance with section 68(10) of this Act in relation to that ground.

(8) Where the sheriff specifies a date for the termination of a supervision requirement in accordance with subsection (7)(a)(ii) above, he may, before such termination, order a variation of that requirement, of any requirement imposed under subsection (6) of section 70 of this Act, or of any determination made under subsection (7) of that section; and such variation may take effect—

    (a) immediately; or

    (b) on such date as he may specify.

(9) Where the sheriff orders the termination of a supervision requirement in accordance with subsection (7)(a) above, he shall consider whether, after such termination, the child concerned will still require supervision or guidance; and where he considers that such supervision or guidance will be necessary he shall direct a local authority to provide it in accordance with subsection (10) below.

(10) Where a sheriff has given a direction under subsection (9) above, it shall be the duty of the local authority to comply with that direction; but that duty shall be regarded as discharged where they offer such supervision or guidance to the child and he, being a child of sufficient age and maturity to understand what is being offered, is unwilling to accept it.

DEFINITIONS

    "child": s.93(2)(b).
    "children's hearing": s.93(1).
    "local authority": Local Government etc. (Scotland) Act 1994, s.2.
    "relevant person": s.93(2)(b).
    "supervision requirement": ss.70(1), 93(1).

GENERAL NOTE

    Though the 1968 Act was aimed at creating a unified and comprehensive code for dealing with children who may be in need of compulsory measures of care, the very novelty of the system it set up meant that certain gaps and omissions were inevitable. Some of these gaps were filled by amending legislation (such as the provisions introduced by the Children Act 1975 (c. 72) relating to safeguarders); and some have been left to the imagination of the Court of Session. One such omission concerned what was to happen when new evidence came to light after the sheriff had found a ground of referral to exist, which cast doubt on that original finding. There was no provision in the 1968 Act permitting the reopening of the question of whether a ground of referral existed or not, and appeal from a sheriff's decision was available on a point of law only. In *R. v. Kennedy*, 1993 S.L.T. 910 parents of a child subject to a supervision requirement, who had all along disputed the grounds of referral found established by the sheriff, petitioned the *nobile officium* for an order requiring the sheriff to consider anew whether or not the grounds of referral had been made out, in the light of new evidence (which took the form, in this case, of a retraction by the child of her original allegations against her father of sexual abuse). The Inner House held that such a petition was incompetent since to allow a rehearing would be a judicial supplement to the statutory procedure laid down in the 1968 Act. However, in *L, Petrs (No. 1)*, 1993 S.L.T. 1310 and *(No. 2)*, 1342 (the so-called "Ayrshire Child Abuse Case") a similar petition to the *nobile officium* was granted. The parents in that case had alleged that new expert evidence was available which cast considerable doubt on the original expert evidence upon which the sheriff had based his findings, and that there was currently a much greater awareness since the Clyde Report into the Orkney Case of the need to be especially careful in interviewing children alleged to be the victims of abuse, which awareness had not been shown in the present case. The Inner House accepted that this justified them ordering the sheriff to examine again the question of whether the ground of referral existed or not, but the procedure under which this rehearing took place and the effect it had on any extant supervision requirement had to be determined by the Court of Session without any statutory guidance.

The effect of these two cases (which are probably irreconcilable) was to leave the law in a state of considerable doubt. The level of evidence required to persuade the court to exercise the *nobile officium*, the effect on supervision requirements, the role of the Court of Session, the issue of title to sue, the availability of appeal, and many other matters remained to be determined. The present section is designed to put the process for re-examining the grounds of referral on to a statutory basis, to clarify the grounds upon which rehearings can take place, and to specify what is to happen to any supervision requirement that has been made on the basis of a ground of referral which is subsequently found not to have been made out. An appeal from any decision of the sheriff under this section can be made in terms of s.51(11) above to the sheriff principal or the Court of Session.

Subss. (1) and (2)
When a sheriff has found any ground of referral in relation to a child established, whether the application for proof had been made because the child or parent denies the ground or because the child has been found by the children's hearing to be too young to understand the ground, an application can be made to the sheriff by any of the persons specified in subs. (4) below to reconsider the establishment of that ground. Such an application can be made whenever the applicant makes the three claims listed in subs. (3) below. The section does not place any limitation on when this application can be made, except implicitly that it must be after such a finding has been made. However, it might be made either before a children's hearing have imposed a supervision requirement upon the child, or after (even, as in *L, Petrs*, some years after), or, indeed, after a children's hearing have decided that no supervision requirement is justified in the case. This last would be rare, but the section provides for a challenge to the sheriff's finding and not to the imposition of a supervision requirement, and it follows that the challenge is competent even when the children's hearing discharge the referral or terminate the supervision requirement. A challenge might be made in these circumstances as a means of clearing a person's name, unjustly impugned by the original sheriff's finding.

Finds that any of the grounds of referral is established. An application under this section cannot be made when there has been no finding by the sheriff, such as when the child and parent accept the ground but later wish to retract that acceptance. An application can be made when the sheriff has dispensed with hearing the evidence under s.68(8), for he still makes a finding in that situation.

Subs. (3)
The applicant under this section must claim and, if the application for a review of the establishment of the grounds is to be successful must establish, each of the three conditions listed in this subsection, that is to say that material evidence was not considered by the sheriff at the original proof hearing, that the evidence is likely to be credible and was admissible, and that there is a reasonable explanation for the failure to have led that evidence at the original hearing.

Evidence which was not considered. This might include evidence which the sheriff did not hear because he dispensed with hearing the evidence under s.68(8) above.

There is a reasonable explanation. This is a lesser test than the Court of Session required for an application under the *nobile officium*, for in *L, Petrs* it was held that evidence could be heard only if the circumstances which had arisen were "exceptional and unforeseen". A reasonable explanation might include the non-availability of the evidence, for whatever reason (so long as that reason is not directly attributable to the applicant), or because of new understandings which have developed since the original finding.

Subs. (4)

Title to seek a rehearing on the basis of new evidence inheres only in the child and in any relevant person (*i.e.* any person with parental responsibilities or parental rights, or any person who ordinarily has charge of or control over the child) and no other person can challenge a finding of the sheriff that a ground of referral in relation to the child exists.

Subs. (5)

The onus is on the applicant to establish, to the satisfaction of the sheriff, the validity of all three claims made under subs. (3) above, and that may be challenged by the reporter or any person who would have title to raise an action under this section. If any one or more of the claims is not established then the application must be dismissed. There is no provision for the hearing of evidence to establish these claims, and the sheriff must make his determination on the basis of argument put before him. This will be directed towards an examination of the nature of the evidence and how it has come to light, but the evidence itself will not be, at this stage, challengeable.

Subs. (6)

If the sheriff determines that all three of the claims made in subs. (3) above are established then the application for a review of the original finding will be granted, and the sheriff must then move on to consider the new evidence which the applicant claims to have. The sheriff may hear the parties and allow further procedure as he thinks fit before hearing the evidence: A.S. 1997 rr. 3.63 and 3.64. Having examined the evidence and heard such parties as are entitled to and wish to make representations to the sheriff, the sheriff must then decide whether the original ground, or any of the original grounds, of referral is, or are, established.

Paragraph (a). If the sheriff is satisfied that none of the original grounds of referral has been established he must discharge the referral. If the application has been made before any supervision requirement has been imposed by a children's hearing then none can be imposed thereafter in respect of these grounds, if the child has already been made subject to a supervision requirement in respect of the grounds then on the discharge of the referral the sheriff must deal with that requirement in accordance with the rules in subs. (7) below.

Paragraph (b). If the sheriff is satisfied that any one or more of the original grounds of referral has been established he may remit the case to the reporter to arrange a children's hearing. The use of the permissive "may" here must be read in the light of s.68(10) above, under which the sheriff "shall" remit the case to the reporter on a finding that grounds of referral have been established. If the child is not currently under a supervision requirement in respect of the grounds found (again) to be established because a hearing has not yet been arranged then the sheriff has, it is submitted, a discretion only in the sense that he may decide not to remit the case to the reporter when the reporter is already in the process of arranging a children's hearing. If the child is not under a supervision requirement because the children's hearing discharged the referral in respect of the grounds now confirmed (but challenged, say, to clear someone's name) the sheriff may decide to remit the case back to the reporter if he thinks that the original decision of the children's hearing was not justified in all the circumstances of the case, or if the circumstances have changed sufficiently, or if new circumstances have come to light in the course of the rehearing, to justify the hearing looking at the matter afresh. Similarly, the sheriff will have a discretion when the child is currently subject to a supervision requirement in respect of the grounds confirmed to exist. A remit to the reporter in these circumstances will normally be redundant, but it might be appropriate when the child is already subject to a supervision requirement if the evidence presented to the sheriff satisfies him that the requirement ought to be reviewed.

Subs. (7)

When the original grounds of referral have been shown to be not made out, the sheriff must then go on to decide whether any other ground of referral is made out. If not, his choices are governed by para. (a) of this subsection, and if so, he must act in accordance with para. (b).

Under para. (a), if the child is currently subject to a supervision requirement, the sheriff may either terminate the supervision requirement immediately, or terminate it on a date he may specify. It is not within the discretion of the sheriff to do anything other than these two listed options, such as continuing the supervision requirement, for a child cannot be kept subject to a supervision requirement in the absence of an original ground of referral except where its termination is being postponed under this paragraph.

Under para. (b), if the sheriff determines that a ground of referral has been made out, though not the one originally established, then he may remit the case to the reporter to arrange a children's hearing for the consideration of the case based on that new established ground. As in subs. (6) above, the permissive "may" is to be read in light of the "shall" used in s.68(10) above. It is submitted that in all cases in which this paragraph applies the sheriff ought to remit the case to the reporter to arrange a children's hearing which in effect will be a review of the supervision requirement that the child is currently under (and which cannot be terminated under this paragraph: para. (a), which permits termination, is conjoined with this paragraph by "or"). If the sheriff has found a ground of referral to exist which is different from the original ground, then that amounts to a finding that the basis for the original supervision requirement was false and that requirement therefore stands in need of urgent review. If the child is, for whatever reason, not currently under a supervision requirement but a new ground is established then the question arises as to whether compulsory measures of supervision are required (see the terms of s.52(1) above). For the sheriff not to remit the case to the reporter for the arranging of a children's hearing would, in effect, be for the sheriff to answer that question and therefore to usurp the role of the children's hearing.

On such date as he may specify. The decision to postpone the termination of the supervision requirement must be made on the basis of the welfare of the child as expressed in s.16(1) above. It is to be noted that this was one of the effects of the Inner House's decision in *L, Petrs* (above), where it was considered to be against the children's interests to be returned home since they had been separated from their parents for a very long time and this is the sort of reason why a termination might appropriately be postponed. There is no limit specified on how long the sheriff can postpone the termination of the supervision requirement for, but it is submitted that it would be inconsistent with the provisions determining the duration of supervision requirements contained in s.73 above to allow the sheriff to specify a date beyond the time at which a hearing must sit to review that requirement. Otherwise the sheriff would be prolonging an order, that was made upon the basis of false information, beyond its natural life. If the child's interests require further compulsory measures of supervision then new grounds can surely be formulated by the reporter.

Being a ground which was not stated in the original application. It is not necessary that the new ground which the sheriff finds established is one based on a different paragraph in s.52. Rather it must be based on different circumstances which amount to a ground of referral in accordance with any of these paragraphs. So the sheriff may find that the original ground (for example, the commission of the offence of assault) has not been made out but that a quite separate offence (say, that of theft) has been made out. Or the sheriff may find that the child has not been a victim of a Sched. 1 offence (a ground under s.52(2)(d) above) but lives in the same household as such a victim (a ground under s.52(2)(c) above).

There is nothing to prevent this finding being based on the same facts that founded the original finding: for example the sheriff may find that the facts do not justify a finding that the child has committed the offence of assault, but do justify a finding that the child has committed a breach of the peace.

Subs. (8)

If a sheriff is satisfied that none of the original grounds of referral is established but has decided, in the child's best interests, to postpone the termination of the supervision requirement, he may vary that requirement in any way he thinks fit (being guided again by the child's welfare), or vary any condition attached to it, or any requirement to keep the child's address secret, or any determination by the children's hearing concerning the length of time which the supervision requirement is to last. In other words, once the sheriff has determined that the supervision requirement is to be terminated, but that termination is to be postponed, every aspect of that requirement is under the control of, and open to variation by, the sheriff. There is no requirement that the sheriff takes account of the views of the child under s.16(2) above (nor, indeed, that the child attend at the rehearing), but good practice suggests that the sheriff should do so in appropriate circumstances.

Subs. (9)

If a supervision requirement is to be terminated the sheriff must go on to consider whether the child should be offered voluntary supervision and guidance. If he considers that such supervision and guidance is necessary for the child he must direct the local authority to provide it.

A local authority. This provision is not limited to the local authority in whose area the child was first brought to a children's hearing but may be any local authority specified by the sheriff.

The local authority directed under subs. (9) above to provide supervision and guidance must do so, but need not do so when the child is unwilling to accept such supervision and guidance and the child is of sufficient age and maturity to understand what is being offered.

CHAPTER 4

PARENTAL RESPONSIBILITIES ORDERS, ETC.

Parental responsibilities orders

Parental responsibilities order: general

86.—(1) On the application of a local authority the sheriff may make an order transferring (but only during such period as the order remains in force) the appropriate parental rights and responsibilities relating to a child to them; and any such order shall be known as a "parental responsibilities order".

(2) A parental responsibilities order shall not be made unless the sheriff is satisfied that each relevant person either—

(a) freely, and with full understanding of what is involved, agrees unconditionally that the order be made; or

(b) is a person who—

    (i) is not known, cannot be found or is incapable of giving agreement;

    (ii) is withholding such agreement unreasonably;

    (iii) has persistently failed, without reasonable cause, to fulfil one or other of the following parental responsibilities in relation to the child, that is to say the responsibility to safeguard and promote the child's health, development and welfare or, if the child is not living with him, the responsibility to maintain personal relations and direct contact with the child on a regular basis; or

    (iv) has seriously ill-treated the child, whose reintegration into the same household as that person is, because of the serious ill-treatment or for other reasons, unlikely.

(3) The reference in subsection (1) above to the appropriate parental rights and responsibilities relating to the child is to all parental rights and responsibilities except any right to agree, or decline to agree—

(a) to the making of an application in relation to the child under section 18 (freeing for adoption) or 55 (adoption abroad) of the Adoption Act 1976, under section 18 or 49 of the Adoption (Scotland) Act 1978 or under Article 17, 18 or 57 of the Adoption (Northern Ireland) Order 1987 (corresponding provision for Scotland and Northern Ireland); or

(b) to the making of an adoption order.

(4) A person is a relevant person for the purposes of this section if he is a parent of the child or a person who for the time being has parental rights in relation to the child.

(5) The sheriff may, in an order under this section, impose such conditions as he considers appropriate; and he may vary or discharge such an order on the application of the local authority, of the child, of any person who immediately before the making of the order is a relevant person or of any other person claiming an interest.

(6) An order under this section shall, if not first discharged by the sheriff, terminate on the occurrence of any of the following—

(a) the child attains the age of eighteen years;

(b) he becomes the subject—

    (i) of an adoption order within the meaning of the Adoption (Scotland) Act 1978; or

    (ii) of an order under section 18 (freeing for adoption) or 55 (adoption abroad) of the Adoption Act 1976, under section 18 or 49 of the said Act of 1978 or under Article 17, 18 or 57 of the Adoption (Northern Ireland) Order 1987 (corresponding provision for Scotland and Northern Ireland);

(c) an order is made for his return under Part I of the Child Abduction and Custody Act 1985; or

(d) a decision, other than a decision mentioned in section 25(2) of the said Act of 1985 (decisions relating to rights of access), is registered with respect to him under section 16 of that Act.

DEFINITIONS
"child": s.93(2)(a).
"local authority": Local Government etc. (Scotland) Act 1994, s.2.
"parental responsibilities": ss.1(3), 93(1).
"parental rights": ss.2(4), 93(1).

GENERAL NOTE
Under the provisions of ss.16–18A of the Social Work (Scotland) Act 1968 a local authority could in certain circumstances assume parental rights and powers over a child. This was achieved simply by the local authority passing a resolution, which had the effect of transferring the relevant rights and powers held by the parent in respect of whom the resolution was passed to the local authority themselves. The procedure was frequently, though not invariably, a prelude to adoption. There was no need for any court process before the resolution was made, though if the parent wished to challenge it this could be done by counter-notice which had the effect of putting the onus on the local authority to take the matter to the sheriff court for confirmation of the resolution. (See Wilkinson and Norrie, *Parent and Child* (1993, W. Green), chap. 16 for full details.) These provisions, repealed in Sched. 5, are replaced with the present ss.86–89, which have followed the recommendations of the *Child Care Law Review* (Scottish Office, October 1990). The new rules represent a radical reshaping of the statutory procedure for local authority acquisition of parental responsibilities and parental rights. Among the most significant changes are the following: (1) power to make what is called a "parental responsibilities order" is vested solely in the sheriff and title to apply for such an order inheres solely in the local authority; (2) the grounds upon which such an order can be granted are very substantially simplified and clarified from the grounds upon which a local authority could assume parental rights and powers under the 1968 Act, though the effect of the order is to all intents and purposes the same as the effect of the old resolution; (3) the sheriff is given guidance as to how to come to his decision, for s.16 above provides that the sheriff must apply the three overarching principles listed there; (4) the limitation in the 1968 Act of the assumption provisions to those children statutorily "in care" is removed and the sheriff can make a parental responsibilities order over any child in his jurisdiction; (5) the order is made in relation to the child who needs to be looked after rather than in relation to a parent who has forfeited the right to bring up the child: this means that the order is available only when there is no suitable person available to look after the child (rather than, as before, when one of a number of persons had forfeited their right). Procedure is governed by A.S. 1997, rr. 2.37–2.44.

One noticeable feature of the current provisions is the extent to which things are left unsaid. For example, no section spells out the effect of the order on the parent's parental responsibilities and parental rights, and this is left to implication. Nor are the rights, powers, duties and responsibilities of the local authority in whose favour the order is made spelt out in Chap. 4 of this Part, and we must look both to other chapters in this Part and indeed to other Parts to delimit the extent of the local authority's role. Also, the definition of those parental rights which are transferred is, as we will see, unhelpful in the extreme. Again, contrasting sharply both with the equivalent English provisions (s.94 of the Children Act 1989) and with the provisions in the current statute in relation to children's hearings (s.51 above), there is no provision dealing with the right of appeal from the sheriff's decision. No right of appeal was laid down in the provisions under the 1968 Act dealing with the sheriff's confirmation of a local authority resolution but the competency of such appeals was never doubted (see Wilkinson and Norrie, *Parent and Child*, at pp. 440–441) and it can be assumed that the normal rules of appeals from decisions of the sheriff will apply to decisions under this Chapter also. (Though there is no express provision for legal aid for such appeals in s.92 below, that cannot be taken to suggest that no appeals are competent, for no legal aid is expressly provided in that section for the defending of an application under this section though there is no doubt as to its availability.)

Subs. (1)

A "parental responsibilities order" is an order which is made by a sheriff, on the application of a local authority, transferring the "appropriate parental rights and responsibilities" (defined in subs. (3) below) to the local authority. It is only a local authority who can apply for such an order, and not, for example the parent or the child. In addition it is only to a local authority that the order can transfer parental rights and responsibilities. The statute does not expressly state from whom the rights and responsibilities are transferred, though implicitly it is each "relevant person" referred to in subs. (2) below and defined in subs. (4) below.

An order transferring. Bizarrely, there is no provision in the Act indicating the effect that a parental responsibilities order has on a relevant person's parental responsibilities and parental rights and we must assume an effect similar to that created by the old legislation. The word "transferring" indicates that the relevant person's parental responsibilities and parental rights are removed from that person and vested in the local authority. This was certainly the effect of a parental rights resolution under the 1968 Act and it would subvert the whole point of the order if the present provisions did not also have this effect. It is unfortunate that this important point has been left to implication, though it is submitted that the implication is inevitable. Confirmation that the order removes a person's parental responsibilities and parental rights can be found in s.11(4) above, which denies title to seek a s.11 order to a number of categories of individuals, including those whose responsibilities or rights have been "transferred" by this section: all are clearly meant to cover persons whose responsibilities and rights have been expressly removed. The use of the word "transferring" also suggests on first reading that the local authority obtains only those responsibilities and rights that the relevant person had immediately before the order was made, for there cannot be "transferred" from a person to a local authority that which the person does not have. (Under the 1968 legislation this was explicit in the terms of s.16(3) thereof.) However, subs. (3) below provides that the local authority acquires under the order all parental rights and responsibilities except those listed, with the result that, in some cases, the word "transferring" is inapt. The effect of the order is to remove from each of the relevant persons such parental rights and parental responsibilities as they have and to confer on the local authority all the rights and responsibilities within the meaning of subs. (3) below.

The sheriff. The jurisdiction lies exclusively with the sheriff and the Court of Session cannot make a parental responsibilities order.

A child. Section 93(2)(a) defines child for this purpose as a person under the age of 18 and it follows that an order can be applied for under this section until the child reaches that age. See further, General Note to subs. (6) below.

Subs. (2)

Under the 1968 Act the conditions upon which the parental rights resolution could be passed were long and detailed, and there was some overlap both with the grounds for dispensing with parental agreement to adoption and with the grounds of referral to the children's hearing. The purpose of the new parental responsibilities order is often very different from the purpose of an adoption order (and the effect is radically different), but there are similarities and the order under this provision will very frequently be a step in the process to make long-term arrangements for the care of the child. It was therefore considered appropriate to make the grounds upon which an order could be made similar to the rules in adoption. This subsection lists the conditions at least one of which have to be satisfied. They are, first, that every relevant person in relation to the child agrees to the making of the order unconditionally, freely and with full understanding of what is involved; or secondly that one of the stated circumstances in para. (b) exists. The circumstances in para. (b) are identical to the grounds upon which consent to adoption can be dispensed with by the court. The nature of the two procedures are different, as are their aims, and the grounds must be interpreted and applied by the court in such a way as reflects this. It may well, for example, be unreasonable for a parent to withhold agreement to a parental responsibilities order but not be unreasonable for that parent to withhold consent to adoption (if, for example, the parental responsibilities order is designed to be temporary).

Shall not be made unless. The satisfaction of one or other of the stated conditions is mandatory before a parental responsibilities order can be made, but it does not follow that the making of the order is mandatory if one or both conditions is, in fact, satisfied. Rather, the sheriff must first determine as a matter of fact whether or not one of the conditions is satisfied. If it is not, he cannot make an order; if it is he must then go on to determine, in the light of the three overarching principles in s.16 above and, if the child is subject to a supervision requirement, the report from the children's hearing drawn up in terms of s.73(13) above, whether or not to make the order.

Each relevant person. The "relevant person" is defined in subs. (4) below. Under the 1968 Act the local authority resolution was passed in respect of a particular parent or guardian, and it did not affect the rights and duties of other parents and guardians. The current provisions, on the other hand, provide that the order is made in relation to the child and is available only when every parent and guardian of the child satisfies one or other of the conditions in this subsection. This emphasises that a parental responsibilities order should be sought only when there is no appropriate person who has the responsibility and right to look after the child. It follows that a parental responsibilities order cannot be made which removes one parent's rights and responsibilities but allows the other parent's rights and responsibilities to continue.

Agrees unconditionally that the order be made. Again to emphasise the closeness of this procedure to that of adoption, it is provided that the parental responsibilities order can be granted to the local authority if each one of the persons with rights in relation to the child agrees to its being terminated. There was no analogous provision in the 1968 Act, which was primarily concerned with forfeiture of parental rights rather than their voluntary surrender. If there is a relevant person who does not agree unconditionally to the making of the order, the order cannot be made, unless, in relation to that person, one of the four conditions in para. (b) exists.

Is not known, cannot be found, or is incapable of giving agreement. It will be in unusual circumstances only in which a person with parental rights is not known: the usual case of the unknown parent is the unmarried father, but he does not have parental rights in any case. A person "cannot be found" when it is practically impossible to communicate with her or him. Incapacity can be either legal or factual, though in both cases it should be permanent, or at least long-term.

Is withholding such agreement unreasonably. There have been many cases in relation to the dispensation of parental agreement to adoption on the basis of identical wording in the Adoption (Scotland) Act 1978. Whether the ground exists is not to be determined by the welfare principle (*Central Regional Council v. M*, 1991 S.C.L.R. 300), though that will of course govern the sheriff's decision whether, if this subparagraph is satisfied, the parental responsibilities order should be made. The test is an objective one of whether or not the reasonable parent would have withheld consent in the circumstances (*Lothian Regional Council v. A*, 1992 S.L.T. 858).

"Two reasonable parents can perfectly reasonably come to opposite conclusions on the same set of facts without forfeiting their title to be regarded as reasonable. The question in any given case is whether a parental veto comes within the band of possible reasonable decisions and not whether it is right or mistaken. Not every reasonable exercise of judgment is right, and not every mistaken exercise of judgment is unreasonable. There is a band of decisions within which no court should seek to replace the individual's judgment with its own" (*per* Lord Hailsham in *W (An Infant), Re* [1971] 2 All E.R. 49 at p. 56).

Has persistently failed, without reasonable excuse, to fulfil ... parental responsibilities. On similar wording in s.16 of the 1968 Act, it has been held that "persistently" does not mean deliberately but repeatedly or continuously for some time (*Central Regional Council v. B*, 1985 S.L.T. 413), but the words "without reasonable cause" suggest that some element must be present for which the person can be held responsible. A useful addition to the law is to specify which of the parental responsibilities must be neglected to satisfy this subparagraph.

Has seriously ill-treated the child. Ill-treatment is to be given wide scope, and covers abuse, neglect, and any treatment (or lack of it) which causes serious harm to the child. It might be constituted by either a single event or a course of conduct. Serious ill-treatment is the causing of "significant harm", as that phrase is used in s.57(2) above. In addition to serious ill-treatment it must be shown that there is little possibility that the child can be reintegrated back into the household of the person guilty of that ill-treatment. This subparagraph can apply even when the child has never been a member of the same household as the person who has seriously ill-treated her or him and "reintegration" should be interpreted to include "integration".

Subs. (3)

Subsection (1) above allows the sheriff to make an order transferring the "appropriate parental rights and responsibilities"; this section contains a singularly unhelpful definition of that phrase. To define the "appropriate parental rights and responsibilities" as "all parental rights and responsibilities" subject to stated exceptions tells us nothing more than which aspects of parental responsibility are not transferred to the local authority. The stated exceptions are not parental rights as defined by s.2(1) above which indicates that the phrase "all parental rights and responsibilities" is intended by this section to be wider than the parental responsibilities listed in s.1(1) and the parental rights listed in s.2(1) above. The phrase will certainly include these, but how much further it goes is not clear. "Parental rights and responsibilities" in this section may well include the duty of aliment (but not the duty of child support, since the terms of the Child Support Act 1991 would preclude local authorities being liable). It is surprising that there is no provision analogous to the now repealed s.17(6) of the 1968 Act to the effect that the person whose parental rights are removed is not thereby relieved of any liability to contribute to the maintenance of the child, and it would seem that such an obligation is within the meaning of the phrase "parental rights and responsibilities" and is now removed from the parent and imposed on the local authority. In addition to the responsibilities and rights defined in ss.1 and 2, the phrase "rights and responsibilities" will include the duties of local authorities spelt out in s.17 above. Also, the right and obligation of parents to attend a children's hearing considering the case of the child will be included in "parental rights and responsibilities" with the result that after the making of a parental responsibilities order a representative of the local authority will be obliged to attend any children's hearing considering the case of the child who is the subject of the order, and the parents will have lost their right to attend.

Except... The local authority in whose favour a parental responsibilities order has been made does not obtain the right to agree to or to refuse to agree to the making of an adoption order, the making of an order freeing the child for adoption, or the making of an order vesting parental responsibilities and parental rights in a person who intends to adopt the child abroad. There is no substantive change in the law here from that contained in s.16(3) of the 1968 Act. These rights remain with the person to whom they attached before the making of the order.

Subs. (4)

The "relevant person" who must agree to the order under subs. (2)(a) above or fall within one of the circumstances in subs. (2)(b) above is defined in this subsection as belonging to one of two different classes.

(i) A parent. It is to be noted that "parent" is not defined for the purposes of Pt II. The word probably means mother to the exclusion of father if the parents are not and never have been married, because an unmarried father will have no parental responsibilities and parental rights to be transferred (except the duty of aliment and child support). This would be consistent with the adoption legislation, with which the unmarried father has no right to agree or refuse to agree to the adoption of his child (*A. v. B.*, 1955 S.C. 378, *A. & B. v. C.*, 1987 S.C.L.R. 514: these cases are, however, inconsistent with the decision of the European Court of Human Rights in *Keegan v. Ireland* (1994) 18 E.H.R.R. 342 and ripe for reconsideration).

(ii) A person who for the time being has parental rights. "Parental rights" are defined in s.93(1) to mean those rights listed in s.2(1) of the Act. It is surprising that the statute does not here refer to parental responsibilities and parental rights, as it does throughout Pt I, given that s.2(1) explicitly states that parental rights exist only in order to enable the person to fulfil their parental responsibilities listed in s.1. The omission is likely to be the result of sloppy draftsmanship rather than any attempt to distinguish between a person with parental responsibilities and parental rights for the purposes of Pt I and a person with parental rights for the purposes of Pt II: it is to be noted that s.87(1) below talks of "the transferred responsibilities", which suggests that a person with parental rights is assumed to have responsibilities that can be transferred. It is submitted that any person who at the date of the court action has any (see s.103(1) below) or all of the parental rights or their concomitant responsibilities is a relevant person, who must agree to the order or fall within one of the specified circumstances, and whose rights can be transferred to the local authority under this order.

Subs. (5)

In making a parental responsibilities order the sheriff may impose such conditions as he considers appropriate. This might include, for example, conditions as to the child's residence or medical treatment or even the religious observances to which the child is to be subjected. A condition could determine the length of time the order is to last. The sheriff might also include conditions as to contact between the child and any other person: s.88 below, which deals with contact, applies both during the subsistence of a parental responsibilities order and when it is being made. The sheriff may also vary or discharge the order. His decision in relation to conditions, variation or discharge is to be made having regard to the three overarching principles in s.16, to which reference should be made.

On the application of the local authority. Under the old law the local authority could itself simply rescind the parental rights resolution that it had previously made. The philosophy of the current provision is that the order be kept within the hands of the court, and therefore not only is it only the sheriff who can make the order, but it is only the sheriff who can vary or discharge it. The local authority in whose favour the order has been made, but no other local authority, has title to apply for variation or discharge.

On the application... of the child. The child too may apply for the variation or discharge of the order, and the wording suggests that the child can make such an application on her or his own behalf. Capacity to do so is, of course, determined by the Age of Legal Capacity (Scotland) Act 1991 and it is submitted that such an application by a child who is the subject of a parental responsibilities order can be regarded as a transaction that is commonly entered into by persons in their circumstances. Under the 1991 Act, "commonly" does not refer to numerical frequency (otherwise this new form of application could never be made a first time, however common it was for children to wish to make it): rather it means transactions that are not unusual or surprising in the circumstances (see Norrie, "The Age of Legal Capacity (Scotland) Act 1991" (1991) 36 J.L.S.S. 434). Children with capacity to raise or defend actions can authorise those who used to be their representatives to do so on their behalf: s.15(6) above.

Any person who immediately before ... is a relevant person. Though parental responsibilities and parental rights are removed from a person by the order, that person retains title to seek the variation or discharge of the order.

Any other person claiming an interest. This phrase is to be given wide scope. As in s.11(3) above title to seek the variation or discharge of a parental responsibilities order inheres in any person who has a legitimate concern in the wellbeing of, or established connection with, the child. Unlike s.11(3), there is no limitation excluding title from those whose parental responsibilities and parental rights have been removed by legal action. No such limitation is needed in this context since those who lose their responsibilities and rights by an order in this process have a legitimate claim to be able to use this process to challenge or alter that order.

Subs. (6)

The sheriff may discharge the order under subs. (5) above, but if this has not been done the order terminates on the occurrence of any of the listed events.

Child attains the age of eighteen years. "Child" is defined in s.93(2)(a) as a person under the age of 18 years and a parental responsibilities order remains in effect until the person reaches that age. It is, however, to be noted that on the child attaining the age of 16 years all the parental responsibilities except that to provide guidance come to an end (s.1(2) above), as do all the parental rights (s.2(7) above). The effect of a parental responsibilities order is not, it is submitted, to maintain on behalf of the local authority all these responsibilities and rights until the child is 18, otherwise the statute would have provided for them having more rights than parents. The order may last until the child is 18, but its effect can vary with time, just as the effect of the parent-child relationship varies with time. It follows that the local authority lose those responsibilities and rights in relation to a child that a parent would lose on the child's 16th birthday. However, the duties incumbent on a local authority contained in s.17 above remain until the child's 18th birthday and it can be assumed that the local authority also retain the rights necessary to fulfil their duties under that section.

He becomes the subject of an adoption order. The adoption supersedes and terminates the parental responsibilities order.

He becomes the subject ... of an order under s.18. An order freeing a child for adoption will vest the parental responsibilities and parental rights in the adoption agency (Adoption (Scotland) Act 1978, s.18(5), as amended by Sched. 2) and this supersedes and terminates the parental responsibilities order vesting those responsibilities and rights in the local authority (which may well be the adoption agency in any case).

He becomes the subject ... of an order ... under ... s.49. An order vesting parental responsibilities and parental rights in a person for the purpose of allowing that person to adopt the child abroad supersedes and terminates the parental responsibilities order.

An order is made for his return. An order by a Scottish or English court under the Hague Convention on the Civil Aspects of International Child Abduction will be to the effect that the child is returned to her or his habitual residence forthwith, and the parental responsibilities order cannot interfere with that process. The order for return therefore supersedes and terminates the parental responsibilities order.

A decision ... is registered. The registration in the Books of Council and Session of a custody (but not an access) decision, obtained from the appropriate authorities in any country which is a signatory to the European Convention on Recognition and Enforcement of Decisions Concerning Custody of Children, supersedes and terminates the parental responsibilities order. A custody decision for the purpose of that Convention is "a decision of an authority in so far as it relates to the care of the person of the child, including the right to decide on the place of his residence, or to the right of access to him" (Art. 1, para. 1 of the European Convention, enacted in the 1985 Act, Sched. 2).

Further provision as respects parental responsibilities orders

87.—(1) Subject to subsections (2) and (3) below, where a parental responsibilities order is made as respects a child it shall be the duty of the local authority which applied for it (in this section and in section 88 of this

Act referred to as the "appropriate authority") to fulfil the transferred responsibilities while the order remains in force.

(2) Notwithstanding that a parental responsibilities order has been made as respects a child, the appropriate authority may allow, either for a fixed period or until the authority otherwise determine, the child to reside with a parent, guardian, relative or friend of his in any case where it appears to the authority that so to allow would be for the benefit of the child.

(3) Without prejudice to any other provision of this Part of this Act, where by virtue of subsection (2) above a child is residing with a person, the appropriate authority may by notice in writing to the person require him to return the child to them by a time specified in the notice; and service of such notice shall be effected either by the authority leaving it in the person's hands or by their sending it to him, at his and the child's most recent known address, by recorded delivery service.

(4) For the purposes of any application for a parental responsibilities order, rules shall provide for the appointment, in such cases as are prescribed by such rules—

(a) of a person to act as curator *ad litem* to the child in question at the hearing of the application, safeguarding the interests of the child in such manner as may be so prescribed; and

(b) of a person (to be known as a "reporting officer") to witness agreements to parental responsibilities orders and to perform such other duties as may be so prescribed,

but one person may, as respects the child, be appointed both under paragraph (a) and under paragraph (b) above; so however that, where the applicant is a local authority, no employee of theirs shall be appointed under either or both of those paragraphs.

(5) Rules may provide for a person to be appointed reporting officer before the application in question is made.

DEFINITIONS
"child": s.93(2)(a).
"local authority": Local Government etc. (Scotland) Act 1994, s.2.
"parental responsibilities order": ss.86(1), 93(1).

GENERAL NOTE
Under the 1968 Act it was only children who were "in care" who could be the subject of a resolution assuming parental rights, and that statute imposed various duties on local authorities in relation to children in their care (whether subject to such a resolution or not). The current provisions do not require that the child be "in care", and this section therefore indicates the duties that the local authority will be under in relation to the child in respect of whom a parental responsibilities order has been made at their instance. In addition, the section provides that in fulfilling its responsibilities towards the child, the local authority may permit the child to reside with certain individuals, though if it does so it can always require the return of the child from such an individual. Rules will provide for the appointment of a curator *ad litem* and a reporting officer.

Subs. (1)
Having obtained the order in their favour, the local authority is obliged to carry out their duties in relation to the child. The only duty specified here is the duty to "fulfil the transferred responsibilities". It is surprising that the provision does not read "transferred responsibilities and rights" but it is submitted that a local authority are obliged to exercise the rights they obtain by means of a parental responsibilities order whenever this is necessary in the child's interests. In addition, the local authority will be subject to the duties in s.17 above, that is to say, the duty to safeguard and promote the child's welfare; the duty to make use of such services available to children cared for by their own parents as appears reasonable; and the duty to take practical and appropriate steps to promote personal relations and direct contact between the child and those with parental responsibilities. This last is inept in relation to children subject to a parental responsibilities order since the parent's responsibilities will have been removed and since contact is specifically dealt with in s.88 below.

Subs. (2)

This subsection replaces much of s.17 of the 1968 Act. In fulfilling their responsibilities towards the child the local authority are not obliged to accommodate the child in a residential establishment or with foster carers. Though this may well be the normal case after a parental responsibilities order has been made, it is open to the local authority to allow the child to reside with a parent, guardian, relative or friend of the child, so long as they consider that this would benefit the child.

Parent. There is no definition of this word in this Part of the Act, and though it may sometimes appropriately be defined to exclude the unmarried father (as for example in s.84(4) above), reading the word *ejusdem generis* with the immediately following words, there would be no reason so to restrict it in this context. Parent means parent, whether adoptive or genetic or presumed (under the 1986 Act) or deemed (under the Human Fertilisation and Embryology Act 1990 (c. 37)).

Guardian. This word is not defined, either here or elsewhere in the Act. It should be taken to mean, it is submitted, parent-substitute appointed as guardian under s.7 or s.11(2)(h) above.

Relative or friend. This means a person with some existing connection to the child, whether of blood or affinity in the former case or affection in the latter case.

Subs. (3)

The local authority in whose favour a parental responsibilities order has been made, and who have permitted the child to reside with a parent, guardian, relative or friend, may at any time call for the return to them of the child. They can do so only if the notice to that effect is in writing and specifies a time. No time-limit is laid down.

Subs. (4)

It is to be expected that in the course of the application for a parental responsibilities order a reporting officer, with similar functions to the reporting officer in an adoption petition, and a curator *ad litem* again with similar functions, may be appointed. Rules govern the appointment and functions of these officers and the same person can be appointed to both offices: see A.S. 1997, rr. 2.39 and 2.40.

Parental contact

88.—(1) This section applies where a parental responsibilities order is being made, or as the case may be is in force, as respects a child.

(2) The child shall, subject to subsection (3) below, be allowed reasonable contact by the appropriate authority with—

(a) each person who, immediately before the making of the parental responsibilities order, is a relevant person for the purposes of section 86 of this Act as respects the child; and

(b) where, immediately before that order was made—

(i) a residence order or contact order was in force with respect to the child, the person in whose favour the residence order or contact order was made;

(ii) a person was entitled to have the child residing with him under an order by a court of competent jurisdiction, that person.

(3) Without prejudice to subsection (4) below, on an application made to him by the child, by the appropriate authority or by any person with an interest, the sheriff may make such order as he considers appropriate as to the contact, if any, which is to be allowed between the child and any person specified in the order (whether or not a person described in paragraphs (a) and (b) of subsection (2) above).

(4) A sheriff, on making a parental responsibilities order, or at any time while such an order remains in force as respects a child, may make an order under subsection (3) above as respects the child even where no application has been made to him in that regard.

(5) An order under this section may impose such conditions as the sheriff considers appropriate; and he may vary or discharge such an order on the application of the child, the appropriate authority or any person with an interest.

(6) An order under this section shall, if not first discharged by the sheriff, terminate when the parental responsibilities order to which it is referable does.

DEFINITIONS
"child": s.93(2)(a).
"contact order": s.11(2)(d), 93(1).
"parental responsibilities order": ss.86(1), 93(1).
"relevant person": s.86(4).
"residence order": ss.11(2)(c), 93(1).

GENERAL NOTE
The 1968 Act was amended in 1983 to provide that a local authority which had assumed parental rights and powers could not terminate arrangements for access or refuse to make them without first giving the parent notice to that effect (1968 Act, s.17A), and on receipt of the notice the parent was entitled to apply to the sheriff for an access order (1968 Act, s.17B). The new procedure set out in this Chapter provides that the granting of a parental responsibilities order is in the hands of the sheriff in any case, and this section ensures that there is reasonable contact between the child and her or his parent, who, if dissatisfied with the arrangements made by the local authority, can apply to the sheriff for an order relating to contact.

Subs. (1)
Application can be made to the sheriff for an order relating to contact between the child and any named person at the time of the application for the making of a parental responsibilities order, or at any time while it is in force. This section governs such applications and imposes duties as to contact on the local authority.

Subs. (2)
The format of this subsection is interesting. Contact is not regarded here as a parental responsibility or parental right (though it is expressly stated to be such for the purposes of Pt. I of the Act); rather it is something which is to be "allowed" to the child. Decisions under this section should, therefore, be made looking at the situation through the eyes of the child rather than the parent. It is provided that the local authority are to allow the child reasonable contact (i) with any person who was a relevant person immediately before the making of the order, (ii) with any person in whose favour a residence order or a contact order was in force immediately before the making of the parental responsibilities order (though a residence order will make its holder a "relevant person" in any case), and (iii) with any person who was entitled to have the child residing with her or him under an order of a court of competent jurisdiction. Though the child must be allowed reasonable contact with the stated persons, there is nothing to prevent the local authority allowing the child contact with other persons such as siblings, grandparents, foster carers and friends, so long as the authority are of the view that it is not against the child's interests to be allowed such contact.
Shall ... be allowed. The fact that the child is to be "allowed" contact suggests that the child will have some say in whether or not contact will take place. It is not a right of the relevant person, who cannot insist on contact under this section, even when an order under this section so provides. A child cannot be forced into contact with a person she or he wishes to have no contact with.
Reasonable contact. It is primarily for the local authority to determine what reasonable contact is. "Reasonable" is to be determined according to all relevant factors, including in particular the wishes of the child, the welfare of the child, the long-term plans for the child, and the nature of the relationship between the child and the appropriate person. If any person believes that reasonable contact is not being permitted, or that what the local authority claim is reasonable is not in fact so, then application to the sheriff can be made in terms of subs. (3) below.
Appropriate authority. Though this phrase is nowhere defined, it means the local authority to whom the appropriate parental rights and responsibilities have been transferred.
Relevant person. The two categories of person under s.86(4) who are included in this phrase are any person who is a parent and any person who has parental responsibilities or parental rights in relation to the child: the comments attached to both of these categories in the notes to s.86(4) above should be referred to. In addition, it is to be remembered that the child may, in the discretion of the local authority, be allowed contact with other people by the proper exercise of the local authority's parental responsibilities.
An order by a court of competent jurisdiction. A person entitled to have the child residing with her or him under a residence order granted by a Scottish court since the commencement of this

Act will be covered by subpara. (i) and the present provision therefore will cover persons who have orders obtained under the pre-1995 legislation or orders of courts outwith Scotland.

Subs. (3)

If the child or appropriate person is not satisfied with the contact arrangements made by the local authority or if the local authority feel that they cannot resolve a dispute, application can be made to the sheriff to make an order regulating contact with a child who is the subject of a parental responsibilities order. This subsection gives the sheriff a wide discretion to make any order that he considers appropriate as to contact, on an application by the child, the local authority, or any person having interest. In coming to his decision, the sheriff is obliged to have regard to all three of the overarching principles in s.16 above, notwithstanding that contact orders under s.88 are not mentioned by s.16, for an order relating to contact is either a part of the making of a parental responsibilities order or is the variation thereof, both of which processes are expressly covered by s.16.

Any person with an interest. This phrase is to be compared with "a person who ... claims an interest" as it appears in s.11(3) above and "any other person claiming an interest" as in s.86(5). It means a person with a legitimate concern for the welfare of, or established connection with, the child. Since the person whose parental responsibilities and parental rights have been removed will often be the person with whom contact would be most appropriate, there is no limitation, as there is in s.11(3), on who comes within this phrase. Persons whose responsibilities and rights are removed are excluded from using s.11 to obtain back some of these responsibilities and rights in order to prevent the present public law chapter being subverted by the use of private law remedies. That consideration does not apply in the interpretation of the phrase here and the fact that a person whose responsibilities and rights are removed by a parental responsibilities order is one of those with whom the child is to be allowed reasonable contact under subs. (2) above clearly gives that person interest to make an application under this subsection.

Whether or not a person described. The sheriff may make an order as to contact between the child and any named person, whether the applicant or otherwise. There is no limitation on who the sheriff may name.

Subs. (4)

A sheriff may make an order as to contact under subs. (3) above even when no application has been made to him to make such an order. This rule applies both when the sheriff is making the parental responsibilities order and at any time while such an order remains in force. However, he can make an order regulating contact under subs. (3) only when a matter relating to the parental responsibilities order is before him, such as when considering whether to make the order under s.86(1), or in reviewing the order under s.86(5). It is submitted that this is the extent of the sheriff's power under this provision to act *ex proprio motu* and that in particular he cannot make an order relating to contact under subs. (3) above if the need for such an order comes to his attention in some other process, such as, for example, a referral for proof from the children's hearing: to hold otherwise would be to confuse two quite separate procedures and indeed (in that example) would usurp the role of the children's hearing.

Subs. (5)

Any order made as respects contact may contain such conditions as the sheriff considers appropriate, he having come to his decision taking account of the three overarching principles in s.16 above (see subs. (3) above); and, on the same basis, he may vary or discharge the order on the application of any of the named parties.

Any person with an interest. As in subs. (3) above, this means any person with a legitimate concern for or established connection with the child—including the person whose parental responsibilities and parental rights were removed by the parental responsibilities order (as will any parental responsibility or parental right under Pt I).

Subs. (6)

A contact order made under subs. (3) above is dependent for its existence on the parental responsibilities order to which it relates and it follows that when the latter ceases to have effect, so does the former. Any contact order made under s.11(2)(d) above, which will have been suspended during the currency of the parental responsibilities order, will be reactivated by the termination of the parental responsibilities order (as will any parental responsibility or parental right under Pt I).

Offences in relation to parental responsibilities orders

89. Any person who, knowingly and without lawful authority or reasonable excuse—

(a) fails to comply with a notice under sec

(b) harbours or conceals a child—

    (i) as respects whom a parental respe
       made; and

    (ii) who has run away, or been taken a
       required by such a notice; or

(c) induces, assists or incites a child as respects wh
    been made to run away, or stay away, from a plac
    after or who takes away such a child from that p.

shall be guilty of an offence and liable, on summary conv
exceeding level 5 on the standard scale or to imprisonme.   ..ot
exceeding six months or to both such fine and such impriso

DEFINITIONS

"child": s.93(2)(a).

"parental responsibilities order": ss.86(1), 93(1).

GENERAL NOTE

Certain offences in relation to parental responsibilities orders are created by this section. Summary conviction carries the penalties listed. The offences are as follows: (i) failing to comply with a notice requiring the return of the child to the local authority which has allowed the child to reside with a parent, guardian, relative or friend; (ii) harbouring or concealing a child who is subject to a parental responsibilities order but who has run away or been taken away or whose return has been required by notice as in (i) above (subject to the defence in s.38 above of providing a short-term refuge for a child at risk of harm); and (iii) taking away or inducing, assisting or inciting a child who is subject to a parental responsibilities order to run away or stay away from the place where she or he is being looked after.

Miscellaneous

Consent of child to certain procedures

90. Nothing in this Part of this Act shall prejudice any capacity of a child enjoyed by virtue of section 2(4) of the Age of Legal Capacity (Scotland) Act 1991 (capacity of child with sufficient understanding to consent to surgical, medical or dental procedure or treatment); and without prejudice to that generality, where a condition contained, by virtue of—

(a) section 66(4)(a), section 67(2) or section 69(9)(a) of this Act, in a warrant; or

(b) section 70(5)(a) of this Act, in a supervision requirement,

requires a child to submit to any examination or treatment but the child has the capacity mentioned in the said section 2(4), the examination or treatment shall only be carried out if the child consents.

DEFINITIONS

"child": s.93(2)(a).

"supervision requirement": s.93(1).

GENERAL NOTE

Section 2(4) of the Age of Legal Capacity (Scotland) Act 1991 gives children under the age of 16 legal capacity to consent to any surgical, medical or dental treatment or procedure so long as that child is capable of understanding the nature and consequences of the proposed treatment or procedure. This section ensures that nothing in Pt II of the present Act affects that capacity: so a child subject to a supervision requirement or an assessment order, or kept in a place of safety under a child protection order or a warrant, or subject to a parental responsibilities order, retains the capacity granted by the 1991 Act to the full extent there envisaged. Capacity to consent to medical treatment necessarily includes capacity to refuse consent, just as capacity to consent to adoption given by s.2(3) of the 1991 Act necessarily carries with it capacity to refuse. Lord James Douglas Hamilton accepted in the debate in the Special Standing Committee of the House of Commons that capacity to consent implied capacity to refuse (March 7, 1995, col. 532), as did Lord Fraser of Carmyllie in the Committee of the Whole House in the House of Lords (June 13, 1995, cols 132–134). Sheriff Kelbie has expressed doubts (in a commentary on *Houston, Applicant*, 1996 S.C.L.R. 943) as to whether the matter is as clear cut as suggested here, but concludes by hoping that the matter is indeed as stated.

section protects the child's right to refuse examination or treatment (when capacity under the 1991 Act) even when a warrant granted under the specified ontains a condition requiring such examination or treatment, or when a children's ng make a supervision requirement with a condition attached that the child submits to such examination or treatment. Any force' used against the child, even when such a condition has been made, would amount to assault. However, a children's hearing is not prohibited from imposing such a condition on a capable child: rather, any refusal on the part of the child to satisfy the condition would be a breach of a condition of the supervision requirement and treated in the way that any other breach would be. Such a condition attached to a warrant would be meaningless if the capable child refused the examination or treatment.

It is surprising that there is no express mention of the right of the capable child to refuse any examination or treatment required in terms of a child assessment order granted under s.55 above, but that omission cannot be taken to suggest that such an order be treated any differently from the warrants and requirements expressly mentioned here, for such an order clearly comes within the generality of the present section. See further, notes to s.55 above.

Procedural rules in relation to certain applications etc.

91.—(1) All proceedings to which this section applies are civil proceedings for the purposes of section 32 of the Sheriff Courts (Scotland) Act 1971 (power of Court of Session to regulate civil procedure in the sheriff court).

(2) Any reference in this Part of this Act to regulation or prescription by rules in relation to any proceedings to which this section applies shall be construed, unless the context otherwise requires, as a reference to regulation or prescription by rules made under the said section 32.

(3) Without prejudice to the generality of the said section 32, rules may make provision as to—

(a) the functions of a person appointed by the sheriff under section 41(1) of this Act and any right of that person to information relating to the proceedings;

(b) the circumstances in which any person who has been given notice in accordance with such rules of an application for a child assessment order, or any other person specified in the rules, may apply to the court to have that order varied or discharged;

(c) the persons to whom notice of the making of a child protection order shall be given by the applicant for that order, and without prejudice to that generality may in making such provision require such notice to be given to either or both of the child and any relevant person in relation to that child;

(d) the persons to whom notice of an application for an exclusion order or, under section 79(3) of this Act, for the recall or variation of such an order or of anything done under section 77(2) of this Act shall be given;

(e) the period within which a hearing shall be held under subsection (5) of section 76 of this Act after the granting of an order under subsection (4) of that section;

(f) the service of any exclusion order on the named person and the appropriate person within such period as may be specified in the rules.

(4) In relation to any proceedings to which this section applies, rules may permit a party to such proceedings, in such circumstances as may be specified in the rules, to be represented by a person who is neither an advocate nor a solicitor.

(5) This section applies to any application made to the sheriff, and any other proceeding before the sheriff (whether on appeal or otherwise), under any provision of this Part of this Act.

DEFINITIONS
"child": s.93(2)(b).
"child assessment order": ss.55(1), 93(1).
"child protection order": ss.57(1), 93(1).
"exclusion order": ss.76(12), 93(1).

GENERAL NOTE
In the debate in the Committee of the Whole House in the House of Lords on June 13, 1995, Lord Fraser of Carmyllie said, at col. 135,
> "Part II of the Bill contains a number of provisions for applications and appeals to be made to the sheriff. Some of these provisions contain rule-making powers while others do not. The purpose of this new clause is to ensure that adequate provision is made for all the sheriff court procedure rules necessary to ensure the effective implementation of the provisions of this legislation and, at the same time, to gather all of the provisions for the rules into one clause in the Bill to facilitate reference".

S.I.s ISSUED UNDER SECTION
Act of Sederunt (Family Proceedings in the Sheriff Court) (S.I. 1996 No. 2167).
Children (Scotland) Act 1995 etc. (Revocations and Savings) (Scotland) Regulations 1997 (S.I. 1997 No. 691).

Legal aid in respect of certain proceedings

92. [*Amends s.29 of the Legal Aid (Scotland) Act 1986 (c. 47).*]

Interpretation of Part II

Interpretation of Part II

93.—(1) In this Part of this Act, unless the context otherwise requires,—
"accommodation" shall be construed in accordance with section 25(8) of this Act;
"chief social work officer" means an officer appointed under section 3 of the Social Work (Scotland) Act 1968;
"child assessment order" has the meaning given by section 55(1) of this Act;
"child protection order" has the meaning given by section 57(1) of this Act;
"children's hearing" shall be construed in accordance with section 39(3), but does not include a business meeting arranged under section 64, of this Act;
"compulsory measures of supervision" means, in respect of a child, such measures of supervision as may be imposed upon him by a children's hearing;
"constable" means a constable of a police force within the meaning of the Police (Scotland) Act 1967;
"contact order" has the meaning given by section 11(2)(d) of this Act;
"disabled" has the meaning given by section 23(2) of this Act;
"exclusion order" has the meaning given by section 76(12) of this Act;
"family", in relation to a child, includes—
    (a) any person who has parental responsibility for the child; and
    (b) any other person with whom the child has been living;
"local authority" means a council constituted under section 2 of the Local Government etc. (Scotland) Act 1994;
"local government area" shall be construed in accordance with section 1 of the said Act of 1994;
"parental responsibilities" has the meaning given by section 1(3) of this Act;
"parental responsibilities order" has the meaning given by section 86(1) of this Act;
"parental rights" has the meaning given by section 2(4) of this Act;
"place of safety", in relation to a child, means—
    (a) a residential or other establishment provided by a local authority;
    (b) a community home within the meaning of section 53 of the Children Act 1989;
    (c) a police station; or
    (d) a hospital, surgery or other suitable place, the occupier of which is willing temporarily to receive the child;

"the Principal Reporter" means the Principal Reporter appointed
under section 127 of the said Act of 1994 or any officer of the Scottish
Children's Reporter Administration to whom there is delegated,
under section 131(1) of that Act, any function of the Principal
Reporter under this Act;

"relevant local authority", in relation to a child who is subject to a
warrant granted under this Part of this Act or to a supervision
requirement, means the local authority for whose area the children's
panel from which the children's hearing which granted the warrant or
imposed the supervision requirement was formed;

"residence order" has the meaning given by section 11(2)(c) of this Act;

"residential establishment"—

    (a) in relation to a place in Scotland, means an establishment
(whether managed by a local authority, by a voluntary organisation or by any other person) which provides residential
accommodation for children for the purposes of this Act or the
Social Work (Scotland) Act 1968;

    (b) in relation to a place in England and Wales, means a community
home, voluntary home or registered children's home (within the
meaning of the Children Act 1989); and

    (c) in relation to a place in Northern Ireland, means a home
provided under Part VIII of the Children (Northern Ireland)
Order 1995, or a voluntary home, or a registered children's home
(which have respectively the meanings given by that Order);

"school age" shall be construed in accordance with section 31 of the
Education (Scotland) Act 1980;

"secure accommodation" means accommodation provided in a residential establishment, approved by the Secretary of State in accordance
with regulations made under section 60(1)(bb) of the Social Work
(Scotland) Act 1968 or under paragraph 4(2)(i) of Schedule 4 to the
Children Act 1989, for the purpose of restricting the liberty of
children;

"supervision requirement" has the meaning given by section 70(1) of
this Act, and includes any condition contained in such a requirement
or related to it;

"voluntary organisation" means a body (other than a public or local
authority) whose activities are not carried on for profit; and

"working day" means every day except—

    (a) Saturday and Sunday;

    (b) December 25th and 26th; and

    (c) January 1st and 2nd.

(2) For the purposes of—

(a) Chapter 1 and this Chapter (except this section) of this Part, "child"
means a person under the age of eighteen years; and

(b) Chapters 2 and 3 of this Part—

"child" means—

    (i) a child who has not attained the age of sixteen years;

    (ii) a child over the age of sixteen years who has not attained the age
of eighteen years and in respect of whom a supervision requirement is in force; or

    (iii) a child whose case has been referred to a children's hearing by
virtue of section 33 of this Act;

and for the purposes of the application of those Chapters to a person
who has failed to attend school regularly without reasonable excuse
includes a person who is over sixteen years of age but is not over
school age; and

"relevant person" in relation to a child means—

    (a) any parent enjoying parental responsibilities or parental rights
under Part I of this Act;

    (b) any person in whom parental responsibilities or rights are vested by, under or by virtue of this Act; and

    (c) any person who appears to be a person who ordinarily (and other than by reason only of his employment) has charge of, or control over, the child.

(3) Where, in the course of any proceedings under Chapter 2 or 3 of this Part, a child ceases to be a child within the meaning of subsection (2) above, the provisions of those Chapters of this Part and of any statutory instrument made under those provisions shall continue to apply to him as if he had not so ceased to be a child.

(4) Any reference in this Part of this Act to a child—

    (a) being "in need", is to his being in need of care and attention because—

       (i) he is unlikely to achieve or maintain, or to have the opportunity of achieving or maintaining, a reasonable standard of health or development unless there are provided for him, under or by virtue of this Part, services by a local authority;

      (ii) his health or development is likely significantly to be impaired, or further impaired, unless such services are so provided;

     (iii) he is disabled; or

    (iv) he is affected adversely by the disability of any other person in his family;

    (b) who is "looked after" by a local authority, shall be construed in accordance with section 17(6) of this Act.

(5) Any reference to any proceedings under this Part of this Act, whether on an application or on appeal, being heard by the sheriff, shall be construed as a reference to such proceedings being heard by the sheriff in chambers.

PART III

ADOPTION

Approval of adoption society for specific services

94.—(1) [*Amends s.3 of the Adoption (Scotland) Act 1978 (c. 28).*]

(2) [*Amends s.4 of the Adoption (Scotland) Act 1978 (c. 28).*]

(3) [*Amends s.65 of the Adoption (Scotland) Act 1978 (c. 28).*]

Welfare of child paramount consideration

95. [*Substitutes s.6 of the Adoption (Scotland) Act 1978 (c. 28).*]

Duty of adoption agency to consider alternatives to adoption

96. [*Inserts new s.6A into the Adoption (Scotland) Act 1978 (c. 28).*]

Adoption by person married to natural parent

97.—(1) [*Amends s.12 of the Adoption (Scotland) Act 1978 (c. 28).*]

(2) [*Amends s.15 of the Adoption (Scotland) Act 1978 (c. 28).*]

(3) [*Amends s.39 of the Adoption (Scotland) Act 1978 (c. 28).*]

Further amendments of the 1978 Act; and interpretation of Part III

98.—(1) Schedule 2 to this Act, which contains further amendments of the 1978 Act, shall have effect.

(2) In this Part of this Act, "the 1978 Act" means the Adoption (Scotland) Act 1978.

PART IV

GENERAL AND SUPPLEMENTAL

Registration of births by persons who are themselves children

99.—(1) In paragraph (a) of section 14(1) of the Registration of Births, Deaths and Marriages (Scotland) Act 1965 (duty of father and mother to give information of particulars of birth), for the words "father or mother of the child" substitute "child's father or mother (whether or not they have attained the age of sixteen years)".

(2) Where, at any time after the coming into force of the Age of Legal Capacity (Scotland) Act 1991 but before the coming into force of subsection (1) above, a person mentioned in the said paragraph (a) who had not at that time attained the age of sixteen years purported to fulfil the duty mentioned in the said section 14(1), he shall be presumed to have had legal capacity to fulfil that duty.

(3) [*Amends s.18 of the said Act of 1965 (c. 49).*]

(4) Where, at any time after the coming into force of the Age of Legal Capacity (Scotland) Act 1991 but before the coming into force of subsection (3) above, a person who had not at that time attained the age of sixteen years made a request, declaration, statutory declaration or application mentioned in subsection (1) or (2) of the said section 18 in relation to a child in respect of whose birth an entry was consequently made under the said subsection (1) in a register of births, or as the case may be under the said subsection (2) in the Register of Corrections etc., the person shall be presumed to have had legal capacity to make the request, declaration, statutory declaration, or application in question.

GENERAL NOTE

It is a fact, which until the passing of this Act was given no formal legal recognition, that persons under the age of 16 years sometimes themselves do become parents. Under the Age of Legal Capacity (Scotland) Act 1991 for most purposes a person has no legal capacity until reaching the age of 16; this, however, is subject to a number of stated exceptions. An exception not stated in that Act is capacity to register the birth of a child though, certainly with mothers, it was possible to argue that such registration was a transaction commonly undertaken by persons of the appropriate age and circumstances. Nevertheless an element of doubt existed and this section is designed to put beyond that doubt the legal capacity of a person, who becomes a parent before attaining the age of 16 years, to register the birth of her or his own child. It does so by amending the appropriate provision in the Registration of Births, Deaths and Marriages (Scotland) Act 1965 (c. 49) to make plain that the duty upon parents to give information concerning a birth applies whatever age the parent is. The new rule is given retrospective effect by subs. (2) according to which any person who purported to fulfil the duty in the 1965 Act before the coming into force of the present provision (but after the coming into force of the 1991 Act, which was on September 25, 1991) is presumed to have had that legal capacity which such a person would have now.

Subsection (3) amends s.18 of the 1965 Act. That section deals with the duty to register the birth of a child whose parents are not married (and will therefore deal with the vast majority of parents one or both of whom are under the age of 16). Such a person is given legal capacity to make the requests, declarations, or applications required by s.18 so long as she or he is of sufficient (mental) maturity to understand the nature of the request, declaration or application (in the opinion of the registrar or sheriff). It may be noted that there is no requirement of mental maturity to be fulfilled in order to acquire legal capacity to perform the duties in s.14 of the 1965 Act, capacity for which is given in subs. (1) hereof. A person aged 12 or more will be presumed to have sufficient understanding. That is a mere presumption: a person over 12 may be found to lack the appropriate understanding, and a person under 12 who is a parent may be found to have the appropriate understanding (though a parent under 12 years of age will be very rare indeed). The effect of subs. (4) is to give this rule retrospective effect as from September 25, 1991 (the date of the coming into force of the Age of Legal Capacity (Scotland) Act 1991).

Inquiries into matters affecting children

100. [*Inserts new s.6B into the Social Work (Scotland) Act 1968 (c. 49).*]

Panel for curators *ad litem*, reporting officers and safeguarders

101.—(1) The Secretary of State may by regulations make provision for the establishment of a panel of persons from whom—
  (a) curators *ad litem* may be appointed under section 58 of the Adoption (Scotland) Act 1978 or under section 87(4) of this Act;
  (b) reporting officers may be appointed under those sections; and
  (c) persons may be appointed under section 41(1) of this Act.
  (2) Regulations under subsection (1) above may provide, without prejudice to the generality of that subsection—
  (a) for the appointment, qualifications and training of persons who may be appointed to that panel; and
  (b) for the management and organisation of persons available for appointment from that panel.
  (3) Regulations under subsection (1) above may provide for the expenses incurred by persons appointed from the panel to be defrayed by a local authority.

GENERAL NOTE
    The Secretary of State is given power to make regulations for the establishment of a panel of persons from whom curators *ad litem*, reporting officers, and safeguarders, who perform various functions under the Adoption (Scotland) Act 1978 and the present Act, may be appointed. There will be one panel of persons who are able to perform any of the stated roles, and sometimes a single person may be called upon to perform more than one of these roles. The regulations will also provide how persons are to be appointed to such a panel, and the qualifications and training necessary to perform the appropriate functions. It is expected that these regulations will be similar to but more extensive than the present regulations dealing with reporting officers in the adoption process (Act of Sederunt (Adoption of Children) 1984 (S.I. 1984 No. 1013)), and this will have the effect of enhancing quite significantly the position of the safeguarder in the children's hearing system.

Removal of duty to report on operation of Children Act 1975

102. Section 105 of the Children Act 1975 (which among other things provides that every five years there shall be laid before Parliament by the Secretary of State a report on the operation of such sections of that Act as are for the time being in force) shall cease to have effect.

GENERAL NOTE
    The provisions of the Children Act 1975 which remain in effect are not important in comparison to the provisions of the present Act, but it was felt to be unduly onerous on local authorities to require them to draw up reports on the operation of the present Act. As a consequence the duty under s.105 of the 1975 Act has been repealed.

Interpretation, rules, regulations and Parliamentary control

103.—(1) Any reference in this Act, or in any enactment amended by this Act, to a person having, or to there being vested in him, parental responsibilities or parental rights shall, unless the context otherwise requires, be construed as a reference to his having, or to there being so vested, any of those rights or as the case may be responsibilities.
  (2) Any reference in this Act to something being "prescribed" is, unless the context otherwise requires, a reference to its being prescribed by regulations; and any power conferred by this Act on the Secretary of State or the Lord Advocate to make rules or regulations shall be exercisable by statutory instrument which shall be subject to annulment in pursuance of a resolution of either House of Parliament.
  (3) Rules or regulations made under this Act—
  (a) may make different provision for different cases or classes of case; and

(b) may exclude certain cases or classes of case.

There are various references in the Act to persons having parental responsibilities, and various other references to persons having parental rights. Subsection (2) of this section provides that such references include persons who have one or more parental responsibility or parental right. Some provisions talk of persons having "parental responsibilities and parental rights" and that phrase suggests, it is submitted, a person with all these responsibilities and rights.

S.I.s ISSUED UNDER SECTION
Parental Responsibilities and Parental Rights Agreement (Scotland) Regulations 1996 (S.I. 1996 No. 2549).
Arrangements to Look After Children (Scotland) Regulations 1996 (S.I. 1996 No. 3262).
Children (Scotland) Act 1995 etc. (Revocations and Savings) (Scotland) Regulations 1997 (S.I. 1997 No. 691).

Financial provision

104. There shall be paid out of money provided by Parliament—
(a) any expenses of the Secretary of State incurred in consequence of the provisions of this Act; and
(b) any increase attributable to this Act in the sums payable out of money so provided under any other enactment.

Extent, short title, minor and consequential amendments, repeals and commencement

105.—(1) This Act, which subject to subsections (8) to (10) below extends to Scotland only—
(a) may be cited as the Children (Scotland) Act 1995; and
(b) except for subsections (1), (2) and (6) to (10) of this section, shall come into force on such day as the Secretary of State may by order made by statutory instrument appoint;
and different days may be appointed under paragraph (b) above for different purposes.

(2) An order under subsection (1)(b) above may contain such transitional and consequential provisions and savings as appear to the Secretary of State to be necessary or expedient in connection with the provisions brought into force.

(3) The transitional provisions and savings contained in Schedule 3 to this Act shall have effect but are without prejudice to sections 16 and 17 of the Interpretation Act 1978 (effect of repeals).

(4) Schedule 4 to this Act, which contains minor amendments and amendments consequential upon the provisions of this Act, shall have effect.

(5) The enactments mentioned in Schedule 5 to this Act (which include spent provisions) are hereby repealed to the extent specified in the third column of that Schedule.

(6) The Secretary of State may by order made by statutory instrument make such further amendments or repeals, in such enactments as may be specified in the order, as appear to him to be necessary or expedient in consequence of any provision of this Act.

(7) A statutory instrument containing an order under subsection (6) above shall be subject to annulment in pursuance of a resolution of either House of Parliament.

(8) Sections 18, 26(2), 33, 44, 70(4), 74, 82, 83, 93 and 104 of this Act and this section extend to England and Wales, and those sections and this section (except section 70(4)) also extend to Northern Ireland; but—
(a) subsection (4) of this section so extends—

(i) to England and Wales, only in so far as it relates to paragraphs 8,
10, 19, 31, 37, 41(1), (2) and (7) to (9), 48 to 52, 54 and 55 of
Schedule 4; and
(ii) to Northern Ireland, only in so far as it relates to paragraphs 31,
37, 41(1), (2) and (7) to (9), 54, 55 and 58 of that Schedule; and
(b) subsection (5) of this section so extends—
(i) to England and Wales, only in so far as it relates to the entries in
Schedule 5 in respect of Part V of the Social Work (Scotland) Act
1968, the Maintenance Orders (Reciprocal Enforcement) Act
1972, section 35(4)(c) of the Family Law Act 1986, the Children
Act 1989, the Child Support Act 1991 and the Education Act
1993; and
(ii) to Northern Ireland, only in so far as it relates to the entries in
that Schedule in respect of Part V of the Social Work (Scotland)
Act 1968, the Maintenance Orders (Reciprocal Enforcement)
Act 1972 and section 35(4)(c) of the Family Law Act 1986.
(9) This section, so far as it relates to the repeal of Part V of the Social
Work (Scotland) Act 1968, also extends to the Channel Islands.
(10) Her Majesty may by Order in Council direct that any of the relevant
provisions specified in the Order shall extend, with such exceptions,
adaptations and modifications (if any) as may be specified in the Order, to
any of the Channel Islands; and in this subsection "the relevant provisions"
means sections 74, 82, 83 and 93 of this Act and any regulations made under
section 74 of this Act.

SCHEDULES

Section 39(2) SCHEDULE 1

CHILDREN'S PANELS

Appointment

1. The Secretary of State shall, for each local government area, appoint such number of
members of children's panels as he considers appropriate and from among that number appoint
a chairman and a deputy chairman.
2. A member of a children's panel shall hold office for such period as is specified by the
Secretary of State, but may be removed from office by the Secretary of State at any time.

Children's Panel Advisory Committees

3. Subject to paragraph 8 below, each local authority shall form a body (to be known as a
"Children's Panel Advisory Committee") consisting of two members nominated by the local
authority and three members nominated by the Secretary of State.
4. The Secretary of State may at the request of the local authority provide for an increase in
the membership of the Children's Panel Advisory Committee appointed under paragraph 3
above by such number, not exceeding five, of additional members as the authority specify in
relation to their request, the additional members to be nominated as follows—
(a) the first, and any second or fourth additional member, by the Secretary of State;
(b) any third or fifth additional member, by the local authority.
5. The chairman of the Children's Panel Advisory Committee shall be appointed by the
Secretary of State from among such of the members he has nominated as are resident in the
local government area for which the panel is appointed.
6. It shall be the duty of the Children's Panel Advisory Committee—
(a) to submit names of possible panel members to the Secretary of State;
(b) to advise the Secretary of State, in so far as he requires advice, on the suitability of
persons referred to him as potential panel members; and
(c) to advise the Secretary of State on such matters relating to the general administration of
the panels as he may refer to them.
7. The Children's Panel Advisory Committee shall have power—
(a) to appoint sub-committees;
(b) to appoint to any such sub-committee a person who is not a member of the Children's
Panel Advisory Committee; and

(c) to refer all or any of the duties set out in paragraph 6 above to any such sub-committee for their advice.

Joint Advisory Committees

8.—(1) Two or more local authorities may, instead of each acting under paragraph 3 above, make arrangements to form a Children's Panel Advisory Committee for their areas (a "joint advisory committee").

(2) A joint advisory committee shall not be formed in pursuance of arrangements made under sub-paragraph (1) above unless the authorities concerned have obtained the consent in writing of the Secretary of State.

(3) The Secretary of State may give a direction, in any case where a joint advisory committee has not been formed, to two or more local authorities requiring them to form a joint advisory committee; and they shall comply with any such direction.

(4) Paragraphs 3 to 7, 10(a) and 11(b) of this Schedule shall apply to a joint advisory committee as they apply in respect of a Children's Panel Advisory Committee and, for the purposes of those paragraphs the local authorities acting under sub-paragraph (1) above shall be regarded as a single local authority.

Recruitment and training of panel members

9. The Secretary of State may make such arrangements as he considers appropriate to recruit and train members, or possible members, of the children's panels.

10. Each local authority shall make such arrangements as they consider appropriate—
    (a) to enable the Children's Panel Advisory Committee to obtain names for submission to the Secretary of State as potential panel members; and
    (b) to train panel members or potential panel members.

Expenses of panel members

11. A local authority may pay—
    (a) to a member or a potential member of a children's panel,
    (b) to a member of the Children's Panel Advisory Committee,
    (c) to any person appointed under paragraph 7 above,
such allowances as may be determined by the Secretary of State; and he may determine differently in relation to different cases or different classes of case.

Publication of list of members of children's panel

12. Each local authority shall publish a list of names and addresses of members of the children's panel for their area, and that list shall be open for public inspection at the principal offices of the local authority, and at any place where an electors list for the local government area is available for inspection.

Section 98(1)   SCHEDULE 2

GENERAL NOTE
In addition to the amendments to the Adoption (Scotland) Act 1978 made in Pt III above, this Schedule contains various other amendments to that Act. Most of the changes are terminological, to take account of the shift in Pt I from the notions of "custody" and "access" to "residence" and "contact", but in addition there are a number of important substantive changes, particularly in relation to the grounds for dispensing with parental agreement to adoption. These changes have been incorporated into the 1978 Act. For details see Plumtree's annotations at para. A.444 *et seq.*

Section 105(3)   SCHEDULE 3

TRANSITIONAL PROVISIONS AND SAVINGS

1. Where, immediately before the day appointed for the coming into force of section 25 of this Act, a child is by virtue of section 15 of the 1968 Act (duty of local authority to provide for orphans, deserted children etc.) in the care of a local authority, the child shall on and after that day be treated as if he had been provided with accommodation under (and within the meaning of) subsection (1) of the said section 25.

2. Sections 29 and 30 of this Act shall apply in respect of a person who, at the time when he ceased to be of school age (as defined in section 31 of the Education (Scotland) Act 1980) or at any subsequent time, was—

(a) in the care of a local authority by virtue of the said section 15 or of section 16 of the 1968 Act (assumption of parental rights and powers); or

(b) subject to a supervision requirement (within the meaning of section 44(1) of the 1968 Act),

as they apply in respect of a person who at such time was looked after (within the meaning of Part II of this Act) by a local authority.

3. Where the parental rights in respect of a child have, by a resolution under the said section 16 or under section 16A of the 1968 Act (duty of local authority in cases of necessity to assume parental rights and powers vested in a voluntary organisation), vested in a local authority and immediately before the day appointed for the coming into force of section 86 of this Act those rights remain so vested, the resolution shall on and after that day have effect as if it were a parental responsibilities order transferring the appropriate parental rights and responsibilities (as defined in subsection (3) of the said section 86) relating to the child to the authority; and any access order made under section 17B of the 1968 Act in relation to the child (with any order made under section 17C of that Act as respects the access order) being (in either case) an order which immediately before that day remains undischarged, shall on and after that day have effect as if it were an order made under section 88(3) of this Act as respects the child.

4. Where the parental rights in respect of a child have, by a resolution under the said section 16, vested in a voluntary organisation (as defined in section 93 of this Act) and immediately before the day mentioned in paragraph 3 above those rights remain so vested, the resolution shall, notwithstanding the repeal by this Act of the said section 16, continue to have effect until one of the following occurs—

(a) the child attains the age of eighteen years;

(b) the resolution is rescinded by the local authority because it appears to them that their doing so would promote the child's welfare;

(c) the period of six months commencing with that day expires;

(d) an order is made by virtue of section 11(2)(b), or under section 86(1), of this Act in relation to the child;

(e) an order is made under section 12 (adoption order) or 18 (order freeing for adoption) of the Adoption (Scotland) Act 1978 in relation to the child.

5. Where the circumstance by virtue of which a resolution under the said section 16 ceases to have effect is that mentioned in sub-paragraph (c) of paragraph 4 above, the appropriate parental rights and responsibilities (defined as mentioned in paragraph 3 above) in relation to the child shall transfer forthwith to the local authority in whose area he resides; and for the purposes of sections 86(6) and 87 to 89 of this Act the transfer shall be deemed effected by a parental responsibilities order applied for by that authority.

6. While a resolution continues to have effect by virtue of paragraph 4 above, sections 17(3A) and (6) to (10), 17A, 17B, 17D, 17E and 20(3) of the 1968 Act (together with the code of practice last published under subsection (5) of the said section 17E) shall continue to have effect in relation to the child in question notwithstanding the repeal by this Act of those sections.

7. Where an order made under—

(a) section 10 (power of court in actions of divorce etc. to commit care of child to local authority) or 12 (power of court to provide for supervision of child) of the Matrimonial Proceedings (Children) Act 1958;

(b) section 11 of the Guardianship Act 1973 (orders relating to care and custody of children); or

(c) section 26 of the Adoption (Scotland) Act 1978 (provision for supervision or care where adoption order refused),

committed the care of the child to, or as the case may be placed the child under the supervision of, a local authority and immediately before the repeal by this Act of the section in question (the "relevant repeal") that order remained undischarged, the order shall continue to have effect notwithstanding the relevant repeal until one of the following occurs—

(i) the period of six months commencing with the date of the relevant repeal expires;

(ii) the Court of Session direct, or the sheriff directs, that the order be discharged; or

(iii) there is an event in consequence of which, but for the provisions (apart from this paragraph) of this Act, the order would have fallen to be discharged.

8.—(1) Where relevant proceedings in relation to a child have been commenced and on the relevant date have not been concluded, the provisions of Part III of the 1968 Act shall continue to apply to those proceedings until the proceedings are concluded, notwithstanding the repeal of any of those provisions by this Act.

(2) For the purposes of this paragraph, "relevant proceedings" means any proceedings at a children's hearing under Part III of the 1968 Act, any application to the sheriff under that Part for a warrant or under section 42(2)(c) of that Act to establish any ground of referral, and any appeal under section 49 or 50 of that Act; and a reference to the commencement, or to the

conclusion, of such proceedings shall be construed in accordance with sub-paragraph (3) or, as the case may be, (4) below.

(3) Relevant proceedings are commenced when one of the following occurs—
- (a) a children's hearing is arranged under section 37(4) or section 39(3) of the 1968 Act;
- (b) an application under section 42(2)(c) of that Act is lodged;
- (c) an appeal to the sheriff under section 49 of that Act is lodged;
- (d) an application under section 50(2) of that Act is made.

(4) Relevant proceedings are concluded when one of the following occurs—
- (a) the sheriff discharges the referral under section 42(5) of the 1968 Act;
- (b) a children's hearing discharge the referral under section 43(2) of that Act;
- (c) the period of three weeks after a children's hearing make a supervision requirement under section 44 of that Act or on remission to them under section 49(5) of that Act, expires provided that no appeal has been lodged within that period against that decision under section 49 of that Act;
- (d) subject, as respects a decision under section 49(5)(b) of that Act, to head (c) above, the period of twenty eight days after the sheriff has disposed of an appeal under section 49(4), (5) or (6) of that Act expires provided that no application has been made within that period to him to state a case under section 50(2) of that Act;
- (e) the period of twenty eight days after the sheriff has disposed of a case remitted to him under section 50(3) expires provided that no further application under the said section 50(2) has been made.

9. Where a child has been taken to a place of safety, or is being detained in such a place, in accordance with section 37(2) of the 1968 Act before the relevant date, and the first lawful day for the purposes of subsection (4) of that section is on or after that date, the child's case shall be proceeded with as if that day had been before the relevant date.

10.—(1) Where on the relevant date a child is subject to a supervision requirement imposed under section 44 of the 1968 Act, he shall be treated as if the requirement had been imposed under section 70 of this Act; and in calculating any period of time for the purposes of section 73 of this Act, that requirement shall be deemed to have been imposed on the day on which the requirement was imposed under the said section 44 or, as the case may be, was last reviewed or varied under the said Act of 1968.

(2) Where any relevant proceedings are concluded as mentioned in paragraph 8(4)(c) above, a supervision requirement imposed under section 44 of the 1968 Act shall have effect as if it were made under section 70 of this Act.

(3) Where before the relevant date, or in any relevant proceedings, the sheriff has in relation to a supervision requirement made an order under section 49(6) of the 1968 Act, that order shall have effect in relation to the supervision requirement deemed to have been made under section 70 of this Act as it would have had effect in relation to the supervision requirement made under section 44 of the 1968 Act.

11. In this Schedule—
"the 1968 Act" means the Social Work (Scotland) Act 1968;
"the relevant date" means the date on which the repeal of Part III of the 1968 Act by this Act takes effect; and
"relevant proceedings" shall be construed in accordance with paragraph 8(2) above.

Section 105(4)   SCHEDULE 4

MINOR AND CONSEQUENTIAL AMENDMENTS

Lands Clauses Consolidation (Scotland) Act 1845 (c. 19)

1.—(1) The Lands Clauses Consolidation (Scotland) Act 1845 shall be amended in accordance with this paragraph.

(2) In section 7 (which makes provision for certain persons to have full power to sell and convey land)—
- (a) after the word "husbands," insert "persons who, within the meaning of Part I of the Children (Scotland) Act 1995, are entitled to act as the legal representatives of a child,";
- (b) after the words "guardians for" the words "persons under a legal disability by reason of nonage" shall cease to have effect; and
- (c) after the word "whether", the words "persons under legal disability by reason of nonage" shall cease to have effect;
- (d) after the word "such" where it appears for the sixth time, insert "legal representatives,"; and
- (e) after the word "such" where it appears for the seventh time, the words "persons under legal disability by reason of nonage" shall cease to have effect.

(3) In section 67 (certain payments to persons under a disability to be deposited with the Bank)—
  (a) after the word "husband," insert "a person who, within the meaning of Part I of the Children (Scotland) Act 1995, is entitled to act as a legal representative of a child"; and
  (b) the words "persons under legal disability by reason of nonage" shall cease to have effect.
(4) In section 69 (nomination of trustees to whom certain payments of under £200 may be paid)—
  (a) the words "legal disability by reason of nonage" shall cease to have effect; and
  (b) after the word "husbands," insert "legal representatives of a child (within the meaning of Part I of the Children (Scotland) Act 1995),".
(5) In section 70 (sums of under £20 to be paid to certain persons), after the word "husbands," insert "legal representatives of a child (within the meaning of Part I of the Children (Scotland) Act 1995),".

Judicial Factors (Scotland) Act 1849 (c. 51)

2.—(1) The Judicial Factors (Scotland) Act 1849 shall be amended in accordance with this paragraph.
(2) In section 1 (interpretation), the words from "the word "Guardian" to "years;" shall cease to have effect.
(3) In section 10 (duty of accountant to supervise judicial factors and others), for the words "guardians and tutors" substitute ", tutors".
(4) Section 25(2) (guardians to be subject to the provisions of the Act), shall cease to have effect.
(5) In section 27 (limitation by court of amount of caution), the words "guardians and" shall cease to have effect.
(6) In section 31 (power of court to remove tutors etc.), the word "guardian" shall cease to have effect.
(7) In section 32 (provisions of the Act not to alter existing powers, rights and duties of offices), the word "guardian," shall cease to have effect.
(8) In section 33 (power of accountant to obtain information from banks), the words "guardians or" shall cease to have effect.
(9) In section 34 (petitions for discharge of office), in both places where it occurs, the word "guardian," shall cease to have effect.
(10) In section 34A (act of sederunt to provide for other forms of discharge), for the words ", death or coming of age" substitute "or death".
(11) In section 36 (records held by accountant to be open to inspection), the word "guardianships," shall cease to have effect.
(14 In section 37 (accumulation of interest on accounts), the word "guardian," shall cease to have effect.
(13) In section 40 (act of sederunt to regulate *inter alia* application of the Act to offices other than judicial factors), in both places where it occurs, the word "guardians," shall cease to have effect.

Improvement of Land Act 1864 (c.114)

3. In section 24 of the Improvement of Land Act 1864 (representation of persons under disability in certain applications etc.), for the words from the beginning to "feoffee" where it last occurs substitute "Any person entitled to act as the legal representative of a person under legal disability by reason of non age or mental incapacity shall be entitled to act on behalf of that person for the purposes of this Act; and any trustee, judicial factor, executor or administrator shall, subject to any other enactment, have the same rights and powers for the purposes of this Act as if the property vested in or administered by him had been vested in him in his own right; but no such legal representative".

Judicial Factors (Scotland) Act 1880 (c. 4)

4. In section 3 of the Judicial Factors (Scotland) Act 1880 (interpretation), in the definition of "judicial factor"—
  (a) for the word "*absentis*," substitute "*absentis* and"; and
  (b) the words from "and" to "required," shall cease to have effect.

Heritable Securities (Scotland) Act 1894 (c. 44)

5. In section 13 of the Heritable Securities (Scotland) Act 1894 (persons to have powers conferred by Act where person subject to legal disability), for the words "and trustees" substitute "and—

(a) any person entitled, within the meaning of Part I of the Children (Scotland) Act 1995, to act as the legal representative of a child; and
(b) trustees".

Trusts (Scotland) Act 1921 (c. 58)

6. In section 2 of the Trusts (Scotland) Act 1921 (interpretation)—
    (a) in the definition of "trustee", the words "(including a father or mother acting as guardian of a child under the age of 16 years)" shall cease to have effect; and
    (b) after the definition of "trustee" insert—
        " "curator" and "tutor" shall have respectively the meanings assigned to these expressions by section 1 of the Judicial Factors Act 1849;
        "guardian" shall not include any person who, within the meaning of Part I of the Children (Scotland) Act 1995, is entitled to act as the legal representative of a child;".

Children and Young Persons (Scotland) Act 1937 (c. 37)

7.—(1) The Children and Young Persons (Scotland) Act 1937 shall be amended in accordance with this paragraph.
(2) In section 12 (cruelty to persons under sixteen)—
    (a) in subsection (1), for the words from "has the custody" to "that age" substitute "who has parental responsibilities in relation to a child or to a young person under that age or has charge or care of a child or such a young person,";
    (b) in subsection (2)(a), after the words "young person" insert "or the legal guardian of a child or young person"; and
    (c) in subsection (4), for the words from "of whom" to "or care" substitute "and he had parental responsibilities in relation to, or charge or care of, that child or young person".
(3) In section 15 (causing or allowing persons under sixteen to be used for begging), in each of subsections (1) and (2), for the words "the custody" substitute "parental responsibilities in relation to, or having".
(4) In section 22 (exposing children under seven to risk of burning), for the words from "having the custody" to "seven years" substitute "and who has parental responsibilities in relation to a child under the age of seven years or charge or care of such a child".
(5) In section 27 (interpretation)—
    (a) the first paragraph shall cease to have effect; and
    (b) in the second paragraph, for the words "the custody of" substitute "parental responsibilities in relation to".
(6) In section 110(1) (interpretation)—
    (a) after the definition of "local authority" insert—
        " "parental responsibilities" has the same meaning as in section 1(3) of the Children (Scotland) Act 1995 and includes the responsibilities which a father would have as a parent but for the operation of section 3(1)(b) of that Act;";
    (b) for the definition of "place of safety", substitute "'place of safety" has the meaning give by section 93(1) of the Children (Scotland) Act 1995;"; and
    (c) for the definition of "residential establishment" substitute " "residential establishment" has the meaning given by the said section 93(1);".

Mines and Quarries Act 1954 (c. 70)

8. In section 182(1) of the Mines and Quarries Act 1954 (interpretation), in the definition of "parent", for the words from "means" to "and includes" substitute "means a parent of a young person or any person who is not a parent of his but who has parental responsibility for him (within the meaning of the Children Act 1989) or who has parental responsibilities in relation to him (within the meaning of section 1(3) of the Children (Scotland) Act 1995), and includes".

Matrimonial Proceedings (Children) Act 1958 (c. 40)

9. In section 11(1) of the Matrimonial Proceedings (Children) Act 1958 (reports as to arrangements for future care and upbringing of children), for the words from the beginning to "the court may" substitute "Where the court is considering any question relating to the care and upbringing of a child, it may".

Factories Act 1961 (c. 34)

10. In section 176(1) of the Factories Act 1961 (interpretation)—
    (a) for the definition of "child" substitute—
        " "child" means any person who is not over—

(a) compulsory school age (construed in accordance with section 277 of the Education Act 1993); or

(b) school age (construed in accordance with section 31 of the Education (Scotland) Act 1980);"

(b) in the definition of "parent", for the words from "means" to "and includes" substitute "means a parent of a child or young person or any person who is not a parent of his but who has parental responsibility for him (within the meaning of the Children Act 1989) or who has parental responsibilities in relation to him (within the meaning of section 1(3) of the Children (Scotland) Act 1995), and includes".

Education (Scotland) Act 1962 (c. 47)

11. In section 145(33) of the Education (Scotland) Act 1962 (interpretation), for the words "the actual custody of" substitute "parental responsibilities (within the meaning of section 1(3) of the Children (Scotland) Act 1995) in relation to, or has the care of,".

Registration of Births, Deaths and Marriages (Scotland) Act 1965 (c. 49)

12.—(1) The Registration of Births, Deaths and Marriages (Scotland) Act 1965 shall be amended in accordance with this paragraph.

(2) In section 20(3)(a) (re-registration of birth of person under sixteen), for sub-paragraphs (i) and (ii) substitute ", by any person (whether or not he has himself attained the age of sixteen years) having parental responsibilities in relation to that person;".

(3) In section 43 (recording of baptismal name or change of name or surname)—

(a) in subsection (3), the words from "In this" to the end shall cease to have effect;

(b) in subsections (6)(a) and (7), for the words "the parent or guardian" substitute "the qualified applicant";

(c) after subsection (9) insert—

"(9A) In this section "qualified applicant" means—

(a) where only one parent has parental responsibilities in relation to the child, that parent;

(b) where both parents have such responsibilities in relation to the child, both parents; and

(c) where neither parent has such responsibilities, any other person who has such responsibilities.

(9B) A person may be a qualified applicant for the purposes of this section whether or not he has attained the age of sixteen years"; and

(d) subsection (10) shall cease to have effect.

(4) In section 53(3)(c) (offence of failure by parent to give information concerning birth), after the word "fails" insert "without reasonable excuse".

(5) In section 56(1) (interpretation), after the definition of "parentage" insert—

" "parental responsibilities" has the meaning given in section 1(3) of the Children (Scotland) Act 1995;".

13. Where, at any time after the coming into force of the Age of Legal Capacity (Scotland) Act 1991 but before the coming into force of—

(a) sub-paragraph (2) of paragraph 12 of this Schedule, a person's mother or father, who had not at that time attained the age of sixteen years, purported to apply under section 20(3)(a) of that Act to re-register the person's birth, the mother, or as the case may be the father, shall be presumed to have had legal capacity to make the application; or

(b) sub-paragraph (3)(c) of that paragraph, a person who had not at that time attained the age of sixteen years purported to make an application under any provision of section 43 of that Act ("making an application" including for the purposes of this sub-paragraph, without prejudice to the generality of that expression, signing and delivering a certificate in accordance with subsection (3) of that section) the person shall be presumed to have had legal capacity to make the application.

Law Reform (Miscellaneous Provisions)(Scotland) Act 1966 (c. 19)

14. In section 8 of the Law Reform (Miscellaneous Provisions) (Scotland) Act 1966 (variation and recall of certain orders in respect of maintenance, custody etc.)—

(a) in subsection (1), after paragraph (c) insert—

"(cc) an order under section 11 of the Children (Scotland) Act 1995 (orders in respect of parental responsibilities etc.) or under any earlier enactment relating to the custody, care or supervision of a child, or access to a child;"; and

(b) in subsection (6), in the definition of "sheriff", in paragraph (a), for the words "or (c)" substitute ", (c) or (cc)".

15.—(1) The Social Work (Scotland) Act 1968 shall be amended in accordance with this paragraph.

(2) In section 1(1) (duty of local authority to implement statutory duties not falling on other authorities), after the word "Act" insert "or Part II of the Children (Scotland) Act 1995".

(3) In section 4 (arrangements for provision of assistance to local authorities by other bodies), after "1984" insert "or Part II of the Children (Scotland) Act 1995".

(4) In section 5 (powers of the Secretary of State in relation to certain functions of local authorities)—

   (a) in subsection (1) after the word "Act" insert "and Part II of the Children (Scotland) Act 1995";

   (b) in subsection (1B)—

       (i) before paragraph (o), the word "and" shall cease to have effect; and

       (ii) at the end add "; and

     (p) Part II of the Children (Scotland) Act 1995.";

   (c) in subsection (2), in paragraph (c) for the words "and (o)" substitute ", (o) and (p)"; and

   (d) for subsection (3) substitute—

"(3) Without prejudice to the generality of subsection (2) above, regulations under this section may make such provision as is mentioned in subsection (4) of this section as regards—

     (a) the boarding out of persons other than children by local authorities and voluntary organisations, whether under any enactment or otherwise; and

     (b) the placing of children under paragraph (a), or the making of arrangements in respect of children under paragraph (c), of section 26(1) of the Children (Scotland) Act 1995, by local authorities.

(4) The provision referred to in subsection (3) of this section is—

     (a) for the recording—

       (i) by local authorities and voluntary organisations, of information relating to those with whom persons are so boarded out, or who are willing to have persons so boarded out with them; and

       (ii) by local authorities, of information relating to those with whom children are so placed or with whom such arrangements are made or who are willing to have children so placed with them or to enter into such arrangements;

     (b) for securing that—

       (i) persons are not so boarded out in any household unless it is for the time being approved by such local authority or voluntary organisation as may be prescribed by the regulations; and

       (ii) children are not so placed or, in accordance with such arrangements, provided with accommodation, in any household unless it is for the time being approved by the local authority placing the child or as the case may be making the arrangements;

     (c) for securing that, where possible, the person with whom a child is so placed or with whom such arrangements are made is either of the same religious persuasion as the child or gives an undertaking that the child shall be brought up in that persuasion;

     (d) for securing—

       (i) that a person who is, and the place in which he is, so boarded out by a local authority or voluntary organisation is supervised and inspected by that authority or organisation; and

       (ii) that a child who is, and the place in which he is, so placed or, in accordance with such arrangements, provided with accommodation, by a local authority is supervised and inspected by that authority,

and that he shall be removed from the place in question if his welfare appears to require it.

(5) In subsections (3) and (4) of this section, "child" has the same meaning as in Chapters 2 and 3 of Part II of the Children (Scotland) Act 1995."

(5) In section 5B (requirement to establish complaints procedures)—

   (a) in subsection (4), in paragraph (b), for the words "rights in respect of" substitute "responsibilities and parental rights (within the meaning of section 1(3) and section 2(4) respectively of the Children (Scotland) Act 1995) in relation to"; and

   (b) in subsection (5), at the end of the definition of "child", the words from "and" to the end of the subsection shall cease to have effect.

(6) In section 6 (power to enter certain establishments to conduct examination)—
(a) in subsection (1)—
>> (i) in paragraph (a), after the word "1984" insert "or Part II of the Children (Scotland) Act 1995";
>> (ii) in paragraph (b), sub–paragraph (ii) shall cease to have effect;
>> (iii) in paragraph (c), after the word "person" insert ", other than a child,"; and
>> (iv) after paragraph (c) add—
>>> "(cc) any place where a child is for the time being accommodated under paragraph (a) of, or by virtue of paragraph (c) of, section 26(1) of the Children (Scotland) Act 1995."; and
> (b) in subsection (2), after the words "1984" insert "or Part II of the Children (Scotland) Act 1995".

(7) For subsection (1) of section 6A (power of the Secretary of State to hold inquiries), substitute—
>> "(1) Without prejudice to section 6B(1) of this Act, the Secretary of State may cause an inquiry to be held into—
>> (a) the functions of a local authority under this Act or any of the enactments mentioned in section 5(1B) of this Act;
>> (b) the functions of an adoption society, within the meaning of section 65 of the Adoption (Scotland) Act 1978;
>> (c) the functions of a voluntary organisation in so far as those functions relate to establishments to which sections 61 to 68 of this Act apply;
>> (d) the detention of a child under—
>>> (i) section 57 of the Children and Young Persons (Scotland) Act 1937; or
>>> (ii) section 206 or 413 of the Criminal Procedure (Scotland) Act 1975; or
>> (e) the functions of the Principal Reporter under Part III of the Local Government (Scotland) Act 1994, the Children (Scotland) Act 1995 or any other enactment."

(8) In section 9 (powers of the Secretary of State with regard to training etc.), in subsections (1) and (2), after the word "Act" insert "or Part II of the Children (Scotland) Act 1995".

(9) In section 10(1) (making of grants and loans for social work), for the words "and (l)" substitute ", (l) and (p)".

(10) In section 11(1) (local authority authorised by Secretary of State to purchase compulsorily land), in subsection (1), after the word "Act" insert "or Part II of the Children (Scotland) Act 1995".

(11) In section 12 (general social welfare services of local authorities), for the words from "be given" in subsection (1) to "a person" in subsection (2)(b) substitute—
", subject to subsections (3) to (5) of this section, be given in kind or in cash to, or in respect of, any relevant person.
(2) A person is a relevant person for the purposes of this section if, not being less than eighteen years of age, he is".

(12) in section 28 (burial or cremation)—
(a) in subsection (1), after the word "from," insert "or was a child being looked after by,"; and
(b) after subsection (2) add—
>> "(3) In subsection (1) of this section, the reference to a child being looked after by a local authority shall be construed in accordance with section 17(6) of the Children (Scotland) Act 1995.".

(13) In section 29 (power of local authority to defray expenses of parents etc. visiting persons accommodated by a local authority or attending certain funerals)—
(a) in subsection (1)—
>> (i) for the words from "a person" to "respect" substitute—
>> "—
>>> (a) a person, other than a child, in the care of the authority or receiving assistance from the authority; or
>>> (b) a child who is being looked after by the authority,
>> in respect";
>> (ii) after the words "visiting the person" insert "or child"; and
>> (iii) for the words "the person", where they occur for the second time, substitute "him";
(b) in subsection (2), for the words from "a person" to "for" substitute—
>> "—
>>> (a) a person, other than a child, who had been in the care of the authority or receiving assistance from the authority; for
>>> (b) a child who had been looked after by the authority, for"; and
(c) after subsection (2), add—

"(3) In subsections (1) and (2) above, references to a child looked after by a local authority shall be construed as is mentioned in subsection (3) of section 28 of this Act.".

(14) Part III (children in need of compulsory measures of care) shall cease to have effect, with the exception of subsections (1) and (3) of section 31 and the amendments provided for by the said subsection (3) and contained in Schedule 2 to that Act.

(15) In section 59(1) (provision and maintenance of residential and other establishments) after the word "Act,", where it occurs for the second time insert "or under Part II of the Children (Scotland) Act 1995,".

(16) In section 68 (visiting of persons in establishments)—
(a) in subsection (2), for the words "in the care or under the supervision of the authority under Part II or Part III of this Act" substitute "being looked after by the authority"; and
(b) after subsection (3) add—

"(4) In subsection (2) of this section, the reference to children being looked after by a local authority shall be construed in accordance with section 17(6) of the Children (Scotland) Act 1995.".

(17) In section 78 (duty to make contributions in respect of children in care etc.)—
(a) in subsection (1)—

(i) for the words "has been received into care under Part II of this Act" substitute "is being looked after by a local authority"; and

(ii) in paragraph (a), for the words "his father and mother" substitute "any natural person who has parental responsibilities (within the meaning of section 1(3) of the Children (Scotland) Act 1995) in relation to him"; and
(b) for subsection (2) substitute—

"(2) This Part of this Act applies to any supervision requirement which, under paragraph (a) of section 70(3) of the Children (Scotland) Act 1995, requires the child concerned to reside in a place or places other than his own home.".

(18) In section 78A (recovery of contributions), in subsection (2)(a), for the words "in their care or under their supervision" substitute "looked after by them".

(19) In section 79 (recipients of contributions)—
(a) in subsection (1), for the words "in the care or under the supervision of" substitute "looked after by"; and
(b) in subsection (2), for the words "having the care or supervision of" substitute "looking after".

(20) In section 80 (enforcement of duty to make contributions)—
(a) in subsection (1), for the words from "received" to "requirement" substitute "looked after by a local authority";
(b) in subsection (4), for paragraphs (a) and (b) substitute "throughout the period during which he is looked after by a local authority";
(c) in subsection (5), for the words "is the maintainable child's father or mother" substitute ", being a natural person, has parental responsibilities (within the meaning of section 1(3) of the Children (Scotland) Act 1995) in relation to the maintainable child"; and
(d) in subsection (7), for the words "having the care or supervision of" substitute "looking after".

(21) In section 82(1) (recovery of arrears of contributions), for the words "having the care or supervision of" substitute "looking after".

(22) In section 83(2) (variation of trusts where person in whose care a child has been residing is for the time being residing in England, Wales or Northern Ireland), for the words "having the care or supervision of" substitute "looking after".

(23) After section 83 insert—

"References in this Part of this Act to child being looked after

83A. In this Part of this Act, references to a child being looked after by a local authority shall be construed in accordance with section 17(6) of the Children (Scotland) Act 1995".

(24) In section 86 (adjustments between local authorities as regards certain expenditure)—
(a) in subsection (1)—

(i) in paragraph (a), after the word "Act" insert ", or under section 25 of the Children (Scotland) Act 1995,"; and

(ii) in paragraph (b), for the words from "of services" to "Act" where it occurs for the second time, substitute ", or under or by virtue of Part II of the said Act of 1995, of services and facilities for a person ordinarily so resident (including, in the case of a child, any expenses incurred after he has ceased to be a child, and, in the event of another local authority taking over, under section 25(4) of that Act, the provision of accommodation for him,"; and
(b) in subsection (3), after the words "1989" insert "or provided with accommodation under paragraph (a) of, or by virtue of paragraph (c) of, section 26(1) of the Children (Scotland) Act 1995".

(25) In section 87 (charges which may be made for services and accommodation), in each of subsections (1) and (1A), after the words "1984" there shall be inserted "or under or by virtue of Part II of the Children (Scotland) Act 1995".

(26) Section 88 (duty of parents to notify change of address) shall cease to have effect.

(27) In section 90(1) (power to make regulations, orders or rules), the words "(other than orders under section 52 and 58 and Part V of this Act)" shall cease to have effect.

(28) In section 94(1) (interpretation)—
(a) the definition of "children's panel" and of "children's hearing" shall cease to have effect;
(b) the definition of "compulsory measures of care" shall cease to have effect;
(c) in the definition of "establishment", after the word "Act," insert "or of Part II of the Children (Scotland) Act 1995,";
(d) the definition of "guardian" shall cease to have effect;
(e) for the definition of "parent" substitute—
   " "parent" means either parent or both parents, except that where the child was born out of wedlock and the parents have not subsequently married each other it means the natural mother but not the natural father;";
(f) the definition of "place of safety" shall cease to have effect;
(g) in the definition of "prescribed"—
   (i) in paragraph (a), for the words "sections 3 and 36" substitute "section 3"; and
   (ii) paragraph (b) shall cease to have effect;
(h) in the definition of "residential establishment", after the word "Act" insert "or of Part II of the Children (Scotland) Act 1995";
(i) the definition of "school age" shall cease to have effect;
(j) in the definition of "supervision requirement", for the words "section 44(1) of this Act" substitute "section 70(1) of the Children (Scotland) Act 1995"; and
(k) for the definition of "training school" substitute—
   " "training school" has the meaning assigned to it by section 180(1) of the Children and Young Persons Act (Northern Ireland) 1968;".

(29) In section 97 (provisions of the Act which extend to England and Wales)—
(a) in subsection (1), the words "section 44(1) (except head (b)) and (1A)", "section 58" and "Part V" shall cease to have effect; and
(b) subsections (2) and (3) shall cease to have effect.

(30) In Schedule 2 (general adaptations of Part IV of Children and Young Persons (Scotland) Act 1937), for paragraph 1 substitute—
   "1. Any reference to a child or to a young person shall be construed as a reference to a child as defined in section 93(2)(b) of the Children (Scotland) Act 1995.".

Children and Young Persons Act 1969 (c. 54)

16. In Schedule 5 to the Children and Young Persons Act 1969, paragraphs 57 and 65(1) (which relate to the provision of accommodation for children outside Scotland) shall cease to have effect.

Chronically Sick and Disabled Persons Act 1970 (c. 44)

17.—(1) The Chronically Sick and Disabled Persons Act 1970 shall be amended in accordance with this paragraph.

(2) In section 18(2) (information as to accommodation of younger with older persons), for the words "having functions under the Social Work (Scotland) Act 1968" substitute ", in respect of their functions both under the Social Work (Scotland) Act 1968 and under the Children (Scotland) Act 1995,".

(3) In section 29(2) (modifications of provisions of the Act in their application to Scotland)—
(a) in paragraph (a), at the end add "except that in the case of persons under eighteen years of age such references shall instead be construed as references to duties to disabled children (within the meaning of Chapter I of Part II of the Children (Scotland) Act 1995)"; and
(b) for paragraph (b) substitute—
   "(b) any references to services provided under arrangements made by a local authority under the said section 29 shall be construed as references to services for—
      (i) such chronically sick or disabled, or such mentally disordered, persons provided by virtue of the said section 12; or
      (ii) such disabled children provided under section 23(1) of the said Act of 1995, by a local authority;".

Children (Scotland) Act 1995

Sheriff Courts (Scotland) Act 1971 (c. 58)

18.—(1) The Sheriff Courts (Scotland) Act 1971 shall be amended in accordance with this paragraph.

(2) In section 32(1) (power of Court of Session to regulate civil procedure in the sheriff court), after paragraph (i) insert—

"(j) permitting a person who is not an advocate or solicitor and is not represented by an advocate or solicitor to transmit, whether orally or in writing, the views of a child to the sheriff for the purposes of any enactment which makes provision (however expressed) for the sheriff to have regard to those views;".

(3) In section 37(2A) (remit to Court of Session), for the words "the custody" substitute "parental responsibilities or parental rights (within the meaning of sections 1(3) and 2(4) respectively of the Children (Scotland) Act 1995) in relation to a child or the".

Employment of Children Act 1973 (c. 24)

19. In section 2(2A) of the Employment of Children Act 1973 (supervision by education authorities), for paragraph (b) substitute—

"(b) in Scotland, if he has parental responsibilities (within the meaning of section 1(3) of the Children (Scotland) Act 1995) in relation to the child or care of him.".

Domicile and Matrimonial Proceedings Act 1973 (c. 45)

20.—(1) The Domicile and Matrimonial Proceedings Act 1973 shall be amended in accordance with this paragraph.

(2) In section 10 (ancillary and collateral orders)—
(a) in subsection (1)—

(i) for the words from the beginning to "in connection with" substitute "Where after the commencement of this Act an application is competently made to the Court of Session or to a sheriff court for the making, or the variation or recall, of an order which is ancillary or collateral to";

(ii) the words "as respects the person or property in question" shall cease to have effect; and

(b) after subsection (1) insert—

"(1A) For the purposes of subsection (1) above, references to an application for the making, or the variation or recall, of an order are references to the making, or the variation or recall, of an order relating to children, aliment, financial provision on divorce, judicial separation, nullity of marriage or expenses "

(3) In paragraph 11 of Schedule 3 (sisting of consistorial action)—
(a) in sub-paragraph (1), in the definition of "the relevant order", for the words from "made" to the end substitute "relating to aliment or children"; and

(b) in sub-paragraph (3), for the words "custody of a child, and the education of a child" substitute "arrangements to be made as to with whom a child is to live, contact with a child, and any other matter relating to parental responsibilities within the meaning of section 1(3) of the Children (Scotland) Act 1995 or parental rights within the meaning of section 2(4) of that Act".

Land Compensation (Scotland) Act 1973 (c. 56)

21.—(1) The Land Compensation (Scotland) Act 1973 shall be amended in accordance with this paragraph.

(2) In section 35(3) (disturbance payments where modification of dwelling required for disabled person), in paragraph (a), after "1968" insert "or section 23 of the Children (Scotland) Act 1995".

(3) In section 80(1) (interpretation), in the definition of "disabled person"—
(a) after "means" insert "—
(a)"; and
(b) after "1972" insert "; and

(b) a child in need within the meaning of section 93(4)(a)(iii) of the Children (Scotland) Act 1995".

Local Government (Scotland) Act 1973 (c. 65)

22.—(1) The Local Government (Scotland) Act 1973 shall be amended in accordance with this paragraph.

(2) In section 56(9) (enactments exempted from repeal by virtue of that section), for paragraph (d) substitute—

"(d) paragraphs 3 and 8 of Schedule 1 to the Children (Scotland) Act 1995 (Children's Panel Advisory Committees and joint advisory committees);".

(3) In Schedule 25, paragraph 41 shall cease to have effect.
(4) In Schedule 27, paragraphs 185 and 187 shall cease to have effect.

Rehabilitation of Offenders Act 1974 (c. 53)

23.—(1) The Rehabilitation of Offenders Act 1974 shall be amended in accordance with this paragraph.
(2) In section 3 (special provision with respect to certain disposals by children's hearings)—
(a) for the words "Social Work (Scotland) Act 1968 is that mentioned in section 32(2)(g)" substitute "Children (Scotland) Act 1995 is that mentioned in section 52(2)(i)"; and
(b) for the words "to the satisfaction of the sheriff under section 42 of that Act, the acceptance or establishment" substitute "(or deemed established) to the satisfaction of the sheriff under section 68 or 85 of that Act, the acceptance, establishment (or deemed establishment)".
(3) In section 5 (rehabilitation periods for particular sentences)—
(a) in subsection (3)(b), for the words "43(2) of the Social Work (Scotland) Act 1968" substitute "69(1)(b) and (12) of the Children (Scotland) Act 1995";
(b) in subsection (5)(f), for the words "Social Work (Scotland) Act 1968" substitute "Children (Scotland) Act 1995";
(c) in subsection (10), for the words "Social Work (Scotland) Act 1968" substitute "Children (Scotland) Act 1995"; and
(d) subsection (10A) shall cease to have effect.
(4) In section 7(2) (limitations on rehabilitation)—
(a) for paragraph (c) substitute—
    "(c) in any proceedings relating to parental responsibilities or parental rights (within the meaning of section 1(3) and section 2(4) respectively of the Children (Scotland) Act 1995), guardianship, adoption or the provision by any person of accommodation, care or schooling for children under the age of 18 years;
    (cc) in any proceedings under Part II of the Children (Scotland) Act 1995;";
(b) paragraph (e) shall cease to have effect; and
(c) the words from "In the application" to the end shall cease to have effect.

Criminal Procedure (Scotland) Act 1975 (c. 21)

*   *   *   *   *

Local Government (Scotland) Act 1975 (c. 30)

25. In section 23(2) of the Local Government (Scotland) Act 1975 (bodies subject to investigation by Commissioner for Local Administration in Scotland), for paragraph (d) substitute—
    "(d) any Children's Panel Advisory Committee formed under paragraph 3, or joint advisory committee formed under paragraph 8, of Schedule 1 to the Children (Scotland) Act 1995;".

Children Act 1975 (c. 72)

26.—(1) The Children Act 1975 shall be amended in accordance with this paragraph.
(2) Sections 47 to 49 shall cease to have effect.
(3) In section 50 (payments towards maintenance for children), for the words from "custody" to "authority" substitute "a child under the age of sixteen is residing with and being cared for (other than as a foster child) by a person other than a parent of the child, a council constituted under section 2 of the Local Government (Scotland) Act 1994".
(4) In section 51 (restriction on removal of child where applicant has provided home for three years)—
(a) in subsection (1), for the words "custody of" substitute "a residence order in relation to";
(b) for subsection (2) substitute—
    "(2) In any case where subsection (1) applies, and the child—
    (a) was being looked after by a council constituted under section 2 of the Local Government etc. (Scotland) Act 1994 before he began to have his home with the applicant, and
    (b) continues to be looked after by such a council,
    the council by whom the child is being looked after shall not remove him from the applicant's care and possession except—
        (i) with the applicant's consent;
        (ii) with the leave of the court; or

(iii) in accordance with an order made, or authority or warrant granted, under Chapter 2 or 3 of Part II of the Children (Scotland) Act 1995."; and

(c) at the end add—

"(5) In this section "looked after" and "residence order" have the meanings given respectively by section 17(6) and section 11(2)(c) of the Children (Scotland) Act 1995; and "residence order" shall have the same meaning in sections 52 and 53 of this Act.".

(5) In section 52 (return of child taken away in breach of section 51), for the words "custody of" substitute "a residence order in relation to".

(6) Section 53 (custody order on application for adoption in Scotland) shall cease to have effect.

(7) In section 55 (interpretation and extent), for the words "sections 47 to 54", in both places where they occur, substitute "sections 50 to 53".

(8) Sections 73 to 84, 89, 99, 100, 102 and 103 shall cease to have effect.

(9) Section 107 (interpretation), except in so far as subsection (1) defines "adoption society", "child" and "voluntary organisation", shall cease to have effect.

(10) In Schedule 3 (minor and consequential amendments), paragraphs 52 to 57 shall cease to have effect.

Sexual Offences (Scotland) Act 1976 (c. 67)

*   *   *   *   *

Education (Scotland) Act 1980 (c. 44)

28.—(1) The Education (Scotland) Act 1980 shall be amended in accordance with this paragraph.

(2) In section 36(3) (referral to reporter of case of irregular school attendance), for the words from "may" to the end substitute ", where no requirement arises under section 53(1) of the Children (Scotland) Act 1995 to give information about the child to the Principal Reporter, may under this subsection provide the Principal Reporter with such information.".

(3) In section 44—

(a) subsection (1) (referral by court to Principal Reporter of case involving offence against section 35) shall cease to have effect; and

(b) in subsection (2) (powers of court where no referral to Principal Reporter), for the words "subsection (1) above, make a direction" substitute "section 54(1) of the Children (Scotland) Act 1995, refer the matter to the Principal Reporter"

(4) In section 65B(6) (sending of report in relation to recorded child)—

(a) paragraph (a) shall cease to have effect; and

(b) at the end add—

"and the local authority as education authority shall also ensure that the local authority for the purposes of Part II of the Children (Scotland) Act 1995 receive such a copy.".

(5) In section 135(1) (interpretation)—

(a) in the definition of "parent", for the words "the actual custody of" substitute "parental responsibilities (within the meaning of section 1(3) of the Children (Scotland) Act 1995) in relation to, or has care of";

(b) the definition of "reporter of the appropriate local authority" shall cease to have effect;

(c) for the definition of "residential establishment" substitute—

" "residential establishment" has the meaning given by paragraph (a) of the definition of that expression in section 93(1) of the Children (Scotland) Act 1995;"; and

(d) for the definition of "supervision requirement" substitute—

" "supervision requirement" has the meaning given by section 70(1) of the said Act of 1995;".

Criminal Justice (Scotland) Act 1980 (c. 62)

*   *   *   *   *

Matrimonial Homes (Family Protection) (Scotland) Act 1981 (c. 59)

30. In section 22 of the Matrimonial Homes (Family Protection) (Scotland) Act 1981 (interpretation), in the definition of "child", for the word "accepted" substitute "treated".

Civil Jurisdiction and Judgments Act 1982 (c. 27)

31. In Schedule 9 to the Civil Jurisdiction and Judgments Act 1982 (excluded proceedings), after paragraph 2 insert—

"2A. Proceedings relating to parental responsibilities within the meaning of section 1(3) of the Children (Scotland) Act 1995 or parental rights within the meaning of section 2(4) of that Act.".

Health and Social Services and Social Security Adjudications Act 1983 (c. 41)

32. In Schedule 2 to the Health and Social Services and Social Security Adjudications Act 1983, paragraphs 4 to 6 and 8 (which amend provisions of the Social Work (Scotland) Act 1968 repealed by this Act) shall cease to have effect.

Mental Health (Scotland) Act 1984 (c. 36)

33.—(1) The Mental Health (Scotland) Act 1984 shall be amended in accordance with this paragraph.

(2) In section 10(1) (application of provisions relating to certain patients suffering from mental disorder)—
  (a) in paragraph (a), sub-paragraph (i), and the word "or" immediately following that sub-paragraph, shall cease to have effect; and
  (b) after paragraph (a) insert—
    "(aa) a child or young person in relation to whom parental rights and responsibilities have been transferred to a local authority by virtue of section 86(1) of the Children (Scotland) Act 1995;".

(3) In section 54 (local authority to be deemed nearest relative of certain children and young persons), for paragraph (a) substitute—
    "(a) the parental rights and responsibilities in relation to a patient who is a child or young person have been transferred to a local authority by virtue of section 86(1) of the Children (Scotland) Act 1995;".

(4) In section 55 (nearest relative of child under guardianship etc.)—
  (a) for subsection (1) substitute—
    "(1) Where—
    (a) a guardian has been appointed for a child who has not attained the age of eighteen years; or
    (b) there is in force a residence order, or a custody order, granted by a court in the United Kingdom, or an analogous order granted by a court outwith the United Kingdom (being an order which is entitled to recognition in Scotland), identifying a person as the person with whom a child under the age of sixteen years is to live, that guardian or person shall, to the exclusion of any other person, be deemed to be the child's nearest relative.";
  (b) for subsection (3) substitute—
    "(3) In this section "guardian" does not include a guardian under this Part of this Act or, in relation to a child, a guardian whose appointment takes effect under section 7, or on an order under section 11(1), of the Children (Scotland) Act 1995 where there is a parent who has parental responsibilities and parental rights in relation to the child."; and
  (c) subsection (4) shall cease to have effect.

Child Abduction Act 1984 (c. 37)

34. In section 6 of the Child Abduction Act 1984 (offence in Scotland of person connected with a child taking or sending that child out of United Kingdom)—
  (a) in subsection (1)(a)(i), after the word "person" insert "or naming any person as the person with whom the child is to live";
  (b) in subsection (2)(b), after the words "to him" insert "or naming him as the person with whom the child is to live"; and
  (c) in subsection (3)(a)(i)(b), for the word "(whether" substitute "or who is named as the person with whom the child is to live (whether the award is made, or the person so named is named".

Foster Children (Scotland) Act 1984 (c. 56)

35.—(1) The Foster Children (Scotland) Act 1984 shall be amended in accordance with this paragraph.

(2) In section 2 (exceptions to definition of "foster child')—
  (a) in subsection (1), for the words "in the care of a local authority or a voluntary organisation" substitute "being looked after by a local authority";

(b) in subsection (3), the words "within the meaning of the Social Work (Scotland) Act 1968" shall cease to have effect;
(c) in subsection (5), the words "; or (b) while he is a protected child within the meaning of section 32 of the said Act of 1978" shall cease to have effect; and
(d) after subsection (5) add—
"(6) The reference in subsection (1) above to a child being looked after by a local authority shall be construed as if it were a reference to which section 17(6) of the Children (Scotland) Act 1995 applies.".
(3) In section 3(4) (saving for Social Work (Scotland) Act 1968), for the words "the Social Work (Scotland) Act 1968" substitute "Part II of the Children (Scotland) Act 1995".
(4) In section 7(1) (persons disqualified from keeping foster children)—
(a) in paragraph (b), after the word "1968" insert "or under section 70 of the Children (Scotland) Act 1995"; and
(b) after paragraph (d) insert—
"(dd) his parental rights and parental responsibilities (within the meaning of the Children (Scotland) Act 1995) have been transferred, by an order under section 86(1) of that Act, to a local authority;".
(5) In section 12 (removal of foster children on complaint of local authority), for subsection (5) substitute—
"(5) For the purposes of section 25 of the Children (Scotland) Act 1995 (and for the reason mentioned in subsection (1)(c) of that section) a child removed under this section shall be regarded as requiring accommodation.".
(6) In section 13 (which makes provision as to the effect of a refusal to allow a visit to a foster child or to allow premises to be inspected), for the words from "sections" to the end substitute "section 55 of the Children (Scotland) Act 1995 (child assessment orders) as giving the local authority reasonable cause for the suspicion mentioned in subsection (1)(a) of that section).
(7) In section 21(1) (interpretation)—
(a) in the definition of "residential establishment‘, after the word "1968" insert "or of Part II of the Children (Scotland) Act 1995"; and
(b) for the definition of "supervision requirement‘, substitute—
" "supervision requirement" has the meaning given by section 70(1) of the Children (Scotland) Act 1995;".

Family Law (Scotland) Act 1985 (c. 37)

36. In section 2 of the Family Law (Scotland) Act 1985 (actions for aliment)—
(a) in subsection (2), for paragraph (c) substitute—
"(c) concerning parental responsibilities or parental rights (within the meaning of sections 1(3) and 2(4) respectively of the Children (Scotland) Act 1995) or guardianship in relation to children;"; and
(b) in subsection (4)(c), for sub–paragraph (iii) substitute—
"(iii) a person with whom the child lives or who is seeking a residence order (within the meaning of section 11(2)(c) of the Children (Scotland) Act 1995) in respect of the child.".

Child Abduction and Custody Act 1985 (c. 60)

37.—(1) The Child Abduction and Custody Act 1985 shall be amended in accordance with this paragraph.
(2) In section 9 (suspension of court's powers in cases of wrongful removal), for paragraph (d) substitute—
"(d) making, varying or discharging an order under section 86 of the Children (Scotland) Act 1995;".
(3) In section 20 (further provision as regards suspension of court's powers)—
(a) for paragraph (d) substitute—
"(d) in the case of proceedings for, or for the variation or discharge of, a parental responsibilities order under section 86 of the Children (Scotland) Act 1995, make, vary or discharge any such order;"; and
(b) in subsection (5), for the words "within the meaning of Part III of the Social Work (Scotland) Act 1968" substitute "(as defined in section 93(1) of the Children (Scotland) Act 1995)".
(4) In section 25 (termination of existing custody orders etc.), subsection (6) shall cease to have effect.
(5) In section 27(4) (interpretation), after the word "Wales" insert "or Scotland".

(6) In Schedule 3 (custody orders)—
(a) in paragraph 5—
> (i) for the words "custody, care or control of a child or" substitute "residence, custody, care or control of a child or contact with, or";
> (ii) in sub paragraph (iii), for the words "tutory or curatory" substitute "guardianship";
> (iii) in sub-paragraph (iv), for the words "16(8), 16A(3) or 18(3) of the Social Work (Scotland) Act 1968" substitute "86 of the Children (Scotland) Act 1995"; and
> (iv) for sub-paragraph (v), substitute—
>> "(v) an order made, or warrant or authorisation granted, under or by virtue of Chapter 2 or 3 of Part II of the Children (Scotland) Act 1995 to remove the child to a place of safety or to secure accommodation, to keep him at such a place or in such accommodation, or to prevent his removal from a place where he is being accommodated (or an order varying or discharging any order, warrant or authorisation so made or granted);";

(b) for paragraph 6 substitute—
> "6. A supervision requirement made by a children's hearing under section 70 of the Children (Scotland) Act 1995 (whether or not continued under section 73 of that Act) or made by the sheriff under section 51(5)(c)(iii) of that Act and any order made by a court in England and Wales or in Northern Ireland if it is an order which, by virtue of section 33(1) of that Act, has effect as if it were such a supervision requirement."; and

(c) paragraph 7 shall cease to have effect.

Law Reform (Parent and Child) (Scotland) Act 1986 (c. 9)

38.—(1) The Law Reform (Parent and Child) (Scotland) Act 1986 shall be amend in accordance with this paragraph.
(2) In section 1 (legal equality of children), for subsection (3) substitute—
> "(3) Subsection (1) above is subject to subsection (4) below, to section 9(1) of this Act and to section 3(1)(b) of the Children (Scotland) Act 1995 (parental responsibilities and parental rights of natural father).".

(3) In section 6(2) (consent to taking of sample of blood), for the words from "guardian" to "custody or" substitute "any person having parental responsibilities (within the meaning of section 1(3) of the Children (Scotland) Act 1995) in relation to him or having".

Disabled Persons (Services, Consultation and Representation) Act 1986 (c. 33)

39.—(1) The Disabled Persons (Services, Consultation and Representation) Act 1986 shall be amended in accordance with this paragraph.
(2) In section 1(3) (regulations with respect to appointment of authorised representatives of disabled persons)—
(a) in paragraph (a), for the words from the beginning to "appoint" substitute—
> "may provide for—
>> (i) any person who has parental responsibilities in relation to a disabled person under the age of sixteen ("parental responsibilities" having the meaning given by section 1(3) of the Children (Scotland) Act 1995); or
>> (ii) any other person who is entitled to act as the disabled person's legal representative (as defined in section 15(5) of the Children (Scotland) Act 1995), to appoint"; and

(b) in paragraph (b), for the words "in the care of" substitute "looked after by".
(3) In section 2 (rights of certain authorised representatives of disabled persons)—
(a) in subsection (3)(a), for the words "the words "the parent or guardian of" shall be inserted after the words "if so requested by";" substitute "for the words "by the disabled person" there shall be substituted the words "by any person appointed by virtue of regulations made under section 1(3)(a)(i) or (ii) of this Act";"; and
(b) in subsection (5), after paragraph (bb) insert—
> "(bc) in Scotland, in accommodation provided by or on behalf of a local authority under Chapter 1 of Part II of the Children (Scotland) Act 1995, or".

(4) In section 13(8)(b) (limitation on requirement for assessment of needs)—
(a) for the words "his parent" substitute "any person having parental responsibilities in relation to him"; and
(b) after the word "request" insert "("parental responsibilities" having the meaning given in section 1(3) of the Children (Scotland) Act 1995)".

(5) In section 16 (interpretation)—

(a) in the definition of "disabled person", for paragraph (b) substitute—

"(b) in relation to Scotland, means—

(i) in the case of a person aged eighteen or over, one chronically sick or disabled or one suffering from mental disorder (being, in either case, a relevant person for the purposes of section 12 of the Social Work (Scotland) Act 1968); and

(ii) in any other case, a disabled child ("disabled child" being construed in accordance with Chapter 1 of Part II of the Children (Scotland) Act 1995);";

(b) in the definition of "guardian", paragraph (b) shall cease to have effect;

(c) in the definition of "the welfare enactments", in paragraph (b), for the words "and sections 7 and 8 of the 1984 Act", substitute ", sections 7 and 8 of the 1984 Act and Chapter 1 of Part II of the Children (Scotland) Act 1995"; and

(d) the existing provisions as so amended shall be subsection (1) of the section and at the end of the section there shall be added—

"(2A) In this Act as it applies in relation to Scotland, any reference to a child who is looked after by a local authority shall be construed in accordance with section 17(6) of the Children (Scotland) Act 1995.".

Legal Aid (Scotland) Act 1986 (c. 47)

40. In section 41 of the Legal Aid (Scotland) Act 1986 (interpretation)—

(a) in the definition of "legal aid", for the words "Part III of the Social Work (Scotland Act 1968" substitute "Chapter 2 or Chapter 3 of Part II of the Children (Scotland) Act 1995; and

(b) in the definition of "person", the existing words from "does" to the end shall be paragraph (a) and after that paragraph there shall be added—

"; and

(b) includes a person under the age of sixteen years.".

Family Law Act 1986 (c. 55)

41.—(1) The Family Law Act 1986 shall be amended in accordance with this paragraph.

(2) In section 1(1)(b) (meaning of "custody order")—

(a) for the words "custody, care or control of a child" substitute "residence, custody, care or control of a child, contact with or"; and

(b) in sub-paragraph (iv), for the words "for the custody of" substitute "giving parental responsibilities and parental rights in relation to".

(3) In section 13 (jurisdiction ancillary to matrimonial proceedings)—

(a) in subsection (2), for the words "under section 9(1) of the Matrimonial Proceedings (Children) Act 1958" substitute "in those proceedings"; and

(b) in subsection (4), for the words "under section 9(1) of the Matrimonial Proceedings (Children) Act 1958" substitute "in matrimonial proceedings where the court has refused to grant the principal remedy sought in the proceedings".

(4) In section 15 (duration, variation and recall of orders)—

(a) in subsection (1)(b), for the words "for the custody of" substitute "relating to the parental responsibilities or parental rights in relation to"; and

(b) in subsection (4), for the words from the beginning to "above" substitute "Where, by virtue of subsection (1) above, a child is to live with a different person".

(5) In section 17 (orders for delivery of child)—

(a) in subsection (3), for the words from "is the child" to "other party" substitute ", although not a child of both parties to the marriage, is a child of the family of those parties"; and

(b) at the end of the section add—

"(4) In subsection (3) above, "child of the family" means any child who has been treated by both parties as a child of their family, except a child who has been placed with those parties as foster parents by a local authority or a voluntary organisation.".

(6) For section 26 (recognition: special Scottish rule), substitute—

"Recognition: special Scottish rule

26. An order relating to parental responsibilities or parental rights in relation to a child which is made outside the United Kingdom shall be recognised in Scotland if the order was made in the country where the child was habitually resident.".

(7) In section 33(3) (power to order disclosure of child's whereabouts), for the words "for the custody of" substitute "relating to parental responsibilities or parental rights in relation to".

(8) In section 35(3) (power to restrict removal of child from jurisdiction), for the words "whose custody" substitute "whose care".

(9) In section 42 (interpretation)—
(a) in subsection (1), before the definition of "part of the United Kingdom" insert—
" "parental responsibilities" and "parental rights" have the meanings respectively given by sections 1(3) and 2(4) of the Children (Scotland) Act 1995;"; and
(b) in subsection (4)(b), for the words from "of one of the parties" to the end substitute "who has been treated by both parties as a child of their family, except a child who has been with those parties as foster parents by a local authority or a voluntary organisation;".

Housing (Scotland) Act 1987 (c. 26)

42. In section 61 of the Housing (Scotland) Act 1987 (exemption from secure tenant's right to purchase)—
(a) in subsection (4)(f)(iii) for the words "have left the care of" substitute "as children have been looked after by"; and
(b) after subsection (4) add—
"(4A) The reference in subsection (4)(f)(iii) above to children looked after by a local authority shall be construed in accordance with section 17(6) of the Children (Scotland) Act 1995.".

Criminal Justice (Scotland) Act 1987 (c. 41)

43. In section 49(4)(b) of the Criminal Justice (Scotland) Act 1987 (right to have someone informed when detained), for the words "actual custody" substitute "care".

Civil Evidence (Scotland) Act 1988 (c. 32)

44. In paragraph (a) of the definition of "civil proceedings" in section 9 of the Civil Evidence (Scotland) Act 1998 (interpretation)—
(a) the words "under section 42 of the Social Work (Scotland) Act 1968" shall cease to have effect;
(b) after the word "application" where it first occurs insert "under section 65(7) or (9) of the Children (Scotland) Act 1995";
(c) after the word "established," insert "or of an application for a review of such a finding under section 85 of that Act";
(d) after the word "application" where it occurs for the second time insert "or, as the case may be, the review"; and
(e) for the words "32(2)(g)" substitute "52(2)(i)".

Court of Session Act 1988 (c. 36)

45. In section 5 of the Court of Session Act 1988 (power to regulate procedure etc. by act of sederunt), after paragraph (e) insert—
"(ee) to permit a person who is not an advocate or solicitor and is not represented by an advocate or solicitor to transmit, whether orally or in writing, the views of a child to the Court for the purposes of any enactment which makes provision (however expressed) for the Court to have regard to those views;".

School Boards (Scotland) Act 1988 (c. 47)

46. In section 22(2) of the School Boards (Scotland) Act 1988 (interpretation), in the definition of "parent", for the word "custody" substitute "parental responsibilities (within the meaning of section 1(3) of the Children (Scotland) Act 1995) in relation to him or who has care".

Self-Governing Schools etc. (Scotland) Act 1989 (c. 39)

47. In section 80(1) of the Self-Governing Schools etc. (Scotland) Act 1989 (interpretation), in the definition of "parent", for the words "the actual custody" substitute "parental responsibilities (within the meaning of section 1(3) of the Children (Scotland) Act 1995) in relation to him or has care".

Children Act 1989 (c. 41)

48.—(1) The Children Act 1989 shall be amended in accordance with this paragraph.
(2) In section 31(7)(b)(iii) (restriction on applications for care and supervision orders), for the words "the Social Work (Scotland) Act 1968" substitute "Part II of the Children (Scotland) Act 1995".
(3) In section 51(7) (enactments which do not apply where a child is granted refuge), for paragraph (b) substitute—

Children (Scotland) Act 1995

"(b) sections 82 (recovery of certain fugitive children) and 83 (harbouring) of the Children (Scotland) Act 1995, so far as they apply in relation to anything done in England and Wales;".

(4) In section 79(e) (application of Part X to Scotland), for the words from "in whom" to "vested" substitute "having parental responsibilities (within the meaning of section 1(3) of the Children (Scotland) Act 1995) relating to the child".

(5) In Schedule 8 (privately fostered children), in paragraph 3(b), for the words "the Social Work (Scotland) Act 1968" substitute "Part II of the Children (Scotland) Act 1995".

Local Government and Housing Act 1989 (c. 42)

49.—(1) The Local Government and Housing Act 1989 shall be amended in accordance with this paragraph.

(2) In section 14(5) (restriction of effect of provisions of that section in relation to certain committees), for paragraph (d) substitute—

"(d) a Children's Panel Advisory Committee formed under paragraph 3, or a joint advisory committee formed under paragraph 8, of Schedule 1 to the Children (Scotland) Act 1995;".

Access to Health Records Act 1990 (c. 23)

50.—(1) The Access to Health Records Act 1990 shall be amended in accordance with this paragraph.

(2) In section 3(1) (right of access to health records), for paragraphs (c) and (d) substitute—

"(cc) where the patient is a child, a person having parental responsibility for him;".

(3) In section 4 (cases where right of access may be wholly excluded)—

(a) in subsection (1), for paragraphs (a) and (b) substitute "the patient is a child"; and

(b) in subsection (2), for the words "(1)(c) or (d)" substitute "(1)(cc)".

(4) In section 5(3) (access to records not to be given where record compiled on basis that access would not be available to particular applicant), for the words "(1)(c), (d), (e) or (f)" substitute "(1)(cc), (e) or (f)".

(5) In section 11 (interpretation), for the definition of "parental responsibility" substitute—

" "parental responsibility", in the application of this Act—

(a) to England and Wales, has the same meaning as in the Children Act 1989; and

(b) to Scotland, shall be construed as a reference to "parental responsibilities" within the meaning given by section 1(3) of the Children (Scotland) Act 1995.".

Horses (Protective Headgear for Young Riders) Act 1990 (c. 25)

51. In section 1(2)(a)(ii) (application), of the Horses (Protective Headgear for Young Riders) Act 1990, for the word "custody" substitute "parental responsibilities (within the meaning given by section 1(3) of the Children (Scotland) Act 1995) in relation to, or has".

Child Support Act 1991 (c. 48)

52.—(1) The Child Support Act 1991 shall be amended in accordance with this paragraph.

(2) In section 3(4)(d) (interpretation), for the words from "having" to the end substitute "with whom a child is to live by virtue of a residence order under section 11 of the Children (Scotland) Act 1995.".

(3) In section 5(1) (supplemental provisions as respects child support maintenance), the words "(or, in Scotland, parental rights over)", in both places where they occur, shall cease to have effect.

(4) In section 54 (interpretation)—

(a) for the definition of "parental responsibility" substitute—

" "parental responsibility", in the application of this Act—

(a) to England and Wales, has the same meaning as in the Children Act 1989; and

(b) to Scotland, shall be construed as a reference to "parental responsibilities" within the meaning given by section 1(3) of the Children (Scotland) Act 1995;"; and

(b) the definition of "parental rights" shall cease to have effect.

Age of Legal Capacity (Scotland) Act 1991 (c. 50)

53.—(1) The Age of Legal Capacity (Scotland) Act 1991 shall be amended in accordance with this paragraph.

(2) In section 1(3) (age of legal capacity)—

(a) in sub-paragraph (i) of paragraph (f), for the words "who has no guardian or whose guardian" substitute "in relation to whom there is no person entitled to act as his legal representative (within the meaning of Part I of the Children (Scotland) Act 1995), or where there is such a person"; and

(b) in paragraph (g), for sub-paragraphs (i) and (ii) substitute "exercising parental responsibilities and parental rights (within the meaning of sections 1(3) and 2(4) respectively of the Children (Scotland) Act 1995) in relation to any child of his.".

(3) In section 2 (exceptions to the general rule), after subsection (4) insert—

"(4A) A person under the age of sixteen years shall have legal capacity to instruct a solicitor, in connection with any civil matter, where that person has a general understanding of what it means to do so; and without prejudice to the generality of this subsection a person twelve years of age or more shall be presumed to be of sufficient age and maturity to have such understanding.

(4B) A person who by virtue of subsection (4A) above has legal capacity to instruct a solicitor shall also have legal capacity to sue, or to defend, in any civil proceedings.

(4C) Subsections (4A) and (4B) above are without prejudice to any question of legal capacity arising in connection with any criminal matter.".

(4) In section 5(1) (construction of references to "tutor")—

(a) the words "or tutory" shall cease to have effect; and

(b) for the words from "the guardian", where they first appear, to the end substitute "a person entitled to act as a child's legal representative (within the meaning of Part I of the Children (Scotland) Act 1995), and any reference to the tutory of such a child shall be construed as a reference to the entitlement to act as a child's legal representative enjoyed by a person by, under or by virtue of the said Part I.".

(5) In section 5(2) (restriction on appointment of guardian to person under sixteen), for the words from "section 3" to the end substitute "section 7 of the Children (Scotland) Act 1995.".

Armed Forces Act 1991 (c. 62)

54.—(1) The Armed Forces Act 1991 shall be amended in accordance with this paragraph.

(2) In paragraph (f) of section 17(4) (persons to whom notice of an application for an assessment order must be given)—

(a) after the word "order" insert "—

(i)"; and

(b) at the end insert "; or

(ii) under section 88 of the Children (Scotland) Act 1995".

(3) In paragraph (f) of section 18(7) (persons who may apply for variation etc. of assessment order)—

(a) after the word "order" insert "—

(i) "; and

(b) at the end insert "; or

(ii) under section 88 of the Children (Scotland) Act 1995".

(4) In section 21(4) (which makes provision in relation to a child returned to the United Kingdom under a protection order under that Act) for the words "Social Work (Scotland) Act 1968" substitute "Children (Scotland) Act 1995".

(5) In section 23(1) (interpretation)—

(a) in the definition of "contact order"—

(i) after the word "meaning" insert "—

(a) except in relation to an order made in Scotland,"; and

(ii) at the end, add "; and

(b) in relation to an order there made, given by section 11(2)(d) of the Children (Scotland) Act 1995."; and

(b) in the definition of "parental responsibility"—

(i) after the word "responsibility" " insert "—

(a) except in relation to Scotland,"; and

(ii) at the end add "; and

(b) in relation to Scotland, shall be construed as a reference to "parental responsibilities" within the meaning given by section 1(3) of the Children (Scotland) Act 1995;".

Tribunals and Inquiries Act 1992 (c. 53)

55. In paragraph 61 in column 2 of Schedule 1 to the Tribunals and Inquiries Act 1992 (which specifies certain tribunals in relation to social work in Scotland)—

(a) in sub-paragraph (a), for the words "Social Work (Scotland) Act 1968 (c. 49)" substitute "Children (Scotland) Act 1995 (c. 36)"; and

(b) in sub-paragraph (b), for the words "that Act" substitute "the Social Work (Scotland) Act 1968 (c. 49)".

56.—(1) The Prisoners and Criminal Proceedings (Scotland) Act 1993 shall be amended in accordance with this paragraph.

(2) In paragraph 8 of Schedule 3 (which provides for the definition of certain expressions in relation to the admission of documentary evidence in criminal proceedings), in the definition of "criminal proceedings"—
  (a) the words "under section 42 of the Social Work (Scotland) Act 1968" shall cease to have effect;
  (b) after the word "application" where it appears for the first time insert "under section 65(7)for (9) of the Children (Scotland) Act 1995";
  (c) after the word "established" insert "or for a review of such a finding under section 85 of that Act"; and
  (d) after the word "application", where it appears for the second time, insert "or, as the case may be, the review".

(3) In paragraph 1 of Schedule 6 (which provides for the definition of certain expressions in relation to transitional provisions), in the definition of "existing child detainee", for the words "section 30 of the Social Work (Scotland) Act 1968" substitute "section 93(2)(b) of the Children (Scotland) Act 1995".

57.—(1) The Local Government etc. (Scotland) Act 1994 shall be amended in accordance with this paragraph.

(2) In section 128 (establishment of Scottish Children's Reporter Administration)—
  (a) in subsection (3), for the words from "the 1968 Act" to the end substitute "the Children (Scotland) Act 1995 and any other enactment conferring functions upon him"; and
  (b) in subsection (8), for the words from "the 1968 Act" to the end substitute "the Children (Scotland) Act 1995 and any other enactment conferring functions upon him".

(3) In section 130 (annual reports by Principal Reporter) in sub-paragraph (i) of paragraph (a) of subsection (1), for the words "the 1968 Act and the Criminal Procedure (Scotland) Act 1975" substitute "the Children (Scotland) Act 1995 and any other enactment (except this Act) conferring functions upon him".

(4) In section 132 (duty of Administration to provide accommodation for children's hearings), for the words "section 34 of the 1968 Act" substitute "section 39 of the Children (Scotland) Act 1995".

58. In Article 70(7) of the Children (Northern Ireland) Order 1995 (enactments not to apply where child given refuge), in sub-paragraph (c), for the words "section 71 of the Social Work (Scotland) Act 1968" substitute "section 83 of the Children (Scotland) Act 1995".

59. In section 2 of the Civil Evidence (Family Mediation) (Scotland) Act 1995 (which provides for exceptions to the general inadmissibility of evidence concerning family mediation), in paragraph (d)(ii)—
  (a) for the words "Part III of the Social Work (Scotland) Act 1968" substitute "Chapter 2 or 3 of Part II of the Children (Scotland) Act 1995"; and
  (b) after the word "hearing" insert—
    ", before a sheriff or before a justice of the peace;
        (iia) on any appeal arising from such proceedings as are mentioned in sub-paragraph (ii) above".

60. In section 20 of the Criminal Justice (Scotland) Act 1995 (construction of sections relating to the admissibility of certain evidence)—
  (a) in subsection (3), in the definition of "criminal proceedings"—
        (i) for the words from "under" to "application", where it appears for the first time, substitute "of an application made under Chapter 3 of Part II of the Children (Scotland) Act 1995"; and
        (ii) after the word "child" insert "or for a review of such a finding"; and

(b) in subsection (5), after the words "1968" insert "or by virtue of Chapter 3 of Part II of the Children (Scotland) Act 1995".

Section 105(5)   SCHEDULE 5

REPEALS

Chapter	Short title	Extent of repeal
8 & 9 Vict. c. 19.	Lands Clauses Consolidation (Scotland) Act 1845.	In section 7, the words "persons under legal disability by reason of nonage" in each place where they occur. In section 67, the words "persons under legal disability by reason of nonage". In section 69, the words "persons under legal disability by reason of nonage".
12 & 13 Vict. c. 51.	Judicial Factors Act 1849.	In section 1, the words from "the word "Guardian" " to "years;". Section 25(2) In section 27, the words "guardians and". In section 31, the word "guardian,". In section 32, the word "guardian,". In section 33, the words "guardians or". In section 34, in both places where it occurs, the word "guardian,". In section 36, the word "guardianships,". In section 37, the word "guardian," In section 40, the word "guardians," in both places where it occurs.
27 & 28 Vict. c. 114.	Improvement of Land Act 1864.	In section 18, the words from "nor shall they" to the end. In section 21, the words from "or if the landowner" to "minors"; and the words "or circumstance" in both places where they occur.
43 & 44 Vict. c. 4.	Judicial Factors (Scotland) Act 1880.	In section 3, in the definition of "judicial factor", the words from "and" to "required".
7 Edw. 7 c. 51.	Sheriff Courts (Scotland) Act 1907.	Section 5(2C). Section 38C.
11 & 12 Geo. 5 c. 58.	Trusts (Scotland) Act 1921.	In section 2, in the definition of "trustee", the words from "guardian" to "years)".
1 Edw. 8 & 1 Geo 6 c. 37.	Children and Young Persons (Scotland) Act 1937.	In section 27, the first paragraph.
1 & 2 Geo. 6 c. 73.	Nursing Homes Registration (Scotland) Act 1938.	In section 4(1)(b)(iii), the words "custody or".
14 & 15 Geo. 6 c. 65.	Reserve and Auxiliary Forces (Protection of Civil Interests) Act 1951.	In section 8(1)(d), the words from "or any order" to the end.
6 & 7 Eliz. 2 c. 40.	Matrimonial Proceedings (Children) Act 1958.	Sections 8 to 10. Section 12.
1965 c. 49.	Registration of Births, Deaths and Marriages (Scotland) Act 1965.	In section 43, in subsection (3) the words from "In this" to the end; and subsection (10).
1968 c. 49.	Social Work (Scotland) Act 1968.	In section 5(1B), before paragraph (o), the word "and". In section 5B(5), the words from "and" at the end of the definition of child to the end of the subsection. Section 6(1)(b)(ii). Sections 15 to 26. Part III, except section 31(1) and (3). Part V. Section 88.

Chapter	Short title	Extent of repeal
		In section 90(1), the words "(other than orders under sections 52 and 58 and part V of this Act)".
		In section 94(1), the definition of "children's panel" and of "children's hearing"; the definitions of "compulsory measures of care", "guardian" and "place of safety"; in the definition of "prescribed", paragraph (b); and the definition of "school age".
		In section 97, in subsection (1), the words "section 44(1) (except head (b)) and (1A)", "section 58" and "Part V"; and subsections (2) and (3).
1969 c. 54.	Children and Young Persons Act 1969.	In Schedule 5, paragraphs 57 and 65(1).
1972 c. 18.	Maintenance Orders (Reciprocal Enforcement) Act 1972.	Section 4(3).
1972 c. 24.	Social Work (Scotland) Act 1972.	The whole Act.
1973 c. 29.	Guardianship Act 1973.	The whole Act.
1973 c. 65.	Local Government (Scotland) Act 1973.	In Schedule 25, paragraph 41. In Schedule 27, paragraphs 185 and 187.
1974 c. 53.	Rehabilitation of Offenders Act 1974.	Section 5(10A). In section 7(2), paragraph (e); and the words from "in the application" to the end.
1975 c. 21.	Criminal Procedure (Scotland) Act 1975.	Section 14. In section 168(c), the word "female". In section 177, the words "provided by a local authority under Part IV of the Social Work (Scotland) Act 1968". In section 296, in subsection (3), the words from "and the child" to the end; and subsection (4). Section 323. In section 364(c), the word "female". In section 378, the words "provided by a local authority under Part IV of the Social Work (Scotland) Act 1968". In section 413, in subsection (3), the definitions of "care" and of "the 1968 Act"; in subsection (4), the words "within the meaning of the 1968 Act"; in subsection (5), the words "(within the meaning of the 1968 Act)"; and in subsection (6A), the words "within the meaning of the 1968 Act". In Schedule 9, paragraphs 43 and 44.
1975 c. 72.	Children Act 1975.	Sections 47 to 49. Section 53. Sections 73 to 84. Sections 99 and 100. Section 102. Section 103. Section 105. Section 107, except the definitions, in subsection (1) of "adoption society", "child" and "voluntary organisation". In Schedule 3, paragraphs 52 to 57.

Chapter	Short title	Extent of repeal
1978 c. 28.	Adoption (Scotland) Act 1978.	In section 1(2), paragraph (a). In section 2, paragraph (d). In section 3(3)(a), the words "including in particular its ability to make provision for children who are free for adoption". Section 8. In section 12, in subsection (3)(b), the words "or by"; and in subsection (4) the word "—(a)" and paragraph (b). In section 14(1), the words from "Subject" to "certain cases)". In section 15, in subsection (1), the words from "Subject" to "certain cases)"; and in subsection (3), the word "natural" wherever it occurs. In section 16, subsection (5). Section 26. In section 28(5), the words "or of a voluntary organisation" and "or the organisation". Sections 32 to 37. In section 51, subsections 6(a) and (7) to (11). In section 60(3), the words "or 51(9)". In section 65(1), in the definition of "guardian", paragraph (b); and in the definition of "local authority", the words ", 35(1)". In Schedule 3, paragraphs 13, 14 and 15.
1980 c. 44.	Education (Scotland) Act 1980.	Section 44(1). In section 65B(6), paragraph (a). In section 135(1), the definition of "reporter of the appropriate local authority".
1980 c. 62.	Criminal Justice (Scotland) Act 1980.	In Schedule 7, paragraph 21.
1983 c. 33.	Solvent Abuse (Scotland) Act 1983.	The whole Act.
1983 c. 41.	Health and Social Services and Social Security Adjudications Act 1983.	Section 7. Section 8(1) and (4). In Schedule 2, paragraphs 4 to 6 and 8.
1984 c. 15.	Law Reform (Husband and Wife) (Scotland) Act 1984.	Section 3(2).
1984 c. 36.	Mental Health (Scotland) Act 1984.	In section 10(1)(a), sub-paragraph (i); and the word "or" immediately following that sub-paragraph. Section 55(4).
1984 c. 56.	Foster Children (Scotland) Act 1984.	In section 2, in subsection (3), the words "within the meaning of the Social Work (Scotland) Act 1968"; and in subsection (5), the words "; or (b) while he is a protected child within the meaning of section 32 of the said Act of 1978.".
1985 c. 37.	Family Law (Scotland) Act 1985.	In section 21, the words from "or an order" to "child".
1985 c. 60.	Child Abduction and Custody Act 1985.	In section 25, subsection (6). In Schedule 3, paragraph 7.
1986 c. 9.	Law Reform (Parent and Child) (Scotland) Act 1986.	Sections 2 to 4. In section 8, the definitions of "child" and "parental rights". In Schedule 1, paragraph 3.

Chapter	Short title	Extent of repeal
1986 c. 33.	Disabled Persons (Services, Consultation and Representation) Act 1986.	In section 16, in the definition of "guardian", paragraph (b).
1986 c. 55.	Family Law Act 1986.	In section 15(4), the words from "under section" to "1973". In section 17, in subsection (1), the words "Subject to subsection (2) below"; and subsection (2). In section 35(4)(c), the words "custody or".
1988 c. 32.	Civil Evidence (Scotland) Act 1988.	In section 9, in the definition of "civil proceedings", in paragraph (a), the words "under section 42 of the Social Work (Scotland) Act 1968".
1988 c. 36.	Court of Session Act 1988.	Section 20.
1989 c. 41.	Children Act 1989.	In Schedule 13, paragraph 13.
1989 c. 42.	Local Government and Housing Act 1989.	In Schedule 11, paragraph 15.
1991 c. 48.	Child Support Act 1991.	In section 5(1), the words "(or, in Scotland, parental rights over)" in both places where they occur. In section 54, the definition of "parental rights".
1991 c. 50.	Age of Legal Capacity (Scotland) Act 1991.	In section 5(1), the words "or tutory". In section 9, the definition of "parental rights". In Schedule 1, paragraphs 3 to 5 and 7 to 15.
1993 c. 9.	Prisoners and Criminal Proceedings (Scotland) Act 1993.	In paragraph 8 of Schedule 3, in the definition of "criminal proceedings", the words "under section 42 of the Social Work (Scotland) Act 1968".
1993 c. 35.	Education Act 1993.	In Schedule 19, paragraph 36.
1994 c. 39.	Local Government etc. (Scotland) Act 1994.	Section 139. In Schedule 13, paragraphs 76(6) and (10) to (25); 92(14)(b)(iii); 100(6)(b)(iv); 103; and 161(7)(c).

INDEX

219